JAMES DREVER

A DICTIONARY OF
PSYCHOLOGY

PENGUIN BOOKS

HARMONDSWORTH · MIDDLESEX

Compiled specially for Penguin Books
First published 1952

Made and printed in Great Britain
for Penguin Books Ltd
by C. Nicholls & Company Ltd

PENGUIN REFERENCE BOOKS

R5

A DICTIONARY OF PSYCHOLOGY

JAMES DREVER

PUBLISHERS' NOTE

The compiler of this Dictionary,
Dr James Drever, Emeritus
Professor of Psychology in the
University of Edinburgh, died
while the book was in production.
It has been seen through the
press by Dr James Drever junior,
who succeeded his father in the
chair of Psychology at Edinburgh.

NOTE

Words or phrases which are
printed in italics within the text
of an article are themselves the
subjects of definitions in their
appropriate alphabetical place.

A

AQ: Contraction for *achievement* (or accomplishment) *quotient.*

Aberration: in general sense more or less irregular deviation from normal. *Mental aberration* sometimes used of mental disorder without specification of the particular type. *Aberration of light:* failure of rays of light to converge to a single point focus passing through an optical system, owing either to the different refrangibility of different wave-lengths (*chromatic*) or to the curvature of the surface on which the light falls (*spherical aberration*).

Ability: power to perform an act, physical or mental, either before or after training. Must be distinguished from *aptitude* (q.v.). *General ability:* a general factor present in varying degrees in different individuals, and affecting all kinds of (mental) performance, contrasted with *special abilities,* which manifest themselves only in special types of performance or activity.

Abklingen (Ger.): employed of the fading out of a sensation, more especially of a tone.

Abnormal: diverging more or less widely from the normal. *Abnormal psychology:* that branch of psychology which investigates such divergences of mental phenomena or of behaviour.

Aboral: employed in animal psychology of the region of the body most distant from the mouth.

Aboulia (abulis): inability, usually pathological, to make or to act on decisions.

Abreaction: employed by psycho-analysts for the process of releasing a repressed emotion by reliving in imagination the original experience.

Abscissa: to specify uniquely the position of a point P in a plane two lines (X and Y axes) are drawn at right angles to one another, one horizontal, the other vertical. If a perpendicular is dropped from P to the X axis, the part of the X axis cut off (*x* value) is known as the *abscissa,* and the length of the perpendicular (*y* value) as the *ordinate* of the point P.

Absentmindedness: absorption in thought so as to be largely unaware of surrounding conditions.

Absicht (Ger.): purpose or intention

7

Absolute: in general sense, independent of relations to other objects; specifically of an impression or estimate of intensity, weight, etc., without comparison with other impressions or objects. Employed sometimes also of a *psycho-physical method* (q.v.), where stimuli are presented for estimate or judgment singly, i.e. without any standard for comparison. See also *threshold*.

Abstract: employed usually of a quality or aspect of an object or process thought of in separation from the whole to which it belongs, but also as a verb designating the process of thought involved. Hence *abstract idea, abstract thinking, abstract reasoning, abstract intelligence*, where the word is employed to characterize different phases of the mental activity involved. See *Abstraction*.

Abstraction: (1) synonymous with *absentmindedness* (q.v.), (2) the mental process of forming abstract ideas. *Abstraction experiment* is the name given to a type of experiment where the subject is required to respond verbally, or in action, to common features in objects or situations presented serially.

Absurdities test: a type of mental test in which the subject is asked to point out what is absurd about a statement, story, or picture.

Acatamathesia: inability to comprehend perceived situations, or objects, or language.

Acataphasia: inability to connect words sensibly in sentences.

Acceptance: the phase of *suggestion* (q.v.), which consists in the accepting of the idea, judgment, or belief suggested.

Accessory: additional; employed specially of those parts of a sense organ which have the function of making the reception of the stimulus more efficient, e.g. the lens system or the muscles of the eye in contradistinction to the *essential* (q.v.) parts.

Accidental errors: errors in experimental observations or measurements due to a number of unknown and variable causes, affecting the results as often in one direction as in the other, and eliminated by making a sufficient number of observations, thus corresponding to the 'errors of observation' in the physical sciences.

Accident proneness: individual liability to meet with accidents; accident susceptibility.

Accommodation: two technical senses: (1) changes in the curvature, and therefore focal length, of the eye, effected by the ciliary muscles, with the object of focussing for different distances, and (2) effect produced on sense organs by continuous and unvarying stimulation so that ultimately no sensation is experienced.

Accomplishment quotient: see *achievement*.

8

Acculturation: the acquiring of a culture through contact.

Acephaly: the state of possessing no head. Adj. *acephalous*.

Achievement: performance in a standardized series of tests, usually educational. —— *age:* the chronological age corresponding to any particular level on a scale of achievement tests. —— *quotient:* AQ: the ratio of the achievement age to the chronological age of the individual tested, expressed as a percentage. —— *tests:* tests constructed and standardized to measure proficiency in school subjects. In all cases 'accomplishment' is sometimes used in place of 'achievement'.

Achromatic: absence of *chroma* or colour. In physics, applied to a lens system which is corrected for chromatic *aberration* (q.v.). Applied also to visual sensations in the white-grey-black series. *Achromatism* is sometimes used as a synonym for *achromatopsia* (q.v.).

Achromatopsia: total *colour blindness* (q.v.), frequently accompanied by *photophobia* (q.v.), *central scotoma* (q.v.), and *nystagmus* (q.v.).

Acmaesthesia: sensing sharp points with touch but without pain sensation.

Acoumeter: see *audiometer*.

Acoustics: the science which investigates sound.

Acquired: employed of characteristics and reactions which are not congenital but developed or learned during an individual's lifetime.

Acquisitiveness: impulse to acquire and not infrequently to hoard certain objects – regarded by some psychologists as instinctive.

Acroaesthesia: increased *sensitivity* in the extremities of the limbs, especially to pain. Opposite is *acroanaesthesia*.

Acromegaly: overgrowth of the bones and connective tissue, particularly in the head, hands, and feet, caused by disordered secretion of groups of glands in *pituitary body* (q.v.); must be distinguished from *gigantism* (q.v.).

Acrophobia: dread of or in high places. See *Phobia*.

Actinic rays: light rays of short wave-length – violet and ultra-violet – so named because of their marked chemical effects.

Action currents: electric currents produced by the passage of a wave of excitation along a nerve (or muscle) fibre.

Active therapy: a method of psychoanalytic treatment sometimes used to break down a *resistance* (q.v.).

Acuity: sharpness; applied particularly to sensory perception of stimuli of low intensity, as dependent mainly on the sensitivity of the sense organ.

Acute Hallucinosis: state similar to *delirium* (q.v.), and similarly caused, with hallucinations but without clouding of consciousness.

Adaptation: (1) equivalent to *accommodation* (q.v.); (2) changes in retina and pupil, occurring with changes in intensity of illumination, as in *dark adaptation* (q.v.); (3) process of becoming more effectively adjusted to the conditions involved in work or learning.

Adaptometer: any instrument for measuring sensory adaptation, but occurring most frequently as applied to an instrument for measuring *dark adaptation* (e.g. Nagel's adaptometer), by which the *threshold* (q.v.) of sensitivity to light is measured after varying periods in the dark.

Adequate stimulus: the natural or normal stimulus appropriate to any sense organ or receptor.

Adjustment: in a special sense, of observations and measurements, the modification or *weighting* (q.v.) of a series of results to compensate for or meet special conditions.

Adolescence: the period in human development between the beginning of puberty and the attainment of adulthood.

Adrenal glands: (alternatively *suprarenal capsules*), *endocrine glands* (q.v.), situated over the kidneys, secreting *adrenin* or *epinephrin* (q.v.).

Aerial perspective: term employed to designate the influence of atmospheric conditions on the perception of the distance (and size) of objects.

Aesthesiogenic: producing sensation, specifically of stimuli or suggestions producing sensory effects in hypnotic subjects.

Aesthesiometer: instrument for measuring the *spatial* or *two-point threshold* (q.v.), presenting several forms, but in the simplest form consisting of a pair of compasses with attached millimetre scale.

Aesthete: one who overemphasizes the place of beauty in experience.

Aesthetics: the scientific and philosophical study of the beautiful and the ugly.

Affect: in modern usage any kind of feeling or emotion attached to ideas or idea-complexes. ——, *displacement of,* used by psychologists for the attachment of affect, especially in dreams, to an item or object other than that to which it normally belongs. ——, *fixation of,* used of phenomena in development, where interest, in place of normally expanding and changing as development proceeds, remains attached to objects and ways of thought and action more or less characteristic of earlier phases.

Affection: general term for the feeling (and emotional) aspect of experience. The adjectival form *affective* is frequently used for feeling as an adjective, as in *affective state, affective tone, affective deficiency, affective association* (where ideas are linked on the basis of common feeling).

Affectivity: the tendency to react with feeling or emotion.

Afferent: used of a nerve, or nerve fibre, conducting a nerve impulse inwards from sense organ to centre; synonymous with *sensory*, and contrasted with *efferent* or motor.

After-image: erroneously used for *after-sensation* (q.v.); *memory after-image* is also sometimes used for *primary memory image* (q.v.).

After-sensation: the continuance of the process in the sense receptor, after the external stimulus has ceased, giving rise to further sense experience; the phenomena are very apparent in the case of vision. After-sensations may be either positive or negative, i.e. of the same quality or hue as the original sensation, or of the opposite or complementary quality or hue (cf. *contrast*).

Age: in general sense, the period that has elapsed since an individual's birth, i.e. chronological age; *mental age*, the age corresponding to any particular level on a scale of intelligence tests. A mental age can be determined, and an *intelligence quotient* (*IQ*) calculated by the formula:
$$\frac{\text{mental age}}{\text{chronological age}} \times \frac{100}{1}$$

Ageusis: defect of taste sensitivity.

Aggression: attack on another, usually, but not necessarily, as a response to opposition; in a special sense by the analytical schools, as a manifestation, either of the 'Will to Power' over other people (Adler), or a *projection* of the 'death impulse' (Freud).

Agitated melancholia: state of deep depression with acute anxiety and agitation.

Agitolalia: excessive rapidity of utterance. See *cluttering*.

Agnosia: inability to attach meaning to sensory impressions.

Agoraphobia: dread in, and of, open spaces. See *phobia*.

Agrammatism: incoherent speech; sometimes called *agrammatologia*; variety of *dyslogia* (q.v.).

Agraphia: inability to write as a result of brain lesion.

Aiming test: a test of motor (hand-eye) co-ordination, the best known type being the *target test* (q.v.).

Akinesis: functional loss of movement without any real paralysis of the part affected.

Alalia: mutism, a variety of *dyslalia* (q.v.).

Albedo: the whiteness of a surface, or its diffuse reflecting power.

Albinism: absence of pigmentation in hair, eyes, etc.

Alcheringa: in the mythology of the Arunta tribe of Australia the 'dream time' or period in which lived the subhuman ancestors of the race.

Alcoholic: due to effect of intoxication by alcohol. Chronic effects of such intoxication include *alcoholic dementia* (marked impairment of memory and judgment), *alcoholic hallucinosis* (see *hallucinosis*), various *psychoses* (q.v.), such as *delirium*, *Korsakow psychosis* or *syndrome* (loss of power of retention with confabulation), with general deterioration of judgment and character.

Alcoholism: diseased condition produced by excessive indulgence in alcohol, exhibiting both an acute and a chronic form.

Alexia: inability to read resulting from cerebral lesion – sometimes called *word-blindness*.

Alg(o): Gk. prefix meaning 'relating to pain'.

Algedonic: relating to pleasure-pain experience; a theory of *aesthetics* based on such experience.

Algesia: capacity to experience pain; opposite of *analgesia* (q.v.).

Algesimeter: instrument for measuring sensitivity to pain stimuli, e.g. those received from a prick. Cf. *algometer*.

Algolagnia: pleasure (of sexual character) obtained from pain, given or suffered.

Algometer: instrument for measuring sensitivity to pain stimuli, as of pressure by a blunt point.

Algophobia: morbid fear of bodily pain.

Alienation: a type of faulty recognition where familiar situations and persons appear unfamiliar and strange, apparently of the same order as *déjà vu* (q.v.).

Alienation: (1) *mental*, a synonym for mental disorder, (2) *coefficient of*,—— a measure of the degree in which two variables are unrelated, i.e. of the lack of correlation, given by the formula $\sqrt{1 - r^2}$ where r is the *product-moment coefficient*. (3) a statistical term used to designate the effect on a *correlation coefficient* (q.v.) of *sampling errors* (q.v.).

Alienist: specialist in mental disorders; modern usage prefers *psychiatrist* (q.v.).

Alimentary canal: the system of organs in the body dealing with food, includes oesophagus, stomach, and intestines small and large.

Allachaesthesia: localization of touch sensation elsewhere than the place really stimulated.

Allaesthesia: synonymous with *allacaesthesia* (q.v.).

Allergy: (generally found in adjectival form '*allergic*') condition of unusually high sensitivity to a substance (e.g. food) which **may** produce considerable physical disturbance.

Alliaceous: one of the classes of smell sensations in *Zwaardemaker's* classification; a typical example is the smell of garlic, placed by *Henning* (q.v.) between resinous and foul. See *odour prism.*

Alloch(e)iria: pathological state where touch or pain is localized at the corresponding point on the other side of the body.

Alloerotism: erotic tendencies directed towards other people.

Allopsychosis: delusions (q.v.) attributing to other people malicious thoughts and intentions.

All-or-none response: response (reflex) which is either elicited or not, and when elicited shows full intensity and no grading.

Alogia: form of *aphasia* (q.v.)

Alpha movement: see *apparent movement.*

Alpha tests: series of mental tests used in first World War for testing U.S.A. army recruits.

Alter (Lat.): one's conception of another human being as a distinct person like oneself.

Alternating personalities: see *multiple personality.*

Alternating psychosis: see *manic-depressive.*

Altruism: consideration for the well-being of other people.

Alveolar: spongy (of body tissue, e.g. in gums).

Alzheimer's disease: a disease of the brain, relatively rare, showing itself in premature *senility,* with speech disorder.

Amaurosis: blindness caused by disease in optic nerve, without any perceptible change in eye itself.

Amaurotic idiocy: defective intelligence with *amaurosis,* and usually early death.

Ambi: Latin prefix: 'both'.

Ambidextrality: equal efficiency with either hand.

Ambiguous: capable of two interpretations, as in the case of ambiguous figures or ambiguous perspective, where a figure may be seen in one or other of two perspectives.

Ambivalence: emotional attitude towards an individual involving the alternation of the opposite feeling attitudes of love and hate.

Ambiversion: type of personality, balanced or oscillating, between *introversion* and *extraversion* (q.v.).

Amblyopia: indistinct vision, without any discoverable defect of the *dioptric mechanism* (q.v.) of the eye.

Amblyscope: instrument used to test the degree of *strabismus* or squint.

Ambrosiac: one of *Zwaardemaker's* classes of odours, e.g. musk.

Amentia: *feeble-mindedness* in various degrees; to be distinguished from dementia (q.v.).

Ametrometer: instrument for measuring the degree of *ametropia,* i.e. the refractive error of the dioptric system of the eye.

Amimia: a language defect, involving inability to use significant gestures.

Amnesia: inability to remember, either total or partial; *localized amn.:* inability, usually functional, restricted to special time, place, or group of experiences; *anterograde amn.* or *retroactive amn.:* inability extending to events immediately preceding a trauma or shock.

Amoeba: unicellular organism, without any constant form, or definite organs for locomotion or food-taking.

Amphioxus: a small organism, marking the lower limit of the *vertebrata.*

Amplitude: the maximal displacement from zero position in a wave motion, which is the basis, in the case of sound and light, for the intensity (loudness or brightness) of the sensation.

Ampulla: the swelling at the end of each *semi-circular canal* (q.v.), in the inner ear.

Amusia: inability to recognize (or reproduce) tones.

Anabolism: the process of building up the complex organic substances in living tissues.

Anaclitic: term employed by psycho-analysts of object choice modelled after the first love object.

Anaesthesia: loss, abolition, or depression of sensitivity to stimuli.

Anaesthetic: substance which produces abolition or depression of sensitivity, though functional anaesthesias may be produced by *suggestion* (q.v.).

Anaglyph: a representation of the retinal *disparation* (q.v.) principle by means of pictures printed in two colours (usually blue and red), to be regarded through coloured glasses, red over one eye and blue over the other, thus obtaining a *stereoscopic* (q.v.) effect.

Anaglyptoscope (*anaglyphoscope*): instrument employed to show the part played by shadows in the interpretation of perspective, by lighting an object from a direction opposite from that from which the light seems to come.

Anagogic: term employed by *Jung* for the morally uplifting trends of the unconscious.

Anal eroticism: in psycho-analytical theory, concentration of interest on the anal region as a pre-genital phase of sexual development.

Analgesia: abolition of pain sensation: adjective, *analgesic.*

Analogies test: a common type of mental test of the form: A is to B as C is to – .

Analogous organs: organs superficially similar, but structurally (and developmentally) different.

Analogy, law of : one of the subsidiary laws of learning formulated by *Thorndike,* to the effect that to any new situation an animal or man responds as he would to any situation like it.

Analysis: in its general psychological sense, the determining of the constituents of any total or complex experience, or mental process; frequently used in a special sense of psychoanalysis, and kindred procedures and theories, and even as synonymous with *psychoanalysis* (q.v.).

Anamnesis: recalling to mind; employed also in medical sense of the history of an illness up to the point at which it is taken.

Anaphia: loss of the sense of touch.

Anarthria: defect of articulation due to lesion in motor speech centre.

Androgyny: tendency in a male body to approximate to that of a female, and vice versa.

Anchorages: reference points in a *frame of reference* (q.v.), or generally standards with reference to which judgment takes place in any field of experience.

Anemotropism: orienting of its body, on the part of an organism, to air currents. See *tropism.*

Anencephaly: absence of brain.

Angström unit, Åu: unit employed in designating wave-length of light equal to $1/10$th of a micromillimetre or 10^{-9} mm.

Angular gyrus: a convolution of the *cerebral cortex* at the posterior end of the upper temporal fissure, which, in the left hemisphere, would appear to be associated with some aspect of the language function.

Anhedonia: absence of the pleasure-unpleasure feeling in situations where it is normally present.

Anima: soul: term used by *Jung* for the inner part of the personality, in communion, as it were, with the *unconscious.*

Animal magnetism: early theory regarding hypnotic phenomena, based on the belief that they were due to a subtle fluid of the nature of magnetism passed from the operator to the subject; the theory of *Mesmer.*

Animatism: a primitive view, attributing life to inanimate objects – an earlier stage than *animism* (q.v.).

Animism: belief that objects in nature possess, or are the abodes of, souls or spirits.

Anisometropia: inequality in the refraction of the two eyes.

Anlage (Ger.): inherited organization as basis of development.

Annoyer: Thorndike's term for an unpleasant stimulus which causes the initiation of efforts for its removal.

Anoetic (anoegenetic): primitive consciousness without objective reference.

Anomaloscope: instrument for measuring *colour anomaly* (q.v.) by the *Rayleigh equation* (q.v.).

Anomaly (colour): deviation from normal colour vision, affecting relative sensitivity to red and green, and possibly showing various gradations to complete *red-green colour blindness* (q.v.).

Anomia: difficulty in recalling names of things, a variety of *aphasia.*

Anorexia: loss of appetite or desire.

Anorthopia: distorted vision of objects.

Anosmia: defective sensitivity to smell stimuli.

Anregung (Ger.): incitation or stimulation.

Anschauung (Ger.): direct apprehension in sense-perception.

Antagonistic: used of muscles or reflexes which counteract one another, e.g. flexor and extensor muscles in arm or leg.

Antenna: jointed appendage carrying sense receptors, occurring in insects and crustacea.

Anterograde: used of *amnesia* (q.v.).

Anthropo- (Gk.): prefix meaning 'man'.

Anthropoid: used of the higher apes, as most nearly approaching the human being.

Anthropology: the science which studies the human being in his bodily form (physical), his racial characteristics (folk), and his social development (social).

Anthropometry: measurement of the bodily form and proportions of different races, sexes, ages, etc., of man.

Anthropomorphism: ascribing human characteristics to gods or animals.

Anthroponomy: science of human behaviour.

Anthropopathy: ascribing human feelings and passions to the Deity.

Anticipatory reaction: response by a subject to a stimulus other than the proper stimulus, given by a keyed-up subject, and shown by an extremely short reaction time, in some cases even a zero or almost zero value.

Antipathy: antagonism or strong dislike.

Antirrheoscope: an arrangement for producing illusory sensations and after-sensations of movement, by means of a horizontally lined

band moving behind an aperture in a similarly lined screen –
sometimes called the '*waterfall*' *illusion*.

Antisocial: hostile to social laws or the social organization.

Antrieb (Ger.): impulse or drive – sometimes equivalent to *spurt* (q.v.).

Anus: the lower opening of the alimentary canal.

Anxiety: a chronic complex emotional state with apprehension or
dread as its most prominent component; characteristic of various
nervous and mental disorders.

Apathy: absence of feeling or emotion, indifference; may be a symptom of a pathological condition. The adjective *apathetic* is sometimes
employed of a *temperament* (q.v.).

Aphakia: absence of the lens of the eye as the result of defect, injury,
or operation.

Aphanisis: fear of loss of power of experiencing sexual pleasure.

Aphasia: in strict sense, a disorder of the speech function, resulting
from cortical lesion, and showing itself either as *motor aphasia*, the
inability to use speech, or as *sensory aphasia*, the inability to understand speech, but often used in a wide sense to cover allied disorders
of language such as *alexia, agraphia.* etc, (q.v.).

Aphemia: inability to utter words, due to emotion or psychoneurosis.

Aphonia: inability to utter sounds, owing to defect of vocal cords.

Aphrasia: inability to speak connected phrases, though the individual
is able to utter separate words.

Aphrodisiac: exciting sexual activity (usually of a drug).

Aphthongia: inability to utter words, because of muscular spasm in
tongue.

Apopathetic: used of behaviour 'playing up' to other people, or stimulated by their presence, but not directed towards them.

Apparent: in connection with visual experience used either of the
size of an object perceived at a distance, implying a contrast with
the real size (but see *constancy phenomena*), or of illusory movement,
more or less of the same order as the *phi phenomenon* (q.v.); various
types of such movement have been classified as *alpha* (when parts of
a figure exposed successively show change of size); *beta* (when objects, differing in position or size, exposed in succession, give the
appearance of motion); *gamma* (when expansion-contraction experiences are shown by a figure, exposed or withdrawn suddenly, or
by a sudden change in illumination); *delta* (when motion is perceived by the exposure of a second stimulus more intense than the
preceding); *epsilon* (when a white line on a black ground, changed

into a black line on a white ground in a different position, gives the appearance of motion.)

Appeal: used technically in industrial psychology, in connection with advertising or salesmanship, in the sense of *incentive* or incitation.

Apperception: in original sense (*Leibniz*), clear perception, in particular where there is recognition or identification; in the educational psychology of *Herbart* (q.v.) it is taken as the fundamental process in acquiring knowledge, and the part played by existing knowledge – the *apperceptive mass* – is emphasized.

Appetite: immediate desire; used also of an insistent impulse, inherited or acquired, originating usually in organic conditions, and, when congenital, frequently classed as an *instinctive impulse.*

Applied psychology: the branch of psychology which seeks to apply to practical problems and practical life the methods and results of pure, and especially *experimental* psychology; the term is somewhat wide, including *industrial, clinical,* and *educational* psychology. On the European continent the term '*psychotechnics*' is used, but in a narrower, and more technical sense, of the actual practice, particularly in the industrial field.

Apport: employed, in psychical research, of the supernormal transporting of objects from a distance into a definite enclosed space.

Appreciation: judgment of value, or significance.

Apprehend: (1) become aware of, in the most general sense; (2) fear; the noun *apprehension* is also used in both senses.

Apprehension span: see *span.*

Appunn: see *lamella* and *tonometer.*

Apraxia: inability to manipulate, or deal intelligently, with objects, as a result of brain lesion.

Aprosexia: inability to maintain concentrated attention.

Apselaphesia: disorganization of the sense of touch.

Aptitude: natural ability to acquire relatively general or special types of knowledge or skill; tests to determine such ability are called *aptitude tests.*

Aqueduct of Sylvius: opening in the mid-brain connecting the third and fourth *ventricles* (q.v.).

Aqueous humour: transparent fluid occupying the space between the lens and cornea of the eye.

Arachnoid: the middle of the three membranes covering the brain and spinal cord.

Arbor vitae: the tree-like appearance of the white matter of the *cerebellum* (q.v.), in medial section.

Arborization: the terminal branching of fibrils at the end of the *axon,* or other process of a *neuron* (q.v.).

Archaeology: the study of the physical, anatomical, and cultural remains of ancient (mainly prehistoric) peoples.

Arch of Corti: the arch in the inner ear formed by the *rods of Corti* (q.v.) at their upper ends.

Archetype: Jung's term for the content of the *racial unconscious.*

Arcuate: applied to fibres connecting adjoining regions in the *cerebrum* and *cerebellum.*

Arcus senilis: an arc of greyish or yellowish appearance, near outer margin of cornea of eye, showing mainly in old people.

Argyll-Robertson pupil: a pupil which does not contract, when light falls on it, but which responds with accommodation and convergence of the optic axes for near objects, a characteristic symptom of *locomotor ataxy* (q.v.).

Aridity: used in a religious sense of a painful dullness and depression of spirit, as from (a feeling of) God's withdrawal.

Aristotle's illusion: the illusion of doubling, which is experienced when a small object is placed between the points of the fore and middle fingers crossed.

Arithmetical mean: see *mean.*

Arithmomania: an obsessive interest in counting, and in numerical relations.

Aromatic: one of *Zwaardemaker's* classes of smell sensations, as the smell of nutmeg or camphor.

Array: term used in statistics, of the distribution of values in the row or column of a *correlation grid* (q.v.).

Arteriosclerosis: degenerative changes in the walls of the arteries.

Articular sensations: sensations in joints.

Articulation: production of consonantal sounds.

Artifact: term applied to products of human activity, as against the results of natural processes.

Artistic: used (a) of activities, motived by aesthetic impulses, in producing an aesthetically satisfying product; (b) of appreciation involving an ability to discriminate aesthetic quality.

Arytenoid: used of cartilages forming the back of the larynx.

Ascendance (-ence): tendency to take the leading part, or dominate in relations with others; opposite tendency is *submission* (q.v.).

Ascetic: used of an individual who values lightly sensuous pleasures, or at least denies them to himself: *asceticism* is more or less equivalent to mortification of the flesh in the ordinary religious usage.

Asemasia (asemia): pathological inability to use or to understand language. Cf. *aphasia.*

Aspiration level: see *level of aspiration.*

Assimilation: in general sense, becoming like, or being like; various technical senses according to context: (a) sociologically, becoming in thought and behaviour like the social milieu; (b) physiologically, using food material to build up organic substances, or, as in *Hering's theory of colour vision* (q.v.), merely the building-up of complex molecular structure; (c) psychologically (1) interpreting a new fact, or experience, by bringing it into relation with already existing knowledge (*Herbart*), or (2) as the result of a process akin to *complication* (q.v.), the combining into a whole of direct and reproduced items of immediate experience (*Wundt*) (q.v.); (d) psychologically, of animal behaviour, reaction to a new situation with a response normally given to a familiar situation, to which the new situation presents some points of resemblance (*Thorndike*). Cf. *law of analogy.*

Assimilative illusion: the type of illusion, caused by the context, perceptual or ideational. Cf. *contrast illusion.*

Association: used generally of the principle, in accordance with which ideas, feelings, and movements are connected in such a way as to determine their succession in the mind or in the actions of an individual, or of the process of establishing such connections. This principle and process has been recognized since the time of Aristotle. The laws, in accordance with which connections are established, are known as *laws of association, primary* and *secondary,* the former being the laws of *contiguity* and *similarity* (q.v.), the latter the laws of *primacy, recency, frequency,* and *vividness.*

Association: used adjectivally (a) of areas of the cerebral cortex, whose functions have not been determined; (b) of fibres connecting one area to another within the same hemisphere; (c) of experiments, or tests, in the fields of learning, thought, etc.; (d) of time, in reaction experiments, where the response involves the functioning of associative connections.

Associationism: the name given to a psychological theory, which takes association to be the fundamental principle of mental life, in terms of which even the higher thought processes are to be explained. It is best represented by what is often called the English School (*Hartley,* the *Mills', Herbert Spencer,* etc.) It is usually combined with *sensationism* (q.v.), and is opposed to theories emphasizing an independent activity of the mind.

Associative: employed of learning and memory, where the establishing of connections, or the facilitating of recall, is regarded as dependent mainly on association; also in several special senses, as of *illusions,* where the addition of lines to a figure gives a new perceptual context and produces an illusion, or of a *facilitating* or *inhibiting* effect produced on one association by the formation of another.

Assonance: similarity of vowel sounds.

Astasia: unsteadiness (tremor), in contraction of a muscle, or in maintaining a position; *astasia-abasia,* inability to stand or walk, as a hysterical disorder, when there is no paralysis or disorder of the reflexes.

Astereognosis: inability to recognize by touch the form of solid objects.

Asthenia: lack (or impairment) of strength, as in *neurasthenia* (q.v.) or *psychasthenia* (q.v.).

Asthenic: used of depressive feelings or emotions, or of a type of human physique with small trunk and long limbs, claimed by *Kretschmer* to be associated with *schizoid* mental characteristics.

Asthenopia: weakness of vision.

Astigmatism: a defect of vision, due to irregularities in the curvature of the refracting surfaces, especially that of the *cornea* (q.v.).

Astral body: a shadow body or *aura,* alleged to be visible to certain individuals who have *cryptaesthesia* (q.v.).

Astraphobia: phobia (q.v.) of thunder and lightning.

Asymbolia: inability, owing to cerebral disorder, to use or understand language.

Asymmetry: lack of structural correspondence between the two sides of the body, particularly with respect to paired members, but also used of *vision,* where one eye operates more strongly than the other in convergence.

Asynergia: inability, owing to cerebellar disorder, to carry out complex actions depending on the co-ordination of different muscle groups.

Atavism: reappearance of a character, which has not shown itself for several generations.

Ataxia: marked loss of co-ordination of voluntary movements; *static ataxia* designates the form where an individual tries to maintain a fixed position or posture.

Ataxiagraph: apparatus giving a graphical record of the degree and nature of muscular co-ordination in ataxic conditions.

Ataxiameter: apparatus which gives the total amount of sway at the head laterally, and from front to back, of an individual who is trying to maintain an erect posture.

Ataxic writing: writing showing incoordination of the writing movements.

Athletic: one of *Kretschmer's* types of bodily structure – well-balanced proportion of trunk and limbs.

Atomism: name given to any psychological theory which holds that conscious states can be analysed without loss into elementary units applied more particularly to *associationism, sensationism,* and extreme *behaviourism.*

Atonicity atony) relative or absolute lack of *muscle tonus* (q.v.).

Atropin. a drug extracted from the deadly nightshade plant; used for dilation of the pupil in examinations of the eye; also causes relaxation of smooth muscle in the intestines, and inhibits glandular secretion.

Attensity: term employed by *Titchener* as a synonym for sensory clearness.

Attention: may be defined, either as the selective activity characteristic of the mental life, or as a state of relative monoideism (*Ribot*), or as a state of consciousness marked by levels of sensory or imaginal clearness (*Titchener*), or as *conation* (q.v.) directed towards a clearer cognition of its object (*Stout*); variously described also either, on the analogy of the field of vision, as characterized by a focus and a margin, or, on the analogy of a wave, as possessing a crest of clear consciousness and a trough of inattention. For *fluctuations of attention* see *fluctuations.* For *span of attention* see *span.*

Attitude: a more or less stable set or disposition of opinion, interest or purpose, involving expectancy of a certain kind of experience, and readiness with an appropriate response; sometimes used in a wider sense, but rather less definitely, as in *aesthetic attitude,* in the sense of a tendency to appreciate or produce artistic results, or a *social attitude,* in the sense of being sensitive to social relations, social duties or social opinions; *attitude scales* and *attitude tests* are scales and tests devised to throw light on temperament and personality traits (see *temperament tests*).

Attribute: a fundamental aspect or characteristic of a sensation, with the vanishing of which the sensation vanishes; for example, all sensations must have *quality, intensity* and *duration,* or better *protensity* (q.v.) This is the technical use of the word in psychology.

Atypical: deviating markedly from type.

Aubert diaphragm: a type of diaphragm for controlling the passage of light, by means of a square aperture, between two plates, which are capable of sliding over one another, so as to enlarge, or reduce, the aperture, and which may be provided with a scale, by means of which the amount of light passed can be measured.

Aubert phenomenon: apparent displacement of a vertical line in a direction opposite to a tilt of the head when no other object is present in the visual field. Must be distinguished from the *Aubert-Förster phenomenon*, which is the easier recognition of small objects when near, as compared with larger more distant objects subtending the same visual angle, expressed in the form of a law to the effect that objectively small objects can be distinguished as two at greater distances from the fovea than two larger objects subtending the same visual angle.

Audibility limits and range: employed with reference to the lowest and highest frequency and the range of frequencies, of tones audible by the human ear; the limits are from about 16 to about 20,000 vibrations per second, but the upper limit tends to fall as one gets older.

Audile: term employed of a type of individual relying mainly on auditory imagery. See *imagery.*

Audio-Frequency: see *audibility limits and range.*

Audiogram: graphic record of an individual's auditory acuity through the range of audibility.

Audiometer: an instrument for measuring acuity of hearing. Older forms, usually called *phonometers* or *acoumeters,* were usually based on a standard sound, produced either by a falling ball, or falling hammer, with measurement by the distance of the subject. A more modern audiometer is *Seashore's,* where intensity is varied electrically by the use of a potentiometer, but all audiometers are now superseded by the use of vacuum tubes and oscillators.

Audition: hearing

Audito-oculogyric Reflex: turning the eyes in the direction of a sudden sound.

Auditory: relating to the ear or the sense of hearing, as auditory sensation, auditory stimulus, auditory acuity, auditory threshold, etc.

Aufgabe (Ger.): task or problem.

Aura: subjective feelings preceding an attack of epilepsy. See also *astral body.*

Aural: relating to the ear, but frequently equivalent to *auditory* (q.v.).

Auricle: the external ear.

Aussage Experiment: an experiment to test fidelity of report, where the subject has to report on a picture (*Stern*), or a group of objects (*Binet*), or a series of events, the observation being limited to a period of time, and the report being frequently supplemented by a cross-examination.

Autacoid. substance secreted by *endocrine* (q.v.) or *ductless glands*, and poured directly into the blood. The name suggested by *Schafer* for *hormone* (q.v.), the usual term.

Autism: see *autistic thinking*.

Autistic thinking: mental activity which is controlled by the wishes of the individual, as contrasted with *reality thinking*, controlled by the conditions imposed by the real nature of objects and events; more or less equivalent to *wishful thinking* or *phantasy* (q.v.).

Aut (o): Greek prefix meaning 'self'.

Autochthonous: literally 'belonging to the soil'; employed of ideas which rise in the mind, independently of the train of thought at the time, and foreign to the normal mode of thought – exemplified in *schizophrenia* (q.v.).

Autocompetition: attempt to surpass one's own score or record.

Auto-eroticism: sexual activity with one's own body as sexual object.

Autogenic: originating within oneself.

Auto-intoxication: intoxication, or poisoning by toxins developed within one's own body.

Autokinesis: significant shifts of judgment as subjective modifications or interpretations of objective data, through the operation of *set, attitude,* or *frame of reference* (q.v.).

Autokinesis: movement initiated by stimuli within oneself.

Autokinetic illusion: apparent movement of a bright point observed continuously in darkness.

Automatic: generally 'self-acting'; of animal activities, without consciousness or volition; specially used of complex actions, performed without personal awareness, such as *automatic drawing, automatic writing, automatic speaking*.

Automatism: usually a complex act performed unconsciously, but in psychical research *sensory automatism* is employed of automatic functioning of the senses, which is seemingly of the nature of hallucination, such as *clairvoyance* (q.v.), *clairaudience* and the like.

Automatist is sometimes employed as a synonym for *medium*.

Automatograph: an apparatus for recording automatic movements. See *autoscope*.

Autonomic: means, literally, functioning independently; applied mostly to the parts and functions of the *autonomic nervous system*, formerly called the *sympathetic*, a name now restricted to part only. This system would appear to be wholly *efferent* (q.v.), consisting of a chain of *ganglia* (q.v.), running alongside of the spinal column, with some ganglia in the skull, efferent fibres (*preganglionic*), connecting with the cerebro-spinal system, and networks or *plexuses* round the internal organs: it controls the functions of *smooth muscles* and *glands*.

Autopsychosis: mental disorder in which all ideas are centred round self.

Autorivalry: See *competition*.

Autoscope: an instrument by means of which unconscious and involuntary movements are changed into visible and significant movements, as with the *divining rod* (q.v.) (dousing), *Chevreul's pendulum* (q.v.), *planchette*, or the *ouija board* (q.v.), table turning, etc. Cf. *automatograph*.

Auto-suggestion: suggestion (q.v.), arising from the individual himself.

Autotelic: a term employed of type of character or character trait to indicate the predominance of aims towards self-defence, self-protection, and self-development in an individual's system of purposes.

Avalanche conduction: conduction in which impulses produce an effect out of proportion to the stimulus by spreading from a few to many neurons.

Average: the *arithmetical mean* (q.v.), as a representative value for a series of values; sometimes used loosely for *median* (q.v.) or even *mode* (q.v.).

Average deviation: see *mean variation,* and *standard deviation*.

Average error: see *mean error*.

Aversion: disagreeable feeling, together with impulse to withdraw or avoid.

Awareness: mere experience of an object or idea; sometimes equivalent to consciousness.

Awe: a complex emotional state, regarded by *McDougall* as a fusion of fear and *negative self-feeling* (q.v.).

Axial gradient: the gradual change along any axis of an organism, or an organ, in the intensity of *metabolism* (q.v.), as indicated by electrical potential.

Axillary: relating to the arm-pit.

Axon: that process of a *neuron* (q.v.) along which a nerve impulse passes away from the cell body.

B

B-Type: contraction for *Basedow* type, a type of *eidetic imagery* (q.v.), which is plastic, and also used of an individual who has this type, along with other characteristics of *Basedow's disease* (*exophthalmic goitre*).

Babinski reflex (*phenomenon*)*:* extension in place of flexion of the toes on gentle stroking of the sole of the foot; shown in infancy, but later is a sign of cerebro-spinal disorder, more specifically of depression of the *pyramidal tract* (q.v.).

Backward association: associative connection formed between an item of experience and an earlier item, contrary to the usual forward direction of association, and probably due in all cases to organic relationship between the two items.

Backwardness: see *retardation.*

Baconian: used of the inductive method, as opposed to the deductive, or Aristotelian.

von Baer's Law: a law describing the development of embryos of different kinds of organisms which are at first similar, but diverge from one another at different stages, according to the closeness of their relationship, those which are least closely related diverging first.

Balance: in general sense, maintenance of equilibrium or posture; in the field of *aesthetics,* used of the equivalence of value or weight, on the right and left sides of a picture, or generally in the picture as a whole.

Balance (*Mosso's*)*:* apparatus for recording changes of blood supply, consisting of a tilting board, movable in a vertical plane, on which the subject lies.

Ball and field test: one of the tests in the *Binet-Simon* series (q.v.), in which the subject is asked to show the track he would pursue to find a ball lost in a circular field.

Balsamic: a quality of smell sensations in *Zwaardemaker's* classification, practically identical with the *fragrant of Henning,* though differing from the latter's balsamic.

Band chart: a type of chart, showing, usually by different colours, the relative amounts of certain items or classes, making up a total, generally by percentages of the total.

Bar diagram: a statistical chart, showing by rectangles a series of magnitudes; when the bands are contiguous the figure is called a *histogram* (q.v.).

Barbaralalia: a foreign accent.

Barotropism (——*taxis*)*:* a response to pressure, as of a current. See *tropism.*

Barylalia: thick speech.

Baryphonia: thick voice.

Basal: at the base of, or forming the basis on which something rests; used of *mental age* (q.v.), for the level at which an individual passes all the tests; also of *metabolism* (q.v.), representing the energy expenditure in the vital functions alone, with individual resting, but not asleep; also of the masses of nervous matter or ganglia at the base of the cerebrum (*thalami, corpora striata,* etc.).

Basilar membrane: the membrane in the *cochlea* (q.v.), which separates the *scala media* (q.v.) from the *scala tympani* (q.v.), and on which rests the *organ of Corti* (q.v.).

Bathophobia: unreasoning dread of depths.

Battery of Tests: a series of *group tests* (q.v.) such as *direction tests, analogies tests, vocabulary tests, completion tests, etc.* Several tests are administered in one session, but each test is separately timed.

Bechterev technique: the employment of a protective reflex movement in conditioning experiments, as against the salivary reflex employed by Pavlov.

Beats: regular fluctuations in intensity of sound, when two tones of slightly different frequency or pitch are sounded together, due to interference of the two wave trains, the rate of the fluctuations giving the frequency difference between the two tones; analogous fluctuations in position are obtained when the two tones are led separately to the two ears (*binaural beats*); the *beat tone,* that is the tone carrying the beat, seems intermediate in pitch between the two tones, and gives a characteristic roughness to the sound when the beats are frequent; the *beat tone* is often confused with the *difference tone* (q.v.).

Behaviour: the total response, motor and glandular, which an organism makes to any situation with which it is faced.

Behaviourism: usually applied to a theoretical approach to psychology, which emphasizes the importance of an objective study of actual responses. The extreme behaviourist 'has no use for consciousness or conscious process'.

Bel: unit of level of sound intensity in terms of energy; the unit most frequently employed is the *decibel* (1/10 bel) which may be thus defined: – the intensity of a sound in decibels $= 10 \log 1./1_0$ where 1 is the energy of the sound and I_0 that of the least audible sound of the same frequency; the unit in terms of loudness is the *phon*.

Belief: an attitude involving the recognition or acceptance of something as real.

Benign: employed of tumours, which are not *malignant* (q.v.), and by analogy extended to psychological phenomena, e.g. *stupor* in *manic-depressive psychoses* (q.v.).

Berdache: a man (in certain American Indian tribes) who wears the dress and follows the occupations of a woman.

Beta: 1. a type of *apparent movement* (q.v.); 2. American Army tests for illiterates (First World War).

Betz cells: large pyramidal cell bodies in the *motor cortex* (q.v.).

Bewusstseinslage (*Ger.*): conscious attitude or attitude of consciousness; a special form of *Bewusstheit* or awareness, without sensory or imaginal characters (*Würzburg school*).

Betzold-Brücke phenomenon: change in hue of spectral colours with change in the level of illumination.

Bias: an attitude either for or against a particular theory, hypothesis or explanation, which unconsciously influences an individual's judgment; it may appear in experimental work as the so-called *error of bias*, the bias being due either to prepossession in favour of a particular theory, or previous judgments in the same experiment.

Bidwell's ghost: a visual *after-sensation* appearing with rotated disc, with black and white sectors, under certain conditions of illumination and rate of rotation, as a shadowy white following upon the edge of the black; term sometimes used as synonymous with *Purkinje's after-image* (q.v.).

Bilious: one of the *temperaments* in the old theory of temperaments, as synonym for *melancholic*.

Bimodal: characteristic of a *frequency curve*, or *distribution*, which shows two maxima. See *mode*.

Binaural: used of the two ears functioning together.

Binet-Simon scale: a series of graded tests of intelligence devised by Binet and Simon. Three scales were devised – 1905, 1908, and 1911 – the last two being graded in year groups, and revisions and modifications have been published in many languages.

Binocular: used of the two eyes functioning together; see *flicker*.

Binocular colour mixture: presenting simultaneously two different colours to the two eyes, preferably with the help of a *stereoscope*, when either *fusion* or *rivalry* of the two colours may occur.

Bioc(o)enosis: the relation between organisms which live in association.

Biogenesis: origin and evolution of living forms. The *law of biogenesis* is the principle that all living organisms are derived from a parent or parents. The *biogenetic law* or *law of biogeny* is the principle that the development of each individual recapitulates the evolution of the race – 'ontogeny recapitulates phylogeny'.

Biologism: the type of theory which takes biological utility as the universal and ultimate explanatory principle, in dealing with life at all levels.

Biology: the science which studies living organisms.

Biometry: the application of statistical methods to biological data.

Bionomics: the branch of biology which studies the relations of organisms to their environment.

Biophore: an elementary unit, assumed by Weismann, as the basis of the body structure of organisms.

Biopsychics: alternative term for *psychobiology* (q.v.). The adjective *biopsychic* is used of mental phenomena in their relation to the life of the organism.

Biosocial: used of those social relations which are determined mainly by biological factors, or of organisms which have social significance for the human being, e.g. animals as pets.

Biotype: applied to a group of organisms of common descent, with the same complex of hereditary factors.

Biparental inheritance: inheritance from two parents.

Birth symbolism: employed in psychoanalytic literature for a symbolic representation, which stands for the first separation from the love object as experienced in the separation of the newborn child from its mother.

Birth trauma: anxiety or fear experienced by the child at birth, possibly from the experience of choking; one of the original determinants of fear.

Biserial: in statistics, the relation between two variables, one of which has only two values.

Bisexuality: having the characteristics of both sexes; or being attracted equally by members of both sexes.

Blank experiment: an experiment sometimes introduced into a series, but not reckoned in the results.

Blastula: a stage in the development of the *embryo*. preceding the *gastrula* stage – characterized by cells arranged in a hollow sphere.

Blind spot: the place where the *optic nerve* breaks through the retina as it enters the eye, 12 to 15 degrees to the nasal side of the retina, and almost in the horizontal plane.

Blix's temperature experiment: the first reported experiment on the localization of *cold and heat spots* (q.v.).

Block design tests: intelligence tests, where coloured cubes have to be assembled to make a given design.

Blocking: experience of being impeded, or brought to a standstill, in a train of association or thought.

Blood groups: term applied to the types of blood, distinguishable by the reaction of the red corpuscles to serum; in man there are four such types.

Blue-arc phenomenon: a stimulus (preferably by red) on a dark background, at the centre of the visual field, produces two luminous bluish arcs, connecting the locus of the stimulus with the locus of the blind spot.

Blue blindness: see *tritanopia*.

Blue-yellow blindness: the rarest type of congenital partial colour blindness. See *tritanopia*.

Bogen cage: a test of practical intelligence consisting of a slatted wood box, which is converted into what is essentially a maze by means of a series of internal partitions, the interior being visible through a glass plate. A ball is placed inside, and the subject is required to manipulate this by means of a stick inserted between the slats in such a way as to bring it out through an opening at one end.

Bone conduction: used of the transmission, by the bones of the skull, of sound waves to the receptors in the ear when a tuning fork in vibration is placed on the head or against the teeth; a *bone conduction test*, for the purpose of diagnosing defect in the normal transmission apparatus, is carried out by testing the auditory acuity for bone conduction, and comparing that with the auditory acuity for normal transmission.

Borderline: used generally of individuals who are near the line of division between two classes, as, for example, sanity and insanity, but more specifically, in *mental testing*, of cases near, but not below, the dividing line between dull normal and subnormal (or *feeble-minded*) – IQ 70 to 75.

Boredom: condition of wandering attention and impaired working efficiency, simulating the condition in fatigue, brought about by monotony of work.

Brachycephaly: relatively broad-skulled, i.e. as compared with the length of the skull from front to back.

Brachydactyly: condition of having abnormally short fingers.

Bradylalia (Bradyarthria): abnormal slowness of articulation, due to brain lesion.

Bradylogia: slowness of speech, due to functional, and not organic, disorder or defect.

Braille: device for enabling the blind to read and write, in which an alphabet is employed consisting of various arrangements of raised points, within a framework of six points, arranged in three rows.

Brain: the total mass of nervous matter within the skull, or the *encephalon* (q.v.); the *brain stem* is the term used of the part remaining when the *cerebrum* (q.v.) and *cerebellum* (q.v.) are removed.

Break phenomenon: the sudden modification of behaviour that appears in fatigue experiments, and in athletic contests, when one of two rival stimuli affecting the subject or contestant suddenly, as it were, overpowers the other.

Breton's law: a substitute formula for *Weber's law* (q.v.), to the effect that the relation between stimulus and *just noticeable difference* (q.v.) is expressed by $S = (R/C)^{\frac{1}{2}}$.

Brightness: physically, the amount of light emitted from a surface, measured in terms of *candle-power* or *lamberts;* psychologically (as used by British psychologists) position in the white-black series; for this latter sense the term *brilliance* is preferred by American psychologists. Colours are said to have a specific brightness (brilliance), which is given by the position of that grey on the white-black scale which is determined by the *flicker* (q.v.) or other method to have the same brightness (brilliance).

Brightness contrast: black and white show the same contrast phenomena, both *simultaneous* and *successive*, as the chromatic colours (*see colour contrast*). *Brightness difference thresholds* can also be determined in the white-black series, and the *absolute brightness threshold* can be determined only with white light, and only for the *dark adapted eye* (q.v.). See *threshold*.

Brilliance: see *brightness*.

Broca's convolution: the centre in the cortex for motor speech, located in front of the lower part of the descending precentral convolution, in the frontal lobe of the left hemisphere (in right-handed persons).

Brown-Sequard syndrome: paralysis and *hyperaesthesia* (q.v.) on one side of body, with anaesthesia on the opposite side, caused by lesion in one lateral half of the spinal cord.

Brown-Spearman formula: a formula for estimating the *reliability* (q.v.) of a test, when it has been increased in length.

Bruch's membrane: the layer of the retina next the outer pigmented layer.

Bulimia: morbid hunger.

Bulky colour: colour in three dimensions, as in a semi-transparent coloured liquid.

C

C.A.: chronological age, usually taken in months in calculating IQ.

CAVD test: Thorndike's battery of four mental tests – *completion, arithmetical problems, vocabulary, directions.*

C factor: cleverness factor, a factor in mental ability, alleged to be independent of *Spearman's g factor* (q.v.).

C.G.S. system: centimetre, gram, second, i.e. units of length, mass, and time, the basis of physical measurement.

Cachexis: a morbid condition of general malnutrition.

Cadence: a sequence at the end of a musical phrase.

Calcarine fissure: a deep fissure, mainly on mesial side of a cerebral hemisphere, and in the occipital lobe.

Calibration: the process of fixing, in terms of a known standard, the values of the readings given by any instrument.

Calligraphy: handwriting, especially with reference to its artistic quality.

Calorimeter: an instrument for measuring production or absorption of heat, and thus energy.

Campimeter: an arrangement for mapping out the visual field, particularly for colour. Cf. *perimeter.*

Canal: see *central, semi-circular, scalar.*

Cancellation: a test, employed in the experimental study of perception, attention, or work, in which the subject is required to discriminate and mark particular figures, letters, or forms, irregularly distributed in a mass of similar figures, letters, or forms.

Candle power: a unit employed in the measurement of the luminosity of a source of light.

Cannabis indica: Indian hemp, a narcotic and intoxicant, used for its psychological and medicinal effects, as *hashish, bhang,* etc.

Canon: a principle guiding scientific procedure, e.g. Mill's *canons of induction.*

Capacity: native potentiality generally, or in respect of any function.

Capillary electrometer: an instrument for measuring small electric currents.

Cardinal point: point at which, in a quantitative series, the *difference threshold* begins to increase in accordance with *Weber's law* (q.v.).

Cardiograph: an instrument for recording the heart action, in respect of rate and amplitude of beat.

Cardiotachometer: an instrument for recording, by means of action currents, the rate of the heart-beat.

Card sorting: a type of experiment, used for various purposes – as a *learning experiment,* for the study of *interference* (q.v.), as a test of efficiency of *discrimination* and motor response, etc.

Cartridge weights: a series of weights used for the study of *differential sensitivity* of touch, or for lifting weights.

Case history: a record of an individual's experience, illnesses, education, environment, treatment, and, generally, all facts relevant to the particular problems involved in a medical or clinical case.

Caste system: a social system characterized by classes separated from one another by social barriers.

Castration: removal of sex glands from either sex. In psychoanalytic literature frequent reference is made to *castration anxiety,* anxiety or fear associated with the idea of such deprivation; similarly *castration complex,* a complex caused by threats of such deprivation.

Catabolism: see *Katabolism.*

Catalepsy: state associated with mental or nervous disorder, or with *hypnosis,* where the patient maintains his limbs in any position in which they are placed – *flexibilitas cerea.*

Cataplexy: a condition of immobility, shown in some animals, as a result of fear or shock, or as a defensive reaction.

Cataract: opacity of the lens of the eye; when cataract is ripe or over-ripe a nucleus is formed, and floats in the outer layer of the lens, the condition being known as *morgagnian cataract.*

Catatonia: a state of mental automatism in which the voluntary muscle systems retain any position in which they are placed – includes *catalepsy; dementia precox (or schizophrenia)* (q.v.), where this is shown, is called *catatonic.*

Catechetical method: the Socratic method of instruction by skilful questioning.

Categorical imperative: moral duty, independent of all conditions.

Category: class, usually based on essential or fundamental considerations.

Catelectrotonus: heightened excitability of a nerve or muscle in the vicinity of the cathode, during the passage of a direct electric current.

Catharsis: literally 'purging'; used figuratively in several connections: (1) in connection with play, which is assumed to afford an opportunity of working off, as it were, natural impulses which were at one time in the history of the race biologically important, but are now either useless or inconsistent with the conditions of modern civilized life; (2) in connection with the freeing of repressed emotion, generally spoken of as *abreaction* (q.v.); and (3) as by Aristotle, applied to the purging of fear and anger by seeing the representation of these on the stage in tragedy, an idea further extended to other forms of artistic representation by other writers.

Cathexis: accumulation of mental energy on some particular idea, memory, or line of thought or action (much used in this sense by psychoanalysts).

Cathode: the negatively charged electrode in a vacuum tube. The *cathode ray oscillograph* is a delicate instrument, by which electrical changes are recorded by the deflection of electrons emitted from a cathode, in an electromagnetic or electrostatic field.

Catoptrics: branch of optics dealing with reflection phenomena.

Caudate nucleus: mass of nervous matter forming part of the *striate body* (q.v.), next the *thalamus* (q.v.).

Causality: the presumption of connection between events or phenomena of such a kind that the occurrence or presence of one is necessarily preceded, accompanied, or followed by the occurrence or presence of another or others.

Causal nexus: relation or connection between successive phases of an event, or between two successive events, in a causal series.

Cell: the structural unit of which living organisms are built; in the higher orders taking many forms adapted for many functions.

Cell body: see *neuron;* formerly called simply nerve cell.

Censorship: term employed by *Freud,* to express figuratively the influence of an *endopsychic* (q.v.) selective agency, which functions as a barrier to prevent repressed impulses, memories, and ideas from coming into consciousness.

Cent: in music the 1,200th part of an octave or the 100th part of a *tempered semitone.*

Centile rank: term employed in statistics of a score in a test, giving the percentage of the total distribution falling below that score.

Central tendency: referring, in connection with the employment of a *rating scale* (q.v.), to the tendency for judgments, with regard to a quality or trait, to gravitate towards the middle of the scale.

Cephalagra: headache. Also *cephalalgia.*

Cephalic: relating to the head. The *cephalic index* is a standard anthropometrical measurement, given by the ratio of the maximum breadth to the maximum length of the skull.

Cerebellum: 'little brain'; the mass of nervous matter above and behind the *medulla* (q.v.) at the top of the spinal cord.

Cerebral: relating to *cerebrum* (q.v.). *Cerebral dominance theory*, one of the two hemispheres being the dominant hemisphere, the left in right-handed people, and the right in left-handed people; the theory that any disturbance of this dominance results in speech disturbance, reading difficulties, etc.

Cerebration: physiological activity in the cerebral hemispheres.

Cerebrospinal: applied to the nervous system, the centres of which are contained within the skull and spinal canal (exclusive of certain *ganglia* (q.v.) within the skull belonging to the *autonomic* (q.v.) system). *Cerebrospinal fluid*, a fluid contained in the *ventricles* (q.v.) of the brain and the central canal of the spinal cord.

Cerebrotonia: one of the personality types arrived at by a correlation of physical and temperamental characteristics, the physique showing predominant *ectomorphy* (q.v.).

Cerebrum: the main division of the brain in vertebrates, lying above, and, in man, covering the other masses of nervous matter within the skull.

Cervical: related to the neck region, used particularly of the nerves and vertebrae.

Chain reflex: a series of reflexes so related that the completion of the action of one initiates the next, and so on in a chain.

Chalone: an *autacoid* (q.v.) which produces an inhibitory effect – the opposite of *hormone* (q.v.).

Chance: in statistical sense, the theoretical probability of the occurrence of an event, calculated on the basis of the mathematical theory of probability; in a biological sense, of a *variation*, which appears random or unpredictable.

Character: employed in a biological sense of any feature of an organism in respect of which it can be compared with other organisms. Psychologically employed of that integration of habits, sentiments and ideals which renders an individual's actions relatively stable and predictable: special features in this integration, or revealing themselves in action, are designated *character traits*, and tests devised to bring out such features are *character* or *personality tests*. Psychoanalysts tend to use the term *character traits* in a limited sense of original tendencies persisting throughout life, more or less in the original form or as *sublimated* (q.v.).

Characterization: description of the main features of an object or a personality; in a more special sense used of the development of character through social interaction.

Characterology: that branch of psychology concerned with character and personality.

Charlatan: quack; one professing expert knowledge or skill without possessing it.

Charpentier's bands: when a disc with a white sector on black is rotated at a certain slow rate on a colour mixer a series of dark bands appears at the front edge of the white sector, and of light bands behind the black edge; the same phenomena may be seen when a bright slit is moved across a dark background. Cf. *Bidwell's ghost* and *Fechner's colours*.

Charpentier's law: within the *fovea* (q.v.) the product of the image area and the light intensity is constant for threshold stimuli.

Chemical sense: generally a sense which is affected by a chemical reaction produced in the receptor by a stimulus substance; in lower organisms a combination of what later becomes the separate senses of taste and smell; the term *chemical reflex* is similarly used of a reflex evoked by a chemical process in a receptor.

Chemoreceptor: see *chemical sense*.

Chemotropism: an orienting response to a chemical stimulus.

Chemotaxis: see *tropism*.

Chess-board illusion: a visual illusion of depth produced by a black and white check pattern in a circle, the checks becoming progressively larger towards the circumference.

Cheyne-Stokes respiration: breathing in certain pathological conditions, which shows a rapidly diminishing, followed by a rapidly increasing, rate.

Chiaroscuro: an artistic term for the distribution of light and shade in a picture so as to produce a distance effect.

Chiasma: see *optic*.

Child guidance: a development of methods, chiefly by way of clinics, for dealing with behaviour and educational problems in children. See *guidance*.

Child-parent fixation: term, used mainly by psychoanalysts, for the *fixation* (q.v.) of interest (libido), either in the form of love or hate, on a parent. Cf. *Oedipus complex*.

Child psychology: a branch of psychology which studies the human being in development from birth to maturity.

Cheirognosy: attempt to read character from the lines on the hand.

Cheiromancy: attempt to foretell an individual's future from a study of the lines on the hand.

Cheirosophy: comprehensive study of the lines on the hand, inclusive of *cheirognosy* and *cheiromancy*.

Choc: uncoordinated response elicited by a sudden stimulus, for which the individual has not been prepared by immediately preceding experience.

Choice: a phase of *volition* (q.v.), involving the selection of one of two or more alternatives (sometimes after a period of *deliberation*).

Choice reaction: a form of *reaction experiment* (q.v.), where the subject is instructed to react differently to two or more different stimuli; may be made also the basis of a learning experiment, either with animal or with human subjects.

Choleric: one of the types of *temperament* (q.v.) according to the old or classical doctrine, marked by quick and intense emotional response.

Chord: in music a more or less harmonious combination of tones sounded together.

Chorda tympani: a branch of the facial nerve, mostly sensory, carrying nerve impulses from taste receptors.

Chorea: motor disorder characterized by jerky, spasmodic movements; two types distinguishable – *Sydenham's chorea*, of a rheumatic nature, and *Huntington's chorea*, progressive, and due often to lesions in the *striate* and brain-stem regions. *Choreic* or *choreiform* movements may also be functional and not due to true chorea.

Choroid: the middle coat of the eyeball containing numerous blood-vessels and pigment cells.

Choromania: frenzied dancing, appearing as a social epidemic, belonging with a number of other social phenomena of an analogous nature, and capable of being regarded as a phenomenon of *mass suggestion* and *imitation*.

Christian Science: a religious movement, founded by *Mrs Eddy* in 1866; the chief practical tenet of its creed is that pain and illness are illusions, and are to be treated as such.

Chroma: synonym for hue *saturation* (q.v.), also a musical term, equivalent to semitone (see *chromatic scale*).

Chroma-brightness (brilliance) coefficient: the ratio of hue to *brightness* (*brilliance*), which varies in the spectrum from a maximum in the violet to a minimum in the yellow.

Chromaesthesia: association of particular colours with sounds, or, less frequently, with sensations from other sense departments, sometimes called *psychochromaesthesia.*

Chromatic aberration: error in an optical system, resulting from the different refrangibility of different wave-lengths in the spectrum, and showing itself, unless corrected, as a coloured fringe in objects at the focus.

Chromatic dimming: sudden diminution of the effect of a chromatic stimulus after the eye has been affected by its full intensity for a few seconds, due to the influence of *successive contrast* (q.v.).

Chromatic scale: succession of notes through an octave, each differing from the next by a semitone.

Chromatics: in vision, the science of colour; in hearing, equivalent to *chromatic scale.*

Chromatism: see *photism.*

Chromatopseudopsia: colour-blindness (q.v.).

Chromatopsia: seeing colourless objects coloured as a result of an abnormal condition of vision, as in snow-blindness.

Chromatotropism: orienting response to a certain hue. See *tropism.*

Chromosome: the small body taking part in the cell division in the fertilized ovum, supposed to carry the *genes* (q.v.), the carriers of hereditary traits.

Chronaxy: the minimal duration of a current double the threshold value which is effective in producing excitation, taken as an index of the excitability of a tissue.

Chronic: applied to disorders which persist over a long period.

Chronograph: a device for the measurement of time intervals, by recording graphically the beginning and end of the interval in question, the mechanism, as a rule, either clockwork or motor, running continuously.

Churinga: magic or ritual stones or pieces of wood hidden away in secret places, representing among Australian aborigines the souls or minds of the owners.

Ciliary muscles: muscles attached to the *suspensory ligament* of the lens of the eye, by means of which the curvature, and therefore the focal length, of the eye is controlled.

Cinematograph: apparatus for recording movement photographically, by means of a series of still pictures, separated from one another by short intervals of darkness; popularly used also of the apparatus by means of which these pictures are projected.

Circular psychosis: mental disorder characterized by alternating *excitement* and *depression.*

Circular reaction: reaction, reflex, or response, the end result of which stimulates its repetition.

Circumvallate papilla: see *papilla.*

Circus movements: movements in which the organism tends to move in a circle, owing either to one-sided brain injury or to continuous one-sided stimulation.

Clairaudience: power of hearing sounds and words, conveying information of events at a distance, without the use of the ear. See *cryptaesthesia.*

Clairvoyance: power of seeing, without the use of the eye, events taking place at a distance. See *cryptaesthesia.*

Clang: a musical note in any musical instrument, which is normally a compound of the fundamental tone and *overtones* (q.v.), its quality being given by the relative prominence of certain overtones or groups of overtones, known as the *clang-tint* or *timbre* (q.v.).

Clarke's column: a group of cell bodies in the spinal cord, the axons of which pass to the *cerebellum* (q.v.).

Class interval: in statistics, the designation of the interval between the means of the groups into which a quantitative series is grouped for statistical treatment, or the range of values over which such a group extends.

Class system: form of social organization of which the *caste-system* (q.v.) is the best illustration.

Classification test: a type of mental test, where the subject is required to classify words, designating objects belonging together, either by crossing out one that does not belong, or by underlining those that do; sometimes the term is used less happily for a test or group of tests the purpose of which is to classify, say, pupils in a school.

Claustrophobia: morbid dread of confined spaces.

Clavus hystericus: a pain localized near the middle line on the top of the skull, which is one of the symptoms of *hysteria* (q.v.).

Clever Hans (der kluge Hans): see *Elberfeld horses.*

Climacteric: period of the menopause in women. Mental disorders occurring at this time are known as *climacteric psychoses.*

Clinic: place for the diagnosis and treatment of various disorders, physical, developmental, or behavioural.

Clinical: original usage of bedside observation; now used generally of observation and examination for diagnostic purposes.

Cloaca: the passage in animals through which the discharge of faeces takes place; the theory frequently held by children that birth takes place by this way appears in the writings of psycho-analysts as the *cloaca theory.*

Clonic: see *clonus.*

Clonus: rapid contractions and relaxations of antagonistic groups of muscles. See *convulsion* and *stammering.*

Closure: one of the principles emphasized by *Gestalt* (q.v.) psychologists, describing the process by which percepts, memories, actions, etc., attain stability, viz. the subjective closing of gaps, or completion of incomplete forms, so as to constitute wholes.

Cloud experiment: an experiment or observation by *Fechner,* in illustration of *Weber's law* (q.v.), that if two clouds just noticeably different in greyness are observed through smoked glass, they cease to be distinguishable.

Clouding: used of consciousness in *psychotic* states, when there is some lack of orientation to a present situation.

Coenotropes: types of acquired responses which may be regarded as the product of original nature and an environment shared in common with other organisms; alternatively, common behaviour which results from common social motives.

Cocaine: an alkaloid obtained from the coca plant, used as a local anaesthetic, but also taken as a drug; small doses exercise a stimulating effect, and are alleged to exalt intellectual power; excessive doses produce *cocaine delirium,* a state of high excitement with mental confusion.

Cochlea: part of the inner ear in which are situated the end-organs for hearing; shaped like a snail shell with two and a half whorls, and with a central pillar – the *modiolus* – and three spiral canals – the *scala vestibuli, scala media,* and *scala tympani;* in the *scala media* are the *organs of Corti* (q.v.). See also *ear.*

Co-consciousness: term used by *Morton Prince* to designate dissociated mental phenomena of the same order as conscious phenomena, but outside the individual's personal awareness; usually designated *subconscious* and sometimes exhibiting a high degree of organization, as in the phenomena of *multiple personality* (q.v.).

Code test: a type of mental test in which the subject is required either to translate, by the help of given cues, a secret code, or to write something in a code, the principles of its construction being given.

Coefficient: in mathematics the constant by which a variable is multiplied (e.g. in the algebraic expression $3ax$, $3a$ is the coefficient of the variable x); in statistics an index of the degree in which some characteristic or relation appears in a given case of measurement, as in *coefficient of correlation* (q.v.), of *variability* (q.v.), of *reliability* (q.v.), of *validity* (q.v.).

Coefficient law: see *Fechner-Helmholtz law.*

Coelenterata: the lowest group of the *metazoa*, or many-celled organisms.

Coenaesthesia: common sensibility, or the total undifferentiated mass of sensations, derived from the body as a whole, but more particularly the internal organs.

Cognition: a general term covering all the various modes of knowing – perceiving, remembering, imagining, conceiving, judging, reasoning. The *cognitive* function, as an ultimate mode or aspect of the conscious life, is contrasted with the *affective* and *conative* – feeling and willing – or it is *noesis* (q.v.) as contrasted with *orexis* (q.v.).

Cohesion: a synonym for *association* (q.v.).

Coincidence: used generally of close agreement amounting to point to point correspondence; and specially, of the meeting in practically the same result of two entirely independent series of events, or of the unexpected conjunction or concurrence in time, or space, or both, of two causally independent series or trains of happenings.

Cold spot: small area on skin peculiarly sensitive to stimuli (punctate) below the body temperature.

Collateral: a branch leaving the *axon* of a *neuron* (q.v.).

Collecting instinct: congenital impulse to obtain and hoard certain kinds of objects independently of their usefulness, the actual objects collected being, however, frequently determined by social imitation.

Collective: belonging to a group as a whole, as in *collective mind* or *consciousness* (of a crowd or mob).

Collective imagination: imagination as represented by products such as myths which are definitely the result of cooperative or collective activity.

Collective psychology: synonym for *group psychology*, or for *social psychology*.

Collective unconscious: term employed by analysts for those elements in the individual's *unconscious* derived from the experiences of the race; employed to a considerable extent by *Jung.*

Colligation: a combination in which the units remain distinct, as contrasted with *fusion* (q.v.).

Colorimeter: instrument for measuring colours, especially of liquids.

Colour: employed either generally, of qualities of visual sensations, inclusive of white, black and the greys, or in the more limited sense of the hues or chromatic colours only, the latter being the preferable usage; the different hues are due to the different wavelengths of the transmitted or reflected light.

Colour-blindness: a defect either congenital or acquired, and either total or partial, affecting an individual's ability to distinguish colours; the variations of congenital colour-blindness are fairly well marked; in total colour-blindness – *achromatism* or *achromatopsia* – all the hues are seen as shades of grey; partial colour-blindness – *dichromatism* – involving usually an inability to distinguish reds and greens, or confusion of these colours, presents two types – *deuteranopia,* characterized by a spectrum of normal length, and *protanopia,* marked by a shortening of the spectrum at the red, and sometimes also at the violet, end; a third type of partial colour-blindness – *tritanopia* – occurs so very rarely that dogmatism about it is out of place, except that it is marked by defect in the blues and yellows. Red-green confusion is fairly common among men – perhaps $7\frac{1}{2}$ per cent, 5 per cent *deuteranopes* and $2\frac{1}{2}$ per cent *protanopes* – but very rare among women – perhaps one per thousand – as a congenital condition.

Colour-blindness tests: three types of tests have been used for a rapid diagnosis of colour defect: (1) matching tests, such as the *Holmgren wools,* or the *Nagel cards,* (2) confusion tests in which the subject is required to recognize letters, numbers or forms, printed in confusion colours with the background, such as the *Ishihara, Stilling,* or *Rabkin* tests, (3) coloured lights, presented under different conditions with respect to size and luminosity, such as the *Edridge-Green* or the *Giles-Archer* lantern tests.

Colour circle: disc with sectors in colours corresponding to those of the spectrum, in the proportion required to give a grey or colourless field, on rotation. Not to be confused with *colour cycle* which is also a representation by a circle of the spectral colours in their order and proportions, with the purples and crimsons intervening between the red and the violet.

Colour mixing: the combining of colour stimuli on the same retinal areas, which can be done in various ways: (1) by illumining a white screen by light of the colours to be combined, (2) by rotating

colour discs on a hand- or motor- driven colour mixer or *colour wheel*.
(3) by reflecting one colour on an unsilvered glass plate through
which the other colour is observed, or (4) by using more elaborate
devices such as *spectrometers* or a spectrometer with *anomaloscope*
(q.v.) fitting. In the mixing of pigments, as by the artist, the conditions are more complex, and somewhat different results are obtained, blue and yellow pigments, for example, giving green, in
place of grey, as with lights or rotating discs. See also *binocular
colour mixing*.

Colour pyramid: a schematic representation by a solid figure – usually a
double pyramid with trapezoidal base, though a double cone may
be used – of the whole series of visual sensations, in all their variations of *brightness* (brilliance), *hue*, and *saturation*. Round the base
are placed the fully saturated spectral colours with the purples;
white and black are placed at the ends of the vertical axis, and this
axis represents, through its length, the various shades of grey.

Colour shades: variations of the different hues in *saturation* and *brightness* (brilliance) towards black.

Colour tints: variations of the different hues in *saturation* and *brightness* (brilliance) towards white.

Colour triangle: representation on a plane, of the variations of colour
in hue and saturation, more particularly with reference to the
physics of colour, and the *three-colour theory* (q.v.) of the *primary
colours* (q.v.).

Colour theories: theories of colour vision. See *Young-Helmholtz, Hering,
Ladd-Franklin*.

Colour weakness: defective colour vision, without colour blindness,
affecting one or more colours.

Colour wheel: rotary colour mixer. See *colour mixing*.

Coloured hearing: phenomena occurring in the experience of certain
individuals, where sounds – tunes, vowels, names, etc. – appear
to be coloured – commonest form of *synaesthesia* (q.v.).

Coloured shadows: phenomena of colour *contrast* (q.v.), where, when a
white sheet is illuminated with white light and a coloured light
simultaneously, and a shadow is cast by interposing an object between the coloured light and the white sheet, the shadow appears
coloured with the hue *complementary* (q.v.) to the coloured light,
giving a very striking illustration of *simultaneous colour contrast*.

Columella: a rod in the middle ear of birds and reptiles, which functions like the chain of bones in the human ear, conducting the
sound waves from the drum to the inner ear.

Coma: a state of deep unconsciousness, with non-responsiveness to stimulation.

Combination test: a type of test of intelligence, devised first by the German psychologist *Ebbinghaus* (q.v.); often called *completion* test, since the principle on which it is based is the filling in of blanks in sentences or passages.

Combination tones: additional tones, which are heard when two or more tones are sounded together; these are called *difference* and *summation tones* (q.v.).

Comma: small musical interval, varying slightly with different scales, but always appearing as a difference between two derivations of what ought to be theoretically the same tone, arrived at by different methods of tuning.

Commensalism: type of community life in the animal world where animals of one species live on equal terms with animals of another species.

Commensurable: capable of being measured or assessed in terms of a common unit.

Commissure: a tract of nerve fibres connecting, in the brain and nervous centres, two regions on opposite sides – the fibres are known as *commissural fibres.*

Common sense: apart from the popular use of this expression as meaning practical intelligence based on experience, it was used by *Aristotle,* and revived by *Thomas Reid* to cover the ability to apprehend qualities common to various senses – the 'common sensibles' – such as time, space, number, Reid making this the basis of his reply to the scepticism of *Hume.*

Common sensibility: see *coenaesthesia.*

Comparative psychology: applied usually to *animal* psychology so far as it uses a comparative method.

Compensation: as employed by the analytical schools, a mechanism by which the individual covers up a weakness or defect, by exaggerating the manifestation of a relatively less defective, or more desirable, characteristic. Also employed (in adjectival form for the most part) for movements, often reflex, of one part of the body in order to restore equilibrium – *compensatory movements* and *reflexes.*

Complementary colours: two colours whose mixture produces a colourless or achromatic sensation; for every colour one which is its complementary can be found.

Complete learning method: experimental method in the study of learning, where repetitions are carried on till complete reproduction is secured, an attempt to reproduce being made after each repetition. See *learning* and *saving method*.

Completion test: See *combination test*.

Complex: an idea or associated group of ideas, partly or wholly repressed, strongly tinged with emotion, and in conflict with other ideas or groups of ideas more or less accepted by the individual.

Complication: a mental process involving the combination of the sensations derived from the same object through different senses, in such a way that the experience of one of these sensations later tends to be accompanied by the partial revival of the others, as when the visual impression of an orange drags with it a partial revival of taste and smell sensations formerly experienced from an orange.

Complication experiment: an experiment devised to illustrate the priority in time given to that one of two simultaneous impressions to which attention is directed; an important experiment historically in connection with the analysis of the so-called '*personal equation*'.

Composite: a whole constituted by the features or traits belonging to different individuals, or different experiences, as in composite portraiture (*Galton*) or in the persons appearing in dreams.

Compound eye: the type of eye found in certain insects, which exhibits an alternative method to the lens method of obtaining on a sensitive surface the image of an object, in this case as a mosaic, the eye consisting of a number of separate rudimentary optical systems (*ommatidia* or *ocelli* (q.v.)).

Compound reaction: a type of reaction studied in *reaction time* (q.v.) experiments, where the response is not the simple reaction to a stimulus, but a response depending on the performance of definite mental processes, such as discrimination, choice, etc. before the reaction takes place.

Comprehension: intelligent grasp of the meaning of a situation or an action. A test of comprehension is employed in the *Binet scale* (q.v.), where the testee is asked what he would do, or ought to do, in a given situation. Many other forms of *comprehension test* are used, especially in educational tests.

Compromise formation: a type of *psychic mechanism* (q.v.) stressed by the analytical schools, where a repressed impulse finds issue in a kind of behaviour which more or less represents a fusion between the repressed impulse and the repressing forces, or is at least a satisfaction of the impulse so disguised as no longer to meet with resistance from the repressing forces.

Compulsion: an irresistible inner force compelling the performance of

an act without, or even against, the will of the individual performing it; the action in question may also be performed at the bidding
of another who has the power to compel obedience.

Conation: literally 'striving'; used either as a general term inclusive
of all experienced mental activity, or as itself the experience of
activity as an ultimate type of experience, and not infrequently
with confusion of these two senses.

Concentration: the fixing of attention; or a high degree of intensity of
attention.

Conception: that type or level of cognitive process which is characterized by the thinking of qualities, aspects, and relations of objects,
at which therefore comparison, generalization, abstraction, and
reasoning become possible, of which *language* (q.v.) is the great
instrument, and the product the concept – normally represented
by a word.

Concha: the concavity of the external ear or auricle; sometimes used
as synonymous with *auricle.*

Concomitant variations: a canon or principle of *inductive* (q.v.) reasoning,
where we reason from the concomitance of two circumstances
that there is some causal connection between them.

Concord: harmonious relationship between two or more tones or
musical notes sounding together.

Concrete: applied to a particular object, usually of sense, or to a
particular event, or to some characteristic circumstance, inherent
in such particular object or event, in opposition to *abstract;* sometimes used of the type of intelligence manifested in dealing with
things or practical affairs.

Concussion: physical shock affecting head or spine, and usually producing brief unconsciousness with curious *amnesic* (q.v.) phenomena.

Condensation: term used by *Freud,* and his followers, for the partial
fusion of two or more ideas, occurring particularly in dreams, and
producing a characteristic type of distortion, illustrated by such
words as 'alcoholidays' for the Christmas holidays.

Condition: a circumstance or situation without which a certain event
does not occur.

Conditioning: a process by which a response comes to be elicited by
a stimulus, object, or situation other than that to which it is the
natural or normal response. The term was originally used of the
case where a reflex, normally following on a stimulus A, comes to
be elicited by a different stimulus B, through the constant association of B with A. The phenomena appear to have been first noticed

by Twitmyer, and subsequently followed up by *Bechterev* and *Pavlov* (q.v.), especially the latter, who made the *conditioned reflex*, as he first called it, the principle of explanation of many complex behaviour phenomena.

Conduct: term used for that level of behaviour which is presumably determined by foresight and *volition* (q.v.)

Conduction: used generally of the transmission of energy change along or through a body, and more particularly of the transmission of a nervous impulse along a nerve fibre. When a nerve impulse traverses a fibre in a direction opposite to the normal this is spoken of as *antidromic conduction*. The passage of an impulse from one neuron to another is called *synaptic conduction*. A type of deafness is known as *conduction deafness*, when it is due to some defect in the conducting mechanism – in the drum or in the middle ear.

Cones: elements of the essential receptor layer of the retina, so called from their distinctive shape, as compared with the *rods*.

Configuration: see *Gestalt*.

Conflict: opposition between contradictory impulses or wishes, as a rule producing emotional tension, often highly disagreeable, leading, according to psychoanalytic theories, to *repression* (q.v.) of one of the impulses.

Confluence: the 'flowing together' of different aspects of a situation, producing by the fusion of influences a modification in the apprehension of the situation as a whole. The *Müller-Lyer illusion* (q.v.) may be explained on this basis.

Confusion: employed of a disordered mental condition, involving a *clouding of consciousness*, lack of *orientation*, and tendency to *hallucination*.

Congenital: present in an individual at birth, actually or potentially, and usually inherited.

Congruent: term applied, in connection with vision, to points or figures seen with each eye, but apprehended as single external objects.

Conjugate movements: co-ordinated movements of the two eyes.

Conjunction: the occurring together of two events, phenomena which are made to play the chief role in *Hume's* theory of *causality*.

Conjunctiva: mucous membrane covering the inside of the eyelids, and the front portion of the eyeball.

Connate: used of characteristics appearing at birth or shortly after.

Connection: a wide general term, covering all kinds of relation between mental phenomena.

Connectionism: the theory that all mental processes may be regarded as involving the functioning of inherited or acquired connections between situation and response.

Connectors: that part of the *psycho-organic system* whose function is to connect *receptors* (sense organs) and *effectors* (muscles and glands); otherwise the nervous system.

Connotation: a logical term referring to the qualities, attributes, and characteristics of an object designated by a word.

Conscience: an individual's system of accepted moral principles, or principles of conduct, or alternatively, and usually, the functioning of such system with reference to an act, contemplated or performed, which threatens violation of the principles, involving emotional as well as intellectual factors; the *super-ego* (q.v.) of *Freud* is an attempt at a psychological account and explanation of its origin, nature, development and functioning.

Consciousness: a character belonging to certain processes or events in the living organism, which must be regarded as unique, and therefore as indefinable in terms of anything else, but which can perhaps be best described as a view of these processes or events, as it were, from the inside – the individual is, as it were, inside what is happening; the adjective *conscious* is ordinarily employed as a synonym for 'aware', but this is a popular rather than scientific usage.

Conscious illusion theory: a theory of the nature of *aesthetic* experience, due to *Lange,* which emphasizes its relation to *play* and *make-believe.*

Consciousness of activity: an unanalysable experience, not to be confused with *consciousness of effort.*

Consciousness of effort: an experience made up of sensations derived from various sources, but mainly from the muscles and the internal organs; in the case of effort of attention there may be sensations in the head, as well as sensations from adjustment of the sense organ or organs involved in the particular direction of attention at the moment.

Consensual actions: actions which are involuntary, but accompanied by awareness of their performance.

Consentience: see *anoetic sentience.*

Conservation: the basis of all memory; the term is equivalent more or less, and certainly preferable, to *retention,* as implying nothing beyond the fact, whereas retention implies the preservation of form, and even a hint of agency.

Consistency: sometimes employed in statistics as an alternative to *reliability* (q.v.).

Consonance: harmonious blending or fusion of tones.

Constancy phenomena: phenomena of perception, where psychological laws seem to cut across physical laws, so that perceived objects retain to some extent certain characteristics in relative independence of change in the stimuli affecting the sense organ, the phenomena appearing particularly, though not exclusively, in the case of vision; in such cases the change in the object as perceived is markedly less than the change in the stimulus situation, the characteristics mainly affected being colour, size, shape, as regards visual objects, and weight. Cf. for colour effects, *film colour* and *body colour.*

Constant error: a type of error occurring in psychological experiment, because of some factor, which exercises a constant influence in a definite direction, and which, owing to the conditions under which the experiment must take place, cannot be eliminated. For example, in comparing two tones for pitch the tones must be presented separately, and the comparison may be affected by which is presented first. See *time error* and *space error.*

Constant method: see *method of right and wrong cases.*

Constellation: originally a grouping of ideas, determined by the operating of association, and usually round a main theme; the general usage now is that of the psychoanalysts for a group of emotionally coloured and partially or wholly repressed ideas.

Constitution: the totality of hereditary (and acquired) factors determining an individual's present physical condition and his future development. As an adjective *constitutional* may refer to disorders of various kinds, but the most important psychological reference is to the so-called constitutional types.

Constrained association: a type of association experiment, where the subject's response must bear a certain defined relationship to the stimulus word. Opposite of *free association* (q.v.).

Construct: a term which some writers, such as *Karl Pearson,* have suggested as a substitute for *concept* (q.v.).

Constructive: used as an alternative for *creative* (q.v.) as applied to *imagination*; also applied to thinking which results in arrival at new conclusions, particularly exemplified in invention and discovery. *Constructiveness* is used of behaviour (sometimes of instinctive behaviour), which involves the utilizing of materials to build up objects relevant to the needs of the individual.

Consulting psychologist: a psychologist who gives professional advice.

Consummatory response: the end response of a series bringing final adjustment in a situation which has been partly, or wholly, brought about by preparatory action.

Contact sensations: light touch sensations, without the deformation of the skin surface due to pressure.

Contagion: the spreading to other individuals of forms of feeling or forms of behaviour, through *sympathy* (q.v.), *imitation* (q.v.), or *suggestion* (q.v.).

Contemplation: term used specially of a phase of experience following on the mere having of the experience, or *enjoyment* (q.v.), and involving reaction of the individual in the form of attentive awareness of an object (*Alexander*); used also in a semi-religious sense of the attitude of the mystic.

Content: the material or constituents of an experience, as distinct from the process of experience (or the form); *content* of *consciousness* – better *mental content* – the totality of the constituents of an individual's experience at any time.

Context: the setting in experience of a particular object.

Contiguity: the designation given to one of the primary laws of *association* (q.v.), according to which, when two experiences have occurred together in time or place, the subsequent occurrence, in perception or ideation, of one of them tends to bring the other to mind. It is generally agreed that this law requires considerable qualification.

Contingency: a term employed in statistics for the probability of an association between two facts, qualities, occurrences, or sets of data, as measured by the *contingency coefficient C* which is a quantitative expression based on the mean square contingency ϕ^2 and given by the equation $C=[\phi^2(1+\phi^2)]^{\frac{1}{2}}$. This measures the degree of connection by the extent to which the two are completely independent of one another.

Contractility: a basic property of living tissue in virtue of which it contracts on stimulation.

Contraction: response to stimulation of a muscle.

Contracture: abnormal condition of a muscle when it fails to return to its uncontracted condition, remaining contracted, and in certain cases producing an anatomical deformity.

Contrast: an effect of intensification of difference produced by the juxtaposition of two stimuli and sensations of the same *modality* (q.v.) but differing markedly in quality or intensity; best illustrated by the visual phenomena of *colour* or *brightness* (brilliance) contrast, either *simultaneous* or *successive*, but it is also shown in other sense departments, and with other types of stimuli, or even perceptual objects, as in illusions. In *simultaneous colour contrast* the complementary colour is produced when a colour is observed on a white, grey, or black background (see *coloured shadows*); for *successive colour contrast* see *after-sensations*.

Contrasuggestibility: the tendency, characteristic of some individuals, to respond to attempts at suggestion by another person, by taking exactly the opposite view or course of action to that suggested (must not be confused with *counter-suggestion* (q.v.)).

Control: generally the means taken to validate experimental results; employed of an experiment which is intended to serve as a control over the results of another experiment, and in which, as far as possible, every condition is the same, except that which is under investigation; a *control group* is a group as nearly as possible equivalent to the experimental group, and submitted to all the same conditions except that under investigation; control in analysis may be exercised by one analyst supervising the analysis carried out by another. The word takes a special meaning in psychical research, where the *control* is the spirit (discarnate) purporting to be manifest through the medium.

Control hammer (or pendulum): methods of calibrating the readings of timing apparatus, such as chronoscopes, by apparatus making or breaking circuits, at known and constant intervals.

Controlled association: see *constrained association*.

Convention: social custom arising out of imitation of one's contemporaries rather than one's ancestors, usually recognized as not absolutely binding, and operating normally in minor matters of behaviour and attitude.

Convergence: the turning towards one another of the axes of the two eyes in fixating nearer objects, in order that the images may fall on *corresponding points* (q.v.) in the two retinae.

Convergence theory: the view that seeks to explain psychological phenomena in terms of the convergence (interaction) of congenital (or acquired) specific qualities with specific external situations, as against onesided nativistic or empirical views. Cf. *coenotropes*.

Conversion: a fundamental change of attitude and outlook, usually from opposition or indifference to adherence to an opinion or belief; in the case of religious conversion there is usually, though not necessarily, considerable emotional disturbance. The word has also two special senses: (1) in psychoanalytical literature the transformation into physical manifestation of *repressed complexes*, as in *conversion hysteria*, and (2) in logic the alteration of a proposition by interchanging subject and predicate.

Conviction: belief without any tincture of doubt, but often with an emotional colouring.

Convolution: a fold of the surface of the *cortex* (q.v.) of the cerebrum; a fold in the cerebellum is more accurately called *folium.*

Convulsion: violent and extensive spasm of muscular contraction, caused by processes in the central nervous system.

Co-ordinate: a mathematical term applied to lines of reference (rectangular co-ordinates) or a line and an angle (polar co-ordinates) with reference to which a point is located in a plane surface; by an extension, and by using planes in place of lines the principle may be applied to tridimensional space.

Co-ordination: two distinct senses: (1) of two objects of the same class in the sense of having the same relation to a higher or including class, (2) of muscular or motor regulation or the harmonious co-operation of muscles or groups of muscles, in a complex action or series of actions.

Copro-: prefix meaning 'excrement' or 'dung'.

Coprolalia: uncontrolled or obsessive obscene speech.

Coprophagia: eating of excrement.

Coprophilia: tendency to be interested in faeces.

Coprophobia: irrational dread amounting to *phobia* for faeces.

Cord: the *spinal cord* (sometimes spelt chord).

Corium: the outer part of the *derma* (q.v) underlying the *epidermis* (q.v.).

Cornea: the transparent anterior part of the *sclerotic membrane* (q.v.).

Corneal reflection: reflection of a beam of light from the surface of the cornea, a method of studying and photographically recording eye movements, as in reading.

Corneal reflex: the reflex closing of the eyelids when the cornea or *conjunctiva* (q.v.) is touched.

Coronal plane: the mesial plane of the head passing through the two ears.

Corpora quadrigemina: see *quadrigemina.*

Corpus: body. See *callosum, striatum,* etc.

Correlation: relation between organs, structures, measurements, etc., which vary together; the most important technical use in the psychological field is the statistical one, where the term is applied to the tendency of two series of measurements to vary concomitantly, in consequence of which, knowledge of the one gives us a basis for drawing conclusions regarding the other, according to the extent or degree of the correlation. The degree of correlation is measured by the *coefficient of correlation* when the relation is linear, the *ratio of correlation* when it is not linear. The extension of correlation methods to more than two variables is known as *multiple correlation*. See also *regression, partial correlation, spurious correlation.*

Corresponding points: points in the two retinae which yield single vision when stimulated by a single object (opposite *disparate* (q.v.)).

Cortex: the outer layer of an organ; used especially of the cerebrum and cerebellum; when used alone the reference is always to the cerebral cortex.

Corti: employed in the designation of structures in the inner ear. The *organ of Corti* is composed of the *arches of Corti* formed by the inner and outer *rods* or *pillars of Corti.*

Cortical blindness: see *mind blindness.*

Cortical grey: medium grey – the grey appearing before the *dark-adapted eye* when not stimulated.

Cortical set: see *mental set.*

Cortin: the active principle of the adrenal cortex responsible for the adrenal *hormone* (q.v.), *adrenalin* (q.v.).

Cosmogony: theory, usually mythological, of the origin and early history of the universe.

Cosmos: the universe as an ordered system.

Co-twin control: an experimental method employed in the study of *maturation* (q.v.), and *learning* in twins, the one twin being the subject and the other the *control*. Important from a theoretical as well as a practical point of view.

Counter-suggestion: a suggestion aiming at the counteracting of the influence of a previous suggestion of *fixed idea* (q.v.).

Couvade: the custom prevalent among primitive peoples, in which, on the birth of a child, the father takes to bed.

Covariance: a statistical term in the measurement of the tendency of two series to vary concomitantly; if x and y are the deviations from the means of paired members in the series then the covariance is $\sum (xy)/N$, where N is the number of cases in each series, i.e. the average product of the paired deviations. Cf. *product-moment correlation* formula.

Covert response: implicit response (q.v.).

Coyness: half-serious withdrawal responses, on the part of a female, from amorous approaches by a male.

Cram: a method of preparing for an examination by memorizing the material immediately before the examination, mainly by repetitive methods, and relying on *recency* and *frequency* for success in reproducing the material.

Cramp: violent and painful contraction of a muscle or muscle group maintained for some time.

Cranial: relating to the *cranium* or skull; *cranial capacity,* the cubic content of the cranium; *cranial index, cephalic index* (q.v.); *cranial nerve,* a nerve arising within the cranium.

Craniography: photographing or charting the skull.

Craniology: branch of biological science which studies the characteristics of the (human) skull. See *phrenology.*

Craniometry: systematic measurement of the human skull.

Cranioscopy: study or plotting of areas of skull. See *phrenology.*

Cranium: skull.

Craving: strong and persistent desire or appetite.

Craze: an effect of *mass suggestion* and imitation involving the uncritical, and often irrational, adoption of a style of dress, form of behaviour, etc., amounting sometimes to a *mania* (q.v.); sometimes also used loosely in the case of an individual of an unusual and somewhat irrational attitude or desire. Cf. *fad.*

Creative: producing an essentially new product, constructive (somewhat wider); used of *imagination,* where a new combination of ideas or images is constructed (strictly when it is self-initiated, rather than imitated); also of thought synthesis, where the mental product is not a mere summation.

Cretinism: a condition, endemic in certain localities, of stunted physical and mental development, due to lack of *thyroid* development, appearing in early childhood, and, if treated with thyroid extract at a sufficiently early stage, capable of being greatly ameliorated.

Crime: a grave offence against the law, and punishable as such. Minor offences are called *misdemeanours,* or, in the case of a juvenile, *delinquencies,* while transgression of divine law, or violation of some religious or moral principle is called *sin.*

Criminal psychology: the branch of psychology which investigates the psychology of *crime* and of the criminal (usually extending its field of study to *delinquency*).

Criminal responsibility: a legal term referring to the conditions under which a criminal is, or is not, responsible in the eyes of the law for his act, and liable to appropriate punishment by law determined.

Criminology: the science which investigates *crime* and criminality, of which criminal psychology may be regarded as a branch.

Crisis: a definite turning-point in a course of events.

Criterion: a standard of judgment, or a test of truth or *validity.*

Critical: in general, referring to a point of transition, or a period of suspense; in a special sense, of the minimal rate of succession of stimuli in vision (as in the rotation of discs) at which *flicker* (q.v.) disappears and complete fusion takes place; or statistically, of the ratio of a magnitude to its *standard error* (q.v.).

Critique: systematic examination of a theory or theories in full detail.

Cro-magnon man: a type of early man, represented by skulls found in Western Europe, which indicate a surprisingly high development physically and mentally.

Cross conditioning: a type of *conditioning* (q.v.) arising as a secondary result from entirely irrelevant stimuli received in the course of a response to primary conditioning.

Cross education (*training*)*:* improvement in motor performance as a result of practice in that or a similar performance by one side or part of the body, produced in another side or part, itself unpractised.

Cross-out (*X-O*) *tests:* tests in which the testee is asked to cross out items, according to definite instructions or principles.

Cross(*ed*) *reflex:* a reflex response on one side of the body, elicited by a stimulus on the other side.

Crowd: a group of individuals temporarily presenting a certain unity of feeling and action, owing to the fact that their attention is concentrated on the same object, material or ideal. Because of this mental unity, which is the essential and fundamental characteristic of the crowd, its mentality tends to be more primitive than that of the normal individual member of the crowd, and is therefore spoken of as the *crowd mind,* and the investigation of its characteristics as *crowd psychology.*

Crucial: adjective used of an experiment or test which is decisive, with respect to a judgment, theory, or hypothesis.

Cruelty: disposition to take pleasure, or find satisfaction, in causing suffering to animals, or to other human beings.

Crura cerebri: two columns of nervous substance, or nerve tracts, passing from the *medulla* (q.v.) to the cerebrum, in front of the cerebellum, and behind the *pons* (q.v.).

Cryptaesthesia: a general term covering the varieties of alleged supernormal modes of sensibility, such as *telepathy* (q.v.), *clairvoyance* (q.v.), *clairaudience* (q.v.), and the like.

Cryptomnesia: memory without identification or recognition as previous experience, original experiences being forgotten or repressed, and their reinstatement appearing as a new experience.

Crystal gazing: scrying (q.v.).

Cubital: referring to the region inside the elbow.

Cue: used of an often obscure, secondary stimulus, which functions as a guide to our response, by way either of perception or of action, to a situation, though it may not itself be clearly discriminated.

Cult: a body of beliefs, rites, etc., associated with an object, usually religious, or, more specifically, religious feelings and attitudes expressed in customs, rites, and ceremonies.

Culture: applied usually to the intellectual side of civilization, or with emphasis upon the intellectual aspect of material achievement, or to the degree of intellectual advancement of an individual; more specifically and technically to the sum total of the arts, science, social customs and educational aims of a people, regarded as an integrated whole. *Culture patterns* are constituted by the relative prominence given to different elements in the whole, and the relative degree of advance shown along different lines, with particular emphasis on the educational side. A *culture area* is a geographical area exhibiting closely similar patterns. *Culture* may be used as an adjective of *conflict* or *rivalry* between neighbouring cultures, or of change or development in various aspects of the culture pattern, or of *set* or *attitude*, or of individual characteristics or *traits*, or *elements* in a culture.

Culture epoch theory: the theory that human groups pass through similar types of culture in the same order, as hunting, pastoral, agricultural, industrial. An extension of a similar view to the development of the individual has given rise to the *culture epoch theory* in education. Cf. *biogenetic law.*

Cuneus: a wedge-shaped area on the inner surface of the occipital lobe.

Cunnilingus: a form of sexual perversion consisting of oral stimulation of the female genitalia.

Curare: a vegetable poison which blocks the transmission of impulses along the motor nerves; it is used as an arrow poison by Indian tribes in Central and South America.

Curiosity: a tendency, probably congenital, to be attracted by the novel or strange, and in its developed form to seek knowledge.

Cursive: used of writing, where the letters or characters are connected so that words can be written continuously, without lifting the pen. Contrasted with *uncial.*

Custodial case: an individual requiring supervision and a measure of segregation, because of handicap, defect, mental disorder, or criminality.

Cutaneous: referring or belonging to the skin.

Cutaneous pupillary reflex: the reflex dilation of the pupil of the eye, caused by scratching the skin of cheek or chin.

Cutaneous secretory reflex: reflex activity of the sweat glands caused by any stimulation of the skin.

Cutaneous sense: used inclusively of the sensations derived from the receptors in the skin for *contact, pressure, cold, warmth,* and *pain.*

Cyan: a greenish blue; peacock.

Cycle: a series of events recurring as a whole; applied particularly to a sound wave or any periodic pendular change or movement.

Cycloid: a *personality type,* characterized by oscillation between excitement and depression.

Cyclopean eye: a hypothetical or theoretical single eye, between the two eyes, with reference to which visual objects are located.

Cyclophoria: variety of *muscular imbalance* (q.v.) of the eyes, in which one eye tends to move slightly out of position round the horizontal axis; usually under control during fixation, but showing itself when the stimulus to focus is withdrawn.

Cycloplegia: paralysis of the *ciliary muscle* (q.v.).

Cyclorama: an illusion produced in an enclosed space, where an arrangement of solid objects on all sides in the foreground seems to melt into a painted background, and produces the effect of one's being in the middle of a great area.

Cyclostat: an apparatus consisting of a cylindrical glass case, in which an animal is rotated at varying speeds, the rate of rotation being recorded on a dial.

Cyclothymia: tendency to alternating *excitement* and *depression,* or *manic-depressive* attacks.

Cylindrical lens: a lens provided with a cylindrical surface, used for the correction of *astigmatism* (q.v.).

Cytology: science which studies living cells.

Cytoplasm: protoplasm surrounding the nucleus of a cell.

D

Dactylology: art of communication by means of signs with hands and fingers.

Daltonism: colour-blindness (q.v.), particularly *protanopia* (q.v.), so named from *Dalton* the chemist, who was a protanope.

Damping: in acoustics, the reducing of the amplitude of a vibrating body: the *damping constant* is a quantitative measurement of the rate of decrease of amplitude, given by δ/T, where T is the period.

Dancing Mania: an uncontrollable impulse, which has sometimes appeared in epidemic form, as a result of *mass suggestion* (q.v.), notably in European cities in 1370.

Dancing Mouse: a Japanese breed of mouse, which has been used in *learning* experiments, notably in some of the earlier work.

Dark Adaptation: a condition of vision brought about progressively by remaining in complete darkness for a considerable period, and characterized by progressive increase in retinal (*rod*) sensitivity (see *adaptometer*). A *dark-adapted eye* is an eye in which dark adaptation has taken place.

Darwinism: theory of evolution formulated by Darwin, particularly the emphasis on the principle of *natural selection* (q.v.).

Data: group of known, given, or ascertained facts, from which a conclusion is drawn, or on which a discussion is based.

Day Blindness: a condition of vision in which the individual sees better in dim light, due to impairment of vision in central area of the retina, or central *scotoma* (q.v.).

Daydreaming: type of *phantasy* (q.v.), in which the individual allows his mind to wander aimlessly among pleasant imagery, gratifying wishes ungratified in real life. Cf. *autistic thinking*.

Daymare: acute *anxiety* seizure in the waking state.

Day residues: used by *Freud* and psychoanalysts for emotional or worrying experiences of the preceding day which play a part in forming the content of dreams.

Deaf mute: person unable to learn to speak because of deafness.

Deafness: limited ability to hear sounds through the normal range of hearing: when there is deafness only for the higher frequencies in normal speech we speak of *high frequency deafness*. Deafness may be either organic, i.e. due to structural disease or defect, or functional. *Cortical* or *mind deafness* is deafness dependent on some defect or lesion in the cortical centre for hearing. *Nerve deafness* is caused by defect in the auditory nerve at some point in the path by which sound waves are conducted to the inner ear.

Death feigning: see *tonic immobility*.

Death instinct: according to *Freud's* theory, the impulses aiming at destruction, death, or escape from stimulation on the part of the individual, as contrasted with the *life impulses,* and primarily appearing as the *repetition compulsion,* in consequence of which the individual must seek death only by repeating the normal life cycle.

Decency: the quality of conducting oneself in conformity with social principles of conduct, particularly in the observing of social taboos.

Decerebrate: used of an animal whose cerebrum has been removed; also of that *rigidity* which follows upon *decerebration,* as a result of exaggerated contraction of the extensor muscles of the limbs.

Decibel: the tenth of a *bel* (q.v.), the unit generally employed in the measurement of the intensity of sounds on a logarithmic scale; originally chosen as equivalent to the *just noticeable difference* (q.v.), and under the assumption of the validity of the *Weber-Fechner law* (q.v.).

Decision: where choice of courses of action must be made, the phase of *volition* (q.v.), following normally upon *deliberation,* and preceding action.

Decortication: experimental removal of the cerebral cortex of an animal.

Decorum: conformity to social standards of behaviour and conduct, more particularly as regards the maintaining of one's personal dignity and self-respect in public.

Decussation: the crossing of bundles or tracts of nerve fibres from one side to the other, particularly used of the decussation of the *pyramids* (q.v.) in the *medulla* (q.v.).

Deduction: inferring from premises, or propositions representing already known facts.

Deep pressure sensibility: subcutaneous sensibility to intense pressure applied to cutaneous surface.

Deep reflex: a muscular reflex elicited by tapping the tendon or bone of attachment.

Deep sensibility: sensibility depending on receptors lying deep in cutaneous or subcutaneous tissue.

Defect: failure to come up to the normal, or an agreed, standard. For *mental defect* see *mental.* For visual or optical defect see *myopia, hypermetropia, presbyopia, astigmatism.* For visual colour defect see *colour-blindness.*

Defective delinquent: a young *delinquent* (q.v.), who is also mentally defective, and in whom the mental defect is a contributory factor in the delinquency.

Defence mechanism: involuntary or unconscious measures adopted by an individual to protect himself against the painful *affect* associated with some highly disagreeable situation, physical or mental, of frequent occurrence; may be employed to cover a wide range of the phenomena emphasized by analysts, from *repressions* and forgettings to mannerisms and the like, unconsciously assumed to cover a defect. The term *defence reaction* is sometimes used for the resulting behaviour, but also includes defensive measures adopted more or less consciously to avoid exposing something there is a strong desire to conceal.

Deferred reaction experiment: a type of experiment used in *animal psychology*, to study the kind of learning which involves the functioning of a *memory image* (q.v.), and incidentally to obtain evidence for the presence of such.

Deficiency: more or less synonymous with *defect*, but usually somewhat narrower in referring to lack in some specific substance or single function.

Deflection: psychoanalytic term for the process of unconsciously evading attention to certain ideas or aspects of ideas.

Deformity: a marked deviation from the normal due to development, accident. or disease. Applied figuratively to the mind or the personality.

Defusion: see *instinctual*.

Degeneracy: marked lowering of the level of social behaviour or conduct (or mental functions), either congenital or acquired.

Degeneration: progressive lowering of the efficiency of an organ or organs, or of some aspect of mind or character.

Deglutition: the process of swallowing.

Degradation Law: a principle or law formulated by *Delboeuf*, as a partial substitute for *Weber's law* (q.v.), to the effect that a sensation is always strongest on entry into consciousness, and diminishes in intensity thereafter.

Deiters's Cells: supporting cells in the outer part of the *organ* of *Corti* (q.v.).

Déjà Vu: an *illusion* of recognition, or type of *paramnesia* (q.v.) when one experiences a new experience as if it had all happened before.

Delayed: used of an instinctive response or form of behaviour, which appears only some considerable time after birth, or of a reaction, or reflex, which does not occur immediately on the stimulus, but only after the lapse of a period of time, unusual for a reflex, and sometimes also of the *deferred reaction experiment* (q.v.).

Delboeuf disc: device employed by Delboeuf for determining *difference thresholds* (q.v.) for *brightness* (brilliance), by the method of *equal appearing intervals*. It consists of rotated discs showing three rings, the middle one of which must be varied by the subject, so that it appears exactly midway between the other two in brightness. Since all are grey it is a simple matter to find the white-black ratio for each.

Deliberation: initial phase of choice where two alternatives are presented as possible courses of action.

Delinquent: used generally of the young offender against the law, but also where the offence is not so serious as to be designated *crime.*

Délire du toucher: compulsion (obsessive) to touch objects, illustrated by Dr Samuel Johnson.

Delirium: a condition of clouding of consciousness, accompanied by *illusions, hallucinations,* and incoherent trains of thought, with restlessness and usually high fever. Cf. *alcoholic psychosis.*

Delta movement: see *apparent movement.*

Delusion: false opinion or belief which cannot be shaken by reason; if persistent, regarded as an insane delusion.

Dementia: loss of mental powers, generally owing to organic or functional disorder; a type of degenerative insanity; to be distinguished from *amentia* (q.v.).

Dementia praecox: mental disorder, now usually called *schizophrenia* (q.v.), showing several marked types, all of them characterised by deterioration; sometimes known as *adolescent insanity* because of its most frequent incidence before the age of thirty; varieties: – *hebephrenic, catatonic, paranoid, paraphrenic* (q.v.).

Demography: statistical investigation of populations, inclusive of geographical situation, social status, mental capacity, etc.

Demonology: mythology and folk-lore dealing with demons and evil spirits.

Demonomania: popularly demon possession; delusional disorder manifesting itself in the delusion on the part of an individual that he is under the influence of an evil spirit.

Demophobia: morbid dread of crowds.

Demorphinization: treatment of the morphia habit by the gradual diminution of the dose.

Dendrite: process of a *neuron* (q.v.), usually, though not always, short and branching, but defined scientifically as a process traversed by nerve impulses in the direction of the cell body.

Denotation: logical term signifying the object designated by a term. Cf. *connotation.*

Dentate nucleus: a group of nerve cells in the *cerebellum.*

Dependency: applied to the relation of an individual to another individual or to society, as receiving aid, without which he is presumably unable to maintain himself, or his position as a member of the community – that is *dependent*.

Depersonalization: in the individual, a more or less pathological state in which he loses his feeling of the reality of himself, or of his body, or may feel that he is dead; also used of a philosophy of the universe, which no longer regards natural forces as manifestations of supernatural agents or gods.

Depolarization: physical term signifying the removal or counteracting of the effect of *polarization* (q.v.); sometimes used figuratively in connection with words and ideas which are emotionally coloured – polarized – of analogous removal of such emotional colouring.

Depression: an emotional attitude, sometimes definitely pathological, involving a feeling of inadequacy and hopelessness, sometimes overwhelming, accompanied by a general lowering of psychophysical activity.

Depressor Nerve: used generally of any nerve which depresses the activity or function of a motor centre, and specially of a branch of the *vagus nerve* (q.v.), which causes dilatation of the peripheral blood vessels with lowering of blood pressure.

Depth: used in vision of perceived distance from the eye of an observer, or of the third dimension; the main depth criteria are, for monocular vision, awareness of contraction of the *ciliary muscle* (q.v.) in accommodation, height of object in field of vision, apparent size, and, for binocular vision, experience of convergence, slight *disparation* (q.v.).

Depth psychology: term frequently applied to the explanation of experience and behaviour in terms of phenomena of the unconscious, and especially of the deep unconscious.

Depth psychology: preferably *depth analysis;* used for analytical investigation of the content of the *unconscious*.

Derangement: see *aberration*.

Dereistic: used by Bleuler, as preferable to *autistic* (q.v.).

Derived emotion: term at one time given by *McDougall* to *Shand's* 'prospective emotions of desire' i.e. such emotions as hope, disappointment, despair, etc.

Dermis: the true skin, under the *epidermis*. *Dermal* is synonymous with cutaneous.

Dermatography: the appearance on an individual's skin of figures and letters traced with light contact, owing to extreme irritability of the capillaries in the skin.

Desire: general term for *appetition* (q.v.) with clear consciousness of its object.

Despair: an intensely unpleasant emotional state, associated with the abandoning of hope of a successful issue of one's efforts to attain an end or satisfy a desire; classed by *Shand* as one of the 'prospective emotions of desire' and by *McDougall* as a *derived emotion* (q.v.).

Despondency: an emotional attitude arising from failure, but not yet becoming *despair* (q.v.).

Deterioration: progressive impairment of function.

Determinant: an organic unit composed of *biophores* (q.v.).

Determine: used in various technical and semi-technical senses, most of which involve the notion of making definite, whether positively, or negatively, by limitation. *Determinate* and *determination* represent most clearly the basal meaning of defining or settling a problem, or establishment of a fact. In *determining tendency* there is the additional notion of the thought processes tending, or being made, to take a certain definite line, and the same notion is carried by the word *determiner*, used of a factor in a cell in the embryo, which causes the development of certain characters in the organism. Again *determinism*, as a philosophical theory, means the view that all phenomena are necessary results of previously existing conditions, which is, for a postulate of positive science, and one of the fundamental postulates also of psychoanalysis, particularly relevant to *Freud's* theory of the dream. Cf. *free will.*

Detraction: sometimes used of lessening the degree of concentration, without alteration of the focus, of attention.

Detumescence: subsidence of swelling.

Deuteranomalous: a type of *anomalous* colour vision, differing from the normal, in apparently diminished sensitivity to green, relatively to red, as indicated by the increased amount of green required in the *Rayleigh equation* (q.v.).

Deuteranopia: type of partial colour-blindness, involving red-green confusion, with normal length of visible spectrum, the name being given with reference to the physical theory of three *primary colours* (q.v.), implying the absence of the second colour, viz. green; hence sometimes called *green blindness.* See *colour-blindness.*

Deutoplasm: the yolk of an egg.

Development: progressive change in an organism, continuously directed towards a certain end condition (e.g. the progressive change from the embryo to the adult in any species); *arrest of development* is the checking of the normal course of development; the adjective *developmental* may be applied to the *mechanism* of development, a *scale* for assessing its progress, the *units* in such a scale, the *zero* or starting-point, etc.

Developmental insanities: types of mental disorder related to definite periods of development, as, for example, *dementia praecox.*

Deviation: general sense, variation from some line, norm, or standard of reference; used in a number of technical senses: (1) visually, of one eye failing to assume its position in coordination with the other in fixation of an object, or of an irregularity between the two eyes, especially with respect to the vertical axis or meridian, in either case producing double vision; (2) statistically, of variation from the mean in a series, as *mean or average deviation* (or *variation*), being the mean of the individual deviations from the mean, or *standard deviation,* the square root of the mean of the squares of the individual deviations, usually denoted by σ and given by the formula $\sigma = \sqrt{\dfrac{\Sigma(x^2)}{N}}$; (3) in *quartile deviation,* another measure of variation, which is half the difference between the *quartiles* (q.v.), better called *semi-interquartile range.*

Dexterity: smooth and rapid, or skilful, movement, usually of arm, hand, or fingers.

Dextrad: towards the right, usually of writing from left to right.

Dextral: on, or belonging to, right side of body.

Dextrality: right hand preference, righthandedness; sometimes used more generally for sidedness, and even inclusive of *sinistrality.*

Dextrasinistral: originally left handed, but trained to use the right.

Diagnosis: determination of the nature of an abnormality, disorder, or disease; a *diagnostic test* is a test suitable and used for this purpose.

Dialectic: a systematic train of *deductive* reasoning, particularly with reference to philosophical or metaphysical investigation.

Diaphragm: the muscular separation between thorax and abdomen; also a device for controlling the transmission of light, e.g. the *Aubert* or *iris diaphragm.*

Diaschisis: lowering of the excitability of a nerve centre, by withdrawal of normally exciting stimuli from other centres.

Diastole: the dilation phase of heart action (heart beat).

Diathermy: shock method of treatment of *general paralysis of the insane,* by raising the blood temperature by means of high frequency alternating current.

Diathesis: predisposition in a certain direction, as an inherited liability to a specific disease or defect under certain environmental conditions.

Diatonic: used of musical scales characteristic of Western music, with semitones between the third and the fourth, and between the seventh and the eighth (major), or between the second and the third, and between the sixth and the seventh (minor).

Dicho-: (*Gr.*) prefix meaning 'double', or 'separation into two'.

Dichoglottic: applied to simultaneous stimulation of two different areas of the tongue with different taste stimuli.

Dichorhinic: applied to simultaneous stimulation of the two nostrils with different olfactory substances.

Dichotic: applied to simultaneous tonal stimulation of the two ears with tones of different frequencies.

Dichotomy: classification into two classes, on basis of presence or absence of a certain characteristic, or by paired opposites.

Dichromatism: synonym for partial colour blindness, implying the reduction of the colour system to two fundamental colours, in place of three; alternatives are *dichromacy* and *dichromatic vision*.

Dicrotic: used of a pulse showing a notch in the descending part of the wave.

Diencephalon: the *interbrain*, or region of the *thalamus* with the *hypothalamus* and *epithalamus*.

Difference canon: one of Mill's five canons of inductive reasoning, to the effect that 'if an instance in which the phenomenon under investigation occurs, and an instance in which it does not occur, have every circumstance in common save one, that one occurring only in the former, the circumstance in which alone the two instances differ is the effect, or the cause, or an indispensable part of the cause of the phenomenon.'

Difference threshold (*limen*): the least amount by which two stimuli must differ in order that they should be sensed as different: synonyms *just noticeable difference, liminal difference*.

Difference tone: additional tone heard when two tones, sufficiently different in frequency, are sounded together, its frequency being the difference between the frequencies of the tones; if *clangs* (q.v.) are used, a series of difference tones may be heard, because of the differences between the overtones: the loudest difference tone is heard with the ratio of frequencies at 2 : 3, this tone being an octave below the lower fundamental.

Differential psychology: the branch of psychology which, in its wider sense, studies the differences between individuals, groups, or races, in fundamental psychological characteristics, or, in its narrower sense, is equivalent to the study of individual differences by experimental methods. See *individual psychology*.

Differential sensibility: ability to distinguish between stimuli differing in intensity or quality, as measured by the *difference threshold* (q.v.), or *j.n.d.*

Differentiation: progressive change, in evolution or in development.

Diffraction: the bending of the wave front of a sound wave or light wave, particularly the latter, behind the edge of an obstacle, producing the penumbra effect round a shadow, in the case of both sound and light; by means of a diffraction grating, consisting of a polished surface, ruled by a great number of finely-cut lines, a spectrum may be produced, owing to the different wave-lengths of the different colours combined in white light.

Diffusion: literally 'spread'; used of (1) culture traits; (2) the area of the cutaneous surface affected by a pressure stimulus applied within it – a *diffusion circle*: (3) circle of *brightness* or of colour produced on the retina by rays from a point source because of the inadequate focusing of the lens system (*aberration* (q.v.)).

Digit-span test: method of determining an individual's *memory span*, which is measured by the number of digits he can repeat in order, after a single hearing.

Diglottic: the stimulation of two separate small areas of the tongue simultaneously by the same taste stimulus. Cf. *dichoglottic*.

Dilemma: a situation offering only two alternatives and mutually exclusive courses of action, both presenting difficulties.

Dimension: employed in a psychological sense (suggested by *Titchener*, and adopted by *Boring*) for the attributes of sensation.

Diminishing return: a principle borrowed from the 'law of diminishing return' in economics, applied to the effect of an increase in number of repetitions in committing a series of items to memory, each additional repetition producing, as it were, relatively less effect; the same principle was applied by *Spearman* to additional units of an ability.

Dimming: the effect produced on *after-sensations* (q.v.), by reducing the intensity of the projection field.

Diopter: a unit of measurement of the convergence power of a lens system, in terms of the reciprocal of the focal length in meters.

Dioptrics: the branch of *optics* which deals with the refraction of light, especially in lenses and prisms.

Diotic: used of simultaneous stimulation of the two ears by the same sound. Cf. *dichotic.*

Diplacusis: the production of different pitch impressions in the two ears by the same sound frequency.

Diplopia: seeing the same external object double.

Dipsomania: uncontrollable craving for alcohol, generally occurring in periodic attacks.

Direct: immediate; used in a technical sense in relation to the first phase of the *apprehension* of objects, before any *recognition, identification,* or *elaboration* has taken place; also of association between two items in immediate succession; also of *reflex action,* where stimulus and response are on the same side of the body.

Directed: used of movements or trains of thought controlled or guided by a single definite end or goal.

Direction: used in technical sense in *line of direction,* the line passing through the *nodal points* (q.v.) of a lens system, or the eye, determining the direction of any object which it strikes; or in *sense of direction,* meaning the element or factor in our experience of space, which locates any object in visual space at some definite point in the visual field, and also the unknown factor upon which the migration of birds and their homing would seem to depend.

Directions test: a type of mental test which measures the ability to carry out instructions of different degrees of complexity.

Directive or determining tendency: subjective factors or conditions guiding the course of ideas, sometimes clearly conscious, as a goal or objective, but not necessarily so; or set of organic conditions, influencing the course of behaviour. Cf. *Aufgabe* and *Einstellung.*

Dirhinic: stimulation of both nostrils simultaneously by the same odour. Cf. *dichorhinic.*

Disability: loss or impairment of a function, due usually to some impairment of structure.

Disaesthesia: sensations of discomfort in cutaneous and subcutaneous tissue, e.g. 'pins and needles'.

Disappearing differences method: a modification of the procedure used in *method of limits* (q.v.), in which two appreciably different stimuli are presented, and one of them is either increased or diminished until the difference is no longer noticed.

Disarranged sentence test: a type of mental test in which the subject is required to rearrange a sentence the words of which are presented in haphazard order.

Disbelief: belief that a statement is false. Cf. *unbelief.*

Discarnate: see *disembodied.*

Discernible: noticeable.

Discipline: originally synonymous with *education;* in modern usage the root notion is *control* of conduct, either by an external authority, or by the individual himself; any branch of study; the effect of such study on the mind. The last of these meanings is implied in one of the most interesting and important issues in modern psychological theory, the so-called doctrine of *formal discipline* or *formal training,* the doctrine, namely, that particular branches of study give a *mental discipline* or *training,* which is quite general in that it affects ability in all other subjects. (This doctrine is no longer recognized as tenable in its extreme form; at the same time *training* and *discipline* may be distinguished by restricting the latter to self-initiated effort in performing a certain task, as distinct from merely going through its performance, in which case there may be some truth in the doctrine as regards discipline, in the sense of control.)

Discord: see *dissonance.*

Discrepancy: a divergence between a theory or statement and some fact or facts, the existence of which is a challenge to the validity of the statement or theory.

Discrete: separate, or unconnected, or discontinuous; used of *units* or *measures* on a scale, where that is based on the enumeration of individual items, or objects, or stimulus values, which, from the nature of the case, are not capable of being varied continuously.

Discrimen: a sensory difference which may or may not be noticed.

Discrimination: perception of difference, or differential response, or ability to perceive slight differences. A *discrimination experiment* is an experiment devised to test the presence of the ability to discriminate under certain conditions; a *discrimination reaction* is a variation of the *reaction experiment* (q.v.) where the subject requires to discriminate between two or more stimuli before reacting, his time being called *discrimination time.*

Disgust: feeling or emotion with tendency towards nausea, regarded by *McDougall* as a *primary,* or instinct emotion, associated with the *repulsion instinct.*

Disintegration: loss (usually progressive) of organization, and breaking up into separate items or parts, of any kind of organized material, physical or mental.

Disjunctive: term employed of a statement, or proposition, consisting of two parts which are in direct opposition to one another, as 'either A is B or A is not B'.

Disorganization: a condition of break-down, usually of a temporary character, of an organized unit or group, like a society or family.

Disorientation: loss, sometimes merely temporary, by an individual of his perception of his relationships in space or time.

Disparate: general sense 'dissimilar'; applied usually to points on the two retinae, which are not *corresponding points* (q.v.), or to sensations belonging to different sense departments.

Disparation: used specially of our visual experience of objects not in the *horopter* (q.v.) which, since their images fall on disparate points in the two retinae, are normally seen double, unless the double vision is suppressed. The disparation is *crossed* or *uncrossed,* according as the object is nearer or more distant than the *fixation point,* when crossed the image to the right being that seen with the left eye, and vice versa, and when uncrossed the image to the right being that seen by the right eye, and that to the left by the left eye.

Disparition: disappearance.

Disparity: the characteristic of being dissimilar; used specially of the images of a solid object, near at hand, on the two retinae; one of the cues in the perception of relief; effect of the two dissimilar images illustrated by the *stereoscope* (q.v.).

Dispersion: scatter; two technical senses: (1) statistically, equivalent to *scatter* (q.v.), and measured by the *mean variation,* or *standard deviation,* or *semi-interquartile range;* (2) in connection with vision in relation to the *circle,* usually coloured, produced when the rays of light from a point source are not focussed at a single point on the retina – *aberration, spherical* and *chromatic.*

Displacement: general sense, transfer of an object from one place to another; two technical senses: (1) the distortion of a visual image (*eidetic*), by inversion, confusion of right and left, up and down; (2) (*psychoanalytical*) shifting of *affect* (q.v.) from one item to another to which it does not really belong, particularly in a dream.

Disposition: general meaning, arrangement; employed technically of any arrangement of organic or neural elements (*neural disposition*), or of mental elements (*psychical disposition*), or of both (*psycho-physical disposition*), either innate or the result of experience. Cf. *engram.* Also used of an individual's totality of natural tendencies to act in certain ways – usually with emphasis on the *affective* and *impulsive* aspects.

DISSIMULATION

Dissimulation: concealment or disguise of one's real thoughts, opinions, and ends, by pretending that they are different; feigning.

Dissociation: the breaking off of connections of any kind, in any sort of combination; used in special sense, originally by French school of psychopathology, for a functional interruption of associations or connections in the mind or in the *cortex,* upon which the revival of memories and systems of ideas depends, as well as the personal control normally exercised over various motor processes, and producing forgettings, *negative hallucinations, anaesthesias,* etc., and generally the phenomena produced by Freudian *repression.*

Dissonance: the rough, harsh, and unpleasant effect of two tones sounded simultaneously, which do not blend or fuse, attributed to *beats* (q.v.) which are too rapid to be separately distinguished.

Distal: away from the point of attachment of a limb or part of body.

Distance: applied figuratively by some analytic schools to a psychic detachment, or unapproachableness, of attitude, or emotion, characteristic of certain psycho-neurotic conditions.

Distant: used of receptors which are adapted to receive stimuli from a distance, as the eye and organ of smell; also applied in vision to any point at a greater distance than 10 m., beyond which there is no change in *accommodation.*

Distoceptor: see *distant.*

Distortion: used technically in connection with visual phenomena due to *retinitis,* sometimes known as *metamorphopsia,* and presenting two types: *barrel distortion,* where a square appears with bulging-out sides, and *pincushion distortion,* where it appears with sides curved inwards.

Distraction: condition where concentration of attention is disturbed by irrelevant stimuli, which are sometimes experimentally made in order to test or measure an individual's ability to resist distraction; general condition, often emotionally determined, where concentration of attention is difficult or virtually impossible, which must be clearly distinguished from *abstraction.*

Distribution: employed in statistics for the representation by a table, or graphically, of the frequency of occurrence of scores or measurements in the testing or measurement of a group of individuals with respect to a definite ability or character; also in the psychology of *learning,* for the arrangement of repetitions and sittings, or the timing of practice in a *learning experiment,* the general principle or law having been established that, subject to certain limitations, dependent on conditions affecting working efficiency, the wider the distribution the more efficient and economical is the learning.

Disuse: want of use; a psychological *law of disuse* has been formulated to the effect that, unless a connection, upon which the response to a certain stimulus depends, is exercised or operative, after the lapse of time it will become more difficult for the response to follow on the stimulus.

Diuretic: an agent which increases urine formation, e.g. coffee.

Divergence: used of the visual phenomena in binocular vision as the opposite of *convergence* (q.v.).

Divination: foretelling the future, or revealing the hidden, by magical, mystical, or supernormal means, e.g. *rhabdomancy*, etc.

Divining rod: see *dousing*.

Dizygotic: see *twins*.

Dizziness: sensations of whirling, giddiness, *vertigo* (q.v.), caused by abnormal stimulation of receptors of *static sense* (q.v.), or by rapid movements of visual field, and sometimes accompanied by *nausea* and *nystagmus* (q.v.).

DL: abbreviation for *difference limen* or *threshold* (q.v.).

Dogiel corpuscle: developmental phase or transitional type of end-organ, found in the mucous membranes of the mouth, nose, eyes, etc.

Dogma: theory or doctrine asserted on authority without supporting evidence.

Dolichocephaly: longheadedness, as a characteristic of a human skull; *cephalic index* (q.v.) above 75.

Dominance: three technical senses: (1) used of a type of *personality*, marked by a tendency to seek control over others – the *dominant type;* (2) in *aesthetics*, the emphasizing of a particular element or aspect in a work of art, with relative subordination of other parts or aspects; (3) in *Mendelian inheritance*, the characteristic of the member of a pair of factors having the power of suppressing the appearance of the other (*recessive* (q.v.)) member. See also *cerebral dominance*.

Dominant: the fifth note (Sol) in the *major diatonic scale* (q.v.); or a chord of which this note is the base; also the wave-length of a spectral colour which will match a given colour, when mixed with the appropriate amount of white light; also referring to an emotion or *complex* which governs an individual's behaviour.

Donatism: an early phase of hypnosis, characterized by *cataplexy* (q.v.).

Donders' law: the principle involved in visual fixation, to the effect that, no matter how the position is reached, every position of the *line of regard* (q.v.), of the eyes in relation to the head, corresponds to a definite and invariable angle of torsion of the eyes.

Dorsal: located on the back, behind or below the neck.

Dorso-ventral: the anterior-posterior line of reference or axis. See *sagittal.*

Dot figure: a figure composed of a number of dots, arranged in regular or irregular order, employed in an *illusion* experiment, the dots arranging themselves, on prolonged observation, in definite patterns, frequently changing from time to time.

Dotting Test: experiment or test, devised and used by *McDougall* in the study of *fatigue, attention,* etc., in which the subject is required to mark the centres of small circles passing at a regular rate, but in irregular position, across a slit whose width is adjustable; also a test of the rapidity with which an individual can tap with a pencil or style.

Double alternation: term used of a problem employed experimentally in a *temporal maze* (q.v.), in which the subject is required to respond twice in one way, followed by twice in another, without any external guidance.

Double aspect theory: a metaphysical theory of the relation between mind and body, based on the philosophy of *Spinoza,* to the effect that mind and body, or mental process and physical process in the nervous system, represent two aspects of one and the same series of events.

Double vision: see *diplopia.*

Doubt: absence of definite belief, usually with alternation between belief and disbelief; sometimes obsessional (see *psychasthenia*).

Doubtful judgments: judgments given by a subject in an experiment when he reports uncertainty.

Dousing (Dowsing): using a dousing, or divining, rod, which is usually a forked rod or branch, for the purpose of indicating the location of a spring, metals, or other objects underground, by the alleged persistent turning of the rod.

Drainage: the drawing off of nervous energy from a nerve centre or area, by activity elsewhere in a connected centre or area; based on this notion, the *drainage hypothesis,* as it has been called, has been put forward, as for example by *McDougall,* as a possible explanation of phenomena of *inhibition* (or facilitation), at all levels.

Drawing scale: a scale, consisting of samples of drawing, varying in merit by approximately equal steps, devised for the purpose of assessing the merits of children's drawings.

Dread: an emotional attitude, involving fear, but directed towards the future in highly unpleasant anticipation.

Dream: a train of hallucinatory experiences with a certain degree of coherence, but often confused and bizarre, taking place in the condition of sleep and similar conditions. Cf. *day-dreaming* and *phantasy.*

Dream interpretation: the attempt, mainly by dream analysis through *free association* (q.v.), to explain various features of, and elements in, a dream. In psychoanalytic theory the dream form and the dream material or content are first of all distinguished, and the interpretation consists mainly in explaining the form which the content has been given. Accepting the views of previous workers that the content consists initially of the various sensory impressions received by the sleeper during sleep, together with the worries of the previous day, and exciting experiences, mainly of the recent past, *Freud* and his followers argue that to this content repressed trends or *wishes* from the unconscious tend to attach themselves, but, in order to evade the *censorship* (q.v.), and prevent the sleeper from waking, so performing the function of the dream, which is to *fulfil the wish to sleep,* these trends and wishes modify the existing content, so that they may disguise themselves, the modification taking place in the unconscious, and being called by Freud the *dream work.* See *manifest dream content, latent dream thoughts,* and *wish fulfilment.*

Drive: used as a general term to include instinctive and other impulses, or motive forces, prompting an animal to directed activity towards an end. See *instinct.*

Dropping out: the disappearance, in the process of acquiring a piece of skill, of irrelevant or unnecessary elements or movements with practice and increase in expertness.

Drug addiction: pathological condition of inability to avoid using certain drugs, brought about, initially, by habitual excess with regard to the use of the drugs, the degree of use constituting excess being relative to the drug, and to the individual.

Dual impression: two sensory impressions from a single stimulus.

Dual personality: see *personality.*

Dualism: a metaphysical theory of reality, as consisting of two independent substances, mind and body or matter.

Du Bois Reymond's law: a principle of neural or muscular excitation, to the effect that the efficiency of an electric current passing through neural or muscular tissue depends, not on the absolute strength of the current, but on the rate of change in its density.

Duct: a tube providing for flow of secretion from a gland, or for the flow of a liquid, as *tear duct, lymph duct. Stenson's duct,* employed sometimes in *conditioning* (q.v.) experiments, is a duct inside the cheek for the flow of saliva from the parotid gland into the mouth.

Ductless glands: glands not provided with ducts; see *endocrine.*

Dumb: see *mutism.*

Dunlap chronoscope: a type of *chronoscope* (q.v.) based on a synchronous or phonic motor – alternatively *Johns Hopkins chronoscope.*

Duodenum: the upper part of the small intestine connected to stomach.

Duplicity theory: the theory that vision involves two distinct and separate mechanisms in the retina, one providing for daylight and colour vision, the other for twilight and night vision.

Dura mater: a fibrous membrane, the outermost of the three coverings of the brain and spinal cord.

Dyad (diad): chord in music composed of two tones.

Dynamic psychology: a psychology emphasizing motives and drives; used specially of their psychology by representatives of the analytic schools; to be distinguished from *dynamic theory.*

Dynamic theory: an aspect of *Gestalt psychology,* stressed by *Köhler,* according to which dynamic conditions, rather than structural, in the sensory and central fields, determine the processes taking place in these fields.

Dynamogenesis: initiation of motor activity, as a result of sensory activity; also the principle that every change in sensory stimulation effects a change in muscular activity or tension.

Dynamometer: an instrument for measuring the strength exerted by muscular activity, as in hand grip, the force exerted being shown by a pointer on a scale: this can also be recorded graphically by means of an adjustment making the instrument a *dynamograph.*

Dys-: (Gr.) inseparable prefix conveying the meaning of un- or mis-.

Dysarthria: defective articulation of speech, due to cerebral lesion.

Dysgraphia: defective formation of words in writing, due to cerebral lesion.

Dyslalia: general term for defective speech.

Dyslogia: impairment of speech, due to mental disorder.

Dysparathyroidism: disorder of the *parathyroid gland* (q.v.).

Dysphasia: any impairment of the language function, due to brain lesion.

Dysphemia: group of speech disorders, due to *neurosis* or *psycho-neurosis*.

Dysplastic: applied to type of body build not conforming to any of *Kretschmer's* three types.

Dyspnoea: breathlessness.

Dysrhythmia: defective speech rhythm.

Dysteleology: possession of useless organs; lack of purposiveness of elements of structure.

Dystimbria: defective resonance, or vocal quality.

Dystrophia: defective nutrition.

E

E: contraction for experimenter, usually found in italics.

Ear: organ of hearing, consisting in birds, animals, and man of three divisions, outer, middle, and inner ear, which latter contains the end organs for two senses, hearing (*cochlea*) and the static sense, or sense of equilibrium (*semi-circular canals* with *utricle and saccule*). In animals and man there is an expansion on the outside of the head (*auricle*) at the opening of the tube (*external auditory meatus*) conducting sound waves to the ear-drum (*tympanum*). The vibrations of the drum, produced by the sound waves, are conducted across the middle ear by the chain of small bones (*auditory ossicles*) to the membrane closing the oval window (*fenestra ovalis*) in the wall of the inner ear, by means of which the vibrations are transmitted to the fluid in the *cochlea* (q.v.), the vibrations returning to the middle ear by the round window (*fenestra rotunda*). The pressure in the middle ear is kept approximately at that of the outer air by a tube (*Eustachian tube*) communicating with the throat.

Ecbatic: mere consequence, result, or outcome, as distinct from, or without implying, purpose or intention.

Eccentric projection: localization of sensation at the position in space of the body producing it, rather than at the point stimulated; also of a theory of perception, based upon this as of fundamental significance.

Eccentricity: deviation from normal behaviour, but not usually to such an extent or in such a way as to be regarded as a sign of mental disorder.

Echinodermata: group of marine organisms, characterized by their radial arrangement of parts, and external skeleton.

Echo: sound reaching the ear after being reflected; also used as a prefix for repetition of certain types of behaviour as *echolalia,* or *echophrasia,* reiteration, more or less automatically, of words and phrases (characteristic of infant speech); *echopraxia,* automatic imitation of movements made by other people; *echopathy,* a general term, applied to a nervous disorder, characterized by senseless repetition of words or phrases.

Eclampsia: epileptiform convulsion, dependent upon disturbance in the nervous centres; type of recurrent convulsions occurring during the later stages of pregnancy, usually associated with deficient functioning of the kidneys.

Eclecticism: a type of theory characterized by the attempt to reconcile inconsistent views, or improve on them, by the selective adoption of elements from each, and making of these a more or less self-consistent system.

Ecology: that branch of biology which deals with the relations of organisms to their environment, or, in the case of human ecology, that branch of *sociology* which deals with the social, institutional, and racial distribution of human beings.

Economic: used generally of motives involving earning a livelihood, the accumulation of wealth, and the like; specially, by psycho-analysts, for the production, distribution, and consumption of human energy in accordance with the principle of greatest utility for least expenditure or effort.

Economical: with the minimum of waste of material or energy resources.

Economics: the science which studies the nature, production, consumption, distribution, and exchange of wealth.

Economy: the principles of the arrangement of any organized operative system, particularly so far as wastage is eliminated; used specially in the phrase *economy of effort,* with reference to the tendency of an organism, in acquiring expertness in any repeated performance, to avoid useless movements and needless expenditure of energy; also as a *principle* or *canon of economy,* for the rule to be observed in the interpretation of scientific data, that the simplest or least complex explanation is to be preferred.

Ecphory: term used by *Semon* to designate the revival of a memory trace or *engram* (q.v.).

Ecstasy: rapture; in a special sense, extreme concentration of attention amounting to semi-trance, as a phenomenon or phase of prolonged contemplation of a limited field, in the case particularly of religious mysticism.

Ecto-: Gr. prefix meaning 'outside' or 'outer', in *ectoderm*, the outer germ layer of the embryo; *ectoplasm*, the outer layer of cytoplasm in cells, or, in psychical research, substance assumed to emanate from the medium in a spiritualistic trance; *ectosac*, outer layer of cytoplasm in unicellular organisms.

Ectomorphy: a classification, based on anthropometric measurements, of physical type marked by prominence of long thin bones, and of surface as compared with mass.

Edipus (Oedipus) complex: in psychoanalytical theory, the *complex*, largely unconscious, developed in a son from attachment (sexual in character, according to analysts) to the mother and jealousy of the father, with the resulting feeling of *guilt* and emotional conflict on the part of the son, held to be normal in some form or other in any family circle. Cf. *Electra complex.*

Educational age: corresponding to educational level of the average school child of any given chronological age, as determined by standardized educational tests. (See *age.*) The *educational quotient* is the ratio of educational age to chronological age, expressed as a percentage.

Educational psychology: that branch of *applied psychology*, which is concerned with the application to education of psychological principles and findings, together with the psychological study of problems of education.

Eduction: term employed by Spearman, for either of the two essential features of relational thinking, according to his view – the noting of relations and the discovery of correlates – giving him his second and third *noegenetic principles* (q.v.).

Effect: used technically by *Thorndike*, to designate the law of *learning*, which has usually been called the *law of selection* (q.v.).

Effector: a muscle or gland, as representing that part of the *psycho-organic system* which carries out the response of the organism.

Effeminacy: presence of feminine characteristics of bodily structure, or the manifestation of feminine behaviour characteristics in a man.

Effemination: effeminacy; a variety of *homosexuality*, where the mentality and the sexual feelings of a man are like those of a normal woman. Cf. *viraginity.*

Efferent: used of nerve fibres conducting impulses from the nervous centre outwards to muscle or gland.

Efficiency: ratio of work done to energy consumed in any mechanism.

Effluvium: used technically, in psychical research, of emanations from bodies of spirit origin.

Effort experience: kinaesthetic (q.v.) sensations, arising from the muscles involved in the effort (together with, according to some psychologists, direct experience of *conation*).

Ego: an individual's experience of himself, or his conception of himself, or the dynamic unity which is the individual; used by psychoanalysts, in an objective and narrower sense, of that part of the person which, as superficial, is in direct touch with external reality, is conscious, and includes, therefore, the representation of reality as given by the senses, and existing in the *preconscious* as memories, together with those selected impulses and influences from within which have been accepted and are under control.

Ego-alter theory: a theory seeking to account for the growth of social consciousness and the development of social organization from the interaction between the self and the other.

Ego-ideal: a psychoanalytic conception, more or less a substitute for conscience, involving a standard of perfection set up in the early life of the child, through *identification* (q.v.) with some admired person, e.g. the father. Cf. *superego.*

Ego instincts: used by psychoanalysts of one group of instincts in a two-fold classification of instincts, the other group being sex instincts.

Ego libido: attachment of *libido* (q.v.) to the ego or self.

Ego-syntonic: term employed by psychoanalysts, meaning in harmony with the ego and its standards.

Egocentric: self-centred; interested primarily in oneself and one's own concerns, and indifferent to the concerns of others; *in association tests* (q.v.) responses which are clearly personal are classified as *egocentric responses;* the fact that an individual can interpret the thoughts and acts of another only through his own experience has been called the *egocentric predicament.*

Egoism: a system of ethical and social philosophy based on the view that the fundamental motive underlying all morality and all conduct is in the last resort self-interest; a characteristic of an individual exhibiting and illustrating this view in practice.

Egotism: talking incessantly of oneself, and one's own doings.

Eidetic: term used primarily of a type of vivid *imagery* which is, as it were, projected into the external world, and not merely 'in one's head'; a half-way house to *hallucination* (q.v.); also of the ability or disposition to project images, frequently characteristic of children; an individual who has such an ability is called an *Eidetiker* (Ger.).

Einstellung (Ger.): set or *attitude*, predisposing towards a certain line of thought or action, immediate, temporary, or as a fixed tendency.

Eject: used as a noun or as a verb to express the representing or interpreting another's mind and mental processes as a replica of one's own; the third of *Baldwin's* three stages in the development of a child through imitation he calls the *ejective stage,* where he reaches an understanding of himself and of other people, through imitation of their actions, the other stages being the *projective*, where he is interested in some action he does not yet understand or perform, and the *subjective*, where he comes to understand it through imitating it.

Elaboration: generally, the expanding and combining activities which are characteristic of the higher levels of thought; specially, as *secondary elaboration*, applied by *Freud* to the relating of a dream by the dreamer himself, with particular reference to the influence exerted by his personal interests, his desire to tell a good story, and the like, in modifying the narrative, both in form and in content; Freud's *dream work* might be called the *primary elaboration.*

Elation: an emotional state of intense joyful excitement; by *Hobbes* called 'glory'; by *McDougall* used as the designation of the emotional aspect of *self display*, as an instinct.

Elberfeld horses: several trained horses in Germany (Elberfeld), capable, it was claimed, of carrying out complex and difficult arithmetical operations, such as the extraction of square and cube roots; the training of the first was begun by *von Osten* in 1901, and this horse, *Clever Hans* (der Kluge Hans), attracted a great deal of interest; others were later trained by *Krall.*

Electra complex: attachment of daughter to father, with antagonism towards mother, and more or less a counterpart of the Edipus complex with the son. Cf. *Edipus complex.*

Electric organ: modified muscular tissue in certain primitive fishes, which can give an electric shock on excitation through the nervous system; must be distinguished from the *electric sense*, said to exist in some animal species, which must depend on the reception of electric stimuli by a special receptor organ, sensitive to such.

Electroaesthesiometer: an *aesthesiometer* (q.v.) where the stimulus point is brought into contact with the skin by an electromagnet.

Electrocardiogram: a record by means of an *oscillograph* (q.v.) of *action currents* (q.v.) in the heart.

Electrodiagnosis: generally, the use of electrical instruments to determine pathological conditions in the body; specially, the use of such methods in the examinations of nerves and muscles.

Electroencephalogram: an *oscillograph* (q.v.) record of action currents within the head, arising from activity in the nerve centres.

Electrotaxis: see *galvanotaxis, galvanotropism.*

Electrotonus: altered physical condition (*tonus*) of muscle or nerve during the passage of a constant direct galvanic current.

Elementarism: a type of systematic psychology which attempts to describe mental process in terms of mental elements and their compounding.

Ellis harmonical: a reed instrument of the harmonium type, for demonstrating, and studying experimentally, exact pitches and exact intervals not available with the ordinary harmonium.

Embolism: the forming of an obstruction in a blood-vessel, as by air bubble or clot of blood.

Embryo: the organism (human) at an early stage of its intra-uterine development.

Emergent: in general sense, arising from a combination of several causes, but not explicable as the sum of their individual effects; used in several special senses: (1) of the general properties of a higher unit, as distinct from the specific properties of its constituents; (2) of the result of the modifying influence of a whole, or *Gestalt* (q.v.), on its parts or constituent elements; (3) as descriptive of a type of evolution where something new and unpredictable arises from the interaction and recombination of pre-existing factors.

Emission: used technically of the seminal fluid, especially when it is emitted during sleep.

Emmert's law: an expression of the tendency of a projected image, whether *after-image* (q.v.), or *eidetic image* (q.v.), to increase in size proportionally to the distance of the surface on which it is projected.

Emmetropia (emmetropism): the normal condition of the refractive system of the eye, where rays from a distant object are focused sharply on the retina when the *ciliary* muscle is relaxed; the *emmetropic eye* is the eye of which the refractive system is perfect.

Emotion: differently described and explained by different psychologists, but all agree that it is a complex state of the organism, involving bodily changes of a widespread character – in breathing, pulse, gland secretion, etc. – and, on the mental side, a state of excitement or perturbation, marked by strong feeling, and usually an impulse towards a definite form of behaviour. If the emotion is intense there is some disturbance of the intellectual functions, a measure of *dissociation* (q.v.), and a tendency towards action of an ungraded or *protopathic* character. Beyond this description anything else would mean an entrance into the controversial field.

Emotional: characteristic of, pertaining to, or caused by emotion; used in a semi-technical sense (1) of a *bias*, due to emotional *attitude*, in observation or interpretation of facts; (2) of *expression*, signifying the various motor and glandular changes accompanying emotional excitement, particularly those producing a more or less characteristic and externally observable picture, and (3) of *pattern* in virtually the same sense, but with special emphasis on the actual grouping of the motor and glandular responses.

Empathy: feeling oneself into, and losing one's identity in, a work of art, a characteristic of the essentially *aesthetic attitude* or *emotion*; used sometimes by psychoanalysts of the phenomena of *identification* (q.v.); possibly more generally characteristic of perceptual experience of a situation than has generally been held.

Empirical: in general sense, based on experience; often used in a derogatory sense, suggesting a lack of a wider scientific knowledge arising from systematic experiment and observation: *empirical psychology* is a psychology based on observation and experiment, as contrasted with *rational psychology* based on deduction from general philosophical principles, and sometimes also contrasted with *existential psychology* (q.v.).

Empiricism: the theory that regards experience as the only source of knowledge; as applied to psychological theory, with respect particularly to problems of space perception, the emphasizing of the part played by experience and learning, as against congenital and inherited factors; more generally such theories as *associationism* and *sensationism; empiric,* used as synonymous with quack.

Employment psychology: see *vocational psychology*.

Empyreumatic: a quality of smell sensation, e.g. smell of tar.

Emulation: rivalry in some form of activity, implying also the notion of imitation.

Encephalitis: an acute inflammatory condition affecting the organs within the skull – the *encephalon*.

End: the objective or result aimed at in purposive activity; also the terminal part of a structure or process, as in *end organ, end brush,* the terminal branching of an *axon* (q.v.), *end plate,* the termination in a muscle of a motor nerve, *end spurt*, the rise in performance towards the end of a task, as in experiments on mental or muscular work, or, in the case of voluntary muscles, just before the onset of complete exhaustion.

Endocrine gland: ductless gland which pours its secretion directly into the blood or circulating fluid. See *hormone*.

Endocrinology: the branch of science which studies the structure, functions, and disorders of endocrine glands and their secretions.

Endo-: Gr. prefix meaning 'within', 'inside', 'inner'.

Endogamy: limitation or restriction of marriage within any group, caste, community, or tribe.

Endolymph: fluid contained within the *membranous labyrinth* (q.v.) of the inner ear. Cf. *perilymph*.

Endomorphy: a classification, based on anthropometric measurements, of type of physique, so far as marked by relative prominence of the abdominal regions.

Endophasia: reproduction 'in the mind' of words and phrases – *implicit* utterance.

Endoplasm: the inside soft material of a cell.

Endopsychic: used of processes within the unconscious of a different order from conscious processes like ideas, as, for example, Freud's *endopsychic censorship*.

Endosarc: the inner protoplasm in unicellular organisms.

Endothelium: the inner lining of vessels or cavities which do not open to the outside.

Endowment: natural or innate capacity, physical or mental.

Enelocomorphism: see *anthropomorphism*.

Enervate: in technical sense, the surgical detachment of the nerve connections of any organ.

Engram: altered condition in living tissue, left as an enduring result of excitation to activity, and serving, according to some writers, as the basis of inheritance and of physiological memory; sometimes used more narrowly for *memory trace*. See *neurogram*.

Entelechy: the condition of realization in actuality of a potentiality.

Ento- (*Gr.*): 'within', 'inside'.

Entoderm: the inner germ layer of the embryo.

Entomology: that branch of biological science which studies insects.

Enteroperipheral: term used by *Spencer* of any experience initiated within the body.

Entoptic: term applied to visual experiences due to conditions or processes within the eye itself.

Enuresis: involuntary discharge of urine; *nocturnal*, during sleep.

Environmental factors: all conditions and factors affecting an organism from without.

Enzyme: a complex organic substance causing chemical transformations in plants and animals, such as the conversion of starch into sugar.

Eoanthropus: earliest man, represented by the *Piltdown man.*

Epencephalon: part of the brain lying behind the midbrain, and consisting of the *pons Varolii* (q.v.) and the *cerebellum.*

Ependyma: lining of the neural canal.

Epicritic: term employed of cutaneous sensibility by *Head* and *Rivers,* to designate a developed sensitivity to light pressure, degrees of warmth and coolness, and definite localization. Contrasted with *protopathic* (q.v.).

Epidemic chorea: see *dancing mania.*

Epidermis: the outer layer of the skin.

Epigamic: term applied to characteristics such as colouring, calculated to attract the other sex, preliminary to mating.

Epigastric: applied to the anatomical region over the stomach.

Epigenesis: a theory of the development of the embryo, which, in contrast with *preformism* (q.v.), assumes that the process takes place through successive accretions and modifications brought about through the influence of the environment, and interaction among the parts.

Epiglottis: the leaf-like structure at the entrance to the larynx, forming a lid for it when swallowing.

Epilepsy: falling sickness; a disorder of the nervous system which shows itself in fits or paroxysms at irregular intervals, in which the subject falls to the ground with muscular spasms, losing consciousness, and foaming at the mouth in *grand mal,* and in the case of *petit mal* (q.v.) with little beyond short lapses of consciousness; in some cases the patient, either as an accompaniment, or as a substitute for the fits, shows *epileptic furor,* a blind, violent, often brutal form of behaviour, of which he later has no memory; following upon the fit there is frequently a semi-conscious, inert state, known as *epileptic stupor.*

Epileptiform: used of seizures like true epilepsy, but with a different and generally more specific origin such as a brain tumour.

Epinephrin: adrenalin or *adrenin,* the *autocoid* (q.v.) secreted by the *adrenal glands,* and also obtained as an extract from the glands; acts on the arterial circulation through the *autonomic system* (q.v.).

Epinosic: term used by psychoanalysts with reference to a secondary gain or advantage through illness.

Epiperipheral: term used by Spencer to signify any experience the location of the stimulus for which is outside the body.

Epiphenomenalism: a philosophical theory of the relation between mental and physical, or between mind and body, which holds that mental processes have no causal agency, that is, that the chain of causality is complete on the body side, so that mental processes are merely accompanying phenomena which make no difference to the outcome.

Epiphora: an abnormal overflow of tears, due usually to an obstruction of the tear duct.

Epiphysis (cerebri): the *pineal gland* (q.v.).

Episcotister: an apparatus consisting of a disc with open and closed sectors, which are adjustable, by means of which the *brightness* (brilliance) of a visual field can be reduced to any desired degree; used in the study of flicker, the equating of two fields for *brightness*, etc.

Epistemology: theory of knowledge, or that branch of metaphysics which deals with the nature and validity of knowledge.

Epithalamus: the upper and dorsal portion of the region of the *thalamus* (q.v.).

Epithelium: the lining of cavities and surfaces of the body exposed externally.

Epochal psychoses: types of mental disorder which occur at transitional periods of life, such as *adolescence* and the *menopause*. Cf. *climacteric*.

Epsilon movement: see *apparent movement*.

Equal and unequal cases: a modification of the experimental method of *right and wrong cases* (q.v.) where the first part of the experiment consists in determining a *difference threshold* (q.v.) by the *method of limits* (q.v.), and then this value and the standard are presented to the subject, in accordance with the method of right and wrong cases for the judgment of equality and inequality.

Equal appearing intervals: see *mean gradations*.

Equal sense distances: see *mean gradations*.

Equal-tempered scale: see *scale*.

Equally noticeable: see *just noticeable*, for which it is a synonym, but with the underlying assumption that all just noticeable differences are equally noticeable.

Equilibrium: employed as a psychological term, either for the maintaining of an upright position, or, specially, in the field of *aesthetics*, for balance in a work of art, as dependent on the psychological *weight* (q.v.) of the different parts. The *sense of equilibrium* or balance is dependent on receptors in the semi-circular canals in the inner ear. Experiments on this sense are carried out by means of a *turntable* (q.v.), which should be capable of being rotated at various angles to the horizontal, so that the subject, blindfolded, is rotated with reference to a variety of axes, in different directions, and at different rates; under these conditions various *illusions of equilibrium* appear, so that the subject has the impression of rest when moving, of moving when at rest, and so on. See *Mach rotation frame,* and also *nystagmus.*

Equipotentiality: capacity of one part or of one organ to take the place of another part or organ, with respect to the performance of a function.

Equivalents: see *average error methods.*

Erection: swelling of genital organs from congestion of blood in the sexual act or sexual desire.

Erethism: abnormally high degree of sensitivity in any part of the body.

Ergasia: general term, covering all varieties of behaviour; usually employed compounded with a prefix, as *dysergasia,* etc.

Ergograph: instrument for the experimental study of muscular work and fatigue, which normally provides for the graphical recording of the regularly repeated contraction of a single muscle system, as of finger, hand, etc,. other systems being kept immobile, and sometimes, in addition, for the summing of the work done in a series of contractions; typical forms are those devised by *Mosso, Kraepelin,* etc.

Erogenous (erotogenic) zones: sensitive regions of the body, where tactile and warm stimuli evoke sexual feelings and responses, e.g. genital regions, breasts, mouth: in psychoanalytical literature stress is laid on the fact that such regions function as a substitute for the genital organs.

Erotic: used of sexual stimuli, sensations, or feelings; also of the individual who is mainly interested in such sensations and feelings.

Eroticism (erotism): employed, in psychoanalytical literature as a general term for sexual excitement, and in psychopathology for an exaggerated display of sexual feelings and responses.

Erotomania: pathologically exaggerated *eroticism.*

Error: failure in thought or action to attain the result or end aimed at, such as conformity with fact or some objective condition; employed technically in several connections, as, for example, *error methods,* for which see *average error* and *right and wrong cases, error of recognition*, for which see *déjà vu*; see also *constant errors* and *variable errors*.

Erythrogenic: term used of long-wave light stimuli, i.e. red.

Erythropsia: red-coloured vision of objects, following on over-exposure to intense light.

Estimation error (difference): half the difference between the upper and lower thresholds.

Esoteric: intelligible by the initiated and inner circle only; used, in sense of secret or mystical, of a doctrine or system.

Esprit de corps: group spirit; feeling of community with a group, and *sentiment* (q.v.) of loyalty to the group; the *self-sentiment* (q.v.) of a social group.

Ethereal: one of *Zwaardemaker's* classes of smell sensations, e.g. ether.

Ethical: moral; in conformity with a moral standard.

Ethn(o)-: (Gr.) used as prefix, meaning 'race' or 'people'.

Ethnic: tribal; relating to racial groups.

Ethnocentrism: exaggerated tendency to think the characteristics of one's own group or race superior to those of other groups or races.

Ethnography: the branch of science which studies the distribution and characteristics of races, especially with reference to geographical conditions.

Ethnology: the branch of science which studies the culture, customs, social relationships etc., of peoples and races.

Ethnopsychology: primarily, the psychology of races, and particularly primitive races, usually applied more widely to include the study of the psychological interaction of races and culture contact phenomena.

Ethology: the branch of science which investigates the development of systems of morals; now more generally, the science of human character.

Ethos: the predominant characteristics of a racial culture.

Etiology: investigation of the causes of a given phenomenon or series of phenomena: medically, the investigation of the cause of a disease or diseases.

Eugenics: the branch of biological science which studies the inherited characteristics of human beings, particularly from the point of view of their tendency towards improvement or the reverse; as applied or practical eugenics, it concerns itself with the measures by which improvement may be secured or degeneracy checked; the tendency now is to use the word mainly in the applied sense, the scientific aspect being spoken of as *genetics*.

Euglena: a protozoan organism, of psychological interest as possessing a very primitive eye, a pigment spot sensitive to light.

Eunuchism: condition of a male who has been castrated. A similar condition due to atrophy of the testes is known as *eunuchoidism.*

Euphoria: feeling of well-being; often a pathological condition, marked by unfounded feelings of well-being, strength, and optimism, characteristic of certain types of mental disorder.

Eustachian tube: the tube connecting the *pharynx* and the cavity of the middle ear, which provides for the adjustment of air pressure in the middle ear to allow of free vibration of the *tympanum.*

Euthenics: science applied to the improvement of man by operating through the environment.

Evil eye: a popular superstition, associated with the belief in witch-craft, that some people can harm others, or cause evil of various kinds, by fixing their glance on those others, or on various objects.

Evolution: primarily, progressive series of changes in the structure and behaviour of organisms, taking place through a long succession of generations, and dependent on *variation, natural selection* and *inheritance*; also as *social evolution* in the life and organization of a social group; used also in a more restricted sense of the mental characteristics of an individual; almost synonymous with *development,* except that the latter implies a definite direction of change towards an end state, usually at a higher and more complex level.

Evolutionism: theory maintaining that existing organic species have arisen from earlier, and usually less complexly organized, species, by a series of progressive changes; contrasted with *creationism,* which maintains the separate creation of each species.

Exacerbation: increasing the violence of the manifestations or symptoms of a disorder of health, or of behaviour.

Exaltation: abnormal or pathological increase in the degree of functioning of an organ; subjectively, high elation.

Excitability: property of responding to stimulation, sometimes implying excessive degree.

Excitation: response to stimulation.

Excitement: the state of being excited; the subjective side of excitation; an elementary feeling, *excitement-depression* being one of the dimensions of *Wundt's tri-dimensional theory of feeling* (q.v.).

Exciting cause: the stimulus which, under given conditions, produces the effect; more specially, the stimulating situation which directly produces the outbreak of a mental disorder.

Exercise: repetition in *learning* (as a noun or as a verb); Thorndike's *law of exercise,* as one of the laws of learning, is to the effect that the repetition of a connection between stimulus and response strengthens the connection.

Exhaustion: extreme fatigue; strictly the limiting condition when a muscle ceases to respond to excitation: *exhaustion psychosis,* a delirium state brought about by excessive fatigue as in endurance tests.

Exhibitionism: in general sense, extravagant behaviour of any kind with the object of attracting attention; in special sense, and psychoanalytically, an infantile manifestation of sex, appearing as a sex perversion later in behaviour of a kind calculated to stimulate sex impulses, or even to give sexual gratification, e.g. by indecent exposure.

Existential psychology: a type of psychology developed from a point of view which limits the subject matter of the science to those aspects of experience which can be observed introspectively, which means, in effect, the sensory and imaginal aspects, together with feelings, all as observable mental processes.

Exogamy: custom or law according to which an individual must marry outside his own clan or *totem group* (q.v.). Cf. *endogamy.*

Exophthalmic goitre: disease characterized by enlargement of thyroid, prominent eyeballs, rapid heart action, muscular tremors, and also marked mental effects; *Basedow's disease.*

Exoteric: the public or superficial aspect, as opposed to the *esoteric* (q.v.), as applied to the meaning and interpretation of a system of thought.

Expansion (expansiveness): a personality characteristic, expressing itself in loquacity and lack of reserve about oneself, and grading into the extreme manifestations, symptomatic of one phase of *manic-depressive psychosis* (q.v.).

Expectation: the attitude of waiting attentively for something usually to a certain extent defined, however vaguely; a source of error in psycho-physical experiment, especially with the *method of limits* (q.v.), giving rise to one type of *variable error* (q.v.); used statistically for probability based on mathematical procedure.

Experiment: observation for a scientific purpose, under conditions as far as possible controlled by the experimenter.

Experimental psychology: employment of experimental methods to obtain psychological data or to solve psychological problems.

Experimenter: the individual in charge of an experiment, who is responsible for the arranging and control of the conditions, as contrasted with the subject or observer, upon whom the experiment is carried out; in experimental records they are usually denoted by E and S respectively.

Experimentum crucis: crucial experiment; an experiment aiming at a decision, affirmative or negative, with respect to a specific question of fact.

Explicit: directly stated or directly revealed in data, as against what is *implicit*, implied, and brought to light only by inference or interpretation.

Exploratory: employed technically of the movements of young children, animals, or lower organisms, at the first stage of orienting themselves to the situation at the start of a learning process.

Expression: in general sense, any external sign or response indicative of mental process; sometimes used in a restricted sense of subsidiary changes accompanying a verbal or motor response; sometimes in a comprehensive sense of the totality of motor and glandular changes, inclusive of vocal expressions, taking place when an organism is faced with any situation.

Extensity: the spatial aspect or attribute of cutaneous and visual sensations, which in developed perception becomes extension, and with *volume* or voluminousness forms the basis of the spatial content of all perceptual experience.

External senses: those senses, or receptor systems, whose *adequate stimulus* (q.v.) comes from outside the body.

Exteroceptor: a receptor normally stimulated by physical changes outside the body.

Extinction: term applied in a technical sense to the abolition of a *conditioned reflex* (q.v.), by repeated stimulation, without being accompanied by the normal or unconditioned stimulus.

Extirpation: removal of some organ or part of an organ (generally a receptor or part of the brain) in order to study the effects of such removal upon behaviour.

Extraspectral: term used of colours not in the spectrum, but produced by mixing two colours from the two ends, i.e. red and violet, producing crimsons and purples; may also be used of colours not seen by the human eye, produced by infra-red and ultra-violet rays, especially the latter.

Extraversion: characteristic of type of *personality* (*extravert*), whose interests are directed outwards to nature and other people, rather than inwards to the thoughts and feelings of the self (*introvert*).

Extrinsic: term used in a technical sense of the external muscles of the eye, by which the eyeball is moved.

Eye: the sense organ for the reception of light rays of wave-lengths between 400 *mμ* and 760 *mμ*. The essential receptors are the *rods* and *cones* in the *retina*. The whole organ in its developed form in the higher vertebrates and man consists of a spheroidal body, with optic nerve attached – the eyeball. Round the eyeball is a tough white covering – the *sclerotic* – which in front becomes transparent in the *cornea*. Inside this is the *choroid*, a pigmented membrane for the absorbing of stray rays of light inside the eye, giving place at the front to the *iris* and *ciliary body*, the former being a curtain for controlling the amount of light entering the eye, through the *pupil*, and the latter attached by the *suspensory ligament* to the *lens* controlling the *accommodation* of the eye for different distances. Inside the choroid is the *retina*, composed mainly of nerve cells and fibres in layers, the ninth layer being the *rods* and *cones*. The spheroid is divided into two chambers by the lens, both filled with transparent fluids, the *aqueous humour* in front, and the *vitreous body* behind the lens. The eyeball is moved by three pairs of muscles, the *internal* and *external rectus*, for movement in the horizontal plane, the *inferior* and *superior rectus*, for movement in the vertical plane, and the *superior* and *inferior oblique*, for rotatory or torsional movement.

F

Fables test: a mental test in which the subject is required to interpret certain fables, i.e. explain the lesson taught by the fable.

Facial angle: an angle variously measured, intended to indicate relative cranial development; usually the angle made by a line from the nostrils to the ear, and a line from the nostrils to the forehead.

Facilitation: literally making easier, promoting, or furthering; used in *neurology* for the summation of the effects of two nerve excitations, either successive in the same nerve, or simultaneous (or successive) in two more or less allied nerves, though the connection may be relatively remote; in psychology used for the effect of direction of attention in giving prior entry to the stimulus attended to. See *complication experiment* and *reaction experiment*.

Factitious: not natural or spontaneous; artificial.

Factor: a force, condition, or circumstance, cooperating with others in bringing about a result; the most important technical use in psychology is in connection with mental *capacity* or *intelligence*, with respect to the *factor theories* of intelligence. See *intelligence*.

Factorial analysis: statistical or mathematical analysis of the factors determining mental or physical performance in a series of tests; at present an important aspect of the statistical treatment of test results in the analysis of *correlation* (q.v.).

Factor theories of intelligence: theories of the nature of mental capacity, based on the statistical analysis of test results, the chief being the *multiple factor theory* of *Thorndike*, the *two factor theory* of *Spearman*, and the *sampling theory* of *Thomson*.

Faculty: in general sense, ability, natural or acquired, to perform a certain act; historically, what was known as the *faculty psychology*, illustrated in its most extreme form by the *phrenologists* (q.v.), which sought to explain mental phenomena by referring them to the activity of certain agencies or faculties, such as memory, imagination, will, and the like, as if these were entities, in place of merely general terms for various groups of mental phenomena.

Faith: acceptance of a belief without conclusive or logical evidence, and usually accompanied, influenced, or even determined by emotion; employed as a technical term mainly in the psychology of religion. The term *faith cure* is used popularly to cover phenomena otherwise designated mental healing, mind cure, and the like.

Fall chronometer: instrument used for measuring time intervals by means of the vertical fall of a weight. Must not be confused with *control hammer* or *pendulum* (q.v.).

Familial: having reference or relation to the family.

Familiarity feeling: feeling attaching to certain experiences, that we have had them before; an initial or partial stage in *recognition*.

Family constellation: a term in individual psychology (*Adler*), covering the influences on the individual child, deriving from the number, age, and personal characteristics of the other members of the family, in their relationship to him.

Fanaticism: excessive and irrational enthusiasm for, or devotion to, a theory, belief, or line of action, determining a highly emotional attitude, and missionary zeal, knowing practically no limits.

Fancy: form or type of aesthetic *imagination* (q.v.), distinguished from artistic forms in being relatively unsystematic, and relatively undirected, more or less following the whim of the moment. See *phantasy*.

Fantasm: see *phantasm.*

Fantasy: see *phantasy.*

Farad: unit of electrical capacity, defined as the capacity of a field (electric) which has a charge of one coulomb, when the difference of potential between its boundaries is one volt, or a thousand-millionth part of a C.G.S. electro-magnetic unit. The unit most generally used, at least in the psychological laboratory, is the microfarad, which is a millionth part of a farad. The current in the secondary of an induction coil is often called a *faradic current.*

Far sight: condition of vision characterized by clear vision of distant objects, with difficulty in obtaining clear images of near objects; may be either *presbyopia* (q.v.) or *hypermetropia* (q.v.).

Fashion: a type or phase of social *convention,* characterized mainly by its changing and competitive character.

Fatalism: the belief that all events are predetermined, inclusive of the fate of every individual human being. and particularly the implication that no human will or act can avert what is destined to happen.

Fatiguability: relative rate of onset of fatigue, in an individual or in an organ.

Fatigue: diminished productivity, efficiency, or ability to carry on work, because of previous expenditure of energy in doing work; on the subjective side the complex of sensations and feelings, and the increased difficulty of carrying on, experienced after a prolonged spell of work; must be distinguished from *boredom,* which may be described as a subjective feeling of fatigue, due to monotony or lack of interest, rather than the expenditure of energy. Fatigue may be mental, muscular, sensory, or nervous.

Fault: a defect in procedure, method, or apparatus, affecting the reliability of the results obtained; in a special sense, failure to respond within thirty seconds in a free *association test* (q.v.) for diagnostic purposes.

Faxensyndrom (Ger.): Bleuler's term for a *psychosis* incident to prisoners, characterized by peculiar behaviour, described as clownish, suggestive of *malingering* (q.v.), but really due to *dissociation* (q.v.).

Fear: one of the primitive, violent, and usually crippling emotions, marked by extensive bodily changes, and by behaviour of the flight or concealment character.

Feature profile test: a type of *performance test* (q.v.), where the subject is required to put together seven pieces of wood, into which a head in profile has been dissected, without being informed of the nature of the object.

Febrile: characterizing high fever; used of delirium.

F(a)eces: material excreted from the anus, after passing through the intestines and undergoing digestive processes.

Fechner-Helmholtz Law: the principle applying to visual sensation, that the alteration of the organ produced by stimulation reduces the excitation effect of a subsequent stimulus, approximately to the same extent as if the intensity of the second stimulus were reduced by the same proportional amount.

Fechner's Law: a mathematical formulation of *Weber's law* (q.v.): the steps taken by Fechner were, first, to substitute for the statement by *Weber* that our experience of the difference between two magnitudes depends on the ratio of the difference to the magnitudes the statement that, for a given difference to remain constant, the proportion of the stimuli to one another must remain constant, and then, secondly, to express this in the form: The experienced difference in magnitude or intensity between two stimuli varies as the ratio of the stimuli, which leads to the formula $S = k \log R$, where S is the experienced intensity and R the physical intensity, while k is a constant for the particular sense department, which is Fechner's law. The law holds only approximately through the middle range of intensities, and is often referred to as the Weber-Fechner relation. A simple method of demonstrating the law is Fechner's *shadow experiment*, where two shadows from a rod, cast alongside one another on a screen by two lights, may be varied in intensity at will by altering the distances of the two lights from the screen.

Fechner's paradox: the name given to the phenomenon first observed by Fechner that a figure viewed binocularly increases in *brightness* when one eye is closed.

Feeblemindedness: applied generally, to a mental level below a certain standard, usually taken as an *IQ* (q.v.) of 70, and specially, to the group designated *moron* in America with IQ between 50 and 70, lower levels being designated *imbecility* and *idiocy*.

Feeling: a general term for the affective aspect of experience, i.e. the experience of pleasure and its opposite, interest, and the like, usually inclusive of emotional experience; used popularly in an indefinite sense for any experience, and more particularly for touch sensations: *feeling tone* is used more particularly to mark the pleasantness or the reverse of a sensation (see *hedonic tone*).

Feigning: exhibiting behaviour suggesting a condition of the organism entirely different from the real condition.

Fellatio: a sex perversion involving oral stimulation of the penis.

Feminism: a social movement aiming at the advance, politically and economically, of the female sex; in a special sense the possession to a marked degree by the male of feminine traits.

Feminization: the various changes in structure and behaviour, involved in the acquiring of female characteristics by a male, as a result of the transplanting of ovarian tissue into a castrated male animal; sometimes used of the acquiring by a male of female characteristics, in consequence of social influences.

Fenestra (ovalis and rotunda): see *ear* and *cochlea.*

Féré phenomenon: see *psycho-galvanic response.*

Ferrier's experiment: an experiment devised by Ferrier to prove that we have no direct experience of efferent or motor impulses, or that feelings of *innervation* (q.v.) have no existence, consisting in placing a finger on a trigger, and imaging as vividly as possible the pressing of the trigger, without actually pressing it, when it becomes clear that any sensations experienced are *kinaesthetic* sensations from neighbouring muscles, etc.

Fertility: productivity; used figuratively of imagination, and tested experimentally by the *ink-blot test* (q.v.).

Fetish: originally an object regarded by the natives of West Africa as having magical powers, and used as an amulet, or for enchantment purposes, or regarded as an object of dread; by extension an object regarded irrationally with peculiar reverence or affection or fear; the name *fetishism* is given to this kind of superstition, and has also come to be used of a more or less pathological and sexually determined attachment to objects associated with a sexual object.

Fiat of the Will: expression used by James to designate the final phase, following immediately on decision, and immediately preceding action, in a volitional process.

Fibre: single nerve process, *axon* or *dendrite,* of a *neuron.*

Fibril: thin thread found in cell body and passing out into *axons* and *dendrites,* to form nerve fibres; sometimes called *neuro-fibrils,* and supposed to be the real conducting elements in the nervous system.

Fibrous layer: a retinal layer, the ninth inward, consisting of the axons of the *ganglion* cells which form the eighth layer.

Fiction: in general sense, any imaginative construction, or the product of such; used in a special sense, by Adler, in *directive fiction,* for imaginary situation created to gratify the impulse for power, and accepted as reality, particularly, for example, the imaginary ill-ness, simulated by the neurotic in order to make others treat him as an invalid, or in order to avoid tasks he does not wish to at-tempt.

Field work: a method of studying social phenomena or animal be-haviour by observation under normal and natural conditions, supplementing this by enquiries and interviews in the case of social phenomena.

Figure-ground: a general characteristic of all perceptual experience, specially manifested in the visual field, in virtue of which the field is organized from the beginning, the object being as it were segregated from the ground, and standing out almost as if in relief; the phenomena are well illustrated by reversing figures, or in puzzle picture phenomena, when the object concealed is suddenly revealed.

Filial generations: successive generations from a given parent or parental pair.

Filial regression: principle formulated by *Galton* according to which characters of offspring tend to revert towards the average of the group to which the parents belong, with respect to deviations from the average in the parents.

Filiform papilla: see *papilla.*

Filiform script: cursive writing, and especially small and rapid writing, in which words tail off into a single line without any distinguishable letters.

Film colour: mode of appearance of a colour, when seen in a spectro-meter, or when filling the field of vision, as contrasted with the colour of the surface of an object, the two exhibiting different phenomena with respect to physical changes, and psychological laws apparently cutting across physical laws.

Final: usually applied to the end of a series, but may also have the sense of purposive; in *final cause* the word has the sense of aim, purpose, or goal of a process or series of events; in relation to the nervous system *final common path* signifies the motor neurons on which a number of motor pathways converge.

Finalism: philosophical interpretation or explanation of (life) pro-cesses in terms of their ends or purposes, and this sense is carried over into the psychology of the analytical schools.

Finger spelling: mode of language communication among or with the deaf, by means of manual signs with the fingers of one hand or of both hands.

Finger-thumb opposition: a significant step in motor co-ordination in the development of a child, occurring on the average at or about the age of one year and used in some test scales as a test of such development.

Fire-worship: type of religion in which the main object of worship is fire or the fire principle.

Fission: mode of reproduction in unicellular organisms, in which the parent cell divides into two, each growing into a separate organism.

Fit: succession of convulsive seizures with or without unconsciousness.

Fittest: in the phrase 'survival of the fittest' meaning that those organisms best adapted to the environment, tend, in the *struggle for existence* (q.v.), to survive and propagate their species. See *natural selection.*

Fixation: employed in three distinct technical senses: (1) of vision, to designate the directing and focussing of both eyes (or one eye) on an object or point, so that the image falls on the foveas or fovea; (2) of learning, to designate the process of establishing, by repetition, a memory, or motor habit; (3) of interest or emotional attitude, by analytical schools, to designate the attachment, generally interpreted psychosexually, to an early stage of development, or object at such stage, with difficulty in forming new attachments, developing new interests, or establishing new adaptations.

Fixed idea: an idea, or line of thought, often emotionally entrenched, or even obsessional, which exercises or tends to exercise, a dominating influence, persistent or recurrent, on a person's attitude and mental life.

Flagellata: an order of lower organisms, which moves and secures food by the beating of whip-like processes.

Flagellation: whipping or scourging; particularly by way of religious penance, or to obtain an emotional experience; a *flagellant,* sometimes used in a general sense of one who whips himself or others, but usually in a special sense of a member of a thirteenth-century sect of religious fanatics, who scourged themselves, or had themselves scourged, by way of religious discipline. Cf. *masochism* and *sadism.*

Flat: in music a tone slightly below a standard pitch, or a tone a semitone lower than some natural tone.

Flatworms: an order of invertebrate worm-like organisms – *platyhelminthes* – represented by the planarians.

Flavour: a sensory quality, or impression, involving taste and smell, sometimes together with touch and temperature, but mainly smell, from an object in the mouth.

Flexibilitas cerea: waxen flexibility; a symptom of some types of *schizophrenia* (q.v.) and *hysteria* (q.v.), where the patient retains a posture of body and limbs in which he has been placed.

Flexibility: pliancy, adaptability, plasticity.

Flexion: bending at a joint of part of the body or of a limb, the muscles which produce such a bending being called *flexors*, as contrasted with *extensors*.

Flexure: bending of the body or part of the body, during embryonic development, or generally.

Flicker: phenomena produced by rapid, regularly intermittent stimulation in the visual (or auditory) field; in the visual field, produced by rapid changes also in intensity, in brightness, or in colour: the flicker becomes finer and finer as the rate of change becomes more rapid (for example, with sectors on a rotating disc), until at a certain rate, called the *critical flicker frequency,* all flicker disappears, this frequency varying with the individual, with difference in brightness (brilliance) of the two fields, and with intensity of illumination.

Flicker photometry: a method of determining the relative brightness of two differently coloured fields, or of equating two such fields with respect to brightness, by the rate of rotation necessary to extinguish flicker in either field. See *episcotister.*

Flight of colours: succession of colours obtained with the fading of the *after-sensation* from an intense light stimulus.

Flight of ideas: rapid succession of superficially related, or entirely unrelated, ideas, occurring in *manic states.*

Flowery: see *fragrant.*

Fluctuations: (1) of *attention,* periodic changes in clearness of an object being attended to, in a sensory field, usually studied experimentally by observing and recording the alternate appearance and disappearance of a just perceptible sound or a just perceptible grey circle on a white ground: (2) of *sampling,* in the sense of the changes in a statistical constant, shown in successive but otherwise similar samples.

Fluttering hearts: the name given to an *illusion* experienced when coloured figures, on a differently coloured background, are moved to and fro (e.g. red hearts on a blue ground), the figures appearing to move from side to side.

Focus: the point to which parallel rays converge after passing through a lens system; figuratively, of the field of attention when compared to the field of vision, the object attended to being said to be in the focus; *conjugate foci* are two points so situated that rays coming from the one converge, after passing through the lens system in the other, which is the position as regards the optical system of the eye in near vision.

Folie (Fr.): mental disorder or insanity; in *folie à deux* a delusion or delusional system shared by two individuals, usually a husband and wife, or two sisters.

Folk psychology: psychology of peoples; applied to the psychological study of the beliefs, customs, conventions, etc. of peoples, especially primitive, inclusive of comparative study.

Folklore: traditions, superstitions, customs, myths, and legends surviving from an earlier, and more primitive, stage of social and cultural development.

Folkways: traditional forms of behaviour of a particular social group, having conventional rather than moral validity in the group.

Fontanel (le): area on the top of the skull, which in infancy is still open, i.e. unossified, that is, covered with cartilage in place of bone.

Foot-candle: unit of illumination; defined as the illumination thrown on a surface at right angles to the rays, from a point source of one candlepower, at a distance of one foot.

Foot-lambert: unit of brightness, equal to a uniform brightness of a perfectly diffusing surface, emitting or reflecting one *lumen* per square foot.

Foot-rule: see *Spearman*.

Forced movements: asymmetrical movements, caused by unequal stimulation of the two sides of an organism, or by injury to one hemisphere of the brain.

Forebrain: the part of the brain comprising the *cerebrum, thalami* (q.v.) and *corpora striata* (q.v.) as its main parts.

Foreconscious: see *preconscious*.

Fore-exercise: preliminary practice period in experiment or test, the object being to introduce the subject to the experimental or test situation, and any manipulation required on his part, and sometimes to get a base line, from which to estimate *variability* from day to day, or the effect of the introduction of the variable condition being studied.

Foreperiod: term employed usually in reaction time experiments, for the period between the word 'ready' and the stimulus, with reference particularly to the record of the subject's *introspection*.

Forepleasure: term used by psychoanalysts, for sexual pleasure experienced in excitation of an *erogenous zone* (q.v.).

Forgetting: failure at any time to recall an experience, when attempting to do so, or to perform an action previously learned. A *curve of forgetting* may be drawn on the basis of learning experiments, using either the *learning and saving method* (q.v.) or the *scoring method* (q.v.), indicating the *rate of forgetting,* or the amount forgotten after the lapse of any period of time. The term *forgetfulness* is employed of the tendency to forget.

Form: generally, the nature of a whole with respect to the manner in which the constituent elements are organized, but independently of the nature of the constituent elements themselves.

Form quality: (*Ger.* Gestaltqualität), quality of a whole, but not of any of its constituent elements, e.g. qualities like 'graceful', 'slender', and the like; attention was first called to such qualities by *von Ehrenfels.*

Formal discipline: see *discipline.*

Formant: term employed, of speech sounds (and musical sounds), for elements contributed to the *timbre* (q.v.) of the vowels by the resonance of the mouth cavities.

Formboard: a board with depressions of various shapes, into which the appropriate insets require to be fitted, used as a mental test of the *performance* type.

Formication: a diffuse tactual sensation, as if ants (formicae) or other insects were crawling over the skin.

Formula: a concise statement, in words or symbols, of a relationship, structural or functional, or of a law or principle, generally in abstract terms, and often mathematically.

Fornix: a group or tract of nerve fibres at the base of the brain, below the *corpus callosum* (q.v.), connecting the *hippocampus* (q.v.) with the *mamillary bodies* (q.v.).

Fortuitous: due to chance, or assumed to be so. See *chance variations.*

Forward reference: accounting or explaining features of growth, etc., with reference to a future stage.

Fourier's Law: principle according to which any complex periodic vibration or function may be resolved into a series of simple harmonic functions, or vibrations, of frequencies increasing in the ratios 1, 2, 3, 4, etc.

Fourth: in music, the interval between the first and fourth notes in a scale, as from C to F.

Fovea Centralis: the depression in the centre of the retina, caused by the thinning out, at that point, of the various layers above the cones; the area of clearest vision upon which the image falls when an object is fixated.

Fractionation: used in a psychological sense, of a method of carrying out a detailed introspection by concentrating attention, in accordance with the instructions of the experimenter, on different parts or phases of a total process to be observed in different repetitions of an experiment; in a statistical sense, of the division of mathematical data into groups for separate mathematical treatment.

Fragrant: a quality of smell sensations of which the smells of hyacinth and of violets are examples; also designated *flowery*.

Frame of reference: a characteristic of all experience and behaviour where activity of judging or evaluating is involved, in virtue of which such judging or evaluating is with reference to a series or structure of standards, set up in, and developing with the individual's experience. This characteristic is manifested at all levels from perception to reasoning on the intellectual side, as well as at all levels in the life of feeling and action, and is especially important in social psychology.

Fraunhofer's lines: dark lines seen in solar spectrum, indicating the presence of certain elements in the sun; used by means of the spectroscope for spectral analysis, and also for specifying different regions of the spectrum, as well as for calibrating *spectrometers* (q.v.).

Free association: an association experiment where the subject is required to give the first word that the stimulus word brings to mind: there are two varieties – the word-list type and the continuous type. The first is the usual type of free association experiment, and is the type used by *Jung* in his diagnostic free association test; the second is the *train of thought* (q.v.) experiment, in which the subject is given a word stimulus, and then continuously gives the ideas, as they come to mind, which is in essence the method of *psychoanalysis*. In the list method the *association time* is usually taken.

Free nerve endings: nerve endings, in the skin, of sensory nerves, without special end organs, assumed to be the source of pain sensations.

Free will: conception, which has been the subject of controversy, both psychological and ethical, of *volition* and action, as capable of being determined by the will of the individual, independently of external influence, or internal conditions, or even motives; usually known as *indeterminism* (q.v.), or *libertarianism,* and contrasted both with *determinism* (q.v.) and with *self-determination* (q.v.).

Freeman time-unit: name given by *Saudek* to a time-unit suggested by *Freeman* as the most suitable time between exposures in photography by cine-camera, of the writing movement – unit is .04 sec. and contraction F.T.U. or F.U. is generally used.

Frenzy: violent and disorganized emotional excitement.

Frequency: the number per second of periodic phenomena, such as vibrations or waves; in statistics, employed for the number of cases with a certain value or score, or between certain values or scores, in a tabulation for statistical purposes, and in this sense the term is used of a *distribution,* a curve, or a surface.

Frequency curve: a curve showing graphically the frequency of the various values in a tabulation; *normal frequency distribution* is that represented by a bell-shaped curve.

Frequency polygon: a graphical representation of frequency, by means of a series of lines, equidistant from one another, forming, when the upper ends are joined, a polygon.

Frequency surface: the surface of a solid formed on a *scatter diagram* by raising from each cell a prism, representing the frequency in that cell.

Frigidity: used, in a technical sense, of absence of normal sexual desire, especially with reference to women.

Fringe of consciousness: expression, used by *James,* for the marginal field of consciousness, comprising sensations and feelings not clearly discriminated, but contributing, sometimes to an important extent, to the experience as a whole of the object or idea occupying the centre of the field. Cf. *implicit apprehension.*

Frontal lobe: the part of a cerebral hemisphere lying in front of the *central fissure* (q.v.) or *fissure of Rolando,* and above the *fissure of Sylvius* (q.v.).

Frotteur: one who practises masturbation by rubbing, or a masturbator generally.

Fruity: a quality of smell sensations; one of *Henning's* classes.

Fugue: used in two distinct technical senses: (1) of a period of loss of memory, when the individual disappears from his usual haunts; (2) of a type of musical composition, where a musical theme is stated by one part, taken up and developed by another, and so on.

Fullerton-Cattell Law: a law substituted for Weber's law by *Fullerton* and *Cattell,* to the effect that errors of observation and just noticeable differences are proportional to the square root of the stimuli.

Function: several technical senses: (1) the activity of, or the part played by, any organic structure; (2) activity in general; (3) mathematically, a variable quantity, whose value depends on the values assigned to the one or more variables involved.

Functional disorders: disorders which do not involve any change or disease affecting structure, as contrasted with organic disorders, as, for example, a mental or nervous disorder, which can be formulated in terms of disorder of behaviour, or functional activity, without reference to organic change in any part of the nervous, or organic, system.

Functional psychology: a type of psychology which emphasizes the functions rather than the mere facts of mental phenomena, or seeks to interpret mental phenomena with reference to the part they play in the life of the organism, rather than to describe or analyse the facts of experience or behaviour; or a psychology that approaches its subject-matter from a dynamic, rather than a static, point of view.

Functional selection: type of biological selection, characterized by the survival and development of those functions which are of greater utility to the individual, or the social group, and the disappearance of those functions having less utility. See *natural selection.*

Functionalism: see *functional psychology.*

Fundaments: term employed by *Spearman* in the statement of his *noegenetic laws* (q.v.), meaning the elements or items between which a relation is thought.

Fundamental Formula: generally used of the simplest expression in mathematical terms of Weber's law as: $dS = C[dR/R]$.

Fundamental: the lowest tone in a *clang* (q.v.).

Fungiform papilla: see *papilla.*

Furor: acute emotional excitement involving violent behaviour.

Fusion: combination of two or more stimuli into an unanalysed, and sometimes unanalysable, impression; in *binaural fusion* we have the combination of stimuli presented separately to the two ears; similarly of *binocular fusion,* in the case of the combination of two images falling separately on the two retinas; and similarly in the case of *tonal fusion,* where two or more tones sounding together blend in various degrees with one another.

G

g. factor: general factor, in *Spearman's two-factor theory* (q.v.); generally taken as synonymous with 'general intelligence'.

Galton bar: an apparatus for determining thresholds in the estimation of linear distances; consists usually of a metre rod of square cross section, with a millimetre scale on the side facing the experimenter, when resting with one edge upwards on two uprights, the other faces being painted grey or black. The rod carries riders on the upper edge, one at the centre of the bar, other two on opposite sides of this, the one marking the standard distance, the other to be placed by the subject at a distance he judges equal from the centre. The experiment is a stock experiment in the psychological laboratory, to exemplify the psychophysical *method of mean error* (q.v.).

Galton whistle: a high-pitched whistle, devised by Galton for the determination of the upper limit of tonal hearing, with a tube capable of being altered in length by means of a plunger, and provided with a graduated scale; the form now used is the Edelmann-Galton form, which provides also for a graduated size of aperture.

Galvanic: a steady direct current such as that given by a galvanic battery.

Galvanic skin response: see *psycho-galvanic response.*

Galvanometer: an instrument for measuring the strength of an electric current; the types used in psychological laboratories are generally the *Einthoven string galvanometer,* or a *moving coil galvanometer,* both dependent on the deflection produced by a current passing through a conductor in a magnetic field.

Galvanotropism (Galvanotaxis): an orienting response in a magnetic field, or produced by electrical stimulation.

Game: organized play according to definite rules, with a definite objective, and usually competitive.

Gamete: in reproduction a cell which combines with another to produce a *zygote* (q.v.), from which a complete organism develops.

Gametogenesis: the processes involved in the development of male and female gametes.

Gamma movement: see *apparent movement.*

Gamogenesis: reproduction through union of two *gametes.*

Gang: a group of persons banded together for some common purpose, usually by implication illegal, except in a form of play among children.

Gangliated: used of a nerve in whose course there is a *ganglion.*

Ganglion: any massed group of cell bodies or nerve cells, within or without the cerebro-spinal system.

Ganglioplexus: a group of cell bodies in a network of nerve fibres.

Ganser's syndrome: giving random, irrelevant, and absurd answers to questions, as a symptom of *hysteria* or simulation.

Gastrula: a stage of embryonic development following the *blastula* (q.v.) stage; embryo usually shaped like a hollow cup.

Gegenstandstheorie (Ger.): theory of objects; an attempt to develop a branch of science for the study of objects as such, objects being classified according to the kind of mental activity of which they are objects.

Gemmation: budding; a form of non-sexual reproduction, where the new organism first appears as a bud from the parent organism. From Lat. *gemma,* a bud.

Gemmule: a minute particle supposed by *Darwin* to be given off by each cell in the body as a basis for the reproduction of a corresponding cell in the new organism.

Gemut (Gemutsbewegung) (Ger.): a general term covering the affective and emotional aspect of experience.

Gene: the carrier of a hereditary factor in the *chromosome* (q.v.), in the *germ cell*: a change in a gene, causing a stable variation, is known as *gene mutation.*

Genealogy: the investigation in genetics of the ancestral descent of an individual.

General ability: used of a wide range of mental capacities; or, specifically, of a general factor affecting all mental operations (*Spearman's g*) or as equivalent to *general intelligence,* as tested by intelligence tests.

General consciousness: experiences common to members of a group.

General idea: general *concept* (q.v.), covering all the individuals of a given class, in so far as they all have certain characteristics in common.

General norms: average scores for different ages, classes, etc., in a series of tests, mental or educational, given to a large unselected group, or random samples, and assumed to be general for the whole population or the ages and classes in question.

General paralysis: a degenerative disease following upon syphilitic infection of the brain.

General psychology: a systematic discussion of general principles and laws holding of the mental life in general, as distinct from peculiarities characteristic of the individual.

General will: decision as to a course of action, taken by a social group, acting as such; used also by some writers as an entity characteristic of the group, and distinct from the individual wills of the individual members of the group.

Generalization: a thought process at the *conceptual level,* through which a *general concept* (q.v.) is formed.

Generation: the average period between the birth of an individual of a species and the beginning of reproduction; or the offspring of two parents.

Generating tone: either of the tones which when sounded together give rise to a *combination tone* (q.v.).

Generic: characterizing a genus. See also *image.*

Genesis: coming into being; origin of any rganism; origin of anything.

Genetic: related to the origin and development or evolution of an organism; *genetic psychology,* that branch or type of psychology which studies mental phenomena and behaviour by the *genetic method,* i.e. by investigating the origin and course of development of the various mental phenomena; similarly a *genetic theory* is a theory which seeks to explain a present phenomenon in terms of its origin and historical development.

Geniculate bodies: two swellings, lateral and medial, on the back portion of the *thalamus* (q.v.).

Genital: relating to the organs of reproduction in an animal; used of organs, zones, and sensations.

Genital character: term used by psychoanalysts to designate the adult stage of *psycho-sexual* development, where the partial phases of the earlier stages are fused, under the dominance of the genital erotic phase, which is also spoken of as *genital primacy,* and represents the final stage of organization.

Genius: the highest range of mental ability, either general, or in respect of special capacities of a creative order.

Geno-motives: true motive forces lying behind the *pheno-motives* (q.v.) and equivalent to 'needs' conscious or unconscious.

Gens: anthropological term used to signify line of descent through the father.

Genus: classification group in biology, including under it a number of different species (as a rule), all of which have certain general characteristics, and with other genera constituting a family; transferred to other fields, with the meaning of a group or class, comprising several species.

Geometrical illusion: usually applied to a group of *optical illusions,* of which illusions of distance and direction are the chief, e.g. the *Müller-Lyer illusion* (q.v.).

Geotropism (Geotaxis): orienting response to gravity. See *tropism.*

Germ: a structure which develops into an organism or organ; figuratively of a primitive entity or phenomenon of almost any kind; used also of a bacillus or micro-organism causing disease: used as an adjective (or prefix) with cell or layer of cells in embryonic development, or in *germ-plasm* of the substance which carries the hereditary factors or *genes.*

Germinal vesicle: the nucleus of the *ovum* before the early stages of development show themselves.

Gerontology: the scientific investigation of old age or of the aging processes.

Gestalt (Ger.): form, pattern, structure, or configuration; an integrated whole, not a mere summation of units or parts; gives its name to the type of psychology which is known as *Gestalt psychology,* and which originated in Germany during the early decades of the present century, mainly as a psychology of perception.

Gestalt psychology: a type of psychology which arose as a strong reaction against atomic psychology in all its varieties, equally hostile to behaviourism and to introspectionism; its basal contention is that mental processes and behaviour cannot be analysed, without remainder, into elementary units, since wholeness and organization are features of such processes from the start; starting as a psychology of perception, its investigations were extended so as to cover learning and other aspects of the mental life.

Gestaltqualität (Ger.): form quality (q.v.); allied to, but not recognized among, the doctrines of the Gestalt psychologists.

Gestation: the carrying of the embryo in the uterus; generally used with reference to the period of pregnancy, i.e. from conception to birth, a period which varies in the different animal species.

Gesture: expressive movement, usually of head or hands, for the purpose of communication, but also frequently accompanying the individual's own train of thought; may become systematized into a gesture language, more or less conventionalized, as among deaf-mutes.

Ghost: visual appearance, presumed to be disembodied spirit; sometimes used figuratively of shadowy presentations in other sense departments.

Ghost-soul: primitive idea of the human soul as a shadowy or vaporous likeness of a person, inhabiting the body, and passing out of it at death; the *ghost theory* of the origin of religion derives in part from a belief of this kind.

Giddiness: see *dizziness.*

Gifted: possessing talents of a high order, generally, or in a particular field. Cf. *genius.*

Gigantism: abnormal development of particular bones, or of the skeleton as a whole, conditioned by overactivity of glands in the anterior lobe of the *pituitary* (q.v.).

Girdle sensation: sensation like that produced by a tightly drawn belt, appearing as a symptom in certain diseases, e.g. *tabes.*

Given: see *data.*

Gland: an organ in the body, the function of which is to produce a specific substance, or specific substances, exercising an important influence in the bodily economy; a very heterogeneous group, but falling into two main divisions – duct glands, and ductless or *endocrine glands* (q.v.).

Glandular response: one of the two classes of response of an organism to stimulation from within or without, in the change of the secretory activity of glands, the other being muscular response.

Glass sensation: the visual effect produced by transparent solids, of a filling of a definite space with a colourless substance, in contradistinction from empty space.

Glaucoma: a painful and serious disorder of the eye, or of vision, caused by heightened pressure of fluids within the eyeball.

Glia: see *neuroglia.*

Gliosis: increase of *neuroglia,* due to a diseased condition of the cerebrum, forming a mass called a *glioma,* resembling clinically a brain tumour.

Globus Hystericus: a sensation in the throat, as if a round mass were rising from the stomach into the *oesophagus* (q.v.).

Glossal: related to the tongue.

Glossolalia: a fabricated language or speech in an unknown tongue, occurring in religious ecstasy, in hypnosis, in mediumistic trances, and in certain pathological mental states.

Glossosynthesis: forming of nonsense words.

Glottis: the opening at the upper part of the *trachea* (q.v.), between the *arytenoid cartilage* (q.v.) of the *larynx,* and the vocal cords, and between the cords.

Glowing colour: a colour which is characterized by a luminous mode of appearance, as of colours in flames or incandescent solids.

Glycogen: the reserve hydrocarbon stored in the liver mainly, and used by the muscles and animal tissues in performing work.

Glycosuria: the presence of glucose (sugar) in urine, caused by violent emotion, or by certain diseases.

Goal: the end-result towards which action, muscular or mental, is directed; employed in a special sense, by *Adler* and his followers, of an objective towards the attainment of which the individual consciously or unconsciously strives.

God: an object of worship.

Golden section: the division of a line into two parts, so that one part is the mean proportional between the whole line and the other part, or, geometrically, so that the square on the one part is equal to the area of the rectangle formed by the whole line and the other part; held to have special *aesthetic* value.

Golgi-Mazzoni corpuscles: end-organs in the skin in which nerve fibres terminate; regarded as receptors either for cold or for pressure.

Gonad: gland producing *gametes* (q.v.); *ovary* in female and *testis* in male.

Goniometer: instrument for measuring angles; in psychological laboratory, an apparatus for measuring tendency to sway, consisting of a platform on which the subject stands upright, balanced so that any sway is indicated on a scale.

Gradation methods: term used for psycho-physical experimental methods, where the procedure is by equal steps, i.e. *method of limits, method of minimal changes,* and *method of mean gradations.*

Grade: position on a graded scale; in America, educational level as determined by the year-class reached: *grade norm* is the educational standard of the average performance of any school grade.

Gradient: magnitude or intensity sloping from high to low, or vice versa; sometimes of the rate of change.

Grand mal (Fr.): major epileptic attack. See *epilepsy.*

Grandeur delusions: exalted ideas of importance, or power, characteristic of certain types of mental disorder.

Granular layers: the 5th and 7th layers of the retina.

Granular pressure: term employed by *Goldscheider* to designate a type of pressure sensation from moderately intense blunt stimulation.

Graph: representation of the relation between two variables by straight, curved, or broken lines.

Graphic: usual sense, recorded by means of a graph; in *graphology*, used of characteristics of an individual's hand-writing, e.g. *graphic alignment*, the alignment of letters or words with reference to their relation to a base line; *graphic individuality*, the sum of the characteristics of an individual's writing; *graphic size*, the height of the short letters; *graphic variability*, the range of variation in an individual's writing, or the range of variation between individuals in a group.

Graphic language: written or printed language, inclusive of picture writing.

Graphic rating scale: method of recording an individual's characteristics, especially traits of character and the like, and the degree in which each is present, by the position of a mark on a line, the ends of which represent the two opposites or extremes.

Graphokinaesthetic: relating to the motor sensations involved in writing.

Graphology: the science which investigates handwriting, with particular reference to the physical, physiological, and personality characteristics of the writer; *graphological elements*, the particular points upon which the graphologist depends for his diagnosis, and the final picture deduced from the interpretation of these.

Graphomania: an obsessive urge to write, indicative of some abnormality or some mental disorder, and in the latter case usually resulting in confused, irrational, and rambling statements, or, in extreme cases, in a mere meaningless succession of written words, sometimes nonsense words, known as *graphorrhea*.

Graphopathology: the scientific investigation of changes in, and other characteristics of, handwriting, indicative of physical or mental abnormality or disorder.

Graphospasm: see *writer's cramp*.

Grasping reflex: response by fingers or toes to object brought into contact with them by which the object is held, characteristic of human infant at an early stage.

Gregariousness: the tendency on the part of various species of animals to live together in groups, or gather together in flocks, herds, or packs.

Grey (Gray): type of visual sensation constituting the *achromatic* series from white to black; used of *non-medullated nerve fibres*, and of nervous substance consisting largely of cell bodies – *grey matter* – in the brain and spinal cord.

Grief: an emotional attitude, or a complex emotion, more or less synonymous with *sorrow,* as generally used, but usually implying greater intensity and more specific reference.

Grotesque: term applied to figures, objects, and also, figuratively, to situations, statements, etc., or fantastic combinations of almost any kind, akin to *ludicrous* (q.v.), but without so strong a tendency to excite laughter, except perhaps the laughter of scorn, if the situations are taken seriously.

Group: a number of objects or individuals capable of being regarded as a collective unit, or having a unity of its own; a pattern or configuration of objects perceived as a whole or *Gestalt.*

Group: as an adjective, used in many connections, as in *group behaviour,* behaviour characteristic of a social group as such, or of an individual as a member of a social group; *group consciousness,* consciousness of the group in the individual member of the group, or sometimes consciousness of the group as a group, as if that were a separate entity; *group differences,* differences in characteristics between groups statistically determined; *group fallacy,* the assumption of a collective mind; *group psychology,* the psychology of social groups; *group spirit,* synonym for *esprit de corps* (q.v.).

Group factors: factors coming out in intelligence test results, treated statistically, which appear to influence more than one, but less than all, of the types of efficiency being tested.

Group marriage: a kind of marriage found among certain primitive peoples where a group of individuals, usually members of the same family, marry in common the same number of women.

Group psychotherapy: collective therapeutic treatment of a group of individuals, as in *sociodrama* or *psychodrama* (q.v.).

Group selection: type of selection where the group functions, rather than the individual, in determining *survival of the fittest* – i.e. group – in the *struggle for existence.*

Group test: a test arranged so as to be applied simultaneously to a number of individuals, as contrasted with the individual test, where each is tested separately.

Growth curve: a graphic representation of the natural development changes, taking place in the growth towards maturity of physical or mental structures, characters, or functions, plotted against time.

Guidance: employed in a technical sense in three connections: (1) *child guidance,* meaning the organization and co-operation of medical, psychological, educational, and psychiatric advice and treatment, through special clinics, in dealing with difficult or retarded children presenting either behaviour or educational problems; (2) *educational guidance*, meaning the employment of standardized tests, mental and educational, together with progress records, school reports, etc., as a basis for advice to children and parents, regarding educational courses which should be followed after the child has passed through the primary school; (3) *vocational guidance*, meaning the assistance of the child and the child's parents in choosing a suitable vocation for the child, by means, and on the basis, of a systematic procedure, involving *intelligence tests, educational tests,* special aptitudes and special disabilities tests, school records, tastes and inclinations, information regarding the state of the labour market, etc.

Guiding idea: alternatively 'guiding fiction'; an idea, more or less constant and persistent, which influences, or directs, a train of thought, as it were, creating an attitude, context, or mental background; according to *Adler's* view determining, generally unconsciously, all traits of character, inclusive of neurotic traits, the idea or fiction being of the nature of a goal which is completeness or superiority.

Guilt: sense of wrong-doing, as an emotional attitude, generally involving emotional conflict, arising out of real or imagined contravention of moral or social standards, in act or thought.

Gustatory: relating to taste sensations, as in *gustatory stimuli* or *gustatory qualities.*

Guttural: relating to the throat.

Gynandromorphism: presence of both male and female characters in the same organism.

Gynandry: tendency in female towards male form of body.

Gynophobia: morbid fear of women.

Gyrus: convolution in cerebrum or cerebellum.

H

h: measure of precision in psychophysical experiments, more or less the reciprocal of the *standard deviation* or the *probable error.*

Haab's pupil reflex: contraction of both pupils, when attention is given to a bright object in a darkened room.

Habit: automatic response to specific situations, acquired normally as a result of repetition and learning; strictly applicable only to motor responses, but often applied more widely to habits of thought perhaps more correctly termed *attitudes;* the process of forming a habit is designated *habit formation,* not *habituation,* which is rather synonymous with *accommodation* or *adaptation;* the term *drug habit* is employed for an acquired inability to abstain from certain drugs, usually narcotic – an acquired *appetite* rather than habit – more or less synonymous with *drug addiction;* conflict between two responses to the same situation, one of which has become a habit, and interferes with a second, which may be a new response, necessitated by a minor change in the situation, is spoken of as *habit interference;* the expression *hierarchy of habits* is used where simpler habits have been organized into more complex or higher level habits, in a complex type of learning, a process suggested as an explanation of the phenomena of *plateaus* (q.v.) in a *learning curve.*

Habitat: usual natural surroundings and conditions of animals and plants.

Haemorrhage: rupture of a blood-vessel, and spread of blood over the surrounding tissues.

Hair Aesthesiometer: an instrument for measuring sensitivity to light pressures, consisting of a hair (human or horse) mounted in a case, with a slide by means of which the part projecting can be altered in length, and also a millimetre scale, devised and employed by *v. Frey;* the pressure at which the hair bends can be determined by a chemical balance, and depends on the diameter of the hair and the length of the part projecting.

Hair cells: cells with projecting filaments, found in the *organ of Corti* in the *cochlea,* and regarded as the receptors for sound; the filaments or hairs vary in length, and may be the apparatus by which *discrimination of pitch* is rendered possible; hair cells are also found in the ampullae at the ends of the *semi-circular canals* (q.v.), and somewhat similar cells are found in the *olfactory areas,* and also in the *papillae* in the tongue.

Hair follicle: structure at the roots of the hairs in the skin with afferent nerve end, supposed to be receptor for touch sensations.

Hallucination: an experience having the character of sense perception, but without relevant or adequate sensory stimulation; failure to have a perceptual experience when relevant and adequate stimuli are present is sometimes spoken of as *negative hallucination* (both types, positive and negative, are easily produced experimentally in *hypnosis*); the phenomena are usually thought of as restricted to abnormal or pathological mental conditions, but they are quite frequent, not merely in hypnosis, but also in the state between sleep and waking, just before falling asleep, or before becoming fully awake, being then called *hypnogogic* and *hypnopompic hallucinations* respectively.

Hallucinosis: disordered mental condition subject to the occurrence of hallucinations, without any other necessary impairment of consciousness.

Halo effect: a tendency to be biased in the estimation or rating of an individual with respect to a certain characteristic by some quite irrelevant impression or estimate (good or bad) of the same individual. It is a frequent source of error in employing *rating scale* (q.v.), and similar procedures.

Handedness: preference for using right or left hand. See *dextrality* and *sinistrality*.

Handwriting scale: a scale for measuring or assessing the quality of handwriting, the best known types being the Ayres scale and the Thorndike scale, both of which are based on standardized samples, selected according to principles assumed to determine quality in handwriting.

Haploid: having half the usual number, i.e. one set only, of *chromosomes*.

Haptic: relating to cutaneous sensibility. The branch of science which studies cutaneous sensations is sometimes called *haptics*.

Haptometer: an instrument for measuring touch or pressure sensitivity, consisting essentially of levers, by means of which a weight can be lowered on the skin, and changes of pressure made by altering counterbalancing weights.

Hard of hearing: having a higher threshold for loudness than normal. See *hypacusia*.

Harmonic: overtone (q.v.), whose frequency is a multiple of the fundamental.

Harmonic analysis: a device for resolving a complex periodic curve into its components in accordance with *Fourier's law* (q.v.).

Harmony: a pleasing combination of tones into chords; generally, as a musical term, inclusive of both *consonance* and *dissonance*.

Hashish: Cannabis indica (q.v.).

Hate: a *sentiment* or emotional attitude involving, according to *Shand*, the whole gamut of primary emotions, but with anger, and often fear, predominating.

Haunted swing illusion: an *illusion* of swinging produced by swinging the room, in place of swinging the seat in which the subject sits.

Hawthorne experiment: an experiment on incentives carried out in the Hawthorne works of the Western Electric Company, the general result of which appeared to show that external incentives had a relatively slight influence compared with better morale and the development of an *esprit de corps* (q.v.), arising particularly from the feeling on the part of the worker that the management had a personal interest in him.

Head nystagmus: oscillating movement of head, produced by rotating an animal, the head turning slowly in the opposite direction to the rotation, then being brought back quickly in the direction of the rotation, this movement being repeated after the rotation has stopped.

Healy picture completion tests: performance tests (q.v.), analogous to the *Ebbinghaus completion test,* on the verbal side, in which pictures are used in place of verbal material, squares being cut out of the pictures, and mixed with other squares of the same size, the subject being required to select and place the correct squares. Either of two types of test may be used; in one a single complex picture represents a number of activities and an essential part in each activity is cut out; in the other there is a series of pictures, showing the various events that might occur in a schoolboy's day, and one square in each of the pictures is cut out, and must be found among a number of squares all of which will fit the space; the latter type is generally preferred for the testing of children, but both types give very interesting and useful results.

Hearing: the experiences derived through the receptors for sound in the *cochlea* of the *inner ear; hearing loss,* the percentage below normal hearing at different frequencies, usually indicated in a curve based on *audiometer* (q.v.) results.

Hearing mute: a popular term for an individual with a considerable amount of hearing, who is nevertheless mute – usually a case of *high frequency deafness,* of *congenital aphasia,* or low-grade intelligence.

Hearing theories: theories aiming at the explanation, not so much of hearing as such, but rather, as a rule, of the various phenomena associated with musical sounds – *pitch, combination tones, consonance* and *dissonance,* etc., of which at least three main types have been proposed: (1) the resonance type (*Helmholtz*), which is the orthodox type, according to which the various fibres of the basilar membrane, or possibly the hairs of the hair cells, are tuned to respond to tones of different frequencies, and pick out each its own frequency in the waves traversing the canals of the cochlea; (2) the sound figure or picture type (*Ewald*) according to which sounds of different complexity or different pitch produce each definite and characteristic figures on the basilar membrane, or the tectorial membrane; and (3) the wave-crest type (*Hardisty* and *Watt*) according to which the basilar membrane as a whole takes on the wave forms passing through the cochlea as variations of pressure and reproduces that wave form in its frequency and its complexity.

Heat: (1) the sensory effect of simultaneous stimulation of cold and warmth receptors, possessing a characteristic insistent quality, possibly due to the addition of pain sensations, as in stimulating warmth receptors with a rod at too high a temperature; (2) also used of a female animal at periods of readiness for mating.

Heat spot: see *warm spot*.

Hebephrenia: one of the commonest forms of *schizophrenia* (q.v.) or *dementia praecox*, in which the subject, becoming more and more detached from reality, exhibits silly mannerisms, and becomes untidy and careless of personal appearance.

Hebetic: relating to *adolescence*.

Hederiform terminations: disc-shaped sensory end organs in the skin usually described as free nerve endings, and supposed to be receptors for pain.

Hedonic: in general sense pleasurable, or relating to pleasure; the agreeableness or the reverse of sensations is spoken of as their *hedonic tone*, and *hedonics* is that branch of psychology which investigates feelings of pleasure and its opposite – unpleasure.

Hedonism: psychologically, the theory that man's actions are determined primarily by the seeking of pleasant, and the avoidance of unpleasant, feelings, and, ethically, that type of theory which makes happiness, either individual or 'the greatest happiness of the greatest number', the standard for human conduct.

Heidelberg man: an early type of man represented by a jaw-bone found at Heidelberg.

Helicoid: like a helix or spiral in three dimensions; resembling in shape a snail shell.

Helicotrema: the opening in the *basilar membrane* at the apex of the *cochlea*, where the *scala vestibuli* and the *scala tympani* communicate.

Helix: the border of the outer ear, from its shape.

Hematophobia: morbid dread of the sight of blood.

Hemeralopia: combination of three Greek words meaning 'day', 'blind' and 'vision'; day blindness; applied to a condition where the eyes see indistinctly, or are blind, in daylight, but see reasonably well by night: often, owing to confusion regarding the meaning of the Greek, used for *night blindness* (q.v.); the same confusion occurs regarding *nyctalopia* (q.v.).

Hemi-: prefix meaning 'half' or 'on one side'.

Hemianalgesia: insensitivity to pain on one side of the body.

Hemianaesthesia: insensitivity to touch on one side of the body.

Hemianopia (hemiopia): loss of vision for one half of the binocular field, or restriction of vision to one half of field.

Hemiparesis: paralysis of one side of the body.

Hemiplegia: loss of ability to make voluntary movements, affecting one side of body.

Hepatic: relating to the liver.

Herbartian psychology: type of psychology, and of educational theory based on that psychology, usually spoken of as Herbartianism; a development of Leibnizian theory or philosophy of the universe, as consisting of a plurality of self-active monads, which became, in *Herbart,* self-active impressions and ideas; the central doctrine was the doctrine of *apperception* (q.v.), a term borrowed from *Leibniz,* but, in Herbartianism, having a new role to play, as representing a definite mental activity on the part of existing systems of knowledge – *apperception masses* – and the new idea striving for recognition. This doctrine was substituted for the *association* of the associationist, as the key to all mental process, the result being a pure intellectualism, which has exercised a considerable influence on subsequent psychology, especially educational psychology. *Herbart* may also be credited with the introduction of mathematical concepts and formulae into the psychological field, in his attempt to express mathematically the interaction of ideas.

Herd Instinct: see *gregarious impulse.*

Heredity: the transmission from parents to offspring of physical and mental characteristics; the totality of characteristics so transmitted.

Hering after-image: the first positive *after-sensation* succeeding a brief light or colour stimulus.

Hering greys: a series of fifty greys, graded by subjectively equal steps from white to black.

Hering illusion: one of the geometrical *optical illusions,* where straight parallel lines are seen as curved inwards when they are drawn across a series of lines radiating from points beyond their extremities and intersecting above and below the lines – the converse of an illusion due to *Helmholtz* where parallel lines seem to be curved outwards when drawn across lines radiating from a point between their centres.

Hering theory of colour vision: a theory based on four fundamental or primary colours in antagonistic pairs, red and green, blue and yellow; three photochemical substances in the retina were assumed, in which antagonistic processes, called by *Hering catabolic* and *anabolic,* but interpreted by his followers in terms of reversible chemical reactions, take place, giving white and black, red and green, and blue and yellow, black being thus for *Hering* a positive sensation, not a mere absence of sensation as for *Helmholtz.*

Hering window: a device, due to *Hering,* for demonstrating *simultaneous colour contrast* by means of coloured shadows. One of several interesting devices for demonstrating colour phenomena.

Heritage: in the case of individual heritage, the totality of characteristics transmitted by heredity from parents or direct ancestry; in the case of social heritage (*Wallas*) the totality of law, customs, language, acquisitions, in short, the whole social and ideational environment into which an individual is born, as representative of the modifications of natural conditions, made available for the present generation, but due to the work of previous generations.

Hermaphroditism: presence of both male and female reproductive organs in the same organism: *hermaphroditic dreams* are dreams which are bisexual in character, and evidence, in the opinion of some psychoanalysts, of the bipolarity of the sexual impulse itself.

Hermetics: system of secret knowledge or lore.

Herpes zoster: popularly shingles; an eruption on the skin, following the course of a nerve, and indicative of an inflammatory condition of spinal or cranial ganglia of sensory nerves.

Herring revision: a series of individual intelligence tests, purporting to be a revision of the Binet-Simon tests, but, though using some of these tests and tests modelled on them, differing from the Binet tests, in several important and indeed essential respects, as being a *point scale,* and not a pass or fail scale, and being arranged on radically different principles, e.g. not in year groups, but in five groups A, B, C, D, and E, in such a way that the extent of tests employed varies with the time available, and the degree of approximation desired.

Hetero- (Gr.): prefix meaning other.

Heterochrony: difference of time, or rate, between two processes. Cf. *chronaxy.*

Heterodox: at variance with generally accepted opinions, beliefs, or principles of explanation, at the time; unorthodox.

Heterogeneity: composed of diverse constituents; the opposite of *homogeneity.*

Heteromorphic: differing from normal form or type; deviating from type with respect to form or structure.

Heteromorphosis: development of an organ or structure in a position other than that in which it is normally found.

Heteronomy: subjection to the guidance or rule of another, as in *hypnosis.*

Heterophoria: see *imbalance, muscular.* Cf. *strabismus.*

Heterosexuality: attraction towards opposite sex; also employed in designating a phase or stage of normal sex development.

Heterosuggestion: suggestion (q.v.) dependent on the words, attitudes, or acts of others, or another, as contrasted with *autosuggestion* (q.v.).

Heterotropia: see *strabismus.*

Heterotelic traits: term employed of predominance in an individual of purposes, interests, and aims in the world outside the individual; may also be used of types of character. See *telic.*

Heterozygote: a *zygote* (q.v.) formed by the union of two dissimilar *gametes* (q.v.), i.e. possessing contrasted *Mendelian characters.*

Heuristic method: an educational method, specially applicable, though not confined, to science teaching, the principle of which is to arrange the work so that the pupil discovers laws and principles for himself, rather than learns them secondhand from information supplied by the teacher.

Heymans' Law: the principle, with respect to visual stimuli, that the *threshold value* of a visual stimulus is increased in proportion to an inhibiting stimulus simultaneously operating.

Hibernation: a condition of torpor, characteristic of certain species of animals, most usually during winter.

Hierarchical table: table of *correlation coefficients* which satisfy the *columnar correlation* criterion, i.e. which show, when arranged, regularly diminishing coefficients, from left-hand top corner to the right in each row, and downwards in each column. See *equiproportional tables*, and *tetrad difference*.

Hierarchy of habits: an organization of habits or skills in a complex habit or skill, as for example in typing, telegraphic sending, or learning to speak a foreign language.

Hieroglyphics: characters in *pictographic* or *ideographic* writing.

Higher mental processes: thought processes in strict sense, i.e. comparison, judgment, and reasoning.

Higher units of response: more complex response units, which organize simpler units, or in which simpler units are organized. Cf. *hierarchy of habits*.

Highest audible tone: highest frequency of sound waves audible as a tone by the human ear – about 20,000 c.p.s., but varies with different animal species.

Hind brain: cerebellum, pons, medulla.

Hipp chronoscope: a chronoscope clockwork-driven, reading in thousandths of a second, often known as the Wheatstone-Hipp chronoscope, as embodying features due to both scientists; a standard psychological apparatus for measuring short intervals of time like *reaction time;* the hands are brought into gear by an electrically-operated clutch, acting against the tension of a spiral spring, and adjustment may be made for working, either from make to break, or from break to make.

Hippocampus: region of under part of cerebrum, consisting of two parts, *hippocampus major* or *horn of Ammon*, and *hippocampus minor*.

Hircine: quality of smell, and one of *Zwaardemaker's* classes – smell of cheese is an illustration.

Histogram: the graphical representation of a frequency distribution, which appears as a *column diagram*, the breadth of the column representing the class interval, and its height the number or the frequency within that class; class intervals are usually equal, but not necessarily so.

Histology: the branch of anatomy which deals with the structure of tissues.

Hitzig's girdle: insensibility to pain at the breast level, occurring as a symptom in *tabes dorsalis* (q.v.).

Holmgren wools: a test for colour blindness, involving the matching for hue of skeins of wool.

Homing: term applied to a tendency, and usually ability, on the part of certain animal species, to return to their original home, or former habitat, when removed to a distance.

Homo- (*Gr.*): prefix meaning 'same'.

Homeostasis: term borrowed from physiology, employed by some psychologists for compensatory adjustments to meet any threat to the personality.

Homoerotic: see *homosexual.*

Homogenous: composed of similar constituents throughout.

Homogeny (*Homogenesis*): similarity of organs in different species, indicative of common ancestry.

Homolateral: belonging to the same side.

Homologous: term applied to organs which are fundamentally alike in structure and in development, but may differ in function.

Homology: similarity in the fundamental pattern of structure, indicative of common ancestry.

Homophony: music in one part; melody.

Homoplasy: similarity of organs in different species, not due to common ancestry.

Homosexuality: sexual attraction towards individuals of the same sex; psychoanalysts apply the term *homosexual neuroses* to a group of disorders, regarded by them as originating in repressed homosexual tendencies.

Homozygote: a *zygote* (q.v.), formed by the union of two like *gametes;* an organism of pure heredity, producing only gametes containing identical hereditary factors (W); identical twins (see *twins*) are sometimes spoken of as *homozygotic.*

Hope: best regarded as an emotional attitude, though designated by some psychologists a derived emotion, its predominant characteristic is desire for the attainment of some objective, with some idea that this desire will be satisfied, giving a pleasant *hedonic tone* to the experience.

Horde: a social group, more or less at the crowd level, as regards lack of organization, but with relatively enduring, rather than merely temporary, existence.

Horizontal: at right angles to the direction of gravity.

Horizontal-vertical illusion: a geometrical optical illusion, in virtue of which a vertical length appears greater (with some possible exceptions) than an objectively equal horizontal length, in lines, rectangles, and the like.

Hormic theory: a psychology emphasizing the importance of instinctive impulses and purposive striving, from the Greek word '*horme*' meaning 'animal impulse', translated '*instinctus*' by the Romans.

Hormone: chemical substance secreted by an *endocrine gland* (q.v.), and carried by the blood to another organ, in which it initiates activity; generally used widely to include also substances producing an inhibitory effect. Cf. *autacoid*.

Horn of Ammon: see *hippocampus*.

Horner's Law: the principle that red-green colour-blindness is transmitted from males to males, through females, in whom it is latent.

Horopter: for any particular distance of fixation, in binocular vision, the locus of all points in the external world, the images of which fall on *corresponding*, or identical points in the two retinae.

Horoscope: the position of the planets and other heavenly bodies at the time of an individual's birth, which was the basis upon which astrologers professed to forecast the future of the individual.

Hue: the *chromatic* or colour aspect only of a visual impression, which, under normal physical conditions of illumination, and normal physiological efficiency of the retina, corresponds to the stimulation of the retina by light of a narrow range of wavelengths.

Humor: a fluid in the body, particularly one of those which in the older physiology and psychology were supposed to be the basis of the different *temperaments* (q.v.).

Humour: character of a complex situation exciting joyful, and in the main quiet, laughter, either directly, through *sympathy* (q.v.), or through *empathy* (q.v.).

Hunger: normally appetite (impulse, drive) for food; may refer also to the mass of uneasy sensations from the viscera, and particularly from *hunger contractions* in the stomach, which accompany the appetite; also used specially of sex appetite.

Hunting: used for an impulse, or a form of behaviour, shown by various species of animals and by man, in the former case mainly in search of food, in the latter as a form of sport or play; almost certainly an instinctive impulse or drive; also employed adjectivally, of an early stage in the development of man towards civilization.

Hybrid: offspring of parents differing in species or variety; in particular, with respect to Mendelian heredity, offspring of parents, one of them alone possessing a certain unit character, are regarded as hybrids with respect to that character.

Hydrocephaly: excessive amount of fluid in skull, resulting in abnormal enlargement of head and limited mentality.

Hydrotropism (Hydrotaxis): orientation of organism, or organ, with respect to water.

Hyoid bone: a bone between the root of the tongue and the *larynx,* giving attachment to the muscles of the tongue.

Hyp(o)- (Gr.): prefix meaning 'below' or 'defect'.

Hyper- (Gr.): prefix meaning 'above' or 'excessive'.

Hypacusia: diminished hearing efficiency. Opposite *hyperacusia.*

Hypaesthesia: diminished sensitivity to tactual stimuli. Opposite *hyperaesthesia.*

Hyperalgesia: excessive sensitiveness to pain. Opposite *hypalgesia.*

Hypercritical: excessively critical.

Hyperfeminization: unusual degree of feminization of behaviour, or structure, or both, appearing especially in castrated males in which female sex glands have been implanted.

Hyperfunction: excessive activity of an organ or system.

Hyperkinesis: excessive motor restlessness.

Hypermasculinization: converse of *hyperfeminization;* unusual tendency towards the masculine in structure and function, or behaviour, especially in castrated females in which male sex glands have been implanted.

Hypermetropia (Hyperopia): eye or lens condition, in which parallel rays, with relaxed ocular *accommodation,* are brought to a focus behind the retina.

Hypermnesia: unusual (pathological) degree of retention and recall, especially of details.

Hyperphoria: see *imbalance, muscular.*

Hyperpituitarism: see *acromegaly.*

Hyperplasia: excessive multiplication of cellular elements in an organism; excessive cell-formation.

Hyperpnoea: exaggerated breathing; panting.

Hyperprosexia: exaggerated *enforced attention,* so as to be unable to ignore stimuli.

Hyperthymia: exaggerated emotional excitement.

Hyperthyroidism: excessive production or administration (for experimental purposes) of thyroid secretion (or its active principle), marked by increase in general activity, emotionality, increased reflex excitability, a tendency to insomnia. See *exophthalmic goitre.*

Hypertonicity (Hypertonia): increased *muscle tonus* (q.v.), accompanied by increased excitability of reflexes, especially those involving anti-gravity muscles.

Hypertrophy: excessive growth of tissue in an organ.

Hypno- (Gr.): as a prefix meaning 'sleep'.

Hypnagogic: referring to the drowsy state just before falling asleep;

imagery in this state frequently takes on the character of *hallucination* (q.v.).

Hypnoanalysis: psychoanalysis in the hypnotic state.

Hypnogenic: producing sleep or hypnosis.

Hypnoidal: resembling sleep; used of conditions having some of the characteristics of light *hypnosis,* or on the borders of sleep.

Hypnology: scientific investigation of sleep; used by *Braid* for the study and practice of hypnosis.

Hypnopompic: used of the state between sleep and waking, before one is fully awake.

Hypnosis: artificially induced state, similar in many respects to sleep, but specially characterized by exaggerated *suggestibility* (q.v.), and the continuance of contact or *rapport* with the operator.

Hypnotic: relating to hypnosis; drug producing hypnosis or sleep.

Hypnotism: the scientific study and practice of hypnosis.

Hypochondria: exaggerated or obsessive attention to and anxiety about one's health.

Hypochondriac: sufferer from *hypochondria;* relating or referring to the body surface in the liver region.

Hypodermic: used of the introduction of a drug into the tissues under the skin; the syringe employed for such injection.

Hypofunction: lowered functioning or activity of an organ.

Hypognathous: having the lower jaw projecting beyond the upper.

Hypokinesis: lowered vigour of movement or motor response.

Hypomania: mild condition of overexcitability.

Hypophonia: voice tending towards a whisper.

Hypophrenia: deficiency in mental development.

Hypophysis: see *pituitary.*

Hypothalamus: the region of the forebrain below, and the under-part of, the *thalamus,* including the *mamillary bodies,* the *optic chiasma,* the *hypophysis,* etc.

Hypothesis: a provisional theory to explain observed facts.

Hypothetical: relating to a hypothesis; still unproved.

Hypothymia: lowered emotional response.

Hypothyroidism: insufficient secretion activity of the *thyroid.* See *cretinism, myxoedema.*

Hysteria: nervous disorder characterized by *dissociation,* high susceptibility to *autosuggestion,* variety and variability of *psychogenic,* functional disorders; by psychoanalysts classified as a *psychoneurosis,* arising from conflict and repression, where the repressed impulses and tendencies are expressing themselves in the various symptoms, etc,. which the patient shows, certain characteristic varieties being specially designated *anxiety hysteria, conversion hysteria, fixation hysteria.*

Hysteriform: applied to motor disturbances or convulsions, which are interpreted as manifestations of hysteric origin; a disorder of this type, *hystero-epilepsy,* shows epileptic fits, which are regarded as determined by emotionally charged experiences.

Hysteroneurasthenia: neurasthenia (q.v.) suggesting the underlying mechanism of hysteria.

I

Icon: an image, representative or symbolic.

Iconolatry: worship of images or pictures.

Ictus: stress or accent; also seizure or stroke.

Id: employed by Freud to designate the impersonal mass of inter-acting energies or forces constituting the *unconscious* in a strict sense, or what might be designated the structural unconscious, behind the processes making up conscious life, as inner determinants of these processes; in a certain sense the human organism, regarded objectively and impersonally, but nevertheless psychologically; suggested by *Weismann* for a hypothetical vital unit, consisting of an organization of determinants – the basic idea being more or less the same as that of *Freud,* and possibly its origin, though in the one case referring to a psychological, in the other a biological, entity.

Idea: in some of the older writers, and popularly. the most general word for any mental process on the cognitive side; usually employed, in contrast to *impressions,* for processes on the ideational and conceptual levels, i.e. as inclusive of images and thoughts, but exclusive of percepts. *Plato's* use of the word is metaphysical, not psychological.

Ideal: emotionally coloured thought of a personality, type of character or line of conduct, as representing a goal to be striven after, though possibly not to be attained, by the individual.

Idealism: any one of a variety of systems of philosophical thought, which would make the ultimate reality of the universe expressible or intelligible only in terms of ideas, rather than in terms of matter in space.

Idealization: representing an object in a form coloured by, or in accordance with, our desires or ideals.

Ideation: the forming of ideas; the level of ideal representation, or the ideational level, i.e. the level in the mental life typified by *memory ideas* or *images*.

Ideational learning: learning involving recall in the form of ideas or images, as contrasted with *perceptual learning* (q.v.); or learning in terms of connections of ideas, as contrasted with *motor learning* in terms of movement – learning by heart, as contrasted with acquiring a motor skill.

Idée force (Fr.): term used by *Fouillée,* to express the dynamic aspect of an idea, the implication being that an idea is in the concrete more than a merely cognitive element.

Identical: the same; or similar in every respect.

Identical points: see *corresponding points.*

Identical proposition: a statement in which the predicate is merely a repetition of the subject without adding anything.

Identical series: the name given to a *recognition* method in the experimental study of *learning.*

Identical twins: see *twins.*

Identical visual direction law: in binocular vision, the principle that any pair of corresponding lines of direction in objective space is seen in visual space as a single line of direction, and objects on either line are seen on the single line.

Identification: generally, a phase of *recognition* in remembering; specially, by psychoanalysts, a process by which an individual, unconsciously or partially so, as a result of an emotional tie, behaves, or imagines himself behaving, as if he were the person with whom the tie exists.

Identity: the condition of being the same, or alike in all respects (*identical*); the character of persisting essentially unchanged (see *personal identity*).

Identity Hypothesis: double aspect theory (q.v.).

Ideograph (Ideogram): a character or a figure representing an object or an idea (see *pictograph*), as a unit of graphic language, at an earlier stage of development than the representation, by characters, of the sounds of the spoken language; also used of the graphical record, by means of the appropriate apparatus, of the unconscious movements of a subject, resulting from the direction and course of his thought.

Ideology: in general sense, a world philosophy; more specially a social and political philosophy; a theory of the nature of ideas; a synonym for psychology, prior to the definite fixing of that term for the science.

Ideomotor: in general sense, the guidance of movement by ideas; in a special but more usual sense, as *ideomotor action,* the direct issue of ideas in action, automatically, or without deliberation, as in *absentminded acts.*

Ideoreflex: in general sense, synonymous with *ideomotor,* but applied, more specially, to the issue in action of an idea suggested from within or from without.

Ideoplasy: the influence of ideas on physiological processes.

Idio- (Gr.): as prefix meaning 'private possession'.

Idiogamy: used in psychoanalytic literature for the restriction of male potency to cohabitation with one woman.

Idioglossia: speech so indistinct that it sounds like a foreign language.

Idiographic: relating to the study or description of individual cases or instances.

Idiolalia: private or invented language of individuals of low mentality, covered by the more general term *dyslalia* (q.v.).

Idiopathic: used of a disorder that is primary, and not the result of accident or some other disorder.

Idioplasm: that part of living substance concerned in reproduction.

Idiophonia: individual form of *dysphonia* (q.v.).

Idioretinal: term applied to visual sensations of light occurring in the absence of external stimulation, due to physiological changes in the retina or cortex.

Idiosyncrasy: a characteristic of the mentality or behaviour of an individual, and peculiar to himself, and not assignable to any general psychological factor or factors.

Idiot: the lowest grade of feeblemindedness, attaining, when adult, a mental age of not more than two years, or an IQ not above 25. A feebleminded individual of any grade, who shows remarkable talent in some one direction, has been called *idiot savant.*

Idol: image, effigy, or natural object worshipped as a god; in Baconian sense, a misconception, assumption, or bias, generally resulting from tradition or mass suggestion, and hampering the discerning of truth.

Illicit: contrary to law, or to custom having the force of law; not permitted; meaning transferred to faulty inference.

Illiteracy: inability to read or write, due to lack of educational opportunity, and not to feeblemindedness; the adjectival form *illiterate* is generally used only of adults, and covers relative as well as absolute inability.

Illumination: amount or density of light falling on a surface; unit the *photon* (q.v.). The illumination of a surface varies directly as the intensity of the source of the light, and as the cosine of its angle of incidence, and inversely as the square of the distance.

Illusion: in the case of sense perception, 'a subjective perversion of the objective content', or actual sense data; in the case of memory a subjective falsification by addition, omission or substitution, in the recall of a past experience. See also *optical illusion* and *apparent movement.*

Image: a revived sense experience, in the absence of the sensory stimulation, e.g. seeing with the mind's eye; employed in several technical combinations: *composite image,* an image based on a number of sensory experiences of the same or similar objects, *eidetic image* (q.v.), *generic image,* an image, usually somewhat schematic, capable of representing any one of a class of objects, *hallucinatory image,* an image which has momentarily perceptual character, *hypnagogic image,* for which see *hypnagogic hallucination.* In the term *retinal image* the word has a different meaning, in this case referring to the *optical image* focussed on the retina by the lens system of the eye.

Imageless thought: a thought, or train of thought, devoid of any imagery. It is a matter of controversy, since the time of Aristotle, whether such thought is possible, or at least whether it occurs at all in human experience, though there is a fair mass of experimental data which would appear to support such a view.

Imagination: the constructive, though not necessarily creative, employment of past perceptual experience, revived as images in a present experience at the ideational level, which is not in its totality a reproduction of a past experience, but a new organization of material derived from past experience: such construction is either *creative* or *imitative,* being creative when self-initiated and self-organized, and imitative when following a construction initiated and organized by another.

Imago: two senses: biologically, the perfect stage of an insect after final metamorphosis; psychologically, idealized figure or phantasy of what a person beloved in childhood – usually a parent – stands for, sometimes exercising a marked influence as a control, and as a standard, in later life.

Imbalance, muscular: used of lack of balance in the case of the extrinsic muscles of the eyeball, causing deviation from the point of fixation, when fusion of the two images is prevented by placing a *Maddox rod* before the affected eye, giving rise to *heterophoria*, i.e. deviation in various directions, according to the pairs of muscles involved, the directions being signified by the special terms *esophoria* (inwards), *exophoria* (outwards), *hyperphoria* (upwards), *hypophoria* (downwards) and *cyclophoria* (rotated).

Imbecile: individual with degree of mental defect intermediate between the *idiot* and the *feebleminded*, or mental age between 2 and 7, or IQ between 25 and 50.

Imitation: performing an act seen performed by another, the process being stimulated (and guided) by the seen act.

Immediate: usually, without the intervention of any significant period of time; without intervening phenomena; *immediate association* is a particular instance of the second of these meanings, where one idea gives rise directly to another idea, without the interpolation of any third; in *immediate experience*, the meaning is the direct experience of the individual or individuals, rather than scientific explanation, interpretation, or extension of that experience.

Immobility: state of being (temporarily) incapable of movement, as in *hypnosis*, or the *death-feigning* response. See also *tonic immobility*.

Immoral: violating moral or social law. Not to be confused with *non-moral* (q.v.).

Impedance: the characteristic of an electric circuit which limits the strength of the current passing in it, either through its electrical resistance, or its self-inductance.

Impediment in speech: popularly used for stammering, stuttering or other speech disorders or disturbances.

Imperative: used with reference to actions which an individual is compelled to perform by command, or because of circumstances; obligatory; in morals the *categorical imperative* has reference to the obligatory character of a principle of conduct accepted by the individual, as unconditionally controlling his conduct.

Imperative idea: persistent or *obsessional* (q.v.) idea of acting in a certain way.

Imperceptible: employed of a stimulus or stimulus difference below the *threshold* (q.v.). Popular rather than technical term.

Impersonation: the intentional or willed representation of another person by an individual, usually, if serious, in order to obtain some advantage or privilege.

Implicit: employed with reference to something not directly stated or given, but implied; also in two special or technical senses: (1) in *implicit apprehension,* of items in a total sense experience, which are not themselves discriminated, but which nevertheless make a difference to the total experience, e.g. the ticking of a clock in a room, of which we are unconscious until it stops, and (2) in *implicit response,* of responses of muscles and glands which are not observable directly without the appropriate apparatus or instruments, and also of *inner speech,* or subvocal response by the vocal organs.

Import: meaning, usually inclusive of what is implied in a statement.

Impotence: want of power (usually in a sexual sense and of a male).

Impression: neural and immediate psychical effect of sensory stimulus.

Impression method: term used in the experimental study of feeling for methods, dependent mainly on the introspective report of the subject, with respect to the affective experience, produced or initiated by stimuli of different kinds, this report being intended to throw light upon the nature and course of affective experience itself, or on some of the associated psychological problems; in the *method of paired comparison* (q.v.), the experiment may have either or both of two objectives, on the one hand, the determination of the actual preferences of an individual, on the other hand, the reasons for such preference, and hence, from a practical point of view, this is the most valuable of the impression methods.

Improvement: term employed in the experimental study of *practice,* for the progressive advance towards a certain standard of mastery or skill, as measured by increase in accuracy, or diminution in time taken, or both.

Impulse: tendency to action without deliberation; a natural or instinctive tendency, or a tendency rising suddenly from excitement, habit of reaction, or other circumstance, the important point being that it arises immediately on the presentation of a certain situation; the term is also used of *nervous* or *neural impulse,* in the sense of the wave of active change propagated along a nerve fibre.

Impulsion: practically synonymous with *impulse,* except that it lays stress on the subjective origin and the *drive* aspect.

Impulsive: term referring to the character of an act as immediate, and without deliberation or volition, on the mere presentation of a situation, either in perception or in idea.

Inaccessibility: state of unresponsiveness on the part of an individual;

condition characteristic of certain nervous or mental disorders, notably *schizophrenia* (q.v.), where there is little or no response to efforts to get mentally in touch with the patient.

Inadequacy: inability to cope with a situation in which an individual is placed, either because of the lack of the necessary personal qualities, or the requisite mental ability, or special skill.

Inadequate stimulus: see *adequate stimulus.*

Inattention: scattered attention; educationally, attention to something other than the lesson; may also refer to the marginal, as distinct from the focal, field of consciousness at any moment.

Inborn: present in the individual at birth; innate.

Incantation: a ritual, or form of words, performed or recited in order to produce a magical effect.

Incentive: motive for acting in a certain way; adding a further motive, more or less extrinsic, to a motive already operating; any strengthening of a drive towards an end or objective, by attachment to that objective of additional values of any kind: often equivalent to *drive.*

Incest: sexual relations between individuals of different sexes closely connected by blood kinship, the degree of the kinship being determined by social law.

Incest barrier: term employed by psychoanalysts for the barrier placed upon the development of the *libido* (q.v.), by social law regarding incest, at the same time stressing the feelings of *guilt,* evoked by thoughts, or phantasies, or dreams, involving the breaking down of the barrier.

Incidental: occurring casually or fortuitously in a situation or series of events, without being essential to the situation or the sequence; stimuli of this order, occurring along with the regular stimuli in an experiment, and influencing the subject's response, are spoken of as *incidental cues.*

Incidental errors of observation: errors made by a subject or observer which have no relation to the controlled conditions of an experiment, or the experimental situation.

Incidental learning or memory: learning or remembering without set purpose, or special effort, to learn or recall.

Incipient: referring or relating to the beginning of a process.

Incitogram: the conditions in the nervous system underlying the organization of motor impulses.

Incoherence: lack of systematic connection, or of organization of parts; in speech, unintelligibility because of such lack of connections.

Incommensurable: relating to two characteristics or two phenomena which cannot be measured or estimated in terms of the same unit, standard, or scale.

Incompatible: not consistent or in agreement with one another; incapable of existing together at the same time in the same place; used of statements, phenomena, characteristics or qualities of individuals, in the sense of mutually contradictory.

Incompetent: not possessed of the knowledge, ability, or skill necessary for a particular task.

Inconceivable: used of a statement or theory incapable of being mentally represented as corresponding to an actual situation.

Incongruous: not in keeping with its setting, context, or surroundings.

Inconsistent: used of two characteristics, properties, or statements so related as to be mutually contradictory, or incompatible with one another.

Incontinent: incapable of self-control, as regards the sex impulse in particular, but also as regards any natural body function, such as urination, defaecation, etc.

Incoordination: term used generally of movements in which muscles or muscle groups do not co-operate smoothly or adequately in a complex movement. May also be used by extension of mental functions.

Increment: amount of change or rate of change, where a magnitude is changing progressively.

Incubus: nightmare (q.v.).

Incus: the middle one of the chain of small bones in the middle ear, or the anvil.

Indecency: anything which violates the conventions approved by a society, with regard particularly to sex, caste, mode of dress, behaviour, and language.

Indecision: an attitude, sometimes pathological, where an individual is unable to decide on a course of action, or between two alternative courses of action, and action is accordingly inhibited for a shorter or longer period; sometimes used of a characteristic, more or less enduring, of an individual.

Independent phenomena: phenomena which are not in any way causally connected; used in special sense in *psychical research,* of phenomena occurring without the intervention of physical agency, either on the part of the medium, or of any one present, such as *levitation, slate-writing,* etc.

Indeterminism: a theory of the will, to the effect that it is possible for an individual to act, or to choose a course of action, independently of the stimuli affecting him, or the motives prompting him at the time. Synonymous with *libertarianism*.

Index: generally, a sign directing to a particular statement, fact, or point; a sign indicative of some phenomenal change.

Index of precision: a mathematical quantity, denoted by h (q.v.), indicating inversely the scatter of the judgments in the psychophysical method of *right and wrong cases* (q.v.). Cf. *standard deviation*.

Indifference point: the point of transition between opposites in experience, in feeling between 'pleasant' and 'unpleasant'; the zero point in any series having positive and negative values; in the case of short time intervals, the point at which estimation is most accurate, and there is not a tendency either to overestimate or to underestimate.

Indirect vision: vision of objects stimulating the marginal, or extramacular, area of retina.

Individual differences: variations or deviations from the average of the group, with respect to mental or physical characters, occurring in the individual members of the group.

Individual psychology: the psychology of individual differences, i.e. the systematic investigation, with the measurement, of these differences; or in a special sense, the type of analytical psychology founded and developed by *Adler*.

Individual response: type of response in free association experiments, carried out with standard word lists, which is peculiar to the individual, and not found in standard lists of responses, such as the *Kent-Rosanoff* (q.v.).

Individuality: the sum total of the characteristics of an individual, which distinguish him from other individuals; sometimes wrongly used as synonymous with *personality*, which has, or may have, dynamic and also normative implications, absent in the case of individuality, which is necessarily purely descriptive.

Individuation: the emergence, in the course of development, of individual structures, parts, and organs, together with specific functions, out of homogeneity and mass activity.

Induced colour: a colour change appearing in a retinal field, due to the stimulation with another colour, not of the same field or area, but of another area of the retina. See *simultaneous contrast*.

Induced emotion: see *induction* (of feeling).

Induced hallucination: hallucination occurring as a result of *suggestion* (auto- or hetero-).

Inducing colour: the colour which gives rise to an *induced colour.*

Induction: used in a number of technical senses, which fall under one of two heads: (1) a logical sense involving inference from the particular to the general, or (2) a special physical, physiological, or psychological sense, of the production of an effect elsewhere than at the original locus of activity. In the first sense induction is the basis of scientific method; in the second it may be said to group together phenomena in many different fields, from the physical phenomena of electro-magnetic induction, as embodied in the induction coil, to the psychological phenomena of feeling and emotion, induced in another person through *sympathetic induction* (q.v.).

Industrial psychology: the branch of applied psychology which concerns itself with the application of psychological methods and results to problems arising in the industrial or economic field, inclusive of the selection and training of workers, methods and conditions of work, etc. Sometimes distinguished from *psychology of industry,* which concerns itself rather with fundamental problems of industry, which are not so much problems of application, or of practice, as general psychological problems underlying economic activities in the widest sense.

Inertia: in general sense, the tendency of a body to persist in its state of rest or motion; sometimes used figuratively in psychology, of *perseveration* (q.v.), or of *latent time* (q.v.); similarly in *aesthetics,* of the principle that art tends to perpetuate what has become obsolete practically, owing to changed conditions.

Infancy: the earliest period of post-uterine human life, during which the child is wholly dependent on parental care; strictly should apply to the period before the child begins to speak, but is usually taken to cover the first two years of life.

Infant psychology: the psychology of the period of infancy, but often extended to cover the pre-school period, i.e. in Britain, up to the age of five.

Infantile: relating to the period of infancy; characteristic of the period of infancy with respect to mentality and behaviour, even in the case of older people.

Infantile amnesia: forgetfulness of the experiences of early childhood; interpreted psychoanalytically, at least in certain cases, as due to *repression.*

Infantile birth theories: notions about birth prevalent among young children.

Infantile complex: a pathologically conditioned emotional state occurring in adult life, interpreted psychoanalytically as due to *regression* (q.v.) to modes of thought and behaviour characteristic of early childhood.

Infantilism: arrested development, especially on the mental side, but usually marked also by stunted physical growth.

Inference: the process of drawing a conclusion, or a conclusion reached, on the basis of previously made or accepted judgments.

Inferiority complex: a *complex* (q.v.) arising from conflict between the impulse to seek recognition (positive self impulse), and fear of the hurt arising from frustration frequently experienced in similar situations in the past, resulting in defensive, compensatory, or often aggressive behaviour, unconsciously determined. Must not be confused with *inferiority feeling* (q.v.).

Inferiority feeling: the normal feeling of weakness and comparative helplessness or inefficiency experienced by all children, sometimes strongly reinforced by special inferiorities, as in physical health, deformity, or defect, and always stimulating to efforts to secure recognition by others, and even, according to *Adler's* conception, to secure superiority over others, often leading to neurotic symptoms of various kinds, including an *inferiority complex.*

Infinitesimal: a quantity less than any definite quantity, however small.

Infinite: a quantity or magnitude greater than any definite quantity or magnitude, however great; the opposite of *infinitesimal.*

Influence: any past or present condition, experienced as or actually playing a part in determining one's behaviour, or course of thought, in the present; a common type of *delusion* (q.v.).

Information: knowledge of facts or about things; often used with the implication of being unsystematized, or derived from hearsay rather than from direct experience.

Information test: a type of mental test devised with the object of throwing light upon the testee's knowledge of facts in a variety of fields, general and special, and frequently forming one of a battery of intelligence tests.

Infra- (*Lat.*): prefix meaning 'below', or 'in low degree'.

Infraconscious: term suggested by *Lloyd Morgan* for a primitive or primordial psychic state from which consciousness has evolved, which may be regarded as still underlying marginal consciousness; alternative term for *subconscious.*

Inframammary: relating to the region of the body between the breasts (mammary region) and the *hypochondriac* (q.v.) region.

Infundibulum: the stalk of the *pituitary* (q.v.).

Ingestion: the process of taking food in mass into the body as in the case of *amoeba* (q.v.).

Inguinal: related to, or located in, the groin.

Inherent: essentially belonging to, or existing in.

Inherit: receive from parents, or ancestors, as a natural characteristic, or endowment. Cf. *heritage.*

Inheritance: the characteristics passed on from parents to offspring, or from ancestry to descendants. The term *alternative inheritance* is employed when one of two corresponding characters in the parents appears in the offspring to the exclusion of the other, while *blending inheritance* is employed where two characteristics in the parents are blended or fused in the offspring so as to produce a stable characteristic, which is capable of being passed on, as such, to subsequent generations.

Inhibition: condition where a function, or functions, or some circumstance prevents the manifestation of some other function, or activity, or mode of expression; the phenomenon may be either peripheral, i.e. in muscle, gland, or sense organ, or it may be central, i.e. in cortical or subcortical areas, and may be physical or mental in origin, or in manifestation; the extinction of a *conditioned reflex* (q.v.) may be regarded as inhibition, and, as such, classified as *internal* or *external,* according as the extinguishing condition is internal or external. See also *retroactive.*

Initial: referring to, or located at, the beginning of a process or activity, as, for example, *initial reflex,* the first reflex evoked by a series of stimuli, gradually increasing in strength from a first stimulus, below threshold strength; or in *initial spurt,* frequently shown in a *work curve* (q.v.)

Initiation: the process of beginning an activity or movement; in a special sense, of the preparation, usually ending with a ritual or ceremony, for entrance into some society, or on the enjoyment of certain privilege, e.g. as a full or adult member of the social group or community.

Initiative: the action of an individual in starting a series of events, e.g. a social movement; the capacity for taking independent action of such a kind.

Injury: damage to an organism from other than natural biological processes, resulting in impairment of structure or function; in the case of injury to a tissue a *current of injury* is set up by the development of an electromotive force between the uninjured parts of the tissue and the locus of the injury.

Ink-blots test: a test, sometimes described as a test of fertility of *imagination*, where a series of irregular figures, such as ink-blots, is presented to the subject, and he is required to say what objects he sees, or can imagine, in the figures, the result depending generally on the number of objects he can report in a given time, though the kind of objects he reports may also be significant. See *Rorschach test.*

Innate: present in the individual at birth; generally implies inheritance.

Innate Ideas: a doctrine originating in the *notitiae communes* of the Stoics, and appearing in modern philosophy under the latter name, as, for example, in *Lord Herbert of Cherbury's 'De Veritate'*, and as the *innate ideas* of *Descartes* – one of the three classes into which he divides ideas – strongly attacked in that form by *Locke,* but reappearing in a different form in *Leibniz* and *Kant,* as well as in *Reid. Locke's* contention that, in a psychological sense of the words, no ideas are innate, remains valid, but the distinction between what is *a priori,* and what is *a posteriori,* in our systematized knowledge, remains useful, however much philosophical controversy it may provoke.

Inner psychophysics: term originating with *Fechner* (q.v.), who distinguished two branches of *psychophysics* (q.v.), inner and outer, the former dealing with the relation between neural processes and sensory experiences, and the latter with the relation between physical stimuli and sensory experiences.

Innervation: the supply of efferent nerves to a muscle or gland; the actual excitation of a muscle or gland, through an efferent nerve.

Innervation feelings: experiences, at one time alleged to exist, of the outgoing nervous impulse to a muscle; but such experiences are now attributed to the receptors in the muscle which contracts, and the afferent nerves, rather than directly to the outgoing impulse.

Insanity: a medico-legal and popular rather than a scientific term, covering forms of mental disorder which involve legal irresponsibility and incompetence.

Insect: a class of invertebrates including ants, bees, wasps, etc., distinguished from other members of the same branch – the arthropods – by possessing, when developed, only three pairs of legs; psychologically the highest of the arthropods.

Insensibility: absence, either temporarily, or generally, of some quality, class, or mode of sensation.

Insight: general meaning, 'mental discernment'; in *introspective psychology*, direct apprehension of the meaning or bearing of something; in *Gestalt psychology*, awareness of the relevance of behaviour to some end or objective; in *psychopathology*, awareness of one's own mental condition.

Insistence: the quality of enforcing attention; employed by some psychologists as a technical term, of doubtful value, for a higher order attribute of sensation, produced by the concurrence of two or more simple attributes, e.g. quality and intensity, which is marked by this enforcement of attention.

Insistent idea: see *fixed idea*.

Insomnia: sleeplessness; generally used of a chronic condition.

Instability: term employed in two semi-technical senses: (1) as lack of steadiness of aim, steadiness of control, effectiveness in action, due to what is popularly termed 'nervousness'; and (2) a more important usage, as *emotional instability*, in the sense of a definite defect, characterized by excessive and variable manifestations of emotional excitement.

Instinct: in its original sense 'animal impulse' (Gr. ὁρμή, Lat. instinctus); hence a general term for natural or congenital impulse; erroneously used in modern times for forms of behaviour, rather than the underlying congenital impulse (behaviour may be spoken of as *instinctive* (q.v.), but not as 'an instinct'); more or less equivalent to innate or congenital 'drive' or 'need'; actual usages in present-day psychology are: (1) the original sense, (2) unlearned complex adaptive response, (3) congenital impulse plus specific emotional excitement. A *delayed instinct* is a term employed usually in (2) for one which does not operate until some time after birth (or hatching), or until a certain stage of development has been reached; *instinct maturation* is employed for the process of development of bodily organs, mechanisms, and connections, underlying unlearned forms of behaviour; a *transitory instinct* is claimed by some writers to be one which can be elicited only at a certain stage in an animal's life.

Instinctive: usually corresponds to innate or congenitally determined, with reference to an organism's activities, as in *instinctive behaviour, instinctive impulse, instinctive tendency*. *James* also uses the expression *instinctive stimulus*, for the stimulus, or perceived situation, which elicits instinctive behaviour.

Instinctual Fusion: expression used by psychoanalytical writers for the theory that all mental processes result from the fusion of the *life and death instincts*.

Institution: an organization representing an established phase or aspect of social, political, or religious life, with a body of laws and principles, and subordinate rules and regulations; a custom, or group of customs; or a practice; but in all cases having a degree of permanence not possessed by a fashion or convention. Popularly the name is often applied to the building housing the organizations.

Instruction: systematic imparting of knowledge by oral speech, written language, or in any way appropriate to the content imparted; one of the two aspects of education, the other being training or *discipline* (q.v.).

Instrumental error: a constant error, due to some defect or deviation from standard of a precision instrument, and corrected for, after calibration, by a constant factor.

Insula: a lobe of the cerebrum. See *island of Reil*.

Insulin: a hormone, or *autacoid,* secreted by the *islands of Langerhans,* in the pancreas; when deficient, the individual suffers from diabetes, for which it is a specific, as a drug.

Integral: in mathematical sense, the result of *integration,* a *definite integral* being the result of integration between definite limits; more generally, referring to an integer or whole number; used in a non-mathematical sense in *integral part,* an essential part of a complex whole.

Integration: in mathematical sense, the summing of a differential series, represented by the symbol ∫; more generally, the process by which organic, psychological, or social material is combined and organized into a complex whole at a higher level; psychoanalytically, two types of psychological integration are marked by the terms *primary* and *secondary integration,* the first being the development, in the young child, of the recognition of his body as distinct from the objects in the environment, and the second the organization into the complete *psycho-sexual unit* of its *pregenital* components, in earlier stages of development.

Intellect: mind in its cognitive aspect, and particularly with reference to the higher thought processes.

Intellection: the conceptual and rational processes; or the higher thought processes generally – conception, comparison, abstraction, generalization, reasoning.

Intellectualism: the tendency in psychology to emphasize the intellectual or cognitive aspect, and to neglect the emotional and volitional, or to attempt to explain them in terms of the intellectual, e.g. the psychology of *Herbart*.

Intelligence: the relating activity of mind; *insight* as understood by the *Gestalt* psychologists; in its lowest terms intelligence is present where the individual, animal or human being, is aware, however dimly, of the relevance of his behaviour to an objective; many definitions of what is really indefinable have been attempted by psychologists, of which the least unsatisfactory are: (1) the capacity to meet novel situations, or to learn to do so, by new adaptive responses, and (2) the ability to perform tests or tasks, involving the grasping of relationships, the degree of intelligence being proportional to the complexity, or the abstractness, or both, of the relationships. For *measurement of intelligence* see *measurement.*

Intelligence quotient: IQ (q.v.); ratio of *mental age* to *chronological age,* expressed as a percentage. See *age.*

Intelligence scale: any series of *intelligence tests,* normally arranged in order of difficulty, by means of which an individual's mental level, or mental development, can be determined.

Intelligence test: a task or problem of some kind, as an item in a scale or alone, by means of which an individual's stage of mental development can be estimated or measured.

Intelligible: capable of being understood.

Intend: to have a purpose to attain a clearly defined aim or goal; to set up a definite objective for oneself; the first movement or phase of conation, which might be said to manifest itself in *intention,* and which differentiates it from mere foresight, or anticipation, or awareness that we are going to act in a particular way; to mean or refer to an object, for which sense see *intentionalism.*

Intension: see *connotation.*

Intensity: the quantitative aspect of sensation (or attribute of sensation), or the how much of a particular sense quality; must not be confused with the magnitude or size in a spatial sense, or with the intensity or quantity of the physical stimulus, to which, however, it is related according to the *Weber-Fechner law* (q.v.) (with certain qualifications); the *intensity threshold* or *limen* is the lowest intensity of the physical stimulus, which gives rise to a sensation – the just noticeable stimulus; the *intensity difference threshold* or *limen* is the *just noticeable difference* of intensity; the former threshold is a measure of the acuity of a receptor, the latter of its discrimination.

Intensity theory of tropisms: a theory which seeks to account for tropisms in terms of the unequally intensive stimulation of corresponding or symmetrical points on opposite sides of an organism.

Intentionalism: a type of psychological theory, sometimes referred to as *act psychology*, which emphasizes as the most fundamental characteristic of psychical process or of the mental life the act of *intending* or referring to an object.

Interactionism: a theory of the relation between mind and body, which assumes interaction or reciprocal causation between the two – that mind acts on body and body on mind – as the solution of the *psychophysical problem;* this involves a philosophical dualism, which need not prevent the psychologist adopting it as the simplest working hypothesis.

Interbrain: see *diencephalon.*

Intercalation: a verbal phenomenon of the nature of a *tic*, which manifests itself in the insertion, irrelevantly, of a given word between syllables, words, or phrases, when speaking.

Intercolumnar correlation: the *correlation* between columns of *correlation coefficients* in a correlation table; employed by *Spearman* to prove his *two-factor theory,* before he adopted the *tetrad difference method.*

Interest: term employed in two senses, functional and structural; (1) designating a type of feeling experience, which might be called 'worth-whileness', associated with attention to an object, or course of action; (2) an element or item in an individual's make-up, either congenital or acquired, because of which he tends to have this feeling of 'worth-whileness' in connection with certain objects, or matters relating to a particular subject, or a particular field of knowledge, as, for example, psychology. What has been called the *doctrine of interest* in education is the theory that education must be based on the interest of the child, always starting from its existing interests, and seeking to develop new interests on the foundation of these.

Interest-attitude tests: see *X-O tests.*

Interest measurement: the technique of assessing an individual's interests by the various methods available, such as *questionnaires, X-O* and *checking tests,* etc.

Interference: employed in two main senses: (1) what might be called a physical sense, in connection with two series of waves or wave systems, reinforcing or neutralizing one another, as in the case of light and sounds, and producing special sensory phenomena, such as *colours* or *beats* (q.v.); and (2) in a more purely psychological sense, in the field of *learning* and *association,* where one piece of learning or one association may inhibit another, as in the case of *retroactive inhibition* (q.v.).

Interference tube: an arrangement of a conducting tube, with branches of different lengths, closed at the outer ends, used for the purpose of eliminating certain components in a complex sound, and thus obtaining a tone of any degree of purity required, the effect of the branch tubes being to cut out, through interference, those particular tones in the complex to which they are tuned.

Interjection theory: the theory which traces the origin of spoken language to exclamatory sounds.

Intermittence tone: see *interruption tone.*

Internal secretion: secretion of *endocrine glands* (q.v.).

Internal sense: any sense the receptors of which respond to stimuli within the body.

Internal speech: verbal imagery accompanying silent reading, or writing; sometimes called inner speech.

International intelligence tests: a series or battery of tests, due to Brigham and Dodd, intended to be entirely free from any dependence upon language, even with respect to instructions, developed for the American Research Council.

Interoceptive system: receptors situated within the body, as distinguished from *exteroceptors,* situated at or near the surface of the body, and responding to external stimuli, and *proprioceptors,* located within the body tissues.

Interocular distance: the distance between the centres of the pupils of the two eyes.

Interpolation: calculating, graphically, or by mathematical formula, a value between two values in a series of measurements.

Interpretation of dreams: usually employed of modern methods of dream analysis. See *dream.*

Interquartile range: the range in score, or measurement value, between the first and third *quartiles* (q.v.), or between the 25th and 75th percentile in a distribution table.

Interruption tone: a tone produced by regular and sufficiently rapid interruption of an otherwise continuous tone, the pitch of which corresponds to the frequency of the interruptions – most easily produced with sirens.

Intersex: term employed of an individual intermediate between a male and a female, in a normally bisexual species.

Intertone: the tone which seems to be carrying the *beats* (q.v.), intermediate between the two tones producing the beats.

Interval: generally, the period of time between two events, or the space between two objects; in music, the difference in pitch between two notes or tones, whether sounded simultaneously or successively, usually expressed in terms of the two frequencies; in the phrase *interval of uncertainty* used for the space between upper and lower thresholds in difference judgments.

Intoxication: condition of an organism, manifesting itself in unusual or abnormal behaviour, produced by drugs or poisons.

Intra-(Lat.): prefix meaning 'within' or 'inside'.

Intracranial: within the cranium, but usually with reference to the brain.

Intra-ocular modification: change, produced within the eye itself, in stimuli entering the eye, by defects in the optical system or other structure of the eye, and affecting vision.

Intrapsychic conflict: employed, by psychoanalysts, for emotional tension produced by conflicting tendencies within the unconscious. (A preferable term would be *endopsychic*.)

Introception: the adoption by an individual, into his own system, of motives or standards set by the social group.

Introjection: psychologically, the ascribing to inanimate objects of characteristics of living creatures; psychoanalytically, absorbing into oneself environmental influences and characteristics, but more particularly, the personal characteristics of other persons, and reacting accordingly to external events; a partial form of *identification* (q.v.).

Introspection: observation by an individual of his own mental processes; systematic self-observation; as employed in psychological experiment, it is most frequently immediate retrospection, rather than introspection in any strict sense.

Introspectionism: the view that the introspective method is the fundamental method of psychological investigation.

Introspective psychology: a system of theoretical psychology based on introspection – now obsolete; the psychological data obtainable by introspection.

Introversion: term employed by *Jung* for the direction of interest inwards, rather than outwards to the external world of men and things; a type of *temperament* or *personality*, characteristic of individuals whose interest is in their own thoughts and feelings, rather than in the world around them.

Introversion-extraversion test: a type of test, usually of the questionnaire type, designed to bring out an individual's general direction of interest, inwards or outwards.

Intuition: immediate perception or judgment, usually with some emotional colouring, without any conscious mental steps in preparation; a popular rather than scientific term.

Intuitionism: the theory which stresses the immediacy of knowledge of certain fundamental truths, particularly, in *ethics*, with regard to right and wrong, or in *aesthetics*, with regard to the beautiful.

Invagination: the pushing in of part of the surface layer of a cell so as to form a cavity.

Invalidism: chronic ill health, particularly where it is essentially neurotic, or neurotically exaggerated.

Invariable colour: a colour, or portion of the spectrum, not affected by the *Betzold-Brucke phenomena* (q.v.) with change of illumination.

Invariance: tendency of an image to retain its original size, independently of the distance of the surface upon which it is projected, in contradiction to *Emmet's law.*

Inverse square law: a general physical law applying to a stimulus reaching a sense receptor from a distance, to the effect that its intensity varies inversely as the square of the distance of the receptor from the source; of special significance in vision and hearing.

Inversion: reversal of order; *sexual inversion,* reversal of normal sexual role, or the assumption of the characters of the other sex, or, psychoanalytically, making a sexual object of an individual of the same sex.

Involuntary: referring to an action, inclusive of attention, taking place independently of an individual's will, but not necessarily in spite of it.

Involution: retrograde movement in development; decline or degeneration; return to normal condition after increase in size due to physiological processes, as in pregnancy.

IQ: intelligence quotient; the ratio of the mental age to the chronological age, as a percentage.

Iris: circular curtain in front of lens of eye with aperture in centre – the *pupil* – of which the area is controlled by muscle fibres in the iris itself, the stimulation of which takes place through the light rays entering the eye and falling on the retina; a form of *diaphragm,* employed in photography, for controlling the amount of light entering the camera and falling on the film or plate. Cf. *pupillary reflex.*

Irradiation: used in several technical senses, all of which involve the notion of 'spread'; (1) in the *visual* field a white or bright area, say a square, on a black or dark background, seems larger than a similar black or dark area on a white or bright background; (2) a *nerve impulse* in an afferent nerve tends to spread to other neurons, as it passes through the central nervous system; (3) a *conditioned reflex,* to the stimulation of a limited cutaneous area, tends to be elicited by the stimulation of neighbouring areas; (4) a *reflex response* tends to spread to larger motor fields, with increase in the intensity of the stimulus; (5) quite analogous phenomena occur in the initial stages of *trial and error learning,* where at the start the subject's responses vary over a wide field.

Irradiation theory: an attempt to base a theory of *learning* on irradiation phenomena, with the gradual selection of useful, and elimination of useless, responses, as in *trial and error learning.*

Irrational: inconsistent with reason, or with the normal behaviour of a rational being.

Irreciprocal conduction: one-way conduction, as in the nerve pathways underlying reflex action, or conduction in any neuron, where the excitation passes always towards the cell body in the dendrites, and away from the cell body in an axon; the phenomenon is probably due to conditions at the synapse and not in the nerve fibres themselves. The general characteristic may also be described as the *irreversibility of conduction.*

Irrelevant: not relative to the problem in hand, whether that is a problem of thought or of action.

Irritability: the character of being capable of stimulation.

Irritant: an agent which produces irritation or inflammation in a tissue; used also figuratively of something which produces an analogous mental effect.

Island of Reil: part or lobe of the *cortex* (cerebral), lying deep in the *fissure of Sylvius* (q.v.) – *insula.*

Islands of Langerhans: small masses of cells in the *pancreas,* which secrete *insulin.*

Islands of Hearing: see *tonal islands.*

Iso-(Gr.): prefix with meaning 'equal' or 'same'.

Isochronism: correspondence of two processes, with respect to time, or frequency of occurrence, or having the same *chronaxy.*

Isolation: separation from others of the same species; used of groups or organisms existing separate from other groups of the same species, either geographically, or with respect to reproductive maturity, in either case with the effect of preventing interbreeding.

Isolation mechanism: psychoanalytic term for a symptom characteristic of *compulsion neuroses,* which are marked by the interposition of a blank pause after a highly unpleasant or personally significant experience.

Isometropia: equality of the two eyes, with respect to refractive state.

Isomorphism: term employed, in *Gestalt psychology*, for structural correspondence between the brain areas activated, and the conscious content.

Isoscope: instrument devised by *Donders* for testing his *law of rotation*, consisting of an arrangement for presenting two vertical wires to one eye, and a single wire to the other eye. This wire is seen binocularly along with the other two wires, and can be inclined in either direction until it appears parallel to the others.

Isotropic: term employed, in optics, of transparent media having similar properties in all directions with respect to the transmission and refraction of light.

Isthmus: name given to the narrow part of the brain stem, between the mid-brain and the hind-brain.

Itch: an uneasy sensation of irritation, or light prick-pain, in a cutaneous area, accompanied by an impulse to scratch the area.

Ivanov-Smolensky technique: a *conditioning* (q.v.) technique employed with children where the response is the squeezing of a rubber bulb and the stimulus a piece of chocolate sliding past an opening, the squeeze if properly timed giving the child the chocolate.

J

J.n.d.: contraction for *just noticeable difference;* difference *threshold.*

Jacksonian epilepsy: form of *epilepsy,* with localized spasms in one limb, or on one side of body, and usually without loss of consciousness; taken as indicating irritation in *motor zones* of cortex.

Jackson's Law. the name sometimes given to the principle that, in the impairment or loss of mental acquisitions, the more recent are the first to be affected or to disappear; that the order of degeneration is the reverse of the order of development or acquisition.

Jacquet chronometer: an instrument of precision for recording seconds and fifths, provided with a lever by which a corresponding time record can be marked on a smoked drum.

James-Lange theory a theory of *emotion,* developed in modern times by *William James* and *C. G. Lange,* the Danish philosopher, but in its essentials found as early as *Descartes,* to the effect that our experience of emotion is really our experience of the bodily changes 'following on the perception of an exciting fact', so that it is nearer the truth to say we are afraid because we run away than that we run away because we are afraid.

Jastrow cylinders: a series of weighted, hollow, rubber cylinders, for determining thresholds for pressure and kinaesthesis, in lifting.

Java man: see *Pithecanthropus erectus.*

Jealousy: a complex emotional state, involving a sentiment of hate by one person for another, because of the relations of both to a third; commonest form sexual jealousy.

Jehovah complex: a megalomaniac identification of oneself with God.

Jendrassik reinforcement: a method of increasing, by *facilitation,* the *patellar reflex* (knee jerk), by hooking the two fore fingers and pulling.

Job analysis: a characteristic procedure in *industrial psychology,* where an occupation is being studied in order to devise methods for selecting or training workers, in which the psychologist seeks to analyse the actual work to be performed into the various jobs or tasks involved, and to correlate these with the various qualities, abilities, etc., required in the workers.

Johns Hopkins Chronoscope: see *Dunlap chronoscope.*

Joie de Vivre (Fr.): 'joy of living'; exhuberant spirits, freely expressed.

Jordan curve: a curve, bounding an area, which does not cross itself. See *topology.*

Jost's Law: the principle that with two associations of equal strength, but unequal age, repetition increases the strength of the older more than that of the younger.

Joy: in the older classifications of the emotions, represented as one of the primary emotions; in *Warren,* appears as a sentiment or emotional attitude; better regarded as one of the two poles of emotion (the other being '*sorrow*'), between which the emotional life, as it were, oscillates; as *Darwin* points out, it tends to express itself in *laughter.*

Judgment: in a wide sense, may be regarded as an essential aspect of all cognition, in so far as it refers to an object; in a narrower and probably more usual sense, the act of relating something to something else.

Jukes: a fictitious name, given to the various representatives and branches of a family, studied through several generations, first by *Dugdale,* and later, in a further follow-up, by *Estabrook,* including altogether some 2,820 persons, of whom half were feeble-minded, and large numbers criminals, prostitutes, vagabonds, and paupers.

Just intonation: the production of tones, in accordance with their frequency in a natural, rather than tempered, scale.

Just noticeable difference: the least difference, mainly, though not exclusively, in a quantitative aspect, between two stimuli which enables the subject to say that they are different; statistically, the difference one senses exactly as often as one fails to do so; the *j.n.d.* or *difference threshold* or *limen.*

Juvenile: referring or relating to a young person, usually below the age at which compulsory attendance at school ceases.

K

k: symbol generally used, mathematically, for a constant; statistically, used for *coefficient of alienation,* given by the formula $\sqrt{(1 - r^2)}$ where *r* is the *correlation coefficient.*

Kallikak family: a fictitious name given by *Goddard* to the two branches of a New Jersey family (same father, two mothers), of which one branch (496 individuals) showed, almost without exception, a record of good citizenship, and in many cases distinguished service to the community, while the other (480 individuals) presented a picture, almost unrelieved, of feeblemindedness, degeneracy, and criminality. Cf. *Jukes.*

Kalotropic: relating, or referring, to the influence of an individual's own aesthetic tastes on the content of his imagery.

Karyokinesis: see *mitosis.*

Karyoplasm: the *protoplasm* of the cell nucleus.

Kelvin scale of temperature: the absolute scale, starting from a zero at −273 degrees centigrade.

Kent-Rosanoff List: a list of 100 stimulus words, for a *free association test,* the frequency of the different associates to each word being given, on the basis of an extensive investigation carried out by the authors, so that by the use of the list one may determine the normality or eccentricity of an individual's imagery or train of thought.

Keratometer: an instrument for measuring the curvature of an individual's *cornea;* or an instrument for measuring the diameter of the cornea.

Keratoscope: see *Placido's disc.*

Kiesow's painless cheek-area: a small area in the inside of the cheek, which appears insensitive to pain, while sensitive to other cutaneous stimuli.

Kine- (*Gr.*): prefix meaning 'relating to movement'.

Kinephantom: an illusion of direction of movement, or its pattern, when a movement is seen in silhouette shadows; *kinephantoscope*, an apparatus for projecting the shadows.

Kinesimeter: an instrument for measuring thresholds for movement sensations.

Kinaesthesis: general term covering sensations of movement of any part of the body, arising from stimulation of receptors in joints, muscles, tendons, and sometimes inclusive of sensations from the *semi-circular canals* of the inner ear, and therefore of the sensations belonging to the *static sense*.

Kinaesthetic memory: memory in terms of ideal representation of movement sensations.

Kinetoscope: instrument for projecting mechanically on a screen, for observation purposes, the record obtained by the cinematographic film. The *kinetoscotoscope* is an analogous apparatus for projecting the movement of bones as shown in X-ray photographs.

Kinehapt: a type of *aesthesiometer* (q.v.), for presenting tactual stimuli, at controlled temporal and spatial intervals, devised to study apparent movement.

Kirschmann's contrast law: the principle that the saturation of a contrast colour varies in proportion with the saturation of the inducing colour.

Kleptomania: an obsessive impulse to steal, not infrequently shown in stealing objects for which the individual has no desire.

Knee jerk: see *patellar reflex.*

Knox cube test: a *performance test* (q.v.) of memory span, given by a pattern of taps on four cubes with a fifth; sometimes called *cube imitation test.*

Koenig cylinders: a series of short metal cylinders, devised by König for testing the upper threshold for pitch.

Korsakow syndrome: a mental disorder, or group of symptoms, usually accompanying *polyneuritis* (q.v.) (alcoholic or other types), marked by weakness or loss of retention, with consequent disturbance of orientation, and fondness for tall and circumstantial 'stories'.

Korte's laws: laws formulating the optical conditions for obtaining apparent motion with two stationary stimuli given in succession.

Kraepelin ergograph: a form of *ergograph* (q.v.), the chief feature of which is the continuous lifting of the weight.

Krause end bulbs: sensory receptors in the skin, generally assumed to be for cold.

Kundgabe: (*Ger.*) statement about a mental process in place of a description of it; information. The *Kundgabe error* is the name given to such a statement about, in place of description of, an experience in an introspective protocol; what is known as the *stimulus error* is a particular case.

Kundt's rule: term applied to two different principles: (1) the principle that divided distances appear greater than objectively equal undivided distances (particular case of *filled and empty spaces* (q.v.); (2) the principle that in attempting to bisect a line (horizontal) in monocular vision, there is a tendency to place the middle towards the nasal side.

Kundt tube: a physical apparatus for determining the frequency, or wave-length, of a sound wave.

Kurtosis: a type of *frequency distribution,* showing a divergence from normality in the parts intermediate between the mean and the extremes. A curve is *platykurtic, mesokurtic,* or *leptokurtic,* according as this divergence at intermediate parts is great, average, or small. Pearson's formula for the *coefficient* of *kurtosis* is μ_4/μ_2^2 (the fourth moment divided by the square of the second moment).

Kymograph: an apparatus consisting essentially of a rotating drum, usually covered with smoked paper, for obtaining graphic records of physiological and psychological processes.

L

LS: contraction for *liminal sensitivity.*

Labour mobility: the ease with which workers can move from one place to another, or from one occupation to another; also the rate of movement into and out of an industry.

Labour turnover: the number leaving and engaged in a definite period of time – say a year – in an industrial undertaking, together with the rate at which change of workers takes place, or the average length of time a worker remains in that employment.

Labyrinth: a maze; specially, the cavity of the inner ear in the petrous temporal bone (the *bony labyrinth*) and the mass of tubes and sacs within that cavity (the *membranous labyrinth*).

Labyrinthine sense: the static sense (q.v.).

Lachrymal glands: the glands secreting tears.

Ladd-Franklin theory: a theory of colour vision, mediating between the *Helmholtz* and *Hering theories* (q.v.), though based on the former. The essential idea underlying the theory is of a single photo-chemical retinal substance, capable of existing in three forms of molecular aggregation or organization: in the first, or most primitive form, it gives rise on stimulation to the white-black or achromatic series; in the second to blue and yellow; in the third to blue and yellow, red and green. In total colour-blindness or *achromatic* vision, the first form alone is present; in *dichromatic* vision – red-green blindness – only the first and second; in normal colour vision all three. There are certain facts of *dichromatic* vision which are not easily reconciled with the theory, e.g. the 'greenish-reds' and 'reddish-greens' seen by many *dichromates*, where they ought to see 'yellow', if the theory is to hold.

Lag: the interval between the cessation of a stimulus and the cessation of its effect; sometimes used for *latent time* (q.v.), the interval between the actual stimulation, and the production of its sensory effect.

Lagena: a primitive organ of hearing, or *cochlea,* found in lower vertebrates.

Lalling: continuous repetition of a single sound, as in infants and idiots.

Lalopathy: any disorder of speech.

Lalophobia: great distaste, amounting almost or quite to a *phobia* (q.v.), for speaking.

Lalorrhea: see *logorrhea.*

Lamarckianism, Lamarckism: theory of evolution involving the *transmission of acquired characteristics*, as one main explanatory principle.

Lambert: unit of *brightness*, which is the uniform brightness of a perfectly diffusing surface, which emits or reflects one *lumen* per sq. centimetre.

Lambert's law: the cosine law of the incidence, emission, and reflection of light, viz. that the illumination or intensity of incident, emitted, or reflected light varies directly as the cosine of the angle of the rays to the perpendicular to the surface.

Lamella: a thin plate; *Appunn's lamella* is a thin plate tipped with a disc, which is used to determine the lower threshold of pitch, i.e. the lowest audible tone; a lamella is also frequently used in place of a tuning fork to give short time intervals for various recording purposes.

Langerhans cells: free nerve endings in the skin, supposed to be the pain receptors.

Language: means of communication; the psychological definition is : 'A conventional system of expressive signs functioning psychologically, in the individual, as an instrument of conceptual analysis and synthesis, and, socially, as a means of intercommunication', from which it follows that the unit of language is a sentence or 'statement'.

Languo(u)r: a complex of mental and neuro-muscular conditions, with, on the one side, organic and general sensations akin to those of fatigue, with disinclination for active employment, and, on the other, a state of relaxation.

Laryngograph: an arrangement by means of which a graphic record can be obtained on a *kymograph* of the movements of the larynx in speech, etc.

Laryngoscope: an apparatus for examining the larynx, the essential part of which is a system of mirrors.

Larynx: the organ at the top of the *trachea* containing the vocal cords, the essential mechanism for producing voice.

Lassitude: languor (q.v.).

Lat(t)ah: a mental disorder with characteristically high *suggestibility*, prevalent among Malay women.

Latency period: in psychoanalytic literature, a period of sexual development between the age of 4 or 5 and the beginning of adolescence, separating infantile from normal sexuality.

Latent time: the time between the giving of a stimulus and the beginning of the (sensory) response.

Latent dream thoughts: see *dream.*

Latent process: term used by some of the earlier writers for subconscious or subliminal processes, or for *unconscious cerebration.*

Lateral line canal: an organ in fishes of uncertain function, possibly auditory, but more probably *static* or *kinaesthetic.*

Laughter: an emotional response, expressive normally of joy, in the child and the unsophisticated adult. The joy in question may vary between wide limits.

Leadership: the exercise of authority in a social group; the quality or qualities upon which such exercise of authority depends, varying with the nature of the social group, and the circumstances in which leadership is displayed or established.

Leading tone: the seventh note in a musical scale, so called because of its relation to the tonic.

Learning: modification of a response, following upon and resulting from experience of results; must be distinguished from *remembering,* which involves the *recall* of previous experience, and is therefore narrower, and learning may take place without remembering, as normally occurs in the acquiring of a motor skill; a graphic representation of progress in acquisition or learning, through progressive periods of learning, or practice, is known as a *learning curve. Laws of learning* have been formulated by many psychologists, the best known being those of *Thorndike;* recognized laws are: *recency, frequency, vividness* (see secondary laws of association), *effect, exercise, readiness, assimilation.*

Learning types: individual types of learners, as distinguished by the kinds of imagery on which they tend to rely, or the methods they employ, as, for example, building up a series step by step progressively, or gradually building up within a framework or *scheme.*

Least resistance: in phrase 'line of least resistance': borrowed from physics and used figuratively, for a course of action offering least apparent obstacles, inner or outer, or most apparent attractions.

Least squares method: a mathematical method of obtaining the best fitting curve to a series of quantitative data, or the best fitting normal equation to a series of empirical equations.

Lefthandedness: see *sinistrality.*

Legibility: quality of the writing or printing of material, which makes it easily and accurately read.

Lehmann Acoumeter: see *audiometer.*

Lens: sometimes *crystalline lens;* the essential part of the dioptric system of the eye, the function of which is to form an image on the retina of the object regarded.

Leptokurtic: a type of *kurtosis* (q.v.).

Leptosome: an individual with an *asthenic,* or slender, type of body structure or physique.

Lesbian: homosexual female.

Lethargy: general meaning, 'morbid drowsiness'; used technically, by *Charcot* for the earliest stage of hypnosis with some *anaesthesia* and muscular limpness.

Letter square: a type of material used in memory experiments, with particular reference to imagery, consisting of a square divided into compartments, in each of which a letter (or figure) is placed, which must be reproduced accurately by the subject as regards both rows and columns.

Leucotomy, pre-frontal: see *lobotomy*.

Level: used technically, to denote a plane, standard, or height, with respect to sensory efficiency, motor performance, intellectual capacity, etc.

Level of aspiration: term which is best explained as a *frame of reference* (q.v.) involving self-esteem; or alternatively as a standard with reference to which an individual experiences – i.e. has the feeling of – success or failure.

Levitation: rising in the air without material support, as in dreams; employed in *psychical research* for alleged movement of heavy objects against gravity, due to no observable or known physical agency.

Libertarianism: see *free-will*.

Libido: term, used by psychoanalysts originally, in its usual sense of sexual desire, but later, in the most general sense of vital impulse or 'energy'; the sexual meaning is, however, retained in particular connections, as in *bisexual libido*, fixation of sexual impulse at an early stage, at which it is both male and female, as in some cases of *homosexuality* (q.v.), or in discussion of the stages of *libido development* from the pre-genital phase to complete *psycho-sexual* organization.

Libido damming: frustration of the *psycho-sexual* development.

Lie detector: any type of instrument indicating physiological changes which take place under conditions of emotional tension, in the course of an examination of a suspected individual as, for example, a *sphygmomanometer*, *pneumograph*, or *psychogalvanometer*.

Life instinct(s): term employed rather vaguely by psychoanalysts, usually inclusive of self-preservation and reproduction impulses, and sometimes synonymous with *libido*.

Life space, psychological: the basal concept in *topological* (q.v.) psychology, signifying the totality of facts which determine the behaviour of an individual at any moment (*Lewin*); dynamically 'the totality of possible events' in the behaviour and experience of the individual; everything in the environment or in the individual himself that is exercising any effect whatsoever on the present behaviour or possibilities of behaviour, regarded under the form of space (as in the mathematical representation of a 'life space' inclusive of physical, social, and personal relationships). See *topology* and *topological psychology*.

Light: physically, those frequencies of radiant energy which directly stimulate the organ of vision; *luminous flux*.

Light-adapted eye: term generally employed of the eye in its normal condition for daylight vision, but used sometimes of the relatively extreme case of an eye which has been exposed for some time to light of fairly high intensity, and so has become relatively insensitive to light of lower intensities.

Light dread: see *photophobia.*

Light induction: term used of simultaneous effects on areas of the retina, other than that which is stimulated, and might therefore include *simultaneous contrast* (q.v.).

Limen: see *threshold.*

Limen gauge: an instrument devised by *von Frey,* for applying pressure stimuli to the skin at regular intervals, consisting of a pressure point attached to a lever, which is actuated by a spring, the tension of which is controlled by another lever, displaced by a rotating drum.

Liminal sensitivity: LS; sensory acuity as measured by the lowest value of a stimulus giving rise to sensation.

Limiting membranes (external and internal): the 3rd and the innermost or 10th layers of the retina, from without inwards.

Limits and differences method: a modification of the psycho-physical *method of limits,* due to *Kraepelin,* which consists in treating the judgments obtained by the normal *method of limits* statistically, as. in the *method of right and wrong cases* (q.v.).

Limits method: a standard psychophysical method of determining *thresholds,* in which the procedure consists in beginning with a stimulus, or stimulus-difference, above the threshold, and progressively diminishing it, by constant decrements – called a descending series – until it is no longer sensed, then beginning below the threshold and increasing by constant increments – ascending series – until it is sensed; the threshold is given by the average of the last value, or difference, sensed in the descending series, and the last value, or difference, not sensed in the ascending series. Other names for the method are: *method of just noticeable differences,* and *method of minimal changes.*

Limma: a musical interval equal to the difference between two major tones and a perfect *fourth*; equal to .9 of a *tempered* (q.v.) semitone.

Linear correlation: see *correlation.*

Linguistic: relating to language.

Linkage: the tendency for characters to be linked together in hereditary transmission; sometimes used for the connection between stimulus and response.

Lip eroticism: the sex sensations induced by kissing.

Lip key: a key for making or breaking contact, in reaction experiments, for the purpose of recording response by means of speech.

Lip-reading: method used by the deaf for following speech by observing the movements of the lips of the speaker.

Lisping: form of *dyslalia* (q.v.) or *paralalia* (q.v.).

Lissajou's figures: figures produced by reflection of a beam of light from small mirrors attached to the prongs of two tuning forks vibrating in perpendicular planes to one another.

Listing's Law: a principle or law of eye-movement, to the effect that, if the eye moves from the primary to any other position, the rotation (torsional) of the eye in the new position is the same as if the eye had turned round a fixed axis, at right angles to the initial, and final, lines of regard.

Listlessness: lack of interest and desire; indifference and inactivity.

Lloyd Morgan's Canon: the principle, that, in interpreting the behaviour of an animal, the simplest interpretation, i.e. the interpretation in terms of the lower, rather than the higher, level, must always be preferred.

Lobe: in general sense, a roundish projecting part; employed most frequently in psychology of one of the main divisions of the cerebrum. See also *olfactory*.

Lobotomy: a neuro-surgical operation involving section of tracts of white matter between the pre-frontal lobe and the thalamus, with the object of affecting changes in behaviour, in certain types of case.

Local galvanic reaction: see *psycho-galvanic response*.

Local sign: name given by *Lotze* to a qualitative factor by means of which one point is distinguished from another in a sensitive surface like the retina or the skin – the basis upon which, with movement, discrimination of a position in space depends.

Locality memory: the ability of an animal to identify a particular locality.

Locality survey: characteristic exploratory behaviour in a particular region or locality.

Localization: the mental placing of the source of a particular stimulus, or particular experience, at a particular point in space or time; the *localization of function* in the *cerebro-spinal axis* means the identification of the part or parts associated with a particular sensory, motor, or mental function; the *localization of sound*, the judgment of the distance, or direction, or both, of a sound.

Localized amnesia: see *amnesia*.

Localized stimulus: a stimulus applied to a small area or region of the body.

Locomotor: referring or relating to the organs upon which *locomotion,* or movement from place to place, depends.

Locomotor ataxy: see *tabes.*

Logarithmic curve: a curve, in which one of the co-ordinates is the logarithm of the other, as $y = \log x$.

Logic: the branch of science which investigates the principles of reasoning, deductive and inductive, or, more generally, the principles of thought.

Logic, affective: the control of the sequence of ideas by affective or emotional factors.

Logorrhea: incoherent rush of words; symptom of mental disorder, or a mere language disorder.

Long-circuit appeal: a term used in advertising and salesmanship, for sale publicity and propaganda involving a reasoned account of a product, or article, and its advantages.

Longitudinal: lengthwise, of direction of measurement, or of direction of vibration in the case of wave movement; in the direction of the long axis in the case of stimulation of a limb, etc.

Looking-glass self: the impression of self which an individual obtains from the opinions and responses of other people.

Loudness: the intensity attribute of sounds, correlated with the physical energy of the stimulus; or, usually, the amplitude of the wave movement.

Love: a typical sentiment involving fondness for, or attachment to, an object, the idea of which is emotionally coloured whenever it arises in the mind, and capable, as *Shand* has pointed out, of evoking any one of the whole gamut of primary emotions, according to the situation in which the object is placed, or represented; often, and by psychoanalysts always, used in the sense of *sex-love* or even *lust* (q.v.).

Low: used in a technical sense mainly of sounds, and in that field either of pitch of tones of small or low frequency, or of intensity, where the stimulus-energy and therefore loudness is small.

Lowest audible tone: the low limit of pitch, below which any diminution of frequency involves loss of the tonal character altogether – about 16 c.p.s. for the human ear.

Loyalty: an attitude or sentiment of devotion to a person, group, symbol, duty, or cause, arising out of, or as a modification of, a *love sentiment,* but also involving a personal identification with the object in question.

Lucidity: used technically of a sane interval in a mental disorder;

or, in psychical research, of a supersensory perception of distant or hidden objects.

Ludicrous: referring to a situation calculated to excite mirth, more particularly, perhaps, accompanied by a feeling of superiority, and a tinge of something akin to scorn.

Lumbar puncture: method of withdrawing cerebro-spinal fluid by means of a puncture with a needle between two lumbar vertebrae.

Lumen: unit of *luminous flux* (q.v.); the amount of light within a solid angle of unit size, coming from a light source of one *candlepower* (q.v.).

Luminosity: used rather indefinitely for *brightness*.

Luminous flux: rate of passage of *radiant energy*, estimated on the basis of the experience of the *brightness* produced by it on a surface at right angles to its direction; must be distinguished from *luminous intensity*, which refers to the emission from a given source, measured in terms of *candlepower*.

Lust: sexual desire or appetite.

Lustre: a visual phenomenon of brightness (brilliance), or of colour, apparently experienced when two or more degrees of brightness (brilliance), or two different colours, are stimulating the eye in rapid succession which is not sufficiently rapid for complete fusion; most characteristically produced experimentally with colours by rotating an *episcotister* (q.v.) in front of a colour-mixer with sectors of two different colours, when the two rotations have a slightly different rate, or if one of the two rates differs slightly from being an exact multiple of the other.

Lux: unit of illumination, and equal to the density of *luminous flux* on a surface at right angles to the rays, at a distance of one metre (or one foot), from a point source of one *candlepower*.

Lycanthropy: a symptom of mental disorder, where the individual thinks he is a wolf, or other wild animal.

Lymphatic temperament: see *phlegmatic*.

Lypemania: melancholia (q.v.).

M

M: abbreviation for *mean*.

MA: abbreviation for *mental age*.

Mach rotation frame: an apparatus for the study of bodily movement, consisting of a large rectangular frame, pivoted on a vertical axis, with a chair for the subject mounted at one end in a similar frame pivoted at top and bottom, the chair being arranged so that it can be tilted.

Machine theory: term used by *Gestalt* psychologists for the view that physiological processes are determined by mechanical, in the sense of topographical, as opposed to dynamic, conditions.

Macrocephaly: pathological condition of enlargement of head.

Macrocosm: the physical universe, or human society, as opposed to *microcosm*, the human individual.

Macropsia: see *megalopsia*.

Macrosplanchnic: term employed of a physique in which the volume of the trunk is large in proportion to the limbs.

Macula lutea: or simply *macula*, the yellow spot, a small area in the centre of the retina, coloured yellowish, in the centre of which is the *fovea* (q.v.).

Macula acoustica: type of structure found in the *utricle* (q.v.) and *saccule* (q.v.) in the inner ear consisting of a small group of *haired cells*.

Maddox rod: a glass rod mounted on a disc, for the diagnosis of *muscular imbalance* (q.v.).

Magic: a term applied to primitive superstitious practices, and to explanations of physical processes, based on a belief in supernatural agencies.

Magnetotropism, magnetotaxis: orienting response to lines of magnetic force. See *tropism*.

Maintenance level: a stage in development when growth has virtually stopped and energy is used to keep the condition relatively constant.

Major scale: term used, in opposition to *minor*, of a type of musical *scale* (or mode), where the semitones occur between the 3rd and 4th and between the 7th and 8th.

Major third, sixth, etc.: see *interval* (musical).

Majuscule: a capital letter, as opposed to *minuscule*.

Make-believe: a type of *phantasy* (q.v.), usually manifested in behaviour as if things were as imagined, but with awareness of the self-deception.

Maladjustment: the condition of an individual who is unable to adapt or adjust himself adequately to his physical, occupational, or social environment, usually with repercussions on his emotional life and behaviour.

Malaise: slight bodily discomfort.

Malevolence: disposition or wish on the part of an individual to harm or distress another. The word *malice* is almost synonymous, but implies action against the other person, on a definite occasion or occasions, rather than continued willingness to injure.

Malformation: structural deviation from normality in an organism, or any of its parts.

Malinger: deliberately to feign illness or disability, in order to evade an obligation, or escape some service.

Malleus: the hammer, the outermost of the three ossicles in the middle ear, and that which is attached to the drum.

Malobservation: failure to observe, and record accurately and adequately, an event or series of events, because of divided attention, bias, inexperience in such observation, or other cause.

Malthus' theory: a population theory, to the effect that in any animal species, including the human, population tends to increase geometrically, while means of subsistence increase more slowly, and, apart from deliberate or voluntary restriction of births, is ultimately kept within limits by famine, pestilence, war, etc.

Malthusianism: the theory of Malthus as above; often applied to birth control by moral restraint, or other methods.

Mammalia: the class of vertebrate animals which suckle their young, and which are therefore provided with *mammary glands*.

Mammillary bodies: two small, rounded projections in the *hypothalamus* (q.v.).

Man-to-man Rating Scale: a type of *rating scale* (q.v.), where different degrees of possession of the various traits to be rated are represented by known individuals, and the rater is required to indicate which of these the person to be rated most resembles in the trait in question, and the mark for that person, in that trait, is then the mark assigned in a master scale.

Mana: a vague, religious notion of impersonal sacredness, mystery, and power, attaching to objects, characteristic of certain primitive Polynesian peoples.

Management: the group of executives directing the work in any industrial undertaking.

Mania: mental disorder manifesting itself in high, uncontrolled excitement; *acute mania,* simply a specially high degree; *homicidal mania,* mania manifesting itself as an excited desire to kill.

Manic-depressive psychosis: a type of mental disorder which alternates between periods of excitement and periods of depression, sometimes with intermediate periods of sanity.

Manifest dream content: see *dream.*

Manikin test: a *performance test,* devised by *Pintner,* which consists in piecing together parts of the figure of a wooden man (arms, legs, head, trunk), the pieces being handed to the subjects without any information of what they make.

Manipulation: a type of behaviour involving handling of objects; or, more generally, any practical dealing with objects.

Manitou: the American-Indian religious notion, somewhat akin to *mana,* of an indefinite, mysterious power pervading the universe.

Mannerism: habitual trick of expression or manner, more or less peculiar to an individual, and so characteristic as often to identify him; sometimes developed as a defensive reaction; frequently also shown in *dementia praecox* (q.v.) in the form of gesturing, symbolic of the *phantasies* underneath.

Manometer: an instrument for measuring pressure of a fluid.

Manumetric flame: a method of observing sound waves by the effect of the variation of air pressure in the wave acting on a rubber membrane closing one side of a gas chamber connecting with a gas jet.

Manoptoscope: a truncated cardboard cone, employed for testing *ocular dominance* (q.v.).

Manual method: a method of deaf education, and deaf communication, employing *finger-spelling* (q.v.).

Manuscript writing: see *script* writing.

Marey tambour: an arrangement for recording on a smoked drum, or other moving surface, such physiological processes as breathing, pulse, etc., consisting of a shallow metal chamber, closed with a rubber membrane, on which rests a light lever, communicating by a tube with a receiving tambour constructed on essentially similar principles, but adapted for the particular process to be recorded.

Marginal contrast: the accentuated contrast effect near the boundary field in vision.

Marginal field: see *consciousness* and *retina.*

Marie's disease: see *acromegaly.*

Marsupials: pouch-bearing animals like the kangaroo, with a pouch in which the young are carried.

Martius Disc: an arrangement for determining the black-white value of a grey.

Masculine protest: a term used by *Adler* as an equivalent for the desire for superiority, or completeness, arising out of a felt inferiority, or incompleteness, *femininity* being regarded as incomplete and inferior.

Masculinization: in the case of the human being, a change of personality from predominantly feminine to predominantly masculine characteristics, as a result mainly of environmental and social influences; in the case of animals, structural and functional changes taking place as a result of implanting testicular tissue in castrated females.

Masked epilepsy: a type of epilepsy where the convulsions are replaced by integrated, but automatic and unremembered actions, and the period of unconsciousness is brief.

Masking: the partial or complete obscuring of one sensory process by another; in particular of one tone or sound by another.

Masochism: pleasure, particularly sexual pleasure, in suffering physical pain; interpreted psychoanalytically, in terms of the destructive or *death instincts,* erotically bound.

Mass action: the principle, emphasized by *Lashley,* that learning, and intelligence so far as it depends on learning, is conditioned, not by special localities or special connexions in the *cortex,* but by the functioning of large areas, and, in the case of injury or operation, learning is affected not by the part that is injured or destroyed so much as by the mass of cortical tissue remaining intact.

Mass methods: descriptive term, used of methods of experimental measurement, testing, and investigation, where large numbers of individuals are examined simultaneously, as, for example, in *group testing,* it being contended that data so obtained are not so accurate and reliable as in the case of smaller numbers dealt with individually, though they have certain advantages from a statistical point of view, additional to any practical advantage they may have from time-saving.

Massed learning: see *entire learning.*

Masselon test: a test used initially as an 'imagination' test, later as an 'intelligence' test, and essentially a *projection test* (q.v.), where the testee is required to make a meaningful sentence which will contain three given words.

Masson Disc: a white disc, with a radius drawn as a series of black rectangles or squares, devised originally for the determination of the *difference threshold* for *brightness* (brilliance), now generally employed in the study of *fluctuations of attention* (q.v.). When rotated, such a disc presents a series of concentric grey circles, which

161

become dimmer and dimmer as one passes towards the circumference, owing to the greater and greater amount of white mixed with the black.

Masturbation: producing the sex orgasm by manipulation, or other artificial stimulation of the genital organs.

Matched groups: see *parallel groups.*

Materialism: metaphysical theory that matter is the only reality; applied to the *psychophysical problem,* it becomes *epiphenomenalism* (q.v.).

Materialization: the alleged forming of material objects, or parts of the human body, by superhuman means – one of the phenomena studied by *psychical research.*

Maternal behaviour: behaviour towards offspring, characteristic of a mother, and usually regarded as instinctive in animals.

Mating behaviour: the series of actions of animals, leading up to *sexual selection* and connexion.

Maturation: in general biology, the attainment of maturity, or the completion of growth; in psychology, rather the process of growth and development itself, as contrasted with the learning process.

Maximal sensation: that intensity of sensation which is not further increased by increasing the intensity of the stimulus, usually giving place to pain.

Maxwell's Demons: a figurative method of discussing physical phenomena, adopted by *Clerk Maxwell,* in which physical forces and concepts are figured as minute demons, with various human attributes.

Maze: a term inclusive of various devices for studying intelligence and learning, particularly *trial and error learning,* (q.v.), in animals and human beings, consisting of a pathway requiring to be traversed or traced to a definite goal, but complicated to a varying degree by additional pathways, which are blind alleys; with human subjects verbal mazes are sometimes employed in which the subject is presented verbally with two alternatives corresponding to the divided paths in the concrete maze.

Mdn.: abbreviation for *median.*

Mean: an intermediate value between extremes; usually, when no adjective is added, *arithmetical mean* is intended.

Mean deviation: see *standard deviation.*

Mean variation: average variation of individual measurements from the mean.

Mean gradations: a psychophysical method, or rather a modification of either of two fundamental methods as regards procedure – the *method of limits* and the *method of mean error* – employed to investigate the problem of equal sense distances.

Meaning: the psychology of meaning is a somewhat controversial field, owing largely to the variety of senses in which the word may be used. There are two fundamental senses, intention and significance, and theories of meaning vary accordingly. The real psychological problems centre round the *significance* sense, and in this case the main controversy arises between those who regard meaning as primarily *cognitive,* and those who regard it as primarily *affective.*

Measure: in music, a short series marked by a single stress; a result obtained by applying a scale to something.

Measure of precision: a quantity varying inversely as the scatter of measurements; usually denoted by *h.*

Measurement methods: quantitative methods in psychological experiment, inclusive of the *psychophysical methods,* and the *measurement of intelligence,* either by scales, or by test scores, treated statistically.

Meatus: the name given to two canals, external and internal, in the temporal bone of the skull, the external leading from the outside to the middle ear cavity, the internal from the cavity of the inner ear to the interior of the skull; the former is the pathway for sound waves to enter the ear, the latter carries the auditory and facial nerves with blood-vessels.

Mechanical aptitude: inborn capacity for learning to deal with machines and machinery; sometimes called *mechanical intelligence,* which emphasizes the understanding aspect, but *aptitude* seems the preferable term.

Mechanics of ideas: Herbart's term for his doctrine of the interaction of ideas.

Mechanism: general meaning, machine-like interrelation of parts and operations; in psychoanalytical literature, semi-automatic reaction patterns issuing from repressed emotional complexes, and directed towards ends determined unconsciously, e.g. *defence mechanism:* a mental mechanism within a dream, criticizing the dream or part of it, is sometimes spoken of as a *neutralizing mechanism.*

Mechanistic theory: psychologically, the interpretation of psychological processes on a mechanical basis, and denial of the reality or efficacy of ends and purposes.

Mediacy: employed of the rise of an idea from a stimulus indirectly through intermediate associated ideas which may or may not come into clear consciousness.

Medial plane: in the human being, the vertical plane perpendicular to the line joining the ears, dividing the body into two superficially symmetrical halves; the corresponding plane in animals; synonymous with *sagittal plane.*

Median: the middle value in a series of values arranged in order of magnitude; given by the formula: $(n + 1)/2$, where n is the number of values; in short series a better representative value than the *mean.*

Median grey: see *middle grey.*

Mediate association: see *mediacy.*

Medicine man: see *shaman.*

Medico-legal: term applied to problems which are at once legal and medical, i.e. problems where medical knowledge is necessary to clear up the legal situation; relating to the application of medical science to legal problems, as, for example, the responsibility for their actions of individuals suffering from a mental disorder or defect.

Medium: an individual alleged or professing to be controlled, while in a trance condition, by a disembodied spirit or spirits, and to be able to receive and convey, through such control, messages from departed spirits; such phenomena are investigated by *psychical research.*

Medulla: in a general sense, the inner part of an organ; in a special sense, as an abbreviation for *medulla oblongata* or *bulb* at the top of the spinal cord, continuing the cord upwards into the *crura cerebri* (q.v.).

Medullary: see *myelin.*

Medullated: covered with the medullary sheath or *myelin.*

Medusa: a jelly-fish stage in the life history of many Coelenterata.

Megalomania: excessive overestimation of one's own importance, abilities, etc.

Megalopsis: enlargement of visual objects, owing to retinal or accommodation conditions.

Megrim: see *migraine.*

Meiosis: a stage in the development of germ cells, in which the cells are divided, and the number of chromosomes in a cell is reduced by half.

Meissner corpuscles: receptors, usually regarded as pressure receptors, found mainly in the soles of the feet and the palms of the hands.

Melancholia: a type of mental disorder with marked feelings of depression, and showing several varieties of motor phenomena.

Melancholic: one of the *temperaments,* in the classical four temperaments; attributed to black bile in the body, from which the name is derived.

Melanism: unusually copious development of pigment in hair, eyes, and skin.

Melody: a succession of musical notes in regular rhythm, or rhythmical phrases expressing a musical idea.

Membership character: term used by the *Gestalt* psychologists to express the effect on the individuality of an item of experience, sensory or ideational, when it becomes a constituent in a whole.

Membrane theory of conduction: theory which accounts for the transmission of the nerve impulse in terms of electrochemical properties of the membrane enclosing the nerve fibre.

Memorize: commit to memory.

Memory: in the abstract and most general sense, that characteristic of living organisms, in virtue of which what they experience leaves behind effects which modify future experience and behaviour, in virtue of which they have a history, and that history is recorded in themselves; that characteristic which underlies all *learning,* the essential feature of which is retention; in a narrow sense it covers *recall* and *recognition* – what we call remembering – but there may be *learning* without *remembering.*

Memory apparatus: an apparatus, employed in the study of memorizing to present in regular succession, and at the desired intervals, the material to be memorized.

Memory colour: effect of past experience of a coloured object in modifying the experience of the colour as presented under different conditions. See *constancy.*

Memory image: revival of former experience of an object in the absence of the object itself; the *primary memory image* is the very vivid memory image revived immediately after the perceptual experience of the object.

Memory levels: term employed in *eidetic* theory of the graded series of memory images, eidetic images, after-images.

Memory span: the number of individual items – usually digits or syllables – an individual can reproduce correctly and in order immediately after a single presentation; the test of this is called the *memory span test.*

Memory system: an artificial system devised to facilitate recall of what must for any reason be memorized.

Memory time: scoring time. See *scoring method.*

Mendel's law: a principle or law of hereditary transmission of *unit characters* (q.v.), to the effect that these are inherited according to a definite ratio, known as the *Mendelian ratio,* between *dominant* and *recessive* characters; in the first generation the proportion is *three* dominants to *one* recessive.

Mendelism: the theory of inheritance according to *Mendel*; now greatly extended, and somewhat modified.

Meninges: the membranes covering the brain and spinal cord, the *pia mater*, *arachnoid*, and *dura mater*.

Meningitis: inflammation of the *meninges*.

Meniscus: in optical sense, a lens convex on one side and concave on the other.

Menopause: the period of life at which *menstruation* (q.v.) stops: the 'change of life' in women.

Menstruation: the monthly discharge of menstrual fluid, which accompanies the discharge from the ovaries into the womb of an ovum in the case of the human female.

Mental: referring to mind or the mind.

Mental activity: in general sense, any mental operation; in special sense, alertness and quickness of thinking.

Mental Age: the measurement of the mental level of an individual in terms of the average chronological age of children showing the same mental standard, as measured by a scale of mental tests.

Mental capacity: the native mental ability of an individual independent of training or education.

Mental chemistry: expression first used apparently by *John Stuart Mill*, on the analogy of a chemical reaction, to signify that two items may be joined by association, in such a way that it is no longer possible to recognize in the union the original items.

Mental content: the total constituents of an individual's experience at any moment.

Mental deafness: cortical deafness (q.v.).

Mental defective: general term, inclusive of all individuals whose level of mental development is such that they are unable, as children, to profit from the ordinary type of school education, and as adults, to maintain themselves in anything but the simplest of environments, even in the case of the highest grades – inclusive, therefore, of the *feebleminded* or *moron*, the *imbecile* and the *idiot*.

Mental deterioration: progressive degeneration of mental abilities and functions.

Mental development: progressive appearance and organization of mental abilities and functions, in the course of the individual's passage from birth to maturity.

Mental discipline: see *discipline*.

Mental element: simple, and at present unanalysable, mental fact.

Mental evolution: progressive advance in *mentality,* manifested as we pass up the scale of animal life from the lowest organisms to man.

Mental examination: the applying of mental tests, either in order to determine an individual's mental level or status, or to diagnose mental disorder.

Mental function: any mental operation or process.

Mental healing: used mainly of the curing of disorders by *suggestion.*

Mental hygiene: investigation of the laws of mental health, and the taking, or advocacy, of measures for its preservation.

Mental imagery: generally employed in connection with the type of image predominant in an individual's trains of thought, or preferred by an individual. See *image* and *type.*

Mental maturity: the attainment of complete mental development as far as an individual is concerned; placed at various ages by different writers.

Mental measurement: applied to the use of the psychophysical methods; also used of mental or intelligence testing.

Mental mechanism: see *mechanism.*

Mental organization: the organized totality of mental operations in an individual; sometimes used of the underlying physiological organization, but the usage is not a desirable one.

Mental process: correctly applied to all processes of the mental life, conscious and *endopsychic* alike, though most frequently referring only to the former.

Mental phenomena: any and all phenomena characteristic of, and peculiar to, mental life.

Mental science: term, now obsolete, or nearly so, for philosophy and psychology, as a single field of thought.

Mental set: see *attitude* and *Einstellung.*

Mental synthesis: term due to *John Stuart Mill*; see *mental chemistry.*

Mental test: a standardized procedure for investigating mental capacities and characteristics, which may be either qualitative or quantitative, i.e. have as its aim either the determination of presence or absence, or the measurement of the degree in which present.

Mentality: a generalization of all those characteristics distinctive of mind; sometimes used in a sense more or less equivalent to mental capacity, or a concrete mind.

Meridian: term employed topographically, for the specification of directions in the visual field, relative to the fixation point, in terms of lines passing through that point, or of planes passing through that point, and the nodal points of a single eye.

Merkel corpuscles: cells in the tissues under the mucous membrane, in the mouth and tongue, possibly receptors for pressure.

Merkel's law: the principle stated by Merkel, that equal differences between sensations correspond to equal differences between the stimuli; this appears to conflict with Weber's law if that is extended so as to cover all differences, and not merely threshold differences.

Mescal: a narcotic drug prepared by fermentation of the juices of the American aloe; a strong intoxicant, producing hallucinations, chiefly of vision.

Mesencephalon: the midbrain; part developed from the middle cerebral vesicle of the embryo, including the *crura cerebri* and the *corpora quadrigemina.*

Mesmerism: an early name for *hypnotism.*

Mesoblast: the *mesoderm,* or middle germ layer of the embryo.

Mesognathous: a skull shape, which recedes somewhat, but not greatly, from the plane of the jaw; neither *prognathous* nor *orthognathous.*

Mesokurtic: see *kurtosis.*

Mesomorphy: a classification, based on anthropometric measurement, of type of physique, as marked by relative prominence of bone, muscle, and connective tissue.

Metabolism: the changes, chemical and physico-chemical, which go on in the living body. The term *metabolic gradient* is used of differences in degree of metabolic activity from one part to another (or from one organ to another). See *basal metabolism, anabolism,* and *catabolism.*

Metagenesis: alternation of distinct forms in successive generations.

Metagnomy: term employed in *psychical research,* for the apparent acquisition of knowledge by supernormal means, such being attributed to disembodied spirits.

Metakinesis: term suggested by *Lloyd Morgan* for the prototype of consciousness, as manifested in the lowest types of organism; also employed in a phase of *mitosis* (q.v.).

Metallic: a quality of taste sensation, obtained by the contact of certain metals with the tongue, but not usually regarded as a simple or elementary taste quality.

Metallophonia: a metallic voice.

Metamorphopsia: distortion of appearance of visual objects, due to parts of the retina being pathologically displaced.

Metamorphosis: term applied to the radical change of nature and form undergone, in the course of development, by certain organisms, particularly insects.

Metaphysics: strictly the branch of speculative philosophy which deals with the ultimate nature of things, or *ontology*, but generally applied more widely to include the theory of knowledge, or *epistemology*, and at one time inclusive also of psychology.

Metapsychics: general term inclusive of supernormal phenomena, both physical and psychical; spiritualistic phenomena in general, together with telepathy, clairvoyance, etc.

Metapsychology: term employed by *Freud* for the extension of investigation beyond the psychological field proper to speculative consideration of the phenomena from three general points of view, *dynamic, topographical* and *economic.*

Metazoa: many-celled organisms and animals.

Metempirical: not open to empirical investigation.

Metempsychosis: transmigration of souls.

Metencephalon: according to present views, that part in the embryo from which the *medulla* (formerly also the *pons*) develops.

Methectic: term employed in *psychical research* of communication between one stratum and another in the *personality,* e.g. in *automatic writing.*

Methodology: a branch of logic, which deals with methods of scientific research.

Metric: relating to measurement in general; more specially, measurement based on the metre; still more specially in the expression *metric formula,* the formula used by *Fechner* as the mathematical expression of *Weber's law,* viz. $S = K \log R$.

Metronome: an instrument for marking off short periods of time, and employed for timing various operations; sometimes fitted with contacts for giving graphical records.

Meyer's contrast experiment: a common method of demonstrating visual contrast, by placing a strip of grey or white paper on a sheet of coloured paper, and covering the whole with tissue paper.

Microcephaly: abnormal smallness of head and brain.

Microcosm: small universe; used figuratively of the human being; also sometimes of the world revealed by the microscope.

Micron: the millionth part of a metre; the thousandth part of a micron is a *millimicron* or *micromillimetre,* used as a unit for specifying wave-lengths of radiation (light, etc.).

Microorganism: organism invisible, or nearly so, to the unassisted human eye, and examined by the microscope.

Microphone: instrument for intensifying or amplifying faint sounds.

Microphonia: abnormally weak voice.

Micropsia: diminished size of visual objects, due to abnormal condition of retina.

Microsplanchnic: a type of physique with relatively small trunk as compared with limbs.

Micturition: discharge of urine.

Midbrain: see *mesencephalon.*

Middle ear: chamber in ear, between the drum or tympanum, and the wall of the inner ear. See *ear.*

Middle grey: a grey standing midway between white and black in the white-black scale or scale of brightness (brilliance).

Midperiod: the period in an experiment following upon the *foreperiod,* with reference to systematic introspection.

Migraine: severe headache, often on one side only, with nausea and depression.

Migration: seasonal change of habitat of some species of birds and animals, often through great distances; psychologically interesting from the point of view of the underlying impulse, and the orientation problem involved.

Milieu: immediate environment, physical and social, but usually, in psychology, with emphasis upon the latter.

Mill's Canons: the five principles or laws of inductive reasoning, formulated by *John Stuart Mill* — agreement, difference, agreement and difference, residues, and concomitant variations.

Mimesis (Gr.): meaning imitation, with respect to both form and action; in *aesthetics,* a theory of Art as imitative or mimetic.

Mimetism: the assuming by one animal of the characteristics of another — shape, colour, movements, etc. — for concealment.

Mimicry: close imitation of an act or series of acts; in special sense, the close resemblance taken on by one organism to another, or to an inanimate object, which serves as a protection (see *mimetism*).

Mind: the organized totality of *psychical* (q.v.) structures and processes, conscious, unconscious, and *endopsychic;* philosophically, rather than psychologically, the entity or substratum underlying these structures and processes.

Mind blindness: inability to grasp the meaning of objects seen; *cortical blindness.*

Mind-body problem: see *psychophysical problem.*

Mind cure: see *mental healing.*

Mind-dust theory: the speculative theory of the existence in the universe of particles or atoms of a mind substance.

Mind reading: the grasping by one individual of what is passing in the mind of another by signs involuntarily given by the other; sometimes called *thought reading,* and employed as a parlour game, when it is usually *muscle reading.*

Mind-stuff theory: essentially the same as the *mind-dust theory.* In this case there is, however, the addition usually of the view that this mind-stuff is experienced as matter.

Miner's nystagmus: see *nystagmus.*

Minimal change method: see *method of limits.*

Minor: as a musical term, used of scales, and intervals. See *scale.*

Minuscule: a lower case (small) letter, as distinguished from a capital.

Miotic (myotic): a drug which contracts the pupil of the eye. See *myosis.*

Mirror drawing: a type of psychological experiment (or test), where the subject is required to follow a drawing, when he sees the drawing and his hand only in a mirror; a form of learning experiment – the acquiring of a new co-ordination of eye and hand.

Mirror writing: writing produced in the laterally reverse direction – from right to left – which appears as normal when seen in a mirror; frequently in children a result of mixed laterality, with respect to hand and eye, and a not infrequent source of educational retardation.

Misdemeanour: a minor violation of law or local regulation.

Miso- (Gr.): as a prefix meaning hating.

Misogamy: hatred of marriage.

Misogynist: woman hater.

Mistuned Forks: tuning forks, which are intentionally made slightly out of tune with one another for experimental purposes, either by filing or loading one of them; used in testing pitch discrimination, the difference between the two ears, demonstrating beats, etc.

Mitosis: cell division, with division of the *chromosomes* (q.v.) and various other changes in the *cytoplasm* and the *nucleus.*

Mixoscopia: excitement caused by witnessing a sexual act.

Mneme: term employed by *Semon* to designate basic memory in the individual or the race; the conservation characteristic pervading all life.

Mnemic theory: the theory of heredity as a kind of memory.

Mnemonics: term employed usually of artificial systems for aiding memory and recall, particularly with regard to specific types of material.

Mob: the most elementary type of social group, if it can be so regarded, where an aggregate of individuals, under the influence of emotion (and suggestion), act as a single unit for a temporary purpose.

Modality: qualitative attribute or aspect of sense experience as belonging to a specific sense department; two sensations are said to differ in modality when it is impossible to pass by gradations of quality from one to the other, as, for example the colour 'blue' and the tone 'middle C'; *modal sensitivity* is the range of stimuli within a particular modality to which an organism is sensitive – denoted by MS.

Mode: in general sense, manner of appearance; used in several technical senses: (1) statistically, for the most frequently occurring value in a series, or the peak or peaks in a *frequency curve;* (2) musically, for the arrangement of notes and intervals in a scale; (3) in the phrase *mode of appearance* for the different ways in which sensory phenomena, especially colours, present themselves, e.g. as film colours, surface colours, volume or bulky colours, etc.

Modiolus: the central pillar or core of the *cochlea.*

Modulus: a constant multiplier by which one series of numbers may be transformed into another.

Mogiarthria: a defect of speech, due to a lesion in the nervous system, which causes a failure in co-ordination of the vocal muscles.

Molar: in the mass, as contrasted with molecular, in the individual molecules or particles.

Mollusca: a group of unsegmented invertebrates, usually with a hard shell.

Moment: measure of a force by its effect in producing rotary movement in a body; statistically, the sum of the deviations from the mean in a series, each deviation being raised to a certain power, divided by the number in the series, thus $\Sigma (x^n)/N$, where Σ is the sum of the deviations, each raised to the nth power, and N the number in the series. The *method of moments* is a method of fitting a curve to an observed distribution.

Mon(o)- (Gr.): prefix meaning 'alone', 'only', 'single' and the like.

Monad: term used by *Leibniz* (borrowed from *Pythagoras*), in his metaphysical doctrine of the universe as composed of a plurality of self-active independent individuals or monads.

Monaural hearing: hearing with one ear alone.

Mongol(ian): a type of congenital defective (*moron* or *imbecile*), so named because of facial characteristics.

Monism: metaphysical theory that the universe consists of aspects or modes of a single substance, e.g. *Spinozism.*

Monochord: one-stringed musical instrument, used for testing pitch discrimination.

Monocular vision: sometimes 'uniocular'; vision with one eye.

Monoecious: having both sexes in one individual.

Monogamy: durable mating, or marriage, between two individuals; one husband and one wife.

Monogenism: theory that the differing races of man are all derived from one ancestral stock.

Monoglottic: term used of a single taste quality obtained by stimulating a small area of the tongue.

Monogony: asexual reproduction, e.g. by budding.

Monograph: a more or less exhaustive discussion of a single limited topic.

Monoideism: a condition, usually pathological, where the mind is fixed on a single idea, or where the individual is constantly reverting to the same topic; a *fixed idea.*

Monomania: mental disorder characterized by a fixed idea; no longer used as a technical term. See *paranoia.*

Monoplegia: paralysis of one limb only, or one member of the body.

Monorhinic. applied to smelling with one nostril only.

Monotone: speech, or other sound, in one pitch throughout.

Monotony: lack of inflection in speaking; figuratively, and more usually, continuance of a single uninteresting operation, or situation, or occupation.

Monotreme: a primitive or egg-laying mammal, represented by the duck-billed platypus, with a single opening for alimentary and uro-genital canal.

Monozygotic twins: see *twins.*

Mood: an affective condition or attitude, enduring for some time, characterized by particular emotions in a condition of subexcitation, so as to be readily evoked, e.g. an irritable mood, or a cheerful mood.

Moon-blindness: see *night blindness*; sometimes used popularly for *amblyopia.*

Moon illusion: the visual illusion of size, when the moon appears larger at the horizon than at the zenith.

Moral faculty: the capacity to distinguish between right and wrong; a term in popular rather than scientific usage; sometimes *moral sense.*

Moral imbecile: a legal rather than psychological term for an individual, apparently with pronounced criminal tendencies, with or without mental or intellectual defect.

Moral judgment: judgment as to the rightness or wrongness of an act or of conduct.

Morale: term employed of an individual, or of a group, signifying the condition with respect to self-control, self-confidence, and disciplined action.

Morbid: involving an abnormal, disordered, or diseased condition.

Mores: comprehensive term, applied to a social group, and covering, over and above recognized principles of conduct, those laws and customs regarded as essential and vital by the group.

Morgan's Canon: see *Lloyd Morgan's canon.*

Moron: usual American term for *feebleminded.*

Morphin(e): a chief alkaloid constituent of opium; narcotic and analgesic.

Morphinism: addiction to abuse of morphin(e).

Morphological index: an anatomical measure obtained by dividing the volume of the trunk by the length of the limbs.

Morphology: the branch of biology which investigates the form and structure of organisms.

Mosaic eye: the *compound eye;* called 'mosaic' because it images objects as a mosaic pattern.

Mother complex: the *Oedipus complex* (q.v.).

Motile: applied to organisms capable of moving about; also used for a type of individual whose preferred type of imagery is *motor.*

Motion illusion: appearance of motion in a motionless object; sometimes due to relative movement, and sometimes of the nature of an *after-sensation,* following a continuous movement of the individual or visual experience of continuous movement. See also *apparent movement.*

Motion study: a development of *industrial psychology,* in the study of repetitive movement, with a view to the elimination of unnecessary movements, and the determination of the most efficient and least fatiguing movement or combination of movements. Elaborate methods have been developed, using stereophotography and cinematography.

Motivate: to provide an incentive; to act as an incentive.

Motivation: term employed generally for the phenomena involved in the operation of incentives or drives.

Motive: an affective-conative factor which operates in determining the direction of an individual's behaviour towards an end or goal, consciously apprehended, or unconscious.

Motoneuron: a neuron (q.v.), directly exciting or inhibiting the activity of a muscle or gland, and directly in connection with it.

Motor area: the ascending precentral convolution (in front of the central fissure or fissure of Rolando), in the frontal lobe of the cerebrum.

Motor: employed as an adjective, referring to structures or functions connected with the activity of muscles, or with the response of an organism to a situation. Thus we have: *motor experience, motor habit, motor learning, motor nerve, motor organ, motor reflex,* etc.

Motor sensation: sensations derived from receptor organs in muscles, tendons, and joints; sometimes inclusive of sensations from the receptors of the *static sense* (q.v.).

Motorium (infrequent term)*:* the cortical and subcortical centres and areas, controlling directly the activity of the voluntary or striped muscle system.

Movement illusion: illusion of movement of a non-moving part of the body. Cf. *motion illusion* and *apparent movement.*

Moving average method: a statistical method of smoothing a series by replacing frequencies, in successive groups, by the average of a number of neighbouring groups.

Müller-Lyer illusion: one of the geometrical optical illusions, known as the 'arrow-head and feather' illusion; an illusion of length or distance, in which two objectively equal lines appear unequal when other lines are drawn, making acute angles at the ends of one, and obtuse angles at the ends of the other. An essentially similar illusion, called *Müller-Lyer rectangles,* has squares marking off one space, and non-square rectangles the other space which is equal to it.

Multimodal theory of intelligence: the theory that intelligence is a pattern of a multiplicity of factors, in contrast to the *two-factor theory* of *Spearman.*

Multiple choice method: a test, in which a problem is presented to the subject, offering a choice of two or more solutions of which only one is correct; the same problem in principle may be employed as a learning experiment with animal and human subjects.

Multiple sclerosis: a disease which is characterized by hardening at various points in the brain and spinal cord, resulting in increasing motor incoordination.

Multipolar cell: a nerve cell with three or more processes.

Munsell colours: a standardized series of greys and colours in all hues, saturations, and brightnesses (brilliances), each associated with a symbol, making possible an exact specification of a grey or colour.

Muscae volitantes (Lat.): 'flying flies'; phenomena of vision, in which specks flit about in the field of vision, owing to the presence of small particles in the lymph between the vitreous humour and the retina.

Muscle balance: the extent to which either eye retains its position in fixation, when it is covered. Cf. *imbalance.*

Muscle reading: the apprehension of ideas in the mind of a person by another in physical contact through unconscious signs given by the former by way of movement or resistance.

Muscle spindles: sensory nerve endings in muscles.

Muscular reaction: type of response in a reaction experiment when the subject's attention is directed towards the making of the response.

Muscular (muscle) sense: see *kinaesthesis.*

Musculature: the contractile tissue of the body which produces movements; consists of two groups: the *skeletal, striped,* or *voluntary* muscles, controlled by the *cerebro-spinal system,* and the *smooth* or *involuntary* muscles, controlled by the *autonomic system.*

Mutation: in biology, a variation which appears suddenly, and is transmitted to offspring.

Mutism: lack of appearance of speech, usually due to deafness, general or *high frequency* (q.v.).

M.v.: used as abbreviation for *mean variation.*

Mydriasis: extreme or abnormal dilation of pupil of eye; *mydriatic,* a drug which causes such dilation.

Myelencephalon: either the cerebro-spinal system as a whole, or, in the embryo, the portion of the *medulla* below or behind the *pons* and *cerebellum.*

Myelin: the white fatty sheath which covers *medullated* nerve fibres (*white fibres*).

Myelinization: the formation of the medullary sheath.

Myelitis: inflammation of the spinal cord.

Myogenic: originating in the muscle tissue.

Myograph: apparatus for recording graphically, or photographically, muscular contractions.

Myology: the part of anatomy dealing with the muscles.

Myopia: a refractive condition of the lens system of the eye, which results, in the resting condition of the eye, in the focussing of parallel rays in front of the retina.

Myosis: extreme contraction of the pupil, due to disease or drugs.

Mysophobia: irrational or morbid dread of dirt. See *phobia.*

Mysticism: belief in the attainment, through contemplation, of truths inaccessible to the understanding; sometimes used of philosophical theories assuming agencies of which a rational account cannot be given.

Myth: a narrative or tradition, without historical or scientific basis, embodying a popular idea regarding natural phenomena, or historical events, or deeds of gods, heroes, etc. *Mythology:* a body of such narratives or traditions.

Mythomania: tendency towards the narration of imaginary adventures; elaborations of suggestions given, frequently exhibited in hypnosis.

Myxoedema: disease involving diminished functioning of the *thyroid gland* (q.v.), usually accompanied by marked increase of adipose tissue, with degeneration of intellectual powers towards definite mental deficiency.

N

Nadir: the lowest point.

Naïve: used of an attitude, childlike, simple, or unsophisticated.

Nancy school: a school of *psychopathology* and *psychotheraphy,* founded at Nancy by *Bernheim,* specially characterized by views regarding hypnosis, their main contention being that hypnosis is merely a condition of exaggerated suggestibility artificially induced; in more recent times stress has been laid on *auto-suggestion* (q.v.) as the fundamental type of suggestion. Cf. *Salpetrière school.*

Nanism: dwarfism; abnormally small size.

Narcissism: extreme self-love; regarded by psychoanalysts as an early phase of *psychosexual development,* where the sexual object is the self, persisting, or representing a regression in the *narcissistic type* of individual; in all cases of narcissism the excessive preoccupation with oneself and one's own concerns is the essential characteristic.

Narcolepsy: uncontrollable inclination for sleep.

Narcosis: a state of stupor induced by certain drugs, tending to pass into *paralysis* with *insensibility.*

Narcotic: a drug tending to produce narcosis; also used as an adjective.

Nares: nostrils and nasal passages, inclusive of the posterior passages connecting with the mouth cavity.

Narrative method: method of obtaining data by allowing an observer to give in his own way an account of events; formerly the main method of *animal psychology,* and in general very unreliable.

Nasal cavities: the right and left chambers in which the receptors of the sense of smell are found, situated above the roof of the mouth.

Nascent: referring to the first stages or phases of development.

National intelligence scale: two series (A and B) of *group tests* of the *battery* type, devised for the National Research Council of America.

Native: inborn; used of congenital characteristics of structure or function; the sum of an individual's inborn capacities is known as his *native endowment;* any inborn characteristic is known as a *native trait.*

Nativism: emphasis on the inborn rather than acquired character of certain factors in our experience, particularly in regard to *space perception;* such a theory is called a *nativistic* in contrast to a *genetic,* theory.

Natural. employed in certain technical senses: (1) of a reaction in which the subject is not instructed to direct his attention either to stimulus or to response; (2) of a musical *scale,* which is not *tempered;* (3) of sciences which are biological, as against physical, or biological and physical, as against social.

Natural selection: the process by which, according to *Darwin,* the evolution of species takes place; the struggle for existence, with the survival of the fittest, i.e. those best adapted to a particular environment, such advantage being by chance variations.

Naturalism: a philosophical attitude or theory of the universe and man's place in it, which lays stress on the operation of natural forces and natural laws, and tends to neglect or deny all else.

Naturism: a term applied by anthropologists to a very primitive form of religious or quasi-religious belief in *mana* as attached indefinitely to natural phenomena.

Nausea: a complex of sensory experiences, in which intestinal sensations predominate, with an unpleasant affective tone, and a tendency to vomit.

Neanderthal man: an extinct type of man, bones of whom were first discovered at Neanderthal, and later in several places, with considerable geographical range; a man belonging to the period of the Middle Stone Age in Western Europe.

Near-sighted: see *myopia*.

Necromancy: that branch of magic which professes to work through communication with the dead.

Necrophilia: morbid attraction, allegedly sexual, to dead bodies.

Need: a condition marked by the feeling of lack or want of something, or of requiring the performance of some action.

Negative: used in a technical sense in: (1) *negative adaptation*, gradual ceasing of a response to a continuous or repeated stimulus; (2) *negative response*, behaviour directed away from the stimulus; (3) *negative self-feeling*, feeling of submission, or of inferiority; (4) *negative sensation*, an imaginary sensation, the stimulus for which is below the *threshold;* (5) *negative therapeutic reaction*, resistance to recovery, as from a *neurosis* caused by feelings of *guilt*; (6) *negative transfer*, transfer of training, resulting in impeding another action or operation.

Negativism: an attitude of resistance to suggestions coming from other people.

Neo - (Gr.): prefix, meaning 'new'.

Neo-catharsis: a *therapeutic* method, sometimes used by psychoanalysts, which consists in making conscious childhood relations.

Neo-encephalon: the new brain, i.e. new in evolutional history – the *cerebrum*.

Neolalia: speech containing many words coined by the speaker, i.e. *neologisms*.

Neo-lamarck(ian)ism: a theory of evolution, involving the *inheritance of acquired characteristics*, as against the *Neo-Darwinian* theory, which bases evolution on chance *variation* and *natural selection*.

Neonate: newly born; in the case of the human child, used of first few weeks.

Neopallium: the part of the central nervous system of most recent phylogenetic development, i.e. the *cerebral cortex*, apart from the *olfactory* area.

Neper (Napier): a unit of sound intensity, equal to 6.686 decibels.

Nernst-Lillie theory: a theory of cell and fibre excitation and conduction, to the effect that this depends on electrical polarization, and changes in the permeability of the enclosing membrane.

Nerve: a bundle of nerve fibres.

Nerve, nervous, and neural: all used almost interchangeably as adjectives, referring to structures, processes, and conditions of the nervous system.

Nerve cell: the cell-body of a *neuron* (q.v.).

Nerve fibres: the processes (*axons* or *dendrites*) of *neurons* (q.v.).

Nerve-muscle preparation: an excised muscle, with attached nerve – usually the *gastrocnemius* muscle and *sciatic* nerve of a frog – employed in the physiological study of nerve and muscle phenomena.

Nerve ring: the most primitive form of nervous system, found as a double ring of cells and fibres, round the margin of the disc of the jellyfish.

Nerve root: a group of nerves in a bundle, passing directly out of brain or spinal cord.

Nerve tract: see *tract*.

Nervous disorder (disease): a general term, covering a variety of types of *psychosis, psychoneurosis,* and often *neurosis.*

Nervous prostration: see *neurasthenia.*

Nervous system: the totality of the *neurons,* inclusive both of those belonging to the *cerebro-spinal* system, and those belonging to the *autonomic.*

Nesting: the complex, and apparently instinctive, behaviour of insects, birds, and some mammals, which takes the form of making nests or habitations.

Neural arc: see *sensori-motor arc.*

Neural conduction: nerve conduction; the transmission along a nerve fibre of a wave of excitation.

Neural crest: a band of cells, lying along the line in which the neural folds meet to form the neural tube, in the embryo.

Neural groove: the groove which marks, in the embryo, the site of the developing neural tube.

Neural pattern: the functional arrangement and interconnection of cells active as a result of stimulation from without or within.

Neural plate: the thickened part of the ectoderm in the embryonic disc, where the *neural groove* forms.

Neural rivalry: competition between reflex activity and cortical control, for the dominance of some *final common path.*

Neural tube: the tube which develops from the *neural plate* to form the central nervous system in the embryo.

Neuralgia: a disorder, generally in a single nerve, characterized by acute but not usually continuous pain.

Neurasthenia: a state of excessive fatiguability, or lack of vigour, both bodily and mental, often accompanied by *hypochondria* and sometimes by *phobias.*

Neuraxis: the brain and spinal cord.

Neurilemma: the tough outer covering of a nerve fibre; in the case of the *medullated fibres,* over the *medullary sheath.*

Neurin: the chief protein constituent of nerve tissue; also used of the energy postulated to account for nerve activity.

Neuritis: painful inflamed condition in a peripheral nerve fibre; the term *central neuritis* is proposed by *Adolf Meyer* for a condition of diffuse degeneration in central fibres present in certain nutritional deficiency conditions.

Neurobiotaxis: the principle that *neurons* exhibit a form of *galvanotropism,* in that the *dendrites* of a neuron are electrically stimulated to grow towards other neurons from which stimulations come, provided there is simultaneous activity on both sides of the synapses.

Neurofibrils: minute threads or fibrils in the nerve fibres, and also in the cell bodies, regarded as the essential conducting elements in the nervous system.

Neuroglia: the supporting tissue in the brain and spinal cord, consisting of *glia* cells.

Neurogram: the enduring effect left behind, as a result of activity in the nervous system, as, for example, the activity involved in any series of sensory experiences, which forms the basis of memory, and so of *personality.*

Neurohumoral: relating to the interaction of nervous processes and chemical substances, in the integration of nervous impulses and *hormonic* action in bodily activities.

Neurology: the branch of biological science which studies the structure and functions of the nervous system; usually includes also the practical or applied aspect, in the diagnosis and treatment of disorders of the nervous system, which lie outside the field of the psychiatrist.

Neuromere: a segment of the *neural tube* in the embryo.

Neuromotor apparatus: interconnected fibrils in unicellular organisms, probably functioning in the manner in which the nervous system functions in higher organisms.

Neuromuscular junction: the surface of contact, at the *end-plates,* between the fibres of a motor nerve and the fibres of the muscle which it innervates.

Neuromuscular spindles: see *muscle spindles.*

Neuron: the structural unit of the nervous system, consisting of a cell body with its processes; of many different forms and sizes.

Neuropathy: diseased condition in the nervous system.

Neurophysiology: the branch of physiology, which deals with the physiology, i.e. the functional aspect, of the nervous system; in particular, the investigation of the nature and transmission of the nerve impulse.

Neuropil(e): network of unmedullated or *non-medullated* neurofibrils, at the *synapses* (q.v.).

Neuropsychiatry: branch of medicine, dealing with the treatment of nervous and mental disorders, particularly those of a structural rather than functional character.

Neurosis: in the old sense, any activity in the nervous system; in present sense, a functional disorder, psychogenic in origin, of the nervous system, rather indefinitely marked off from *psychoneurosis* (q.v.); by psychoanalysts regarded as a conflict phenomenon, involving the thwarting of some fundamental instinctive urge (they also speak, however, of *actual neurosis,* where there seems to be a physical origin).

Neurotic: term used rather indefinitely of an individual whose behaviour is suggestive of a minor nervous disorder.

Neurotic character: term employed by Adler and his school for an individual who is attempting in various ways to compensate for some *organ inferiority,* or, more generally, to attain superiority, or complete *masculinity.*

Neurypnology (Neurhypnology): term used by *Braid* (q.v.) for the study and practice of hypnotism, his view being that the hypnotic state was a state of the nervous system, akin to the state in sleep.

Neutral: used of a condition between two opposing states of mind; might be designated as the zero of a series, which may vary in either a positive or a negative direction from it.

Newton's Law of colour mixture: the law, formulated by Newton, that, if two colour mixtures give the same sensation of colour (or light), their mixture will also give that sensation; might also refer to another principle stated by Newton, with respect to the mixture of two colours to give an intermediate colour, sometimes called his *law of equilibrium* in colour mixing, to the effect that if A and B are the colours mixed in proportions m and n, then the colour resulting will be at a point on the line joining A and B so that $AO/OB = n/m$.

Nexus: interdependence of two elements, items, or events; usually refers to the causal connection between two events.

Night blindness: a congenital, or acquired, defect of vision, involving diminution of the power, or at least of the range, of *dark adaptation* (q.v.), usually with absence of the *Purkinje phenomena* (q.v.), involving inability or difficulty in seeing objects in moderate darkness; appears sometimes as a functional defect, without marked impairment of dark adaptation.

Night terrors: very disturbing or frightening dreams, from which the individual wakes in a state of terror.

Nightmare: dream, marked by acute anxiety; according to Freudian theory, it represents a breaking down of the *censorship* and the failure of the dream to perform its function of protecting sleep.

Nihil est in intellectu quod non prius fuerit in sensu (Lat.): 'nothing is in the intellect which has not previously been in the senses', the characteristic aphorism of *sensationalism; Leibniz* added 'nisi intellectus ipse', 'except the intellect itself'.

Nihil ex nihilo fit: 'nothing comes out of nothing', a scholastic aphorism asserting universal causation.

Nissl granules: bodies in the cell body of the neuron; possibly food substances.

Nisus: conscious effort against obstacles; striving; akin to *drive* or rather *conation*.

Nociceptive reflex: defensive reflexes to painful stimulation.

Nocturnal enuresis: see *enuresis*.

Noegenesis: a term used by *Spearman* (q.v.), to designate the course which the essential process in cognition, viz. *noesis*, follows.

Noesis: the activity of the mind in knowing an object; the essential characteristic of cognition as such. Mental processes which are basically processes of *judgment* are called *noetic processes*.

Noise: the sensory effect of irregular, or aperiodic, sound waves; undesired auditory stimuli.

Nolism: the will not to do a given act.

Nomadism: a tendency or inclination to wander from place to place.

Nominalism: the name given to one side of a psychological and epistemological controversy, regarding the sense in which a *general concept* exists, a controversy which in one form or another dates back to Ancient Greek philosophy, the characteristic of nominalism being the view that the only thing that is general is the word or name; a phase of the *imageless thought* controversy.

Nomograph (Nomogram): mathematically, a graphic representation of mathematical relationships; statistically, a chart with a series of scales, usually as parallel straight lines, representing the values of related variables; the value of any two of these values being known, a third related value can be determined merely by the use of a straight-edge.

Nomology: that branch of science, or of any one science, which investigates general principles and formulates laws.

Nomothetic: relating to the formulation of laws; legislative.

Non compos mentis: 'unsound of mind'; legally incompetent, owing to mental condition.

Non sequitur: the name given to a logical fallacy, which consists in drawing an illegitimate conclusion from the premises; 'it does not follow'; the phrase is sometimes used as a noun.

Non-conscious: without conscious life; not to be confused with *un-conscious*.

Non-contradiction: term used of a law, or canon of logic; if one of two contradictory statements is true, the other must be false.

Non-ego: everything outside the ego or self; the objective world, as distinguished in experience from the self.

Nonius: see *vernier*.

Non-moral: not capable of being judged as either moral or immoral; outside the application or applicability of moral standards.

Non-rational: not capable of being judged as either rational or irrational, because outside the field of rationality or reason.

Nonsense syllables: artificial combinations of letters, not forming words, employed as material in *learning* experiments, so as to exclude associations possibly already formed.

Non-sensory: outside the sensory field; without sensory character.

Non-verbal tests: intelligence or other mental tests, which do not employ verbal material, or, sometimes, which can be given without employing words, e.g. to the deaf.

Non-social: not coming under the head, or belonging to the sphere, of the social; not to be judged or considered from a social point of view; sometimes equivalent to *asocial*.

Non-voluntary: neither voluntary nor involuntary; where the question of will does not arise.

Norm: a representative or standard value or pattern, for a group or type; statistically the *mean, median,* or *mode,* whichever is taken as the representative value for a group of scores in a test.

Normal: conforming to the standard for a particular type or group; average, or near the average, for a type or group; with respect to intelligence level, intelligence quotients not deviating more from the mean than twice the standard deviation might be regarded as normal, beyond that amount of deviation as *subnormal* (defective) or *supernormal*.

Normal distribution curve (or frequency): that distribution, represented by a bell-shaped curve, which satisfies certain mathematical conditions deducible from the theory of *probability*.

Normative science: a science which seeks to lay down norms or standards for correct thinking or acting, such as *logic* or *ethics*, as contrasted with a positive or empirical science, which observes and records facts.

Normosplanchnic: a physique or body, in which the trunk and limbs are normal, or average, in proportion to one another, with respect to size.

Nosogenesis: term used by psychoanalysts for the classification of a nervous disorder, in accordance with the conditions or character of its onset.

Nosophobia: morbid dread or *phobia* of some particular disease.

Note: term used in music for the complex of tones, or the *clang*, given by the human voice or a musical instrument; a tone with its overtones or harmonics; a tone regarded in relation to its position within the *octave*.

Note-blindness: a rare form of *alexia* or *word-blindness*.

Notochord: a band or rod, forming the primitive basis of the spinal column, in primitive vertebrates, and in the human embryo.

Nous (Gr.): reason, as distinct from sense.

Nuclear complex: the initial complex, according to psychoanalysts, arising from impulses, friendly and hostile, towards other members of the family, particularly the father or the mother.

Nuclear layers: the fourth and sixth layers of the retina, respectively the outer and the inner nuclear layers.

Nucleolus: a small body within the nucleus of a cell.

Nucleus: the centre of life of a cell, consisting of specialized materials, sharply separated off from the rest of the material or *cytoplasm*, in the cell; employed figuratively in various connections, but usually with the sense either of 'core' or 'initial stage' of development of some kind.

Number completion test: a mental test, where the subject is required to complete, or continue, a series of numbers, related according to some definite principle or principles.

Number form: the characteristic of a mental phenomenon or process akin to *synaesthesia*, where an individual, in imaging or thinking of a number, always represents it as having a position in a spatial scheme or form, these forms being relatively constant for the individual.

Nyctalopia: Greek compound of three words, meaning 'night blindness', but sometimes taken as meaning 'day blindness'. Cf. *hemeralopia*.

Nyctophobia: morbid fear of night or of darkness.

Nymphomania: exaggerated sexual desire in a human female, usually as a symptom of mental disorder.

Nystagmus: involuntary jerky movements of the eyes, either in the form of a slow followed by a quick movement in the opposite direction, or rapid oscillations; occurs in total colour blindness, usually when due to a central scotoma, and in normal individuals subjected to definite conditions, as in rotation experiments; also occurs in labyrinthine disorders, and is frequent in miners, owing to long exposure to abnormal visual conditions; can be produced by electrical stimulation of the labyrinth (*galvanic nystagmus*), or by irrigating the ear with warm or cold liquid (*caloric nystagmus*).

O

O: usual abbreviation for *observer*.

o Factor: an *oscillation* factor in cognition, related to fluctuations in mental or cognitive efficiency.

Object: the most general sense, psychologically, is that which is before the mind at any time, perceived, imaged, or thought, as distinct from the act of perceiving, imagining, or thinking; another general sense is something aimed at in action or in thought (see *objective*); there are many derived senses, all coming directly or indirectly under one or other of these general senses; coming under the first meaning we have *object-consciousness* and *object of consciousness*, meaning that of which the individual is aware; we also have *object blindness*, as a disorder of vision where the individual, though able to see, is unable to apprehend visual objects; we have *object odour* or *smell*, where an individual has perception, through smell, of a familiar object, of which he knows the smell, rather than a perception of the smell itself. Derived from the second sense we have the two psychoanalytical terms: – *object cathexis*, where love is diverted from its normal sexual aim, and *object choice*, where a love object is determined by early fixations, as *narcissistic* or *anaclitic*.

Objective: the two general senses of *object* here again determine the derivative senses. The second general sense of object gives the meaning of *objective* as something aimed at consciously, with whatever degree of vagueness; from the first general meaning of object we have the various adjectival meanings of objective, as in *objective psychology,* that type of psychology which studies phenomena that can be observed from the outside inclusive of behaviour and physiological data, or, more generally, mental expressions and products; *objective score,* a score in a test, assessed in accordance with a key; and independently of subjective evaluation; *objective trait,* a characteristic which manifests itself in external behaviour, and because of this is capable of being measured in *objective terms.*

Obligation: a feeling of inner compulsion, from whatever source, to act in a certain way towards another, or towards the community; in a narrower sense a feeling arising from benefits received, prompting to service in return; less definite than *duty,* and not involving, as in the latter, the ability to act in accordance with it.

Oblique muscles: two of the eyeball muscles, attached to the eyeball above and below respectively, and effecting mainly torsional movement of the eyeball. See *eye.*

Obliviscence: forgetfulness, so far as due apparently to lapse of time.

Obscurantism: general tendency to oppose or impede investigation, or enlightenment, or the progress of knowledge.

Observation: careful and attentive examination of phenomena, with a view to a clearer knowledge of the phenomena, for a practical or a theoretical object. For *self-observation* see *introspection.*

Observer: generally equivalent to *subject* in psychological experiment, but with the additional implication that he is expected to furnish a report of his experience, which need not be demanded of a *subject.*

Obsession: a persistent or recurrent idea, usually strongly tinged with emotion, and frequently involving an urge towards some form of action, the whole mental situation being pathological.

Obsessional Neurosis: a *psychoneurosis* (q.v.), characterized by obsessional ideas or urges.

Obsessional type: a type, regarded by psychoanalysts as governed by anxiety, arising from a guilty consciousness.

Occam's razor: see *principle of economy.*

Occasionalism: a metaphysical theory which seeks to explain the apparent causal connection between mental and bodily processes – the psycho-physical connection – by assuming divine intervention to produce bodily movement, on the occasion of the mental idea of movement, or the will to move, and the production of a perception in the mind, on the occasion of the stimulation of a sense organ – a theory which developed out of the Cartesian position.

Occipital lobe: the part of the cerebrum at the back of the head.

Occultism: the doctrine and practice of the occult sciences, such as alchemy, astrology, theosophy, and generally those which involve a control over nature by means of a secret lore, and magical or pseudo-magical procedures.

Occupational: relating or referring to the work an individual performs for a livelihood.

Occupational hierarchy: an arrangement of occupations, and occupational groups, according to the average grade or level of general intelligence required for their successful prosecution, from unskilled labour to the higher professions.

Occupational therapy: the employment of occupations, chiefly of a manual character, for therapeutic or remedial treatment of mental and physical disorders and defects.

Ocellus: a small or simple form of eye; also one of the facets of a *compound eye*; also the eye form in some feathers.

Octave: the pitch interval between tones one of which has a frequency twice that of the other.

Ocular: referring or relating to the eye.

Ocular dominance: the difference, analogous to righthandedness and lefthandedness, between the two eyes with respect to use, preference and efficiency.

Ocular measurement: measurement of visual acuity and visual discrimination, with respect to spatial characters.

Od, or Odylic force: a hypothetical force, alleged to permeate all nature, and to manifest itself to certain sensitive individuals, as a kind of emanation of hot, cold, luminous, or coloured waves or rays.

Odour: sensation due to chemical stimulation of receptors in the mucous membrane of the nasal cavities; classified into nine classes by *Zwaardemaker* (q.v.), and more recently by *Henning* into six – fruity, flowery, spicy, resinous, scorching, putrid – these odours being placed, in his scheme, at the six angles of a triangular prism.

Oedipus complex: see *Edipus*.

Oestrus (-um): periodic heat or rut in female animals.

Ogive (Ogival curve): an S-shaped curve, by which cumulative frequencies of scores, etc. in a distribution can be represented.

Ohm's Law: the physical principle defining electrical resistance as the ratio of electromotive force to current, $R = E/C$; also the principle that a complex sound is analyzed by the ear into a series of simple tones, the frequencies of which correspond to the members of the *Fourier series*.

Olfactie: the unit of olfactory intensity; one *olfactie* is the intensity of the threshold stimulus tested by *Zwaardemaker's olfactometer*.

Olfactometer an arrangement, devised by *Zwaardemaker* (q.v.), for measuring thresholds for smell; it consists essentially of a glass tube, or tubes, fitting into the nostril, or nostrils, at the one end, and at the other end, fitting into a larger cylinder, containing the odorous substance, which itself is in tube form, and can be pushed over the inhaling tube to any desired extent, the exposed extent being measured by an attached scale.

Olfactory: referring or relating to smell.

Olfactory area: the area of the cerebral *cortex*, in which are located the centres for smell.

Olfactory bulb part of the olfactory area, projecting from it at the base of the *frontal lobe*.

Olfactory cells: the receptors for smell stimuli; spindle-shaped cells in the mucous membranes of the nasal cavities, really neurons, with a projection carrying hairs or bristles, on the surface of the mucous membrane.

Olfactory nerve: the first cranial nerve, connecting the olfactory cells with the olfactory region in the cerebrum.

Olivary bodies: raised regions on the anterior surface of the *medulla*.

Omen: a phenomenon supposed to foreshadow a future event, the two having no causal connection.

Ommatidium: one of the divisions of a *compound eye*.

Omnibus test: a type of *group intelligence test,* in which items of different kinds are mixed together in place of being arranged separately as in the *battery type* of test and there is one timing for the whole test.

Omnipotence of thought: a conviction that a mere wish is effective in producing the event; characteristic of the thinking of early childhood, the beliefs of primitive peoples, superstitious beliefs, and of the *obsessional neuroses,* which attach exaggerated and magical powers to thoughts or imaginations.

Onanism: masturbation.

On(e)irology: interpretation of dreams; the study of dreams.

Oneiromancy: divination by means of dreams; equivalent to older meaning of oneirology.

One-way screen: screen used in the observation of children and animals, made by close wire netting or thin cloth, brightly lighted on one side and dark on the other, and observed from the dark side.

Onomatomania: obsessive interest in words and names, frequently with the attaching of special significance to certain words.

Onomatopoeic theory of origin of language: theory of the earliest words in language being imitative words, or imitative sounds, derived from the sounds in nature, or made by animals.

Ontogenesis: the evolution and development of the individual, in contrast with *phylogenesis,* the origin and development of the race.

Ontogeny: virtually the same word and meaning, except that ontogeny refers rather to general problems of individual development, whereas ontogenesis refers to the development of a particular individual. Contrasted with *phylogeny*.

Ontology: that branch of metaphysics which concerns itself with the problem of the nature of existence or being.

Ontotropic: referring to the tendency of imagery, particularly *eidetic imagery,* to agree, with respect to content and colour, with natural objects.

Oogenesis: the development of the ovum or female sex cell.

Oogonium: botanically, the female organ in the lower cryptogams; also the original *germ cell* from which the female ovum is derived.

Ophthalmia: inflammation of the *conjunctiva,* or more generally of the superficial tissues of the eye.

Ophthalmometer: instrument for measuring the curvature of the *cornea* of the eye along different meridians, with a view to the determination of *astigmatism*.

Ophthalmometry: the determination of the optical constants of the eye.

Ophthalmoplegia: paralysis of the muscles of the eye.

Ophthalmoscope: an instrument for observing the retina and the interior of the eye, consisting essentially of a mirror with a hole in its centre for reflecting a beam of light through the pupil of the eye, and so enabling the observer to examine the interior of the eye.

Ophthalmotrope: an arrangement for demonstrating the movements of the two eyes, in which a series of strings functions in place of the eye muscles.

Opiumism: addiction to the use of opium, a drug derived from one of the poppies, of which the chief constituent is *morphine*.

Opposites test: a type of mental test in which the subject is required to give the opposites of the stimulus words.

Optic: referring or relating to vision, or to the organ of vision, or the science of light (optics).

Optic chiasma: see *chiasma*.

Optic disc: the head of the optic nerve as it appears in the *ophthalmoscope*.

Optic lobes: name given to the two upper *corpora quadrigemina*.

Optic thalamus: see *thalamus*.

Optic tract: group of nerve fibres passing from the *chiasma* to the *thalamus*.

Optical illusion: an illusion of vision; usually refers to an illusion affecting spatial relations, especially of the group designated the *geometrical optical illusions*.

Optical pendulum: an arrangement for presenting visual stimuli by means of a pendulum carrying a moving slit, which gives the necessary exposure.

Optical system: the parts of an optical instrument, inclusive of the eye, which have to do directly with the refraction (or reflection) of light.

Optimism: an attitude on the part of an individual towards life, or towards certain events, which tends, sometimes to an excessive extent, to dwell on the hopeful side; a philosophy of life, and of the universe, characterized by the view that 'this is the best of all possible worlds'.

Optometry: eye-measurement, as a science, and as a practice.

Oral: relating to the mouth; the *oral cavity*, the cavity of the mouth from the lips to the *pharynx*.

Oral erot(ic)ism: term used by psychoanalysts, with reference to the view of nursing at the breast as representing an early pre-genital stage of sexual development.

Oral neurosis: psychoanalytic term, applied to stammering, as representing unconscious motivation from the oral *libido*.

Oral sadism: psychoanalytic term, and interpretation, for the tendency in infants to introduce into the mouth, and suck or bite, objects.

Oral stage: psychoanalytic term for the infantile stage of psycho-sexual development.

Orbital: referring or relating to the eye cavities.

Ordinate: the vertical axis of reference of a curve, with reference to rectangular co-ordinates.

Orectic: referring to *orexis* (q.v.); organic processes initiating or stimulating orexis are sometimes termed *orectic processes*.

Orenda: in American Indian (Iroquois) religion, a word conveying very much the same idea as *mana* (q.v.).

Orexis: the conative and affective aspects of experience – impulse, appetite, desire, emotion.

Organ: (1) in the musical sense a wind and key instrument, producing the notes by series of pipes, or, in the American organ, by reeds; (2) a bodily structure performing a particular function.

Organ inferiority: defect in some organ or organs. See *inferiority.*

Organelle: an organ within a cell, or a part of a cell performing a particular function.

Organic: belonging to, or characteristic of, an organized structure – primarily body structure, but figuratively any structure.

Organic memory: alteration of living tissue, resulting from any activity in it, involving its functioning in any way, persisting as a condition modifying subsequent activity.

Organic psychosis: mental disorder involving, or based on, structural changes in the cerebral cortex.

Organic selection: influences in evolution, supplementing *natural selection,* arising from use or disuse in successive generations of particular slight functional or structural variations, which survive or disappear, because of such use or disuse, not because they have or have not survival value in themselves.

Organic sense: the sense or senses, associated with receptors within organs or tissues of the body, inclusive of *visceral, kinaesthetic,* and *pain* sensation, though sometimes restricted to the first of these.

Organism: an organized system of interrelated and interdependent parts, sharing a common life, and capable of maintaining its existence as a unitary system; usually applied to the living animal, or, figuratively, to the organized social group.

Organismic: relating or referring to organisms, as in *organismic psychology,* or an organismic point of view, where emphasis is placed upon the phenomena as phenomena in or of organisms.

Organization: differentiation of parts and functions, and integration into a systematic interconnected whole.

Organogenic: arising from the activity of a particular organ.

Organon: a body of principles, determining procedure in the acquiring, producing, and extending of knowledge, and the guidance of thinking; in effect a logic.

Orgasm: the culminating point in sexual intercourse; culmination of emotional excitement generally.

Orientation: two psychological senses: (1) awareness of one's spatial, temporal, practical, or circumstantial situation, with reference particularly to *mental orientation* in various connections; (2)

assuming a position in space, with reference to an external stimulation having direction, or an *orienting response,* as shown in the *tropism* and *taxis* of lower organisms.

Original nature: the sum total of the native or inherited characteristics of an organism.

Orthodox: in accordance with official or generally recognized principles.

Orthogenesis: the theory or view that evolution is not random, but directed along definite lines, irrespective of *natural selection.*

Orthognathous: used of a form of skull which does not show excessive protrusion of the jaw beyond the forehead; a facial angle of about 90 degrees.

Oscillation: o factor (q.v.).

Oscillator: for *audio-oscillator* (q.v.).

Oscillograph: an instrument of which there are various forms, for giving a record of the wave-forms of electrical oscillations.

Ossicles: minute bones; generally used for the auditory chain of small bones in the middle ear, consisting of the *malleus,* or hammer, the *incus,* or anvil, and the *stapes,* or stirrup.

Ostwald colours: a series of standard colours, with tints and shades.

Otoconia: otoliths (q.v.).

Otocyst: the vesicle developing into the ear in the embryo; sometimes used for *statocyst* (q.v.).

Otoliths: small solid particles – crystals of calcium carbonate – in the *endolymph* of the *utricle, saccule,* and *semi-circular canals* of the inner ear.

Otology: the science of the ear and its disorders.

Otosclerosis: a form of progressive deafness, due to hardening of the moving parts, particularly the chain of ossicles, in the auditory mechanism.

Ouija board: an apparatus, used by mediums to obtain spirit messages, consisting of a board with letters and numbers, etc., on it, and a traveller, moved involuntarily, the general principle being the same as that of an arrangement used in the psychological laboratory to study involuntary movement.

Ovary: the gland in the female which produces *ova.*

Over-: prefix meaning 'excessive' or 'beyond'.

Overcompensation: reaction in excess of the necessary amount, to allow for a tendency in himself in a certain direction, of which the subject has knowledge; also attempt to make up for a known defect, the attempt being determined sometimes by the *unconscious.*

Overdetermination: a psychoanalytic term used to signify the co-operation of more than one factor, or influence, in producing a neurotic symptom, where any one of the factors by itself would be sufficient; similarly an item or element in the *manifest dream content* may be, as it were, a meeting-place of more than one influence from the *latent dream thoughts*; the term is used somewhat differently by *Baudouin*, in connection with his view of affectively determined associations, where he argues that such associations are always determined also by some other associative bond.

Over-individual: term employed by some writers on *group psychology*, with reference to the contention that factors which are not of the individual mind must be considered in accounting for the behaviour of social groups.

Overlapping: employed in several connections: (1) of several factors affecting scores obtained in mental tests; (2) of distributions of scores obtained from two groups, falling partly within the same limits; (3) of responses, when a second is initiated before the first is completed. In all cases the meaning is essentially the same, of the partial coincidence in space or time of two separate things or events.

Over-learning: learning in which repetition or practice has proceeded beyond the point necessary for the retention or recall required; such over-learning may, however, be necessary in view of factors likely to affect recall, which are bound to enter subsequently from the circumstances of the case.

Overt response: any response that can be observed by another person.

Overtone: any one of the tonal elements present in a *clang*, except the fundamental.

Ovum: female germ cell; plural *ova*.

P

p factor: perseveration factor, a factor varying from individual to individual, which shows itself in a characteristic of mental process, analogous to inertia in the physical world, which affects especially the facility in turning from one activity to another, and therefore acts against the *o factor* (q.v.).

Pacini corpuscle: a type of receptor in the cutaneous surface, and within the joints, for touch sensations.

Paidophilia (Paedo- or Pedo-): love for children; often used in a pathological sense, of a form of sex perversion, or the tendency towards it (love for boys).

Pain: a definite sensation, not to be confused with unpleasant feeling. Some psychologists, to prevent confusion, prefer to use the term *unpleasure,* as the opposite of pleasure.

Pain sense: a special, or preferably 'organic', sense, found in all parts of the body, free nerve endings being the supposed receptors; points can be localized in the skin especially sensitive to pain stimuli, which are usually called *pain spots.*

Paired associates: materials used in certain types of learning experiments, where words or nonsense syllables are presented in pairs, and the learning is tested by presenting the first member of each pair, to which the subject is asked to reply with the second. See *scoring method.*

Paired comparison: one of the *methods of impression* (q.v.), employed in the experimental investigation of feeling; also employed to determine an individual's preferences, as for colours. The principle of the method is to present each item with every other item, in chance order – and each pair in each spatial order – and determine the order of preference by the number of preferences given to each item.

Palaeoencephalon: the most primitive parts of the brain, i.e. those appearing earliest in the course of evolution.

Palaeopsychology: the investigation of primitive features of mentality, persisting from a previous stage of evolution.

Palingenesis: the stages in the development of the individual, so far as they present an epitome of the stages in the evolution of the species or race.

Pallaesthesia: (sometimes palmaesthesia); sensitivity to vibration, especially in regions of prominent bones.

Pallium: the cortical layer of the forebrain. See *neopallium.*

Palmar: referring to or located in the palm of the hand.

Palmistry: an attempt to read character from the lines on the palm of the hand; as a branch of *cheiromancy,* the attempt to predict the future on this basis.

Palp, palpate: to touch lightly with the fingers; to examine by the sense of touch, as a method of medical diagnosis.

Palpable: directly observable; easily perceived.

Palpedral: referring to, or located in, the eyelids.

Palpitation: rapid and strong action of the heart.

Panasilinic telegraph: telegraphic communication by means of the rapport of two snails – a hoax perpetrated in the early days of the electric telegraph, and still used as an illustration of credulity.

Pancreas: a large internal gland, situated near the stomach, part of which secretes gastric juices, and part with an *endocrine* function, secreting substances, particularly *insulin,* which regulate *metabolism. See islands of Langerhans.*

Pangenesis: a speculative theory, propounded originally by *Darwin,* and modified by von Kries, to account for heredity, based on the assumption of the existence of small organic units, named *gemmules* by Darwin, and *pangens* by von Kries.

Panmixia: unrestricted interbreeding between members of various species.

Panpsychism: the metaphysical theory that the real is ultimately psychic, or of the nature of mind.

Panum phenomenon: if two parallel lines near together are presented to one eye, and a single line parallel to them to the other eye, and then the single line is stereoscopically combined with either of the other two, the result is the experience of two lines in different planes, i.e. at different apparent distances, the apparently nearer being that of the combination.

Papillae: small elevations found associated with various sense receptors: in the tongue (*lingual*), as the *circumvallate, foliate, fungiform,* and *filiform* papillae, the first three containing *taste buds,* and the last without taste buds, but probably functioning as receptors for touch; in the skin (*tactile*), containing touch receptors; in the inner ear of lower vertebrates (*acoustic*), becoming the *organ of Corti* in higher vertebrates.

Papilloedema: swelling of *optic disc,* usually due to brain lesion.

Papillitis: inflammatory condition of the *optic disc,* due to pathological condition in the optic nerve; to be distinguished from *papilloedema,* which is non-inflammatory.

Para- (Gr.): prefix with the usual meaning of 'deviating from normal', or the more literal meaning 'beside'.

Parabiosis: partial fusion of two animals, with resulting mutual physiological influence; temporary cessation of functioning of a nerve.

Paracentral gyrus: convulution on the middle surface of the hemispheres, and round the upper end of the *central fissure.*

Paracentral vision: vision with the area of the retina just outside of the *fovea.*

Paracusis: anomalous apparent increase of acuity of hearing, generally agreed to be illusory, when there is in addition a noise, and to occur only in the case of individuals who are partially deaf to low tones, because of the fact that those who speak to them raise their voices to overcome the noise.

Paradox: a statement apparently involving inconsistency; or a phenomenon involving conflict with what might have been expected.

Paradoxical cold: a sensation of cold, obtained with a rod at about 43 degrees Centigrade, when a cold spot is stimulated.

Paradoxical warmth: sensation of warmth, with a stimulus about 30 degrees Centigrade, normally a cold stimulus.

Paraesthesia: abnormal, distorted, or wrongly localized sensation.

Parageusia: distorted taste sensation, or a taste *hallucination*.

Paragraphia: the insertion of unintended and wrong words in what is being written, as a result of pathological cortical conditions.

Parakinesis: term employed in *psychical research*, with the assumption or suggestion of supernormal forces, for *levitation* with mere contact.

Paralalia: form of *dyslalia*, involving the distortion of speech sounds, as in *lisping*.

Paralexia: the misreading of words and phrases, as a result of a pathological cortical condition.

Parallax: one of the conditions upon which the perception of relative distance depends, when movement at right angles to the line of vision alters the relative position of two unequally distant objects; also of a similar difference in point of view between the two eyes, when the distance between the eyes is of significance, relative to the distance of the objects.

Parallel Law: a psychophysical principle, formulated by *Fechner*, to the effect that the sensed ratio of the difference between two stimuli remains constant with diminished sensitivity, as a result of long-continued exposure of the receptors to the stimuli.

Parallel movements: movements of the eyeballs, in which convergence and divergence do not play any part, as in looking at distant objects.

Parallelism: a shortened form of '*psycho-physical parallelism*', a theory, or a working hypothesis, regarding the relation between brain process and mental process, to the effect that they vary concomitantly, without either affecting the other; factually equivalent to the double-aspect theory of *Spinoza*, or the pre-established harmony theory of Leibniz, interpreted psychologically.

Paralogia: a form of *dyslogia*, where there is difficulty in the expression of ideas in speech, and consequent illogicality or irrelevance.

Paralogism: a piece of false reasoning, the reasoner being unaware of the fallacy; unintentional and unconscious fallacy.

Paralysis: impairment or loss of motor function, due to disorder in some part of the neuro-muscular mechanism; also used of impairment or loss of sensory function.

Paralysis agitans: a disorder, usually of senility, characterized by tremor, delay of muscular contraction and movement, with unusual position of head and limbs. *Parkinson's disease.*

Paralytic dementia: see *paresis.*

Paramoecium: one of the ciliate protozoa, shaped somewhat like a cigar, studied by *Jennings* (q.v.), and frequently referred to as an illustration of the difficulty of accounting for the behaviour, even of protozoa, without assuming factors of the psychological order.

Parameter: mathematically, a constant occurring in the equation of a curve, by the variation of which the equation can represent a whole family of such curves; psychologically, used of any of the constants in *learning,* or growth curves, which differ with conditions, subjects, material, etc.

Paramnesia: distortion or falsification of memory or recognition. See *déjà vu.*

Paranoia: mental disorder, characterized by persistent *delusions,* often with *hallucinations.*

Paranoid dementia: mental disorganization, with systematized *delusion* formation.

Paranosic: term used by psychoanalysts for the primary advantage derived from an illness.

Paraphasia: insertion habitually of wrong words in speaking, usually of pathological origin; term sometimes used of normal individuals incidentally introducing wrong words in speaking.

Paraphemia: psychoneurotic employment of wrong sounds in speaking; neurotic lisping.

Paraphonia: morbid changes of voice.

Paraphrenia: general term inclusive of *paranoia* and *schizophrenia.*

Paraplegia: paralysis of the lower limbs.

Parapraxis: general term, inclusive of slips of the tongue and pen, errors in action, forgettings, and the like, resulting from faulty mental functioning; attributed by psychoanalysts to the expression of unconscious wishes.

Parapsychology: see *metapsychics.*

Parasympathetic: term applied to cranial and sacral parts of the *autonomic nervous system.*

Parataxis: maladjustment, especially with respect to emotions, a term suggested by T. V. Moore.

Parathyroid: term applied to four small bodies situated on the two lateral lobes of the *thyroid* (q.v.).

Paresis: applied generally to incomplete paralysis; specially, and most frequently, employed of the various results of *syphilitic infection* of the cerebral cortex, without the involving of other parts of the cerebro-spinal system.

Parietal: referring to lobe of cerebrum, between *frontal* and *occipital* lobes, and above the *temporal.*

Parisian line: a unit of measurement, employed in Weber's time, equal to 2.25 mm.

Parotid gland: the largest salivary gland in man, situated in front of the ear.

Parsimony Law: see *economy principle.*

Parthenogenesis: development of a new organism from an unfertilized ovum.

Partial activity: see *piecemeal activity.*

Partial correlation: see *correlation.*

Partial colour-blindness: see *colour-blindness.*

Partial tone: see *overtone.*

Particular complex: psychoanalytic term for a *complex* based, not on one of the fundamental instincts (universal), but on some circumstance or event incidental to the life history of an individual.

Particulate inheritance: term suggested by *Galton* for a type of inheritance shown by offspring presenting something of a mosaic of characteristics from both parents, which do not fuse or blend.

Part-whole test: a type of association experiment or test, where the subject is required to specify the whole of which the name of a part is presented.

Passion: used by the older writers for emotion in general, but now reserved for violent emotional outbreaks.

Passive: being acted upon, rather than acting; inactively showing the result of external influences.

Passivity feelings: delusional feelings of being acted upon by various forces or influences, electrical, hypnotic, etc., characteristic particularly of *schizophrenia.*

Past-pointing: the method of testing the normal response to rotation of a subject who has been rotated, in which he tends to point with his finger at a point past that indicated by the finger of the experimenter.

Pastoral stage: a stage in the development of civilization, between the hunting stage and the agricultural stage, when the form of culture consisted in the keeping of herds and flocks.

Patellar reflex: the knee jerk; reflex produced by blow just below the patella, or knee-cap, with the leg relaxed and bent at the knee, which is normally an upward kick, caused by the contraction of the *quadriceps* muscle.

Pathogenesis: the development of a disease or of a morbid condition.

Pathography: the study of *personality* in the light of the disorders and ailments from which an individual suffers or has suffered.

Pathological lying: a tendency to relate, sometimes very circumstantially, without apparent motive, imaginary tales as true, characteristic of some types of mental disorder. Cf. *Korsakow syndrome.*

Pathology: branch of biological or medical science, which concerns itself with abnormal and diseased conditions in organisms.

Pathoneurosis: a *neurosis* following on disease or injury, and interpreted psychoanalytically as withdrawal from the external world and concentration on the diseased or injured part, on the part of the *libido.*

Pathophobia: morbid fear, or rather dread, of suffering or disease.

Pattern: functional union, operating as a whole, of distinguishable parts.

Pavlov's experiment: the experiment, or series of experiments, associated with Pavlov's name, consisting in diverting, through an external fistula, a dog's flow of saliva, so that it could be observed and measured, then studying the phenomena of the conditioning of the salivary reflex by this means.

P.E.: probable error.

Peacock: a blue-green colour; *cyan* blue.

Peccatophobia: morbid fear of sinning or having sinned.

Pecking experiment: experimental investigation of the pecking of newly or recently hatched chicks, in the study of the relationship between *maturation* and *learning.*

Pedagogical psychology (experimental pedagogy): see *educational psychology.*

Pederasty: a form of homosexual sex perversion.

Peduncle: a band of nerve fibres passing into a large organ in the brain. See *crura cerebri.*

Peking man: an early form of man, represented by remains found near Peking; closely related to *Neanderthal man.*

Pelagic: employed of organisms living near the surface of the sea, far from shore.

Pellagra: a nutritional skin disease, often involving mental depression.

Pendulum: a body swinging freely from a fixed suspension point; used for many purposes in psychological investigation; the *control pendulum* is a large pendulum swinging between contacts, and released and stopped by electromagnets, employed for the calibration of chronoscopes, and other purposes; *Chevreul's pendulum* is a small bob, suspended by a thread, the end of which is held in the hand, with outstretched arm, when it functions as an *autoscope* (q.v.), and, as the *pendule explorateur,* is used in psychical research to answer questions, etc.

Pendulum chronoscope: a chronoscope for measuring short time intervals, based on a pendulum, of which there are several forms. One of the earliest chronoscopes devised for psychological experiments was Sanford's *Vernier Chronoscope,* where two pendulums are employed, with slightly different known periods of swing, the first related by the stimulus, the second by the response, and counting the number of swings till the two swings are together gives a basis for calculating the reaction time; Helmholtz's *pendulum myograph* may also be employed, with a tuning fork to give a time scale, and an electromagnetic marker, the pendulum being released and stopped by electromagnets; the best known pendulum chronoscope is probably the *Bergström,* where the stimulus is arranged to free the pendulum, and the response to stop it, and a scale is provided, with a marker or pointer.

Penology: the scientific study of the problems of legal punishment.

Pentatonic scale: musical scale divided into five intervals. See *scale.*

Percentile rank: statistically, an indication of the position of a value or a score, in a series arranged in order of magnitude, by the percentage of the values or scores falling at or below that position.

Percentile curve: a curve, the ordinate of which gives percentiles, and the abscissa, the scores; for normal distribution an *ogive* or S-curve.

Percentile scale: a scale giving percentiles for each score.

Percept: the mental product of the act of perceiving; the mental modification which comes into existence when we perceive; must not be confused with the thing perceived.

Perception: the process of becoming immediately aware of something; usually employed of sense perception, when the thing of which we become immediately aware is the object affecting a sense organ; when that object is recognized or identified in any way perception passes into *apperception.*

Perception time: the time which elapses between the presentation of the object, and the indication by the subject, say by naming it, that he has perceived it.

Percipient: generally the person perceiving; used in *psychical research* for the person receiving a telepathic message.

Performance test: a type of mental test in which the subject is asked to do something, rather than to say something, the use of language being greatly reduced, if not entirely eliminated; the type of test which throws light on the ability to deal with things, rather than symbols – concrete intelligence.

Perilymph: one of the fluids in the inner ear, external to the sac in which the *endolymph*, the other fluid, is contained.

Perimeter: a form of apparatus for mapping the retinal field (for colours), consisting essentially of an arm or moving part, which can be rotated about an axis on the line of vision, the rotation being in a plane at right angles to the line of vision, this arm carrying the stimulus, which in turn can be moved so as to be presented at any angle to the line of vision, and in all directions from the fovea. The mapping of the retina in this way is known as *perimetry*. Cf. *campimetry*.

Periodic: mathematically, of a function which repeats the same values at regular intervals, as the variable increases or decreases uniformly; used also of a *psychosis*, or mental disorder, which recurs or passes through different phases at more or less regular intervals.

Peripheral: a relative term, the opposite of *central*, applied to the surface of any organ or of the body as a whole, central, in the latter case, meaning in, or towards, the cerebro-spinal axis; in the case of the retina peripheral means away from the *fovea; periphery* bears the same relative meaning in the noun form.

Peripheral nerve: any nerve directly connecting receptors or effectors with the cerebro-spinal axis; and *peripheral nervous system,* the totality of these nerves.

Peristalsis: wave-like contractions which propel its contents along the alimentary canal.

Peristomial: referring to, or located in, the region about the mouth in invertebrates.

Pernicious trend: term employed by psychoanalysts for indications in an individual's thinking – of marked *regression* from normal modes of thought to an earlier pregenital stage, exhibited in *schizophrenia*.

Persecution delusion: symptom of mental disorder, or tendency towards mental disorder, where an individual interprets lack of success on his part, frustrations, and, in more extreme cases, his own experiences, often imaginary, and his feelings of an unpleasant colouring or character, to working or plotting against him on the part of others. See *projection*.

Perseveration: primarily, the tendency of an impression to leave an influence on subsequent experience, which dies down slowly, but at different rates with different people (see *secondary function*); following from this primary meaning, the tendency of an idea, feeling, or mode of activity to recur after we have had the original experience, this tendency being stronger in inverse proportion to the time that has elapsed, this being a factor which may determine recall or *reinstatement*, independently of association.

Person: an individual human being, with individual characteristics, and unique social relationships.

Persona: term employed by *Jung*, in contrast to *anima*, to express the 'function-complex' which determines an individual's reactions with reference to an object or situation.

Personal equation: historically, a time disagreement between two equally competent observers observing and recording the same astronomical event, attributed, before experimental analysis had thrown light on the phenomena, to personal characteristics of the observer; subsequently found to be due to several factors, the most important being the direction of attention. See *complication experiment*.

Personal identity: psychologically, the sense or feeling of being the same person, based mainly on *common sensibility* and continuity of aims, purposes, and memories.

Personalism: the emphasizing of the *person* as central in philosophy and psychology.

Personality: a term used in various senses, both popularly and psychologically, the most comprehensive and satisfactory being the integrated and dynamic organization of the physical, mental, moral, and social qualities of the individual, as that manifests itself to other people, in the give and take of social life; on further analysis it would appear in the main to comprise the natural and acquired impulses, and habits, interests, and complexes, the sentiments and ideals, the opinions and beliefs, as manifested in his relations with his social milieu; *dual* and *multiple personality*, where these elements are organized into separate and different systems, afford the clearest evidence of the constituent elements in the personality; in such cases the more stable and normal system or phase is spoken of as the *primary personality*, the other systems or phases as *dissociated* or *secondary personalities*.

Personality types: attempted classifications of individuals according to the different aspects of their make-up or the response patterns in their behaviour, which are prominent; the best known of such classifications is that of *Jung,* according to direction of interest, into *extraverts* and *introverts*: all such classifications, however, tend to take as types what are really extreme deviations in one direction or another from the general, normal, or average man; most of them are also classifications of *temperaments* (q.v.), rather than of personalities.

Personation: assuming for some purpose the identity of another person.

Personal document analysis: the analysis of personal documents such as diaries, letters, literary works in order to obtain insight into the personalities of which they are the products.

Personalistic psychology (*personalistics*): emphasis upon the personal world of the individual as a point of departure in the study of his experience and behaviour.

Personification: attributing, seriously or figuratively, personal characteristics and qualities to inanimate objects, or to the various forces and phenomena of nature.

Personnel: the staff or body of employees of a factory, business, or institution.

Personnel management: the supervision of the selection, training, placement, promotion, etc., of the personnel of an undertaking or institution.

Personnel research: the study of the human being in relation to his occupation, and the conditions, physical and social, under which the occupation must be carried on, inclusive of the various problems with which *personnel management* is faced.

Personology: sometimes employed to cover the study of the various aspects of *personality,* as a distinct branch of psychology.

Perspective: the appearance presented by visible objects with respect to relative position, apparent distance, etc.; the perception of visible objects, in their relative magnitudes, positions, and distances; sometimes used figuratively of the appreciation of the relative importance of principles, ideas, events, etc.; *aerial* or *atmospheric perspective* is the name given to the part played by light and shade, and atmospheric phenomena generally, in visual space perception, particularly with respect to distance or depth; *binocular perspective* and *monocular perspective* refer respectively to the various phenomena, so far as they appear in vision with both eyes, or with one eye, with respect particularly to depth or distance, in both cases (see *depth perception*); *temporal perspective* is a transference by analogy of the notion to the memory of events and their relative position in time.

Perspicacity: acute or clear understanding.

Perspicuity: great clearness of statement or expression.

Persuasion: the process or art of influencing, or seeking to influence, an individual's opinions and actions, ostensibly by reasoning or intellectual appeal, though depending for its effectiveness in most cases on non-rational factors.

Perturbation: a disturbed and unpleasant emotional state, usually with some mental confusion.

Perversion: distortion away from the real end or purpose; specifically of a pathological deviation from normal behaviour, more particularly in sex habits. An individual manifesting perversion, particularly sex, is called a *pervert*.

Pessimism: an attitude towards life, or philosophy of life, expressing itself in the view that it is better not to be than to be, or that man is born to misfortune.

Petit mal: (*Fr.*) a type of epilepsy, where there is merely a brief lapse of consciousness, often, however, with progressive mental degeneration.

Phakoscope (Phaco-): an instrument for observing changes in the accommodation of the lens, by means of reflected images from its surfaces.

Phallic phase: according to psychoanalysts, a belief in early childhood that a phallus is a normal possession of both sexes.

Phallus: an image of the male generative organ, venerated in various religions as a symbolic representation of the generative power in nature.

Phantasm: a subjective visual presentation of forms or absent persons, or what is taken for a disembodied spirit.

Phantasy: a form of creative imaginative activity, where the images and trains of imagery are directed and controlled by the whim or pleasure of the moment.

Pharynx: the cavity behind the nose and mouth opening into the *larynx* and *oesophagus*.

Phase: the value, at a definite moment, of a magnitude, varying periodically with reference to one of its values chosen as starting point; psychologically, applied mainly to sound waves, two of which are said to be in phase when the displacement of any point and the direction of its movement in one are similar to the displacement and direction of movement of the corresponding point in the other; in opposite phases when the displacements are the same but the movement in opposite directions, or when any point in one attains its maximum displacement in one direction at the same moment as the corresponding point in the other attains its maximum displacement in the opposite direction.

Pheno-motives: motives of which the individual is conscious, defined by Stern as 'anticipatory ideas of goals antecedent to voluntary action'.

Phenomenalism: the philosophical view that human knowledge is confined to phenomena, and never attains to the real nature of things.

Phenomenology: the systematic investigation of conscious experience as experience, regarded as the true method of approach to psychology.

Phenomenon: a possible datum, or group of data, of experience at any moment.

Phi-gamma function: an *ogive* or S-shaped curve, plotted for a normal probability (or *normal distribution*) curve, on the basis of *cumulative frequencies*, assumed as the basis for the calculation of thresholds in the *Method of right and wrong cases* (q.v.). See *percentile curve*.

Phi-phenomenon: the movement aspect of objects perceived in motion, or the impression of movement, as given by presenting two objects in quick succession in two different but neighbouring positions.

Philosophy: the branch of learning which investigates the ultimate nature of existence, of knowledge, and of the good – comprising ontology, epistemology, and ethics, and at one time – not very remote – inclusive also of psychology.

Phlegmatic: one of the four classical *temperaments*, characterized by sluggishness and emotional coldness; sometimes called also *lymphatic*.

Phobia: dread, or uncontrollable fear, generally of a morbid or even pathological character, of some object or situation.

Phon(o)- (Gr.): prefix meaning 'sound'.

Phonation: production of sounds by voice.

Phonautograph: instrument for recording graphically sound waves, consisting essentially of a stylus or lever attached to a membrane, which vibrates with the sound, while the stylus records on a smoked drum.

Phoneidoscope: instrument for making sound waves available for visual observation by reflection of a beam of light from a soap film in the path of the sound.

Phonelescope: instrument for observation, and also measurement, and photographic record, of sound waves, consisting essentially of a telephone receiver, to the diaphragm of which a thread is attached, carrying a mirror, which reflects a beam of light on a drum or photographic film.

Phonetics: the branch of science which investigates vocal sounds.

Phonodeik: an instrument for recording or projecting sound waves with greater accuracy and sensitivity than either the *phonautograph* or the *phonelescope,* the latter of which it resembles in principle.

Phonometer: an instrument for measuring auditory acuity. See *audiometer.*

Phonophobia: morbid fear of speaking aloud.

Phonoprojectoscope (Phonoscope): instruments and arrangements of various kinds, for allowing of the visual observation of sound waves.

Phoria: a suffix sometimes used as a word, in the sense of *muscle balance* of the eye muscles.

Phorometry: measurement of the degree of imbalance of eye muscles.

Phosphene: bright area or ring in the field of vision produced by pressure on the eyeball.

Phot(o)- (Gr.): prefix meaning 'light'.

Photerythrous: referring to the brightness or visibility of the red end of the spectrum, which is characteristic of the *deuteranope* (q.v.), of partial colour-blindness.

Photism: hallucination of bright light; also used of a form of *synaesthesia* (q.v.), in which a visual perception of colour is apparently attached to certain sensations from other sense departments, notably hearing.

Photochemical: employed of substances in which chemical changes are produced by light, or of the chemical changes, with particular reference to such substances and such chemical changes in the retina.

Photochromatic interval: the interval between the threshold for light perception, and the threshold for colour, with respect to stimulus intensity, extensity, or duration; with low values for these a colour stimulus may give only a light sensation.

Photo-electric cell: a delicate instrument for detecting and measuring faint light. See *photometer* and *selenium cell.*

Photographic observation dome: an enclosure arranged for the observation of infants, the walls of which are provided with *one-way vision screens,* and adjustable cameras, and other recording apparatus inside the enclosure.

Photokinesis: activity in certain lower organisms produced by light.

Photokymograph: a camera for recording movements, as of the eyes in reading, either by photographing shadows of moving pointers or reflected beams from moving surfaces.

Photoma: visual hallucination of flashes or sparks of light.

Photometer: any optical arrangement for measuring light intensity, the simple forms usually depending on equating with known brightness, as in *grease spot,* or *shadow* photometer, or on *flicker* phenomena.

Photon: unit of visual effect of light, defined as the illumination on the retina from a surface brightness of one candlepower per square metre, seen through a pupil of area of one square millimetre.

Photophobia: avoidance of use of eyes in strong light, as in albinos and the totally colour-blind; morbid dread of strong light.

Photopic vision: daylight vision; more specifically vision under such conditions of illumination as make possible the discrimination of colours.

Photoreceptor: receptor specially adapted to respond to *radiant energy* of wave-lengths within the band of the visible spectrum.

Phototropism (-taxis): orienting responses to light.

Phrenology: by derivation, science of the brain or mind; used for the system of doctrines developed by *Gall* and *Spurzheim,* the characteristic tenets of which were that the brain consists of a number of organs, corresponding to the various faculties of the mind, that the size of an organ is the measure of its power, and that it is possible to determine mental characteristics and capacities by observation of the prominence of areas on the external surface of the skull; at first called *craniology* and later practised as *cranioscopy.*

Phrictopathetic sensations: term employed of tactual sensations, indefinitely localized, and of tingling and peculiarly irritating character.

Phylogenesis: origin and evolution of races or species; the term *phylogeny* is used with practically the same meaning, except that it is rather more concrete.

Phylum: one of the general divisions of the animal kingdom.

Physical anthropology: the study of man's place in nature, with respect to his physical structure.

Physico-social: employed with reference to social relations, so far as these are determined by the physical environment.

Physiognomy: the principles according to which the capacities and characteristics of an individual can be determined from the features of the face, or from the form and structure of the body generally; sometimes taken as identical with, and sometimes as inclusive of, *phrenology.*

Physiological age: rating, on the analogy of *mental age,* of an individual, on the basis of a scale determined by the condition of important physiological systems – vascular system, reproductive system, etc. – averaged for unselected groups of different chronological ages.

Physiological gradient: line of increasing or decreasing vital activity or *metabolism.*

Physiological limit: usually the maximum speed or efficiency attainable in a motor act, or series of acts, because of the physiological nature of the neuromuscular mechanisms involved.

Physiological psychology: historically, equivalent to experimental psychology; now used mostly of the borderland between psychology and neurology.

Physiological time: time taken for a stimulus to produce its excitatory effect on a receptor – *latent time* – plus the time taken for the propagation of the nerve impulse from receptor to centre, and again from centre to effector, as a total to be deducted from a reaction time, to give the time for the central process to take place – the *reduced reaction time* (q.v.).

Physiology: the branch of biological science which investigates the functioning of the different parts, structures, and organs in a living organism.

Physique: general body structure.

Pia mater: the closely fitting innermost membrane, covering the brain and spinal cord; often abbreviated to *pia.*

Pictograph (pictogram): a drawing representing an object or idea, as an element in a non-verbal, graphic form of language; characteristic of the earliest forms of written language, and sometimes used still as a form of puzzle – *rebus.*

Picture completion test: a type of intelligence test in which the subject is required to find the missing parts in a picture, or series of pictures, all the missing parts being of the same shape, and mixed with other picture fragments, also of the same shape; a performance form of the *completion test.* Must not be confused with the *dissected picture test.*

Picture interpretation test: a type of intelligence test in which the subject is required to say what a picture is about, the grade of mentality being assessed according to the nature of the response – enumeration, description, interpretation.

Piecemeal activity: the designation proposed by *Thorndike* for a subsidiary principle of animal learning, to the effect that a part or aspect of a situation may come to be connected with a response, with ignoring of some or all of the other parts, so that the response may still be given when these other parts are altered; also called *partial activity.*

Pigment layer: the layer next the *rods and cones* in the retina; the first layer, the *rods and cones* layer being the second.

Piltdown man: one of the earliest types of man, represented by a skull found at Piltdown in England; also known as Sussex man.

Pineal body or gland: epiphysis cerebri; a small glandular body, which may have an *endocrine* function in early childhood, but in some of the lower vertebrates is a third median eye; situated in the midbrain projecting backwards above the *corpora quadrigemina*; according to Descartes the location of the soul, or the point at which it was in contact with the body.

Pinna: the *auricle* or external ear.

Piston recorder: an instrument for the graphical recording of pulse, etc., where a piston in a cylinder takes the place of the ordinary tambour.

Pitch: a characteristic of tone sensations, arranging them in a series from low to high, and at least to some extent differentiating them from *noises,* which if they have this characteristic at all do not have it in any marked degree, except in so far as they involve tonal components. What is known as *standard pitch* is the pitch of a tone selected as standard for the tuning of musical instruments. There are several recognized standards; the *scientific* or *philosophical pitch standard* is a middle C of 256 vibrations per second; the standard for *concert pitch* is an A of about 450 vibrations, and of *international pitch* an A of 415. In the actual tuning of musical instruments, as well as for giving a keynote for singing, a *tuning* or *pitch fork* of C or A is used, or as an alternative a *pitch pipe* containing a reed. Individuals who have an accurate memory for pitch and can reproduce any note specified are said to have *absolute pitch.*

Pithecanthropus (erectus): an extinct ape, closely resembling the human being or *Homo sapiens,* identified and represented by a skull found in Java.

Pithecoid: resembling a monkey or ape.

Pithiatism: hysteria (q.v.); also the treatment of nervous disorders by *persuasion.*

Pituitary gland: hypophysis cerebri; an *endocrine gland* in the skull, connected with the *thalamus* under the cerebral hemispheres, and secreting at least two important *hormones* (q.v.) playing a part in development, structural and sexual.

Placido's disc: a white disc with concentric black circles, and an aperture in the centre, by means of which the reflection of the disc in the cornea can be observed, employed for the observation of irregularities in the surface of the *cornea.*

Planchette: a board which may be suspended above, or rest on, a smooth surface, provided with a style or pencil, for marking on paper on the surface, employed for the recording of involuntary movement, to obtain automatic writing, or for very much the same purposes as the *ouija board.*

Planimeter: an instrument for measuring the area of an irregularly shaped plane figure.

Plantar reflex: flexion of toes produced by softly stroking the sole of the foot. Cf. *Babinski reflex.*

Plastic art: production of art objects by moulding, modelling, or carving.

Plastic: capable of progressive change, in adaptation to changing conditions; employed of *responses, images,* etc.

Plasticity: the characteristic of being *plastic;* an important characteristic of an organism's responses, so far as they are modifiable to meet changing conditions, and, in the case of the human being so far as such modification is under control; also an important characteristic of images, especially *eidetic images* (q.v.).

Plateau: a temporary halt in progress, and flattening of the learning curve, in the process of acquiring a complex piece of skill, involving habits and skills of different orders, such as learning to play a musical instrument, to use a typewriter, or to speak a foreign language.

Platonic affection: friendship between two individuals of different sexes, apparently independent of sex attraction.

Platykurtic: see *kurtosis.*

Play: activity, physical or mental, existing apparently for its own sake, or having for the individual as its main aim the pleasure which the activity itself yields; usually involving also a detachment from serious aims and ends, involving a measure of *dissociation.*

Pleasantness – unpleasantness: the two *polarities* of simple feeling; one of the three dimensions of feeling according to *Wundt's tridimensional theory* (q.v.); the *hedonic tone* of experience.

Pleasure – pain: see *pleasantness – unpleasantness.*

Pleasure principle: the tendency inherent in all natural impulses or 'wishes' to seek their own satisfaction independently of all other considerations; according to Freudian theory the principle ruling the individual at the start, and remaining always as the guiding principle in the *unconscious.*

Plethysmograph: an apparatus for recording variations in the volume of different parts of the body.

Plexus: a network of nerve fibres, outside the central nervous system, and usually forming part of the *autonomic* system, and occurring in the regions of the main internal organs.

Pluralism: a system of philosophy, which holds, as against *monism*, that the ultimate reality of the universe consists of a plurality of entities – atoms, monads, or persons – for example, the philosophy of *Leibniz.*

Pluralistic behaviour: a type of response to a specific stimulus situation, exhibited universally by the members of a group or species; the term *multi-individual behaviour* was later preferred by the originator of the term.

Pneumograph: an apparatus or arrangement for recording the breathing by means of a recording tambour.

Pneumo-dynamograph: a *dynamograph* for the recording of air pressure produced by breathing.

Pneumophonia: a voice with the sound of the breathing prominent in it.

Poggendorff illusion: one of the *geometrical optical illusions*, produced by an oblique line passing, at an acute angle, as if below two parallel lines, when the two parts of the oblique line do not seem to be in the same straight line.

Point of regard: see *regard.*

Point of subjective equality: that value of a variable which will be judged equal to the stimulus more frequently than any other point or value; or the point where the curve of 'greater' judgments intersects the curve of 'less' judgments; or the point midway between the upper and lower *thresholds.*

Point scale: a method of arranging and scoring a series of mental tests, which gives as its result a number of points for an individual, from which, by reference to a table of norms, his exact status is determined, in terms of mental age, I.Q., or *percentile rank;* the same test material as in the *Binet scale* may be used, but the scoring is not on a pass or fail basis, but on a certain number of assigned points for credit or partial credit in each test, e.g. the *Yerkes-Bridges Point Scale*.

Polarity: characteristic of a phenomenon which varies between opposites, e.g. feeling between pleasant and unpleasant, or emotion between joy and sorrow.

Poltergeist: popular term for an alleged spiritistic manifestation, which is characterized by throwing things about, and mischievous pranks of various sorts.

Poly- (Gr.): prefix meaning 'many'.

Polyandry: marriage between one woman and several men.

Polydactylism: the possessing of extra fingers or toes.

Polygamy: marriage of one man to two or more women, or of one woman to two or more men.

Polygraph: apparatus for recording simultaneously, and side by side, a number of processes, such as pulse, breathing time, etc.

Polygyny: marriage between one man and several women.

Polylogia: continuous, and usually incoherent, talking.

Polymorphism: the occurrence of several types of individual organism, or animal, in the same colony or community, and derived from the same parent.

Polymorphous perverse: term applied by psychoanalysts to the sexuality of the young child, and also to the sexuality of the sexually perverse adult who exhibits the same varieties of sexual perversion.

Polyneuritis: simultaneous inflammation in several nerves.

Polyopia: the formation of several images of an object on one retina, owing to irregularities in the refracting media.

Polyphony: music in two or more parts.

Polytypic: term applied to evolution resulting in the appearance of divergent types.

Pons varolii: part of the hind brain, consisting of a broad band of nerve fibres, arching across the *medulla*, on the opposite side from the *cerebellum*.

Pornography: literature dealing with the obscene.

Porter's Law: the law that the critical frequency for the abolition of flicker – that is, the rate at which flicker is just abolished – in rotating discs varies as the logarithm of the brightness of the stimulus, and independently of wave-length.

Positive after-image: see *after-image*.

Positive and negative cases: see *right and wrong cases method*.

Positive self-feeling: feeling of satisfaction at securing recognition from others.

Positive transference: see *transfer of training*.

Positive Tropism (Taxis): an orienting response, where the organism turns or moves towards the source of the stimulation, or disposes itself in the direction of the stimulation and towards the source from which it comes.

Positivism: type of philosophical thought which limits knowledge to the facts of experience, and refuses to embark on speculation regarding the ultimate nature of things.

Post-epileptic stupor: a comatose, or semi-conscious, condition, following upon an epileptic seizure.

Post-hypnotic suggestion: a *suggestion* given an individual in the hypnotic state to perform an act after coming out of the state, usually on a signal being given; when the suggestion operates, the subject may pass again temporarily into a hypnotic state while he performs the act, or he may perform it consciously, because, he says, 'he can't get any peace till he does it' – a *compulsive idea*.

Postulate: a principle which is provisionally adopted, without any evidence being offered; a presupposition upon which an argument, etc., may depend.

Postural: related to *posture* (q.v.); term employed of the totality of the *reflexes* which together maintain the body in a given attitude, or of *experiments* involving posture.

Posture: general attitude or position of the body as a whole.

Potency: usually employed generally, of latent power; in a special sense, of sexual efficacy.

Potential: as an adjective, referring to latent power not manifest at the moment.

Practice: repetition in learning to perform some act, or to acquire some skill.

Practice curve: a graphic representation of the progress in performance, based on the accomplishment at regular intervals.

Practice limit: the highest degree of excellence, speed, or skill that is physiologically possible. Cf. *physiological limit*.

Practice period: a preliminary period, in experimental procedure, before the experiment proper begins, in order to get the subject (and experimenter) accustomed to the procedure, etc., not taken into account in the actual experiment.

Practice theory: the *preparation* theory; a theory of the function of play in the life of the child, to the effect that its biological function is to prepare the child through practice for adult activities; usually attributed to *Karl Groos*, but suggested by other and earlier writers.

Pragmatism: a philosophical doctrine, the essential nature of which is best expressed by the statement that the ultimate test of the right and the true must be looked for in the practical consequences; or that the whole meaning of a conception expresses itself in its practical consequences.

Prägnanz (Ger.): a term employed by the *Gestalt school*, for the tendency of every mental form or structure towards meaningfulness, completeness, and relative simplicity.

Pray's letters: a test for *astigmatism* (q.v.) consisting of letters formed by strokes running in different directions for each letter.

Praxinoscope: an instrument for showing motion by means of a series of pictures of an object, and an arrangement of mirrors, in a box rotating horizontally. See *stroboscope*.

Precipitate: term employed by psychoanalysts in reference to unconscious material ready to function in determining motivation.

Precision: high degree of accuracy and constancy of measurements; the so-called *index of precision* (q.v.) is inversely related to *variability* or *deviation; instruments of precision* are finely adjusted measuring instruments, giving fine and highly accurate measurements.

Precision Law (Präzisierung): a principle, emphasized in *Gestalt* psychology, according to which the organization of the mental content at all levels occurs through the tendency of the content, in perceptual or ideational fields, to become as well articulated as possible. Cf. *Prägnanz*.

Precocity: unusually early development of mental or physical capacities.

Preconception: a view, opinion, or theory in the mind before any or sufficient data are present to support it, leading generally to a *bias*.

Preconscious: used by psychoanalysts with reference to material, which, though at the moment unconscious, is available, and ready to become conscious; also topographically of a region, as it were, in the mind, intermediate between consciousness and the unconscious as such.

Predication: a logical term, signifying any assertion of a relationship between two terms (or psychologically, concepts), as 'A is B.'

Prediction: a statement that an event will occur before its actual occurrence, usually based on some knowledge or hypothesis.

Predisposition: a term employed of a congenital condition in an individual, favouring development in a certain direction or of certain characteristics; or of a tendency, set, or attitude, favouring the acceptance of certain beliefs, or the adoption of certain lines of action.

Pre-edipal phase: according to psychoanalytical views, a phase in the early development of the child, marked by exclusive attachment to the mother, and prior to the development of the *Edipus complex.*

Pre-established harmony: one aspect of the Leibnizian philosophy, which would explain the relation between the mental and the physical as one of parallelism of two independent series of events, so arranged beforehand as to mirror one another.

Preference method: a method of experimentation in the *affective* field, in the case of human beings, and in the sensory field, in the case of animals, in the latter case with the object of determining the nature and limits of their sensory world.

Preformism: the doctrine that characters and capacities, which show themselves in the course of development, are present in the *germ cell* from the beginning, as against the doctrine of *epigenesis* (q.v.).

Pregenital phase of sexuality: term used by psychoanalysts of the early, undifferentiated sexuality of the child, before there is attachment to, or predominance of, the genital zone.

Prehension: taking hold of, or grasping, objects.

Prejudice: an attitude, usually with an emotional colouring, hostile to, or in favour of, actions or objects of a certain kind, certain persons, and certain doctrines.

Premeditation: planning, purposing, or intending an action beforehand, as against acting on the impulse of the moment.

Premonition: the thought, usually with anxiety, of a coming event, derived from some experience or suggestion, which may be quite irrelevant, but is regarded as a warning; in *psychical research* the use of the word implies a revelation from supernormal sources.

Prenubile: term employed of the period of development before reaching the marriageable stage.

Preparatory interval: the interval of time, in a reaction or other experiment, between the word 'ready', or other preparatory signal, and the presentation of the stimulus.

Preperception: the prepared set or attitude of readiness for an expected perception, or other experience, generally involving an anticipatory idea, which intensifies the clearness and vividness of the experience itself, and may shorten the period for its development.

Prepossession: a milder form of prejudice, usually in favour.

Prepotence: the characteristic of a reflex, or habit, in virtue of which it takes precedence over another reflex or habit. Adjectival form, *prepotent*.

Presbyopia: a condition of vision, characterized by lack of elasticity in the lens of the eye, which comes with advancing age, and restricts the possibility of accommodation for near objects, while distant vision may be unimpaired.

Present: psychologically, not a point of time, but a period or space of time, extending under favourable conditions to about 4 seconds, and characterized by the fact that two experiences, say two taps, with this interval between them seem to give a single, temporarily unitary impression; sometimes spoken of as *specious* or *sensory present*.

Presentation: any immediate content of experience, sensory or ideational though sometimes restricted to the former.

Presentationism: see *realism*.

Presentiment: a feeling, usually of a foreboding character, of some impending future event.

Pressure: a type of touch sensation, distinguishable in experience from contact, and usually accompanied by some deforming of the cutaneous area affected by the physical stimulus.

Pressure balance: an instrument for exerting a controlled, variable, and measurable pressure on an area of the skin.

Pressure point: a rod with a blunted point for exploring an area of the skin for *pressure spots*, i.e. spots which have a specially low threshold for pressure.

Pressure pattern: a perceptual experience of relative roughness or smoothness, dependent on simultaneous or successive pressure sensations, within a cutaneous area.

Prestige: an influence or glamour, attaching to an individual, profession, institution, etc., which has the effect of giving opinions, statements and the like, coming from that source, special suggestive value. See *suggestion*.

Prevision: term employed in *psychical research* with special sense of supernormal foresight of future events; 'second sight'.

Prestidigitator: juggler or *conjurer*.

Pride: excessively strong *self-sentiment* (q.v.); exaggerated *self-respect* (q.v.).

Primacy: the fact or state of being first; one of the *secondary laws* (q.v.) of association, to the effect that, other things being equal, first impressions are from that fact favourably placed for retention and recall.

Primal: first in time; employed in a special sense by psychoanalysts of a fragmentary recalled experience or scene from early childhood, the apparent first stage in the production of a *neurosis.*

Primary: first in rank; logically first; frequently used also in sense of first in time.

Primary colours: see *colour.*

Primary function: a term applied, in opposition to *secondary function* (q.v.), to the immediately present experience, following on actual stimulation of the sense organs and the perception of the present situation, without involving any after-effects of previous experience, in sensation, memory, or behaviour.

Primary memory image: term employed for the image revived immediately the sensory experience, with its *after-sensations,* has died away. Cf. *immediate memory.*

Primary position: the position assumed by the eyes, when the head is erect, and the eyes fixated on a distant object straight in front in the median and horizontal planes.

Primary process: term employed by psychoanalysts for the process producing in the unconscious the dream phenomena of *condensation, displacement,* etc. (Freud's '*dream work*'); a better term would be *primary elaboration,* as distinct from the *secondary elaboration* in relating a dream.

Primary qualities: the fundamental qualities of objects; qualities which, as perceived, resemble the actual qualities in the object, according to an old distinction between the primary and secondary qualities of objects, found as early as *Democritus,* and at least as late as *Locke* and the natural realists, the *secondary* qualities being those arising from the relation of the object to the observer, or the effects on the observer of psychologically unknown qualities in the object, such as colour, etc.

Prime: a musical term for the fundamental or the first overtone in a *clang.*

Primitive: employed with reference to the early stages in evolution or development; or with reference to peoples and cultures representing a low stage of civilization, especially those without recorded history.

Primitive credulity: the early stage of belief in the individual, when all experiences are uncritically accepted at their face value.

Primordial: usually employed of first in time, or originally, but strictly means first in rank; generally carries a connotation of hoary antiquity.

Principal: general sense, chief or most important; several technical senses: (1) of the *focus* of an optical system at which parallel rays converge after passing through the system; (2) of a *plane* passing through the *principal points* of a thick lens or optical system; (3) of the two points in a thick lens or optical system, which are such that rays directed towards the one emerge parallel to their line of incidence from the other.

Principle: a uniformity in nature, which may be formulated verbally as a law; an accepted general rule of conduct; a general logical relationship.

Prior entry: the law or principle in connection with attention, to the effect that an object attended to comes to consciousness more quickly than one not attended to. See *complication experiment*.

Prism: in optical science, a wedge-shaped piece of glass or crystal, or a combination of such, in the form of a trapezium, which bends, and at the same time disperses, through refraction, according to their wave-lengths, rays of light passing through it, and thus decomposes white light into the spectral band of colours.

Prism degree: an opthalmological unit of the refractory power of a prism, being represented by a prism the refracting surfaces of which make with one another an angle of one degree.

Prism Diopter: a unit of prism strength, given by the tangent of the angle through which light rays are deflected by the prism, multiplied by 100. Cf. *centrad*.

Probability: in general sense, the degree of likelihood of an event happening, direct evidence for and against being insufficient or absent; statistically, measured on the basis of the mathematical *theory of probability*, where the occurrence of an event is taken as governed by the laws of chance.

Probability Curve: Gaussian curve; *normal frequency curve;* a bell-shaped curve, of which the equation is $y = (N/\sigma\sqrt{2\pi})\, e^{\frac{-x^2}{2\sigma^2}}$ if N is the number of cases, and *e* the base of the natural logarithms.

Probability ratio: the ratio of the number of ways in which a given event could occur to the total number of possible events, equal probability of all being assumed.

Probable error: P.E.; a measure of the limits within which, as calculated from the mean of an unselected or random sample, the chances are equal that any other value, obtained from another sample, would fall.

Problem box: a type of test, represented by a box fastened by relatively complex fastenings, given to be opened by the subject; a simpler type is much used in animal experiment. See *puzzle box*.

Problem solving: general term for a type of experiment, in which an individual, human being or animal, is faced with a situation of some complexity, demanding some initiative and some mental synthesis, if the goal is to be attained.

Procedure: the systematic arrangement of the exact manner in which an experiment or scientific investigation is carried out; in *procedure with knowledge,* the subject knows or is told what to expect, in *procedure without knowledge* this is concealed.

Process: a continuous series of successive, but interdependent, changes or events; sometimes of a single event in such a series, provided it involves some sort of transformation taking place in time; any mental event, regarded as such a change or series of changes.

Process attitude: the attitude of a subject in an experiment, when his attention is directed towards the various mental occurrences which he is experiencing. Contrasted with the *object attitude,* where his attention is given to the stimulus.

Procreation: begetting, from the point of view of the part played by the male.

Prodigy: in general sense, anything that causes wonder; an individual who shows supernormal ability, special or general, particularly at an early age.

Prodrome: a medical term for the preliminary signs, or premonitory symptoms, of a definite disease; sometimes used figuratively, in a more or less general sense, in connection with physiological or psychological process.

Product moment: the average of the products of paired measures; where, as in psychological statistics, these are deviations from a mean it is usually termed *covariance.*

Product moment correlation coefficient: is the *correlation coefficient* calculated from the *product moment,* the formula being (Pearson): $r = \Sigma (xy)/N\sigma_x \sigma_y.$

Proficiency: degree of an individual's acquired knowledge or skill in a particular direction.

Profile, mental or psychological: a graphical representation of an individual's standing, or level, in a series of tests, measuring various aspects of his mentality. See *psychograph.*

Profile test: a type of performance test, where the subject is required to construct a head in profile, from a number of pieces into which it is dissected, without any information being given as to the object to be formed.

Prognathous: employed of a type of human skull, in which the upper jaw projects beyond the forehead.

Prognosis: judgment as to the future course, and termination, of a series of events in process; technically, as a medical term, forecast of the probable course and outcome of a disease or disorder.

Project method: an educational method which seeks to organize school work round definite enterprises undertaken by the children, for the most part in groups; sometimes the employment for such a purpose, of practical activities carried out in the home, or in the neighbourhood.

Progression Law: the formulation, by Delbœuf, of the *Weber-Fechner law,* as the principle that successive sensation increments represent an arithmetical progression, while the stimulus increments show a geometrical progression.

Projection: historically, in the older psychology, the objective reference of sensations, that is, their reference to an object, as the origin or source of the stimuli, or their localization within or without the body; more recently the interpretation of situations and events, by reading into them our own experiences and feelings (see *projection tests*); also recently, by the psychoanalysts, the attributing unconsciously to other people, usually as a defence against unpleasant feelings in ourselves, such as a feeling of *guilt,* or feelings of *inferiority,* of thoughts, feelings, and acts towards us, by means of which we justify ourselves in our own eyes. Cf. *delusions of persecution.*

Projection centre: the region of the cerebral cortex, connecting directly with sensory or motor centres in the *basal ganglia* or spinal cord.

Projection fibres: tracts of nerve fibres, in the cerebrum, passing directly to lower centres, as distinct from the *commissural* and *association* fibres.

Projection, Optical: the formation of an image by any optical system, outside the system itself. For *visual projection,* see *projection* (first meaning).

Projection tests: a type of mental test aiming at the determination of *personality traits* through the completion of sentences, interpretation of ink-blots (*Rorschach figures*), and the like, or interpretation of pictures, making of designs, where, in all cases, there is no right or wrong, but the individual is left free to follow his own inclinations and phantasies.

Prolegomena: systematic introduction to a branch of study, or to a specialized work.

Proliferation: the multiplication of cells in an organism, normal or pathological.

Prompting method: an experimental method of studying learning by heart, where the stage a piece of learning has reached is measured by the number of prompts the subject requires in an attempt at reproduction.

Pronation: rotation of the hand so as to bring the palm downwards.

Proof-reader's illusion: an illusion of visual perception of familiar words, due to the images of the words being evoked by the context, and by slight cues in the word as presented, with the consequent overlooking of typographical errors.

Propaedeutic: preliminary study introducing and leading on to a higher study.

Propaganda: organized efforts to induce certain attitudes in other people or in the public, largely by way of *suggestion* and the utilization of emotionally tinged words.

Propagate: of animals or plants, to cause to multiply or spread; also figuratively of opinions and knowledge.

Propagation: the propagating, as above; also the conduction of a nervous impulse along a nerve.

Propensity: a somewhat archaic word for a *tendency* or *impulse,* inherited or acquired, towards a type of action, or a particular form of behaviour.

Property: an intrinsic quality of an object or process, which may not form part of its definition.

Prophylaxis: protective measures, either individual or social, against disease; figuratively of analogous measures against false opinions, doctrines, etc.

Proportion: employed in an *aesthetic* sense, of the agreeable relations of parts to one another or to the whole.

Proposition: the expression in words of a judgment.

Proprioreceptor: a receptor, or sense-organ, situated within the tissues of the body.

Prosencephalon: the *cerebrum, corpora striata,* and *olfactory lobes,* so-called as the first portion of the embryonic *forebrain.*

Prosopopesis: in *psychical research,* personation, spontaneous or induced, of a discarnate personality, from the characteristics of the individual when living, preserved in the memories of the living, and collected by supernormal (telepathic) means.

Prospective reference: reference of thought in the present, to some future situation, as a partial analysis of *purpose* (q.v.).

Prostitution: offering, as a means of livelihood, or for payment, the body for sexual intercourse; figuratively for any similar abuse of talents, position, or influence.

Prot(o)- (*Gr.*): prefix meaning 'first'.

Protanomalous: a type of colour vision, which differs from the normal in respect of relative insensitivity to red, as compared with green; determined by requiring, or showing, an excess of red in the *Rayleigh equation* (q.v.).

Protanopia: a type of partial colour-blindness, characterized by confusion of red and green, and insensitivity to the extreme red of the spectrum; red blindness; so called because of presumed lack of the first of the three physical primaries. Cf. *scoterythrous.*

Protective colouring: resemblance of an organism in colouring, or in colouring and form, to its usual environment; in some cases, ability to take on colouring resembling that of the environment at the time, or some common object in the environment.

Protensity: the time attribute or aspect of sensation; a term suggested by *Ward,* as preferable to *duration,* which seems to imply a degree of definiteness not initially present.

Protaesthesia: hypothetically primitive sensory experience.

Protocol: the original record of an experiment made by the subject, during, or immediately after, the experiment, and recording his introspective notes.

Protopathic emotion: hypothetically the earliest or most primitive affective or emotional experience of the child, a pure or simple unpleasantness; the first stirrings of interest might equally well be regarded as the earliest experience of an affective character; as regards the earliest emotion there is high probability in favour of *fear.*

Protopathic: term, employed by *Head* and *Rivers,* of a type of sensory response, or sensibility, found by them in certain areas of the cutaneous surface, after, and during recovery from, an experimental section of the sensory nerve supply of that area; the chief marks of this alleged sensory response were its lack of grading, or all-or-none character, and its vagueness, and lack of definite localization; other investigators, notably *Boring* and *Schafer,* have been unable to verify these findings; an ungraded type of emotional response, approximating to the all-or-none character, is found in the case of intense emotion, and the term has also been applied to such response.

Protoplasm: living substance, as in the cytoplasm, or nucleus, of a living cell.

Prototype: primarily the earliest form of an organism, or an organ; by extension, applied also to patterns of response.

Protozoa: unicellular organisms; the earliest and most primitive forms of animal life.

Proverb test: a type of intelligence test, the essential point of which is the understanding or interpreting of a well-known proverb.

Proximoceptor: a receptor which can be stimulated only through contact with it, or its accessory parts.

Pseud(o)- (Gr.): prefix meaning 'false' or 'misleading'.

Pseudaesthesia: by derivation, any sensory *illusion* or *hallucination;* usually employed more specifically of sensory experiences located in an amputated limb.

Pseudochromaesthesia (sometimes *psychochromaesthesia*): a species of *synaesthesia* (q.v.); more particularly, *coloured hearing.*

Pseudoclonus: rhythmical contractions of ankle muscles on bending toes inwards; occurs in excessive fatigue, hysteria, and toxic conditions.

Pseudodementia: extreme apathy, without intelligence defect.

Pseudoisochromatic: term employed, of charts or plates, printed in confusion colours for testing colour vision.

Pseudologia fantastica: obsessive, or constitutional tendency to lying circumstantially, and to an excessive extent.

Pseudomemory: false memory, as of an experience that had no existence.

Pseudomnesia: pathological *pseudomemory.*

Pseudomyopia: a condition of lowered visual acuity, which causes the individual to hold objects nearer the eyes, as if suffering from *myopia.*

Pseudonystagmus: nystagmus-like movements of the eyes, without real *nystagmus* (q.v.).

Pseudoparalysis: apparent loss of muscular power, or power of movement, as in paralysis, but without real paralysis.

Pseudophone: an apparatus for studying the localization of sound, by producing illusions of localization, using various methods, as, for example, by sound reflection, sound-proof tubes passing over the head to the other ear, etc.

Pseudopresentiment: an experience akin to *déjà vu* (q.v.), with the difference that an experience, more or less startling, carries with it the irresistible conviction that one has previously had the feeling, in the form of a warning that just this event was impending.

Pseudopsychology: a system of doctrine, professing to be psychology, but involving principles and methods of procedure inconsistent with the recognized principles of the science.

Pseudoscope: an instrument which, usually by means of prisms, reverses normal optical relationships, so that, for example, a solid object is seen as hollow.

Psittacism: a parrot-like verbal statement, without regard to the meaning of the words.

Psychasthenia: a term somewhat variously used, but covering ordinarily a group of mental disorders of an obsessive and anxiety type.

Psyche: originally the principle of life, but used generally as equivalent to mentality, or as a substitute for mind or soul.

Psychergograph: an apparatus for presenting stimuli in such a way that the correct response to one brings on the next, the time in each case being recorded; employed in fatigue and discrimination reaction experiments.

Psychiatrist: one who professes and practises *psychiatry* (q.v.); equivalent to the older term *alienist* (q.v.).

Psychiatry: a specialized study and practice dealing with mental and nervous disorders; generally employed in a somewhat wide and indefinite sense, inclusive of *psychopathology,* and even some branches of *psychology.*

Psychical: generally equivalent to mental, but with special reference to the non-sensory processes.

Psychic: a popular rather than scientific term for an individual possessing or capable of developing occult powers. Used either as a noun or as an adjective.

Psychic blindness or deafness: inability to see (or hear) because of cerebral lesion or functional disorder, the sense organs being unimpaired; most properly limited to the latter, i.e. functional; must be distinguished from *mind blindness,* which is failure to understand or interpret what is seen.

Psychic determinism: the postulate of Freudian psychology that the mental life, and all aspects of the mental life, are causally determined, in the same sense as are events in the physical world; or that nothing in the mental life is due to chance, any more than in the physical universe.

Psychic(al) distance: degree of detachment of an individual from the practical significance or appeal of an object, particularly, but not necessarily, a work of art.

Psychic force: term applied by some students of *psychical research* to the hypothetical cause of alleged *telekinetic* phenomena.

Psychical communism: similarity in the make-up and the working of human minds, arising from similar environmental conditions and training, and resulting in such agreement, in responses to the same situation, as might be and popularly is taken as evidence for *telepathy.*

Psychical research: the systematic and scientific investigation of supernormal phenomena, associated with *telepathy, spiritism,* and similar debatable borderline topics; sometimes called *metapsychics* or *parapsychology,* or even *psychism.*

Psychoanalysis: a system of psychology, and a method of treatment of mental and nervous disorders, developed by *Sigmund Freud,* characterized by a dynamic view of all aspects of the mental life, conscious and unconscious, with special emphasis upon the phenomena of the *unconscious,* and by an elaborate technique of investigation and treatment, based on the employment of *continuous free association* (q.v.).

Psychoasthenics: a rarely used term for the investigation of *feeblemindedness.*

Psychobiology: the investigation of psychological problems in the field of general biology.

Psychodiagnostics: the attempt to assess personal characteristics through the observation of external features, as in *physiognomy, craniology, graphology,* study of voice, gait, etc.

Psychodometer: a term applied to an early form of chronoscope, for measuring reaction time, by means of a tuning fork, which recorded its vibration on a moving smoked glass, the sound of the fork being the stimulus, and the response lifting the fork from contact with the glass.

Psychodynamics: the study of mental and developmental processes from a dynamic point of view, as a branch of psychology.

Psychogalvanic response (reflex): P.G.R.; the apparent diminution of the electrical resistance of the skin, due in reality to the production of an electromotive force in the skin, resulting from mental activity; employed as a delicate indicator of such activity, particularly if of an affective or emotional character; the instrumental set-up for the study of the P.G.R., inclusive of a galvanometer, usually of the moving coil type, is often called a *psychogalvanometer,* and may be arranged to give a photographic record.

Psychogenesis: the origin and development of mental phenomena in general, or particular features or peculiarities of mental processes, as manifested in behaviour.

Psychogenic: term usually employed of disorders which originate in mental conditions, though they may come to involve physiological changes, as a result of these mental conditions.

Psychognosis: the study of mental phenomena by means of hypnosis or hypnoidal states; reading of character from anatomical features. Cf. *psychodiagnostics.*

Psychograph: a chart showing an individual's standing, with respect to various *personality* characteristics (see *profile*); also used of a descriptive account, or a biographical sketch, indicating an individual's personal characteristics and capacities.

Psychography: writing, ostensibly produced without the activity of a medium's muscles.

Psychoid: that which manifests itself in the activity of a human body; soul.

Psychologism: the view that philosophy and the human sciences are, or should be, based on psychology; or the more extreme view that psychology is the basis of all science.

Psychologist: one with an expert knowledge of the methods and facts of the science, either generally, or in some special field; an expert in some of the fields of practical application of psychology; in America and in this and other countries, the expert is marked by his status in a recognized Psychological Association or Society.

Psychologist's fallacy: the fallacy of confusing his own knowledge about a mental process, with the subject's direct experience of the process, and reading the former into the latter.

Psychology: as a branch of science, psychology has been defined in various ways, according to the particular method of approach adopted or field of study proposed by the individual psychologist, but a comprehensive definition, which would include all varieties, so far as they can be rightly said to represent aspects of the original and historical meaning of the word, would run in some such way as this: the branch of biological science which studies the phenomena of conscious life, in their origin, development, and manifestations, and employing such methods as are available and applicable to the particular field of study or particular problem with which the individual scientist is engaged; the differences between psychologists are generally philosophical, rather than scientific, differences, and in any case are far fewer, and scientifically far less important, than the points of agreement; the generally recognized branches of psychology are: *abnormal psychology, animal psychology, child psychology, genetic psychology, industrial psychology,* and *social psychology;* the general divisions, according to method of approach, are: *analytic, behaviouristic, Gestalt, hormic, introspective,* and *statistical.*

Psychology, the new: an indefinite term, changing in its reference from time to time, but always referring to some recently developed method of approach, or of research.

Psychometric function: a mathematical formula, expressing the relation between a series of quantitatively different stimuli, and the relative frequencies, on the part of a subject, of the judgments, 'less', 'equal', and 'greater', in comparison with a standard stimulus.

Psychometrics: mathematical or measurement aspects of psychological experiments; more recently, statistical treatment of mental test results.

Psychometry: mental measurement in general; investigation of the time factor in mental processes; in special sense, in *psychical research,* applied to the acquiring supernormally, by a *sensitive,* of knowledge, through the handling of objects, or by *psychometrizing.*

Psychomotor: related or referring to the motor effects of mental (cerebral) processes.

Psycho-neural parallelism: see *psycho-physical parallelism.*

Psychoneurosis: term usually employed, though not always consistently, for the group of functional nervous or mental disorders, less serious and less fundamental than *psychoses,* of which *hysteria* may be taken as the type.

Psychonomic: term employed of conditions and influences affecting mental development; from a social point of view, of mental forces determining or playing a part in social organization.

Psychonomics: the name given to the branch of psychology which studies the relation of the individual, particularly in his development, to his environment, physical and social.

Psychopath (Psychopathic personality): an individual, emotionally unstable to a degree approaching the pathological, but with no specific or marked mental disorder.

Psychopathology: mental pathology, or the pathology of mind; a study of mental functions and processes, under conditions brought about by disorder or disease, physical or mental.

Psychopathy: specific, but unspecified, mental disorder.

Psychopharmacology: the study of the mental effects of drugs.

Psychophysical law: any formulation of the relation between physical stimuli and sensory processes.

Psychophysical methods: a group of experimental and quantitative methods, devised for employment in psychophysical investigation. There are three fundamental methods, viz. *method of limits, method of right and wrong cases*, and *method of mean error* – with modifications.

Psycho-physical parallelism: a theory – or a working hypothesis – which expresses the relationship between mental and physical processes, by assuming that these represent two concomitant, and parallel, series of events, without assuming any causal connection between them.

Psycho-physical problem: generally, the relation between mind and body; psychologically, the relation between mental process and physiological processes in the cerebral cortex.

Psychophysics: the branch of experimental psychology which investigates the functional and quantitative relations between physical stimuli and sensory events; sometimes extended to cover experimental psychology generally, sometimes called *psycho-physiology*, or even *physiological psychology*.

Psychosexual: referring or related to the sex life in a wide sense.

Psychosexual hermaphroditism: a term employed, mainly by psychoanalysts, where the sexual object of an individual may be of either sex.

Psychosis: abnormal or pathological mental state, constituting a definite disease entity; term applied at one time generally to any mental state or process as a whole; a *deteriorative psychosis* is a psychosis showing progressive loss of mental function.

Psycho-social: term employed with reference to social relations dependent on mental factors and functions.

Psychodrama: a method of diagnosis and treatment for personality problems, having considerable affinity with *projection* (q.v.) methods, and still more closely related to *sociometry* (q.v.), consisting essentially in getting an individual to reproduce spontaneously on a stage, and before an audience in some cases, the structure of a situation already discovered to be highly significant for the difficulty or problem being treated or investigated. Other persons – known as *auxiliary egos* – take part in the action on the stage, and an audience may be present selected with reference to the special problem in hand, all under a director, who is normally the psychiatrist having charge of the treatment. This method has also been employed for *group psychotherapy*, and when specifically employed for this purpose it becomes *sociodrama*, though normally the *auxiliary egos* and the audience, where their own problems are being treated in the actions on the stage, cannot but be affected in all psychodrama.

Psychosocial: term applied to phenomena in the individual having a social bearing either in origin or in outcome.

Psychosomatics: the correlation of psychological phenomena, normal, abnormal, or pathological, with somatic or bodily conditions and variations.

Psychostatics: rarely-used term for a branch of psychology which investigates the structure of mental states and functions.

Psychotechnology: branch of science which investigates the general principles underlying the application of psychological methods and results to practical problems; the actual practical application is sometimes called *psychotechnics.*

Psychotherapy: the treatment of disorders by psychological methods.

Ptosis: paralytic drooping of the eyelid.

Pubertas praecox: premature or unusually early development of signs of puberty.

Puberty: the maturing of the sexual functions.

Pubes: the lower part, or hypogastric region, of the abdomen.

Public opinion: the general consensus of opinion in a community regarding a social, ethical, or political matter, or regarding the character and conduct of an individual.

Puerilism: a condition, either of retarded development, or of degeneration, where an individual's mental processes or behaviour remain or become immature, like those of a child or adolescent.

Puerperal: following childbirth.

Pugnacity: see *aggressiveness.*

Pulse: the rhythmical waves of tension in the arteries owing to the action of the heart; the variation of the pulse rate with the level of *metabolism* (q.v.) is known as the law or principle of *pulse metabolism.*

Pulvinar: the projecting hinder part of the *thalamus* (q.v.).

Punctal lens: a trade name for a type of spectacle lens, similar to the *toric* (q.v.).

Punctiform: term employed of a discontinuous distribution in spots or points, as in the case of the cold and heat points or spots in the skin; also of the kind of *exploration* by means of which these are localized.

Pupil: the circular opening in the *iris* of the human eye, by which light rays are admitted to the eye, and the size of which controls the amount of light entering the eye.

Pupillary reflex: the variation of the size of the pupil, depending on the intensity of light falling on the retina, and controlled by muscle fibres in the *iris*.

Pupilloscope: an instrument for testing colour vision efficiency, by measuring changes in the size of the pupil, when the wavelength of the light stimulus is changed.

Pure: not mixed; employed technically in various connections, as a *pure colour,* where the light is as nearly as possible of uniform wavelength; a *pure tone,* where the air waves are of the same frequency, overtones being eliminated; a *pure musical scale,* one which is not *tempered.*

Purkinje after-image: Bidwell's ghost (q.v.).

Purkinje figures: the shadows cast on the retina by the blood-vessels in the retinal layers in front, when the interior of the eye is brightly illumined through the *sclerotic.*

Purkinje phenomenon: the change in the point of maximal brightness in the spectrum, from the yellow towards the greenish-yellow, and the darkening of the extreme red, and to some extent also the extreme purple, which appear as the eye becomes dark-adapted.

Purkinje-Sanson Images: the images on the two sides of the lens seen with the *phakoscope* (q.v.).

Purple: if the spectral colours are arranged on the circumference of a circle, the band of colour joining its two ends, that is, between red at the one end and violet at the other; the colour obtained by mixing blue and violet with red; produced by *Kirschmann* from the decomposition of white light by what he called a 'negative slit'.

Purpose: the thought, in the present, of an end or aim, in the future, with the intention of realizing it; a term which it is impossible to define in merely static terms, activity consciously directed towards a goal, or with a conscious *objective* is *purposive activity;* emphasis on purposive activity is characteristic of the *hormic psychology,* but the extent to which purpose can be adequately dealt with in positive science is highly controversial.

Purposivism: a term employed to describe any psychological theory which claims that purposes are effective determinants of behaviour, as an addition to stimuli.

Pursuit: a series of movements which are adjusted and co-ordinated, so as to keep in accord with a series of changes of movement, acting as a stimulus or series of stimuli.

Pursuitmeter: an apparatus devised to measure the capacity for co-ordinating eye and hand-movement, in following a series of regular or irregular movement changes, controlled in various ways; probably the simplest form is the *pursuit pendulum,* where the movement of a large pendulum is followed with a vessel to catch a stream of water passing through the pendulum, while it is in motion; in other types, an irregularly moving hand on a dial must be followed by the movement of another hand, operated by the subject, either directly by hand, or by means of a wheel or pulley, but there are many types; generally used for testing special aptitudes.

Putrid: a quality of smell sensations, illustrated by smell of H_2S, or decaying matter; foul.

Puzzle-box experiment: a type of learning experiment employed in animal psychology; the animal is placed inside (or outside) a box, with food outside (or inside), the door of the box being fastened with a system of bars and latches, of varying degrees of intricacy and complexity, to be opened by the animal, the time for each success being taken.

Pyknic: a type of body-build, with large trunk, thick neck, and relatively short legs, associated with *cyclothymic* (q.v.) *temperament.*

Pyramidal tract: a band of nerve fibres, passing from the *motor zone* of the cerebrum to the motor *ganglia,* at the lower level.

Pyramids: the name given to regions in front of the *medulla,* on either side of the anterior median fissure.

Pyromania: a type of insanity with tendencies towards incendiarism.

Pyrosis: burning sensation in lower oesophagus and stomach.

Pythagorean scale: see *scale.*

Q

Q: symbol employed for *quartile deviation* or *range* (q.v.).

Quadrate Lobe: an area on the inner surface of the hemispheres of the cerebrum, between the *frontal* and *occipital* lobes.

Quadrigemina (Corpora): four masses of nervous substance forming the back part of the *mesencephalon.*

Quale: the qualitative nature or description, in itself, of an experience, without reference to its meaning or significance.

Quality: a fundamental aspect or attribute of sensory experience, differentiating one experience from another, within the same sensory field, of a non-quantitative character, and independently of all aspects of a quantitative character.

Quarter-tone music: music based on a scale which divides the octave into equal quarter-tone intervals.

Quartile deviation: Q; a measure of the scatter of values in a series, which is half the distance between the 25th and 75th *percentiles,* or between the *quartiles;* often called alternatively the *semi-interquartile range* (q.v.), and *probable error* (q.v.).

Questionnaire (Questionary): a series of questions dealing with some psychological, social, educational, etc., topic or topics, sent or given to a group of individuals, with the object of obtaining data with regard to some problem; sometimes employed for diagnostic purposes, or for assessing *personality traits.*

Quiescence: a feeling of restfulness, the opposite of *excitement,* the two representing one dimension in *Wundt's tridimensional theory* of feeling.

Quincke's tubes: a series of small glass tubes or pipes, which can be used open or closed, for the study of *difference tones* (q.v.).

Quotient hypothesis: an interpretation or formulation of *Weber's law,* to the effect that the ratio of any two successive *just noticeable differences* is constant.

R

R: symbol used for stimulus (Ger. Reiz); also for response in the combination S-R, stimulus-response; also for the coefficient obtained by *Spearman's 'foot-rule' formula* (q.v.).

r: symbol for *correlation coefficient.*

Rabbit-duck figure: an ambiguous figure which may be seen as the head of a rabbit or of a duck, employed in *apperception* experiments.

Race experience: accumulated knowledge, traditions, customs, etc., transmitted from generation to generation in a community.

Race psychology: a branch of *comparative psychology,* dealing with the mental characteristics, etc., of the different races of mankind.

Racial unconscious: see *collective unconsciousness.*

Radiant energy: electromagnetic waves travelling through space at the rate of 186,000 miles per second, a limited range of wavelengths of which affects the human eye as *light.*

Radiation: employed in its usual sense, of divergence in all directions from a centre; also in a special sense, of the spread of excitation in the nervous centres from a directly affected point.

Radiometry: measurement of radiation in terms of energy, by a *radiometer.*

Radix: nerve root, or bundle of nerve fibres at the point of entry into, or exit from, the central nervous system.

Random: employed of haphazard arrangement, or arrangement as if due to pure chance; applied to unselected *groups* of individuals or to *movements* not organized with reference to an end, biological or psychological; or to a *sample* from a larger population, taken in place of the whole, as far as possible at random, so that the sample may be taken to represent the whole.

Range: the interval or distance between two extreme values, inclusive of the extremes themselves, in a series of data, stimuli, sensibilities, variations from the mean, etc.

Rank: position, in a series arranged in order, on the basis of some principle of arrangement, with reference to the other items or values in the series.

Rank correlation: the correlation between two series of measurements, arranged in order of magnitude, and the ranks paired for each individual; *Spearman's* formula is usually employed, which is

$$\rho = 1 - \frac{6 \Sigma (d^2)}{N(N^2 - 1)},$$ where P is the correlation, d the difference between the ranks of an individual in the two series, and N the number of cases.

Ranschburg inhibition: a phenomenon occurring in the tachistoscopic exposure of material, say numbers, when it is found that more digits can be recognized when all are different than when some are alike, like apparently inhibiting like.

Rapport: in a general sense, relationship based on a high degree of community of thought, interest, and sentiment; in a special sense, that relationship which is established between hypnotist and subject, in which the subject is highly sensitive to suggestions from the hypnotist, but insensitive to suggestions from any other source, a somewhat similar relationship being usually established between analyst and patient.

Rapping: a method of alleged communication with a discarnate personality, employed in *psychical research,* where answers are given to questions by means of raps or knocks; a method of *metapsychics.*

Rate: the amount of change in movement, condition, etc., taking place in unit time.

Rating: the assigning of a position, rank, score, or mark, to an individual. See *graphic rating scale.*

Ratio: the quantitative relation which two similar magnitudes bear to one another.

Ratiocination: reasoning, usually deductive.

Rational: capable of reasoning; in accordance with sound reasoning; *rational behaviour* is behaviour which is based on sound reasoning, or logically appropriate to a situation, or founded on intellectual insight.

Rationalism: a philosophical point of view which emphasizes the primacy and adequacy of reason in the search for truth.

Rationalization: the process of justifying by reasoning after the event, as, for example, an act after it has been performed; often a *defence mechanism* against self-accusation, or a feeling of *guilt*; term also employed in the industrial field for the scientific organization of industry; and also in advertising for a type of *appeal,* partly of the *short circuit,* but in the main of the *long circuit* type.

Raw Score: the score in a test based on the performance itself, without any correction being applied.

Ray: a representation by a line of the presence and direction of travel of light or radiant energy.

Rayleigh disc: an arrangement for measuring in physical units the intensity of sound, which consists of a thin mica disc, suspended in a resonator tube by a light fibre carrying a mirror, the measurement being given by the torque on the fibre, registered by a beam of light reflected from the mirror.

Rayleigh equation: the proportion of spectral red to spectral green in a mixture which matches spectral yellow, as given by an *anomaloscope* (q.v.); a test for the determination of *anomalous colour vision* with respect to red or green; an analogous test can be given with rotating discs, different proportions of black requiring usually to be added to the yellow, for different types and different degrees of anomaly.

Reaction experiment (Reaction time experiment): a classical psychological experiment, in which the time a subject takes to respond to a stimulus is measured, generally by some type of *chronoscope;* the stimulus may be any sense stimulus, and the response, in the case of simple reaction time, is usually given by lifting the finger from the button of a *reaction key* or *tapping key;* the signal or stimulus may be complicated in various ways, and to various degrees, in which case we have *compound* or *complex* reaction time as a result, and the response may be made with different and appropriate types of reaction key – *lip key*, *sound key*, etc.

Reaction formation: a term used by psychoanalysts to designate an unconscious mechanism, developed sometimes as a character trait, and manifested in irrational and sometimes excessive or violent action in the opposite direction to an impulse or desire which is being repressed; a kind of self-defence on the part of an individual against an impulse or tendency he experiences, but rejects.

Reaction type: a type of response in a reaction experiment, dependent on the direction of the subject's attention; the recognized types are *sensorial*, *motor* (*muscular*), and *mixed*.

Reactive tendency (*impulse*)*:* an impulse or tendency (instinctive) evoked by, and expressing itself in reaction towards, an external object or situation.

Readiness: preparedness to respond, or react.

Readiness law: one of *Thorndike's* principles of learning, according to which a response is facilitated by the preparation of neural connections to operate, owing to such factors as recency and frequency.

Reading habit: the tendency to look first at the top left hand corner of a page, as affecting the relative value of position in the page with respect to advertisements.

Real: having actual existence; applied to actual objects and relations, as contrasted with illusory or imaginary; psychologically, calling for *motor adaptation*.

Realism: a philosophical term employed with different connotations at different times, but generally involving a view of the real existence of objects experienced, and in some cases of their reality as experienced in sense perception; in an *aesthetic* sense, a view of the criterion of aesthetic or artistic value; in a literary and aesthetic sense, the representation of life and objects as they really are.

Reality: the totality of existing material objects; more abstractly the sum total of the conditions imposed by the external world on the activity of the individual, to which *motor adaptation,* on the part of the individual, is demanded.

Reality feeling: is the feeling or consciousness of the need for *motor adaptation,* and is the essential characteristic and earliest form of *belief.*

Reality principle: term employed by *Freud* to designate the conditions imposed on the satisfaction of the *pleasure principle* (q.v.) by the physical and social environments, particularly the latter.

Reason: general term for the higher intellectual processes; more narrowly the capacity for explicit thought with reference to an end.

Reasoning: a process of thinking involving inference, or of solving problems by employing general principles.

Reasoning tests: types of mental test where the subject is required to draw conclusions from certain data, or to check conclusions already drawn.

Rebirth phantasy: according to psychoanalytic teaching, a characteristic phantasy, symbolizing one's birth, motived by an unconscious wish, and expressing itself in dreams and day-dreams of swimming or emerging from water.

Rebus writing: type of graphic language, which represents, as it were, a stage in the development of graphic language between the *ideograph* and the representation of sounds by symbols or letters, where the sounds of words and word-elements, but not the meanings, are represented by pictures, or pictures and letters, as, for example, the representation of 'disclaim' by a circle and the picture of a man on crutches.

Recall: to revive or reinstate in memory, verbally, or in concrete imagery, a past experience.

Recall method: a method of measuring retention, or the rate of forgetting, by the percentage of items recalled after various intervals of time since these were learned.

Recapitulation: repeating in order a course of events already gone through.

Recapitulation theory: the theory or doctrine that the individual in his development recapitulates the stages or types which have been passed through in the evolution of the race, or, in brief, that *ontogeny* recapitulates *phylogeny*.

Recency: the name given to one of the so-called *secondary laws of association,* to the effect that recent impressions or recently formed associations have, other things being equal, an advantage for recall.

Receptor: an apparatus in which a sensory nerve terminates, which is specially adapted to certain types of stimulus.

Receptor field: the collection of points, or the area by the stimulation of, or within, which a reflex may be elicited.

Recessive character: that one of two Mendelian characters, the other being the *dominant,* which when crossed with the other, does not appear, but is latent in the first generation, but may appear in subsequent generations.

Recidivism: the tendency to become convicted of crime repeatedly, or to become a habitual criminal.

Reciprocal innervation: the principle that two motor centres so connected that one supplies one of a pair of antagonistic muscles, and the other the other, are in their activity so interrelated that when the one muscle is contracted by an impulse from the one, the other muscle is relaxed, or its contraction inhibited by the action of the other.

Recognition: perceiving (or recalling) an object, accompanied by a feeling of familiarity, or the conviction that the same object has been perceived before.

Recurrent: repeated, or repeating, after an interval or intervals.

Recurrent image: an image which persistently returns; sometimes of an *after-sensation* which keeps repeating for some time after the stimulus has been withdrawn.

Recurrent psychosis: a mental disorder which repeats itself in similar attacks.

Red: term employed loosely of visual sensations obtained from the long-wave end of the spectrum from a wave-length of $620\mu\mu$ upwards; a large part of this range, if not all, is tinged with orange for normal vision, and *pure or primal,* or *Ur-red* is beyond the end of the spectrum towards *crimson,* and is tinged with blue for most normal eyes, though it is the colour placed at one apex of the *colour triangle* (q.v.).

Red-green blindness: partial colour blindness, involving confusion of red and green, of two distinct types called respectively *protanopia* and *deuteranopia,* the latter about twice as frequent as the former, and both together showing a frequency of about 7.5 per cent in males, in this country; a condition not very clearly understood of oversensitivity to red, where objects appear tinged with red, is known as *red-sightedness.*

Redintegration: term suggested by *Sir William Hamilton* for the principle or law of association, exemplified in a whole being reinstated from the perception or idea of a part, but claimed as a fundamental principle, capable of being interpreted so as to cover all the *primary* laws.

Reduced eye: a simplified or schematic eye. See *Listing's reduced eye.*

Reductio ad absurdum: disproving a proposition by showing that it logically involves a conclusion admittedly false or absurd.

Reed: a tongue of wood or metal, whose vibrations produce a musical note; employed in reed instruments of various types.

Re-education: restoring a lost ability or group of abilities; an aspect of the wider process of *rehabilitation.*

Referred sensation: a sensory experience localized at a point quite different from the part affected by the stimulation.

Reflection: physically, the action of surfaces in throwing back light rays, heat rays, sound waves, etc., impinging upon them; psychologically, turning one's mind upon experiences, percepts, ideas, etc., with a view to the discovery of new relations, or the drawing of conclusions for the guidance of future action; considering.

Reflection coefficient: the ratio of the amount of light leaving a reflecting surface, to the amount incident on it.

Reflex: the direct and immediate response of an *effector* (muscle or gland), or group of effectors, to the stimulation of a *receptor* (sense organ); sometimes employed loosely of any apparently mechanical or automatic response to a stimulus, or even to an object.

Reflex arc: see *sensori-motor arc.*

Reflex time (Reflex latency): the time between the stimulus and the beginning of the response.

Reflexogenous zones: the areas of the skin and mucous membranes, the stimulation of which gives rise to more or less generalized motor responses.

Reformism: a term applied to an aggressive attitude, aiming at the reforming of defects in others, as a defensive measure against the detection by others of a tendency towards the same, defects in oneself.

Refracting media: transparent tissues and fluids in the eye, which refract or bend the rays of light entering the eye, so as to form images on the retina.

Refraction: change in the direction of propagation of waves of light, etc., in passing from one medium to another of different density; a function of the angle at which the wave-front encounters the new medium; the angle through which a ray is bent is called the *angle of refraction,* and is relative to the two media concerned, being therefore expressed as a ratio of the sine of the angle of incidence to the sine of the angle of refraction.

Refraction errors: errors due to some irregularity or defect in the refracting media of the eye, which produces a defect or distortion in the image on the retina.

Refractory period: a brief period of time, following the passage of a nerve impulse in a nerve fibre, during which it fails to respond, either absolutely, or relatively, i.e., only to more intense excitation, the absolute phase being followed by the relative phase.

Regard: in general sense, look; in a technical sense, employed in several connections: (1) *field of regard,* the total region of the external world, covered by the moving eye; (2) *line of regard,* the line joining the point of fixation with the centre of rotation of the eye; (3) *plane of regard,* the plane containing the fixation point, and the centres of rotation of the two eyes; (4) *point of regard,* the fixation point.

Regeneration: the restoring or replacing of a lost or degenerated part.

Regional: referring or belonging to a particular area or segment of the body or a part of the body.

Register: in music, the compass or range of frequencies producible by an instrument, or the human voice; specially, a particular range of tones, which can be produced in the same way and with the same quality or *timbre.*

Regression: in general sense, return or reversion to an earlier or more primitive stage, type or phase; three main and distinct technical senses:—

1. The tendency on the part of individual organisms, or social groups, to revert towards the typical form. See *filial regression.*

2. The psychoanalytical usage of the reverting of the *libido* to a channel of expression, belonging to an earlier phase of development, or the reverting of the individual to interests and forms of behaviour characteristic of an earlier or infantile stage, often as a result of *fixation* (q.v.).

3. The statistical usage, with reference to the relation between paired variables, for example, the scores of individuals in two mental tests, where the relation is expressed in the form of an equation – the *regression equation* – which expresses the value of *x* to be expected for a given value of *y*, or the value of *y* for a given value of *x*, the correlation *r* between the *x* and *y* tests being known, giving a *regression coefficient,* expressed by $r\ \dfrac{\sigma_x}{\sigma_y}$ where σ_x and σ_y are the standard deviations in the two tests.

Regression, phenomenal: the tendency towards the real object under normal conditions, when the size, shape, colour, brightness of the object under special conditions is being estimated. See *constancy phenomena.*

Regression time: the interval of time taken by a reader to readjust his fixation to the beginning of the next line, or to readjust to words and phrases he has inadequately perceived within a line, to which he goes back.

Regret: an unpleasant feeling, with reference to a past experience or act, together with the desire that it had eventuated or been performed otherwise.

Regular: in accordance with a definite law or principle.

Reichenbach phenomenon: see *odylic force.*

Reinforcement: the action of one process of nervous excitation in increasing the intensity of a second; term employed by psychoanalysts for a process in which the primary motif of a dream is repeated by a dream within the main dream.

Reissner's membrane: a membrane in the *cochlea* separating the *scala vestibuli* from the *scala media.*

Rejection: a type of avoiding behaviour on the part of an organism; throwing out something that has already been partly taken into the body; mentally a negative attitude towards a judgment, suggestion, or belief.

Rejuvenation: restoration of vitality in a senescent organism.

Relationship system: system of designation, classification, and social significance of kinship, or other relationship, sanctioned by tradition or tribal law among a people.

Relative: dependent upon comparison with other objects or items in the same class or series; employed also of accommodation, as between the two eyes, of sensitivity, of variability, etc.

Relative suggestion: a term employed by *Thomas Brown,* to distinguish a type of association which, as contrasted with a purely mechanical type, brings out new connections in the material and so involves mental activity; the term is also used by *Stout,* but with greater stress on the activity, and less on the association aspect.

Relativity principle or law: the principle that all experiences are relative to simultaneous or preceding experience.

Relaxation feeling: one of the ultimate qualitative variations or dimensions of feeling, in *Wundt's tridimensional theory* – tension-relaxation.

Relaxation principle: an aspect of psychoanalytic procedure, where the analyst, in order to keep the atmosphere easy, adopts the mood of the patient; also employed of muscular relaxation, as a method of treatment of stammering and other conditions involving muscular tension.

Relearning: the reacquisition of some skill or some memory material already acquired, but lost as a result of disease, injury, or obliviscence.

Reliability: used technically, in a statistical sense, of the consistency of a test with itself, i.e. the extent to which we can assume that it will yield the same result if repeated a second time.

Reliability coefficient: a measure of consistency; the *correlation coefficient* between two repetitions of the same test; to save time the correlation between two halves of one test – the *split half method* is often substituted.

Relief: deviation towards the observer of parts of a visually regarded object, from the plane of the remainder; the opposite of *intaglio*.

Religion: either a systematic theory of the superhuman or divine, as a power or influence behind material processes and the general course of events, or an attitude involving a personal belief in such a power, and some determination or modification of conduct in the light of such belief.

Religion, Psychology of: that branch of psychology which investigates the psychological origin and nature of the religious attitude, or religious experience, and the various phenomena in the individual arising from or accompanying such attitude and experience.

Religious instinct: an assumed instinctive tendency in the human being to believe in, and cultivate relations with, superhuman agencies and powers.

Remedial instruction (*training*)*:* attempts to train defectives and delinquents, so as to make them, as far as possible, useful and efficient members of the community.

Remember: to recall, with full *recognition*, a past experience, as a train of imagery, concrete or verbal.

Reminiscence: recall which is passive rather than active; for the latter *recollection* is the preferable term.

Remission: temporary abatement or diminution of a pathological process, particularly one of a paroxysmal character.

Remorse: a painful emotional state, characterized by a feeling of responsibility for an action or event now deeply regretted.

Remote: term employed technically, in connection with exploring movement, of the touch sensations from an object touched, as contrasted with the *resident* sensations, mainly of movement in the moving part or parts; term also used of an association of an item in a series with another item, not contiguous to it.

Renal: referring or relating to the kidney.

Repression: a conception developed initially by *Freud* and the psychoanalysts, which has largely displaced the *dissociation* (q.v.) of the French pyschopathologists, the essential difference from 'dissociation' being that it is dynamic and explanatory and not merely descriptive; applied primarily, with *Freud,* to a mental process arising from conflict between the 'pleasure principle' and the 'reality principle', as when impulses and desires are in conflict with enforced standards of conduct; as a result such impulses and desires with the associated memories and ideal systems, and the painful emotions arising out of the conflict, are actively or automatically thrust out of consciousness into the unconscious, in which, however, they still remain active, determining behaviour and experience, for the most part indirectly, and producing neurotic symptoms of various kinds, as well as determining dreams, both night and day, and underlying many types of deviations from normal behaviour. *Rivers* has suggested that the term 'repression' should be employed in its ordinary sense of 'actively thrusting out of the mind', and the term 'suppression' employed for the automatic process, to which the term is practically restricted by Freud.

Reproduction: the process of reinstatement as imagery of experiences previously perceptual; the essential process, along with *retention,* in remembering.

Reproduction method: a method of testing material learned, with respect to its retention, and its accuracy of reproduction; also sometimes used as a designation for the psychophysical *method of mean error.*

Reproductive: term employed in two quite distinct senses:

1. Of the function involved in both sexes in producing offspring, and arising from that the *selection,* in an evolutionary sense, dependent on relative fertility.

2. Of the type of imagination which seeks to reinstate, as imagery, the exact pattern of previous perceptual experience, and more generally, of the *tendency* towards reinstatement, based on associational, perseverational, and impressional factors (primary and secondary laws).

Repugnance: an emotional attitude towards an action or object, with the impulse towards strong opposition or rejection.

Repulsion: repugnance, with a more or less definite disgust, or even nausea.

Research: systematic scientific investigation in pursuit of knowledge, or confirmation, in any field.

Resentment: an emotional attitude characterized by anger against someone, because of real or imagined obstruction of one's interests, or injury to oneself or one's friends.

Residues method: the fourth of *Mill's* canons of *inductive reasoning*, to the effect that, if we deduct from any phenomenon the part already known to be the effect of certain antecedents, we can infer that the residue is the effect of the remaining antecedents.

Residuum: the remainder left, after certain parts or constituents have been accounted for, in any complex phenomenon; also sometimes, of the trace of any experience left behind.

Resignation: an emotionally tinged attitude shown by the cessation of active response to a situation, which we have previously been making efforts to alter.

Resinous: one of *Henning's* six ultimate qualities of olfactory sensation, of which a typical illustration is the smell of a pine or fir cone.

Resistance: in general sense, opposition, or an opposing force; in psychoanalytical literature, employed of an active opposition of a subject, preventing unconscious material from becoming conscious, or from receiving expression, particularly such unconscious material as has suffered *repression*.

Resistance sensation: a complex of pressure and *kinaesthetic* sensory impressions, when muscles are being contracted against opposing pressure.

Resolution: a decision regarding a line of conduct to be pursued; a firm adherence to a decision that has been taken; a character trait, marked by firmness of purpose in persisting in a course of action decided on.

Resolution law or principle: the principle, formulated by *Jennings*, to the effect that the resolution or change from one physiological state to another becomes easier and quicker after it has taken place a number of times.

Resonance: the vibratory response of a physical object, particularly a stretched string or wire, to a frequency of vibration imposed upon it, which happens with the greater readiness the more nearly the imposed frequency corresponds to the natural vibration frequency of the object.

Resonance box: a resonator consisting of a wooden box, the size of which is appropriate to the tuning fork placed upon it, with respect to vibration frequency.

Resonator: an apparatus for intensifying the loudness of a tone of its natural frequency, consisting usually of a metal sphere, or a cylinder open at one end, or a box as above.

Respect: a sentiment of valuation, or, when active, an attitude involving valuation, either of oneself or of other people, in the latter case accompanied by some slight degree of deference; figuratively applied also to a philosophy or mode of life, system of belief, and the like, involving a measure of appreciation, esteem or deference.

Respiration: the breathing function.

Response: the activity, muscular or glandular, of an organism with reference to a situation with which it is faced, or as a result of stimulation. Cf. *reaction.*

Responsibility: the fact, state, or feeling, of being answerable for, or having an obligation in connection with, someone or something.

Responsible: answerable, or accountable for something, or liable to be regarded as such, from the point of view of age, capacity, position, or mental state.

Rest: cessation, or relative cessation, of serious activity, mental or muscular, as a general rule because of fatigue.

Rest pause: a pause introduced during a working period, with the object of eliminating or reducing fatigue, and usually forming a regular part of the organization of the work.

Restlessness: a general state of the organism, reflecting itself in a feeling which some psychologists have regarded as one of the elementary dimensions of feeling, along with its opposite *quiescence* (q.v.).

Result: a situation or event which is regarded as arising out of certain preceding conditions; the data obtained from a scientific experiment.

Retained members method: a method of experiment in memorizing, useful as a group method, where a measure of retention can be obtained from the percentage of items correctly reproduced after the material has been presented a certain number of times.

Retardation: in general sense, the slowing up of movement or development; applied usually to the mental development of a child, where the mentality is definitely below normal, and even below an *I.Q.* of 70, which is generally taken as the upper limit of *feeblemindedness,* but where the examiner hesitates to label the child as definitely defective; might be employed of any I.Q. between 60 and 90.

Retention: the persisting trace left behind as an after-effect by any experience, forming the basis of learning, memory, habit, and skill, and of all development, so far as it is based upon experience.

Retina: the innermost of the three coats of the eye, on which the images of external objects in the field of vision are formed by the lens system, containing the *rods and cones,* the receptors for vision.

Retinal: belonging or referring to the retina, as in *retinal elements,* the *rods and cones* with the nerve paths leading from them, *retinal horizon,* the horizontal line in the retina on which the external horizon is imaged, with the eyes in the *primary position* (q.v.), *retinal oscillations,* the excitation effect on the retina of a single momentary stimulation, giving a succession of alternating light and dark after-effects, as in *Charpentier's bands* (q.v.), or in *after-images.*

Retinal rivalry: phenomena shown when the two eyes are simultaneously stimulated with different colours, or different figures, as one with red and the other with blue, under which conditions there is alternation in the visual field for both eyes, one colour alternating with the other, that is alternation from the predominance of the one eye to the predominance of the other, one colour, or one figure, occupying the whole field for a period, and then the other for a period, in alternation.

Retinitis: inflammation of the retina, generally causing blind areas, or *scotomata.*

Retinitis pigmentosa: inflammatory or pathological condition of the pigment layer of the retina, affecting colour sensitivity, areas of the colour fields, and *dark adaptation.*

Retinoscope: an instrument for examining the retina, and the refracting condition of the media, consisting essentially of a small mirror, perforated in the centre, by which a beam of light can be thrown on the retina.

Retroaction: effect of a new experience or piece of learning on retention of a previous experience or piece of learning.

Retroactive association: a connection established between an item in a series and another item which has preceded it in the series. See also *facilitation* and *inhibition.*

Retrobulbar: two meanings; the posterior or dorsal side of the *medulla;* behind the eyeball.

Retrograde: moving backwards; degenerating.

Retrospection: looking backwards, to what has been experienced in the past; technically used of *introspection* of an experience that is immediately past, under certain conditions the only kind of introspection possible.

Retrospective falsification: distortion of, addition to, or subtraction from, an experience when recalled, due to the operation of interest on the train of imagery, and confusion between what is remembered and what is imagined.

Retrospective reference: the essential characteristic of remembering, which involves the placing of a remembered experience in its temporal location and context.

Revenge: deliberate infliction of injury upon others, individuals or groups, from whom injury has been received.

Reverberation: repetition through reflection of sounds in an enclosed, or partially enclosed, space.

Reverence: a complex emotional state, in which, according to *Mc-Dougall*, three *primary* emotions at least are fused – fear, negative self-feeling, and tender emotion, with emphasis on the second.

Reverie: more or less aimless trains of imagery and ideas, often of the nature of *day-dreaming* or *phantasy*.

Reversible perspective: a type of geometrical *optical illusion*, experienced with regard to certain drawings which on being regarded for a short time show a change of figure with respect to perspective, and thereafter keep alternating from one aspect to the other.

Reversion: term employed with reference to inheritance of a character or trait which appears in one generation, but was not apparent in the immediately preceding generation, but did appear in an earlier ancestor. See *atavism*.

Revival: the re-presentation of an experience, usually as image or train of imagery, in the absence of the original stimulus.

Rhabdomancy: divining, by means of rods or wands. See *divining rod*.

Rheobase: the galvanic excitation threshold of nerve or muscle tissue. See *chronaxy*.

Rheostat: an arrangement for regulating the strength of current in a circuit, by varying the E.M.F. actuating that circuit, by means of a sliding resistance in a main circuit.

Rheotropism: orientating response to direction of flow or current in water.

Rhinencephalon: the olfactory region of the forebrain, inclusive of the *olfactory lobes*, the *hippocampi*, and other regions, on the mesial sides of the cerebral hemispheres.

Rhinophonia: a nasal voice.

Rhodopsin: visual purple (q.v.).

Rhythm: the regular succession of a given time interval or series of time intervals, marked off by sounds or movements, and with regular accentuation, objective or subjective.

Ridgway colours: a system of pigment colours, 1115 in all, designed for the specification of the plumage colours of birds.

Right and wrong cases method: one of the standard psychophysical methods developed by *Fechner*; employed mainly for the determination of absolute and difference thresholds – the most elaborate, and theoretically least open to objection, of the methods for this purpose; the procedure consists in presenting stimuli near the threshold (or differences) a great number of times, and, on the basis of the results, determining that value which is perceived, or discriminated, as often as it is not perceived or discriminated, i.e. in exactly 50 per cent of the cases, such a value being taken as the *threshold* value; the method of calculation may be graphical, by interpolation, or by utilizing the theory of probability, the last giving the most accurate result.

Right associates method: a method of experiment employed in the study of learning, usually called the *scoring method* (q.v.).

Righthandedness: see *dextrality*.

Righting response: a response of certain organisms, when placed on their backs, in resuming their normal position.

Rigidity: a state of general and persistent muscular contraction, met with frequently in hypnotic states, and also as a result of pathological or experimental interference with motor pathways, in the central nervous system.

Rite: a ceremony, usually of a religious character, established by law or custom; an element in a ritual.

Ritual: a system of religious or magical ceremonies or procedures, frequently with special forms of words, or a special (and secret) vocabulary, and usually associated with important occasions or actions.

Rivalry: competition between individuals or groups for specific objects or distinctions; frequently also used of competition between organs or processes. Cf. *retinal rivalry*.

RL: abbreviation for stimulus *threshold* or *limen*.

rms.: root-mean-square (q.v.) value.

Robot: Russian word meaning 'work'; mechanical arrangement to do characteristically human work; applied figuratively to an unintelligent mechanical worker.

Rod: a receptor for vision in the retina; so-called because of its rod-like shape; the main functioning organ in *dark adaptation*; distinguished from the other retinal receptor, the *cone*, the main organ in daylight and colour vision.

Rod vision: see *scotopic vision*.

Rods and cones: a layer in the retina – the second; the receptors for vision.

Rods of corti: part of the *organ of Corti*, in the *scala media*, in the *cochlea*, in the inner ear, supported on the *basilar membrane*, and containing the hair cells, which are the receptors for sound.

Rolandic fissure, or *fissure of Rolando:* now generally called the *central fissure;* a deep fissure in the cortex on the exterior of each hemisphere, running from the vertex downwards towards the *Sylvian fissure*, and dividing the frontal from the parietal lobe.

Romberg sign: the tendency to sway, when standing with feet together and eyes closed, characteristic of *tabes* (q.v.).

Root-mean-square: the square root of the mean of the squares of the values dealt with; when these are deviations from the mean we have the *standard deviation* (q.v.).

Rorschach test: a *projection test* (q.v.), which is an elaborated form of the *ink-blot test*, with some of the blots in colour.

Roscoe-bursen law: the law or principle that in various visual phenomena response is determined by the product of intensity and the duration of the stimulus, independently of either by itself.

Rossolino method: an early profile method in which a series of 38 tests of intellectual capacities is devised to give a *psychograph* or profile of an individual, from the intellectual point of view.

Rotation chair: a chair, mounted so as to rotate round a vertical axis, employed in the investigation of physiological and psychological phenomena produced by rotation.

Rotation perception: experiences due to the stimulation of the receptors of the *static sense*, in the *semi-circular canals*, in the inner ear, the stimulus being given by positive and negative acceleration of rotatory movement, in the horizontal and other planes, with eyes open or shut.

Rotation table: the type of arrangement generally used for psychological experiments on rotation, in the form of a platform, which may be rotated in any plane, and upon which a chair may be placed.

Rote learning: learning by pure repetition, regardless of meaning, and without any attempt at organization.

Rotoscope: an instrument based on stroboscopic principles, for observing machinery in rapid movement.

Roughness: in tactual experiences, unevenness arising from a number of simultaneous or successive pressure stimuli of varying intensity; in hearing, an experience of sounds rapidly changing in waveform and amplitude, as with *beats*.

Rubin's figure: a reversible goblet-profile figure, employed by *Gestalt* psychologists to illustrate the *figure-ground* phenomena.

Ruffini corpuscle (Cylinder): end-organs in subcutaneous tissue, believed by some to be receptors for warmth.

Rumour: an unverified story, circulating in a community, alleging the occurrence of a certain event.

Russmethode (Ger.): a procedure, by means of smoke-rings, from a small gas jet, deposited on a moving ribbon, to record pulsations of the voice.

S

S: abbreviation usually employed for 'subject' in an experiment; also used for stimulus, with R for response, in the combination SR.

s factor: see *specific factor*.

S.D.: standard deviation.

Saccadic movement: sudden movement of the eyes from one fixation point to another, as in reading.

Saccadic speed: the rate at which saccadic movements take place.

Saccadic time: the sum total of the intervals during which the eye is in movement in reading a line as contrasted, with the fixation time.

Saccule: one of the sacs – the other is the *utricle* – in the membranous labyrinth of the inner ear, attached to the *semi-circular canals*.

Sacred: set apart for some purpose, usually religious; or connected with a god or with worship.

Sacrum: the triangular bone near the base of the spinal column, and forming the back wall of the *pelvis*. Adjective *sacral*.

Sadism: a type of sexual perversion, characterized by obtaining sexual pleasure or gratification from maltreating other individuals of either sex; sometimes used generally of love of cruelty.

Sadness: an emotional mood, tending towards sorrow, characterized by relative passivity and diminished muscular tone, with sighing, and not infrequently weeping.

Sagittal axis or plane: the line of direction passing through the body from back to front, or any vertical plane parallel to the medial plane of the body and inclusive of that plane; often restricted to the medial plane – the plane of the sagittal suture.

St Vitus Dance: see *chorea.*

Salesmanship: the qualities promoting, or the principles underlying, success in effecting the sale of anything; more specifically success as a salesman, and the qualities entering into it.

Saliva: the fluid secreted by the salivary glands, and discharged into the mouth cavity, which assists in mastication, swallowing and digestion.

Salivary reflex: the glandular reflex stimulated by the presence of any substance (normally food) in the mouth, and manifesting itself in the activity of the salivary glands.

Salpetrière school: a school of *psychopathology,* represented in the views of *Charcot* and his followers, taking their name from *Charcot's* clinic at the Salpetrière, Paris; particularly notable for views regarding the hypnotic state.

Salpinx: the oviduct or *Fallopian tube.*

Same-opposite test: see *synonym-antonym test.*

Sampling: the selection, usually at random, of a limited number from a large group or population, for testing and statistical treatment, on the assumption that the sample may be taken as representative, for the particular purpose, of the whole group.

Sampling errors: errors due to the fact that a sample may not be truly representative of the whole group; statistically, the difference between the mean of the sample and the mean of the whole group.

Sanction: the grounds for an individual's action; socially, the means taken to compel individuals to act in accordance with social standards.

Sanford envelopes: set of weighted envelopes, used by Sanford to determine *difference thresholds* for lifted weights.

Sanford's pendulum chronoscope: an early *chronoscope* (q.v.), of the vernier pendulums type, for measuring *reaction time.*

Sanguine: one of the classical temperaments, characterized by optimism, changeableness, freedom from load, activity, and shallow emotions.

Sanity: full possession of faculties; a normal mental condition.

Santonin: a drug, which in large doses produces interesting phenomena of colour vision, notably the rare *blue-yellow* type of partial colour-blindness, or at least an approximation to it.

Sapphism: erotic attachment between women.

Sarcode: the jelly-like protoplasm forming the bodies of *protozoa.*

Satisfaction: the simple feeling-state accompanying the attainment of any goal; the end-state in feeling accompanying the attainment by an impulse of its objective.

Satisfier: any stimulus, situation, or experience, which meets a need, or represents a goal.

Saturation: a dimension of a colour, which might be described, or defined, as the quantity of hue or chroma present in it; the 'hue intensity' of a colour; the degree in which a colour differs from a grey of the same *brightness* (or brilliance).

Saturation scale: a scale, based on the colours of the spectrum, and indicating steps from the most highly saturated colours to grey, of which there are 24 in red and blue, and 17 in yellow, in which numbers are used to indicate degrees of saturation.

Satyriasis: sexual insanity, or an exaggerated sexual desire in human males. Cf. *nymphomania.*

Savart Wheel: a disc with teeth, equally spaced round the circumference, which, when rotated with sufficient speed against a tongue, produces a tone the pitch of which varies with the speed of rotation of the disc, and the frequency corresponding to which is given by the number of teeth striking the tongue per second.

Saving method: a method of quantitative experimentation in memory, for studying in particular the amount remembered and the amount forgotten after the lapse of different periods of time subsequent to the learning by a certain number of repetitions, this number giving the amount of initial learning, while the difference between this number and the number of repetitions required to relearn, after the lapse of any period, represents the 'saving'. Full name is '*learning and saving method*'.

Scala media: the canal in the *cochlea,* between the *scala vestibuli* and the *scala tympani,* containing the *organ of Corti.*

Scala tympani: the canal in the *cochlea,* extending from the apex to the round window – *fenestra rotunda.*

Scala vestibuli: the canal in the *cochlea,* from the oval window – *fenestra ovalis,* to the apex.

Scale, mental: a series of mental tests, so arranged as to give a measurement of the level of mental development, usually in terms of *mental age* or of *intelligence quotient,* particularly where the tests are arranged in order of difficulty, or in age groups, as in the *Binet* and similar scales; a measuring rod for mental development.

Scale, musical: a series of tones, graduated in pitch, with a conventional number and arrangement of intervals or steps, within an *octave,* which is a natural division, in the sense that the octave bears a peculiar relation to the fundamental; the best known scales, at least in western music, are the *Pythagorean,* the *Major* and *Minor Diatonic,* the *Chromatic,* and the *Equally Tempered,* in the first three of which the octave is divided into six tones, and in the last, into twelve equal semitones; apart from the *chromatic* and the *equally tempered* scales, the main difference between the others is the position of the semitones in the scale, which really constitutes the chief difference between major and minor scales; in the *Pythagorean* (*Lydian*) and *Major Diatonic,* the semitones are between the fourth and fifth and the seventh and eighth, while in the *Pythagorean* (*Hypo-Dorian*) and usual *Minor Diatonic,* the first semitone is between the second and the third, and the second between the fifth and sixth. These might all be called 'natural scales'. In the *equally tempered* scale, which represents an adaptation of these scales to keyboard instruments, the octave is divided into twelve semitones, all equally related to one another, the effect being to make the keyboard suitable for all the scales, but at the expense of slightly mistuning all the notes, except for the octaves. Other scales are the *tetrachord* or four-tone scale, used by the Ancient Greeks, the *pentatonic* or five-tone scale of Oriental music, and the *heptatonic* or seven-tone scale.

Scale, tonal: the range of frequencies audible to the human ear – from 16 to about 20,000 vibrations per second.

Scale value: the position of a test item on a scale, as indicated by its numerical designation.

Scapho-cephalic: term employed of a head, or skull, which is keel-shaped.

Scapula: shoulder-blade.

Scatter: the spread or *variability* of a distribution of measurements, scores, etc.

Scatter diagram: a table or chart, showing the distribution of a group of individuals with respect to two characters, or showing the relation between two series of paired measurements; a grid.

Scheiner's experiment: an experiment demonstrating visual *accommodation,* in which, one eye being shut, a card with two pinholes, at a distance apart less than the diameter of the pupil, is placed over the other eye, when all objects nearer or farther away than the fixation point are seen double.

Schema: a mental framework or outline, which refuses to be sharply defined consciously, is of the order of a set or attitude, but less definite, and functions as a kind of vague standard, arising out of past experience, and placing any fresh experience in its appropriate context and relations.

Scheme: a plan, programme or project; in some cases an outline.

Schizoid: a *personality type,* tending towards *dissociation* of the emotional from the intellectual life; a shut-in personality.

Schizophrenia: a type of mental disorder, inclusive of what was formerly called *dementia praecox,* characterized by dissociation, particularly between the intellectual processes and the affective, the latter being also to a great extent disorganized, with many varieties.

Schizothymic: possessing schizoid characteristics within the limits of normality.

Schlaftiefmesser (*Ger.*): 'depth of sleep measurer'; an apparatus for measuring depth of sleep at different intervals of time, by dropping a series of balls of constant weight automatically from different heights on sound boards; the sleeper is instructed to stop the apparatus when he is waked from sleep, and the height from which the last ball was dropped is taken as the measure of the depth of the sleep.

Scientific management: a term employed to designate work begun by Taylor in 1881 – and therefore sometimes called *Taylorism* – which, to begin with, involved simply the adoption of a scientific attitude and objective methods of study with respect to the methods and movements of workers, with a view to increasing output and reducing costs, by introducing changes calculated to promote these objects.

Sciosophy: a term used of systems of thought based on beliefs which are not consistent with modern scientific knowledge, as, for example, *astrology, theosophy,* and to some extent *phrenology,* or at least *cranioscopy.*

Sclerosis: hardening of tissues.

Sclerotic: the tough white outer coat of the eyeball, which in the *cornea* becomes transparent; the white of the eye.

Scope: range; in science usually the whole group of phenomena, processes, or events falling within the limits of the field of any science, enquiry, investigation, or principle.

Scopic method: method of recording quantitative data by visual observation. Cf. *graphic method.*

Scopophilia: deriving a sexual gratification from looking at the naked human form, articles of dress, etc.

Score: the quantitative value assigned to the response to an item in a series of tests, or to the whole series of responses to the whole series of tests; a quantitative mark.

Scoterythrous: term employed of a type of colour-blindness, in which the extreme red of the spectrum is darkened or black; shortened spectrum at the red end, characteristic of total colour-blindness and of *protanopia.*

Scotoma: an area in the retina which is blind or partially blind, usually specified as central, paracentral, etc. The plural is *scotomata.*

Scotometer: an instrument, similar in principle to a *perimeter,* for locating and mapping *scotomata.*

Scotomization: a term employed by some psychoanalysts for a process of depreciating or denying everything conflicting with the valuation of the *ego.*

Scotopic adaptation: dark adaptation, with special emphasis on the functioning of the *rods.*

Scotopic vision: vision under conditions of *dark adaptation;* twilight vision.

Scratch reflex: scratching movements of hind leg of an animal, elicited by scratching, or rubbing, the flank, or side of the neck.

Screen memory: a psychoanalytic term for fragmentary memory items from early childhood, represented by something trivial in processes of *condensation,* in the *manifest dream content.* Sometimes called *cover memory.*

Script: a type of handwriting in which characters intermediate between cursive and print are employed, for which legibility and other psychological advantages are claimed.

Scripture weights: a series of small light discs, each suspended by a light thread from a wooden handle, used, but not devised, by *Scripture,* for the determination of pressure thresholds on the skin.

Scripture's Blocks: name usually given to a well-known ambiguous perspective figure of a pile of cubes which reverses when one starts to count them; and also of a pile of logs of which the ends are exhibited, which produces the same illusion.

Scrying: employing a crystal or a bright reflecting surface, to obtain visual hallucinations, or projected visual (*eidetic*) imagery; crystal gazing.

Séance: a sitting for the purpose of obtaining spiritistic or metapsychical phenomena; usually, though not always, a group assemblage, with a *medium,* in a darkened room.

Seashore tests of Musical Talent (ability): a series of gramophone records for measuring specific fundamental musical capacities, such as *pitch discrimination, tonal memory, rhythm,* etc.

Sebaceous gland: kind of gland secreting an oily liquid, found all over the skin, except on the palm of the hand, and the sole of the foot.

Seclusiveness: the tendency to cut oneself off from social contacts; frequently pathological.

Second sight: term employed for prophetic vision, among Celtic people for the most part. Cf. *clairvoyance.*

Secondarily automatic: term employed of responses which, through frequent repetition, have become practically automatic.

Secondary elaboration: the contribution of the teller of a story, to the story as told; employed primarily in relation to *dream analysis* (q.v.).

Secondary Function: the persistence of a nervous or mental process, or its influence, for some time after its primary function has been, so to speak, performed, as in the phenomena of *perseveration*; one of the differentiating features, marking off types of *temperament* or *personality,* in the opinion of some investigators (*Heymans* and *Wiersma*).

Secondary Qualities: term employed in an old controversy regarding perception, and the properties of matter, epistemological rather than psychological, for those properties of objects which give rise to sensory qualities which do not resemble the properties themselves, as for example wave motion, which gives rise to experience of sound or light or colour; the distinction between *primary* and *secondary* qualities was apparently drawn as early as *Democritus.*

Secondary sex characteristics: characteristics, anatomical, physiological, and psychological, which differentiate the sexes, but apparently play no part in reproduction.

Secretion: the substances produced by glands and other tissues; the activities involved in producing these substances.

Sect: a group of individuals following certain practices, or holding, and usually expressing, certain opinions, the practices and the opinions marking them off from the general community.

Secular: term employed of changes of culture taking place during long periods of time; popularly used also of activities which are not religious.

Security: the condition of being in safety, or free from threat of danger to life, or what is highly valued; employed in special sense by *Adler,* of a condition in which power or conquest is attained without struggle.

Segmental reflex: a reflex involving only one segment – more properly region – of the cord.

Segmental theory: the theory, with respect to the nervous system of segmented organisms, that the segment of the nervous systems in each segment of the body controls the activities in that segment.

Segregation: in general sense, separation or isolation; two distinct technical senses: (1) in *Gestalt psychology*, the appearance of wholes, detached from their surroundings, as a result of dynamic *self-distribution* in the sensory field, and (2) in *genetics*, the reappearance in the second, missing the first, generation, of *recessive characters*, present in one of the parents.

Segregation Law: the principle in *genetics* that characters in which parents differ are segregated in the second generation in a definite ratio, typically into three *dominant* to one *recessive*.

Sejunction: term employed by *Wernicke*, in practically the same sense as *dissociation*, in so far as it affects the *personality*.

Selected group: a group for experimental purposes, selected with reference to a particular character, or group of characters, either intentionally, with reference to the object of the experiment, or accidentally, where a random selection was intended; a *sample* which is not representative of the whole group or population, because of the operation of some selective factor or factors.

Selection: see *natural, social,* and *vocational.*

Selection method: an experimental method in which the subject selects from a series the object or item which he judges equal to the standard object or item presented.

Selectionist: neo-Darwinian; one who holds that *natural selection* is a sufficient explanation of the process of evolution.

Selective agency: any factor or factors operating in such a way as to bring about selection, *natural, social,* or *mental.*

Selective synthesis: the selection manifested in a connected train of thought, involving, as it does, the rejection of irrelevant associations, where, apart from the operation of a selective agency – the aim or goal – such associations might as readily determine the ideas in the mind as those which determine the appearance of the relevant ideas.

Selenium cell: a type of *photometer* for detecting changes in the intensity of light, based on the property of the rare metal selenium, in virtue of which its resistance varies with the amount of light falling upon it.

Selenium dog: a device employed to illustrate the part that may be played by stimuli in determining the direction of movement or response (see *tropism*), consisting of a mechanical dog on wheels, having for its eyes two selenium cells separated by an opaque screen, and arranged so that they operate the wheels, with the result that the dog follows a moving light.

Self: usually in the sense of the *personality* or *ego*, regarded as an agent, conscious of his own continuing identity; often used widely of an animal or even material object regarded as an agent. Employed as a prefix or as a separate word.

Self-abasement: the impulse involved in *negative self-feeling*, or the feeling of inferiority; the normal response of submission or humility.

Self-absorption: a high state of abstraction from external stimuli or events; excessive or even pathological *egoism* or *narcissism*.

Self-accusation: charging oneself with sins or crimes which are frequently purely imaginary; a symptom of pathological depression.

Self-activity: changes within the mental life, consciously produced by, and felt as originating in, oneself.

Self-consciousness: awareness of one's own existence, thoughts and actions; popularly embarrassment or shyness.

Self-consistency: employed of persons, theories, or things, in the sense of not contradicting themselves in any action, phase, or aspect.

Self-control: control exercised by the individual over his own feelings, impulses, and acts.

Self-deception: deceiving oneself. See *rationalization*.

Self-denial: denying oneself the satisfying of wants, wishes, or desires.

Self-determination: guidance, by the individual, of his own conduct; in a wide sense, as an aspect of the *free-will controversy*, implying the causal efficacy of *purpose*.

Self-display: tendency to make oneself prominent; often used, as by McDougall, for the impulse to secure recognition from one's fellows – the *positive self-impulse*.

Self-distribution: term employed by Gestalt psychology of that dynamic in the sensory field which results in the organization of that field.

Self-expression: in a general sense, the expression in behaviour of one's own nature; in a more special sense, applied to the development of an individual, through free expression of his own tastes, interests, and capacities.

Self-impulse: the impulse to seek recognition from one's fellows.

Self-love: egoism in its emotional aspect; *narcissism*.

Self-observation: in its technical sense, equivalent to *introspection*.

Self-preservation: a term, loosely used to cover a group of instinctive impulses – not a single instinct – directed towards the preservation of the life of the individual.

Self-psychology: a type or system of psychology, taking its departure from the *self*, as revealed in *introspection*, and making this, as it were, a point, or line, of reference throughout.

Self-punishment mechanism: a psychoanalytic term for neurotic symptoms arising from excessive reaction of *the super-ego* (conscience), in conflict with impulses from the *id* (primitive nature).

Self-rating: an attempt by an individual to assess his own *personality* by means of a *rating scale* (q.v.).

Self sentiment: the *sentiment* of value, which has the idea of the self as its core: *McDougall's* 'self-regarding sentiment'; in its developed form *self-respect*.

Semantics: the scientific study, and detailed or critical investigation, of the evolution of the meanings of words; the science of meaning generally; in the wider sense, *semasiology, semeiology,* and *semeiotics* are also used.

Semblance: the outward aspect of something; often the appearance of something that is not actually there, or of which the reality is different.

Semi-circular canals: three canals in planes at right angles to one another, in which the receptors of the *static sense* are found; situated in the inner ear. See *ear.*

Semi-interquartile range: a measure of the dispersion or scatter of a distribution by half the difference between the first and third *quartiles,* or 25th and 75th percentiles; sometimes spoken of as the *probable error,* or *quartile deviation.*

Semitone: half a tone, or step, in a musical scale, varying somewhat in the different *scales*; in the *equally tempered scale* represented by the ratio 1 : 2, and in the *diatonic* by the ratio 15 : 16.

Senescence: growing old; the degenerative changes which begin relatively early, but become more marked in old age.

Senile dementia: dementia resulting from shrinking of brain in advanced age.

Senilism: presence of signs characteristic of *senility,* whether in old age or prematurely.

Senility: the impairment, particularly of mental functions, present in old age; the end result of *senescence.*

Sensation: the ultimate and irreducible aspect or element of sense perception, dependent upon the stimulus affecting a sense receptor;

really an abstraction, but generally discussed, especially in physiology and psychophysics, as if it were an elementary experience; the process of sensing.

Sensation level: a term used in the auditory field of the number of *decibels* above the *threshold,* for any sound.

Sensation unit: term employed in the auditory field for a unit of loudness, corresponding to the *decibel*, which is the unit of physical intensity; the abbreviation *SU* is generally employed.

Sensationalism: a type of psychological theory, represented in its purest form by *Condillac* (q.v.), which seeks to reduce all mental processes and contents to their elements as units of sensation, the connecting principle being *association;* usually held along with *associationism.*

Sense: employed generally of sensory experience as a whole, or of the world of sensation, and usually with this meaning, when employed adjectivally; also, specially, of a specific sense department – a sense – differing in *modality,* and in type of receptor or organ, from other sense departments.

Sense datum: what is actually given, as a result of the immediate effect of the stimulus on the sense organ; the specific contribution to sense perception of the sense organ.

Sense-feeling: the pleasantness or unpleasantness of a sensory experience; the *hedonic tone* of a sensation.

Sense illusion: see *illusion.*

Sense impression: synonymous with sense datum, but with rather more emphasis on the objective aspect; sensation.

Sense organ: the special end-organ of sense, inclusive usually of the essential part or parts in the actual receptors, and also the accessory parts, by which reception is facilitated.

Sense perception: the apprehension of situations or objects, determined by, or based on, stimuli affecting the sense organs at the moment.

Sense quality: the specific character of a sensation, which persists through quantitative variations, within a separate and specific sense department; that which makes any sensation, in a special sense, what it is. Cf. *modality.*

Sensed difference: a difference between sensations, which is noticed or apprehended.

Sensibility: capacity of being stimulated by sense stimuli; not to be confused with *sensitivity,* though the two are often used as synonymous.

Sensibilometer: a form or type of touch-key, where the circuit, in a reaction or other experiment, is closed by pressing the key.

Sensitive: in usual psychological meaning, capable of experiencing a particular kind or degree of stimulation; in psychical research, one who is peculiarly susceptible to occult influences – *a medium.*

Sensitive zones: regions of the body specially susceptible to cutaneous stimulation.

Sensitiveness: the characteristic of being peculiarly sensitive, or having a low *threshold* for various types of stimulation, evoking sensations, feelings, or emotions.

Sensitivity: in general sense, susceptibility to stimulation; used more particularly of ability to be affected by, and respond to, stimuli of low intensity, or to slight stimulus differences.

Sensitization: the process in a receptor, or receptors, of becoming or being made more excitable by sense stimuli.

Sensitization period: the interval of time required to become sensitive to a definite stimulus.

Sensori-motor: term employed with reference to structures, processes, or phenomena involving both the sensory and the motor aspects, or parts, of the *psycho-organic system.*

Sensori-motor activity: responses following on and with reference to sensory stimulation.

Sensori-motor arc: the functional unit of the nervous system, as establishing a connection between *receptor* and *effector*, or between the situation with which an organism is faced, and the motor response which the organism makes, thus performing the essential function of a nervous system; consisting normally of two or more structural units or *neurons*, one *afferent*, conducting the nerve impulse from the receptor, and the other *efferent*, conducting the impulse to the effector – muscle or gland.

Sensory: term employed with reference to all the structures and phenomena on the receptor and afferent side of the *psycho-organic system*, the stimuli affecting the receptors or sense-organs, the receptors or sense-organs themselves, the processes in the receptors, the nerves conveying nerve impulses away from the sense organs, and the nerve centres to which these impulses are conveyed.

Sensorium: a term practically obsolete in modern psychology; formerly used for the seat of sensation in the brain; sometimes used for the sensory mechanism as a whole.

Sensory acuity: the degree in which, in any sense department, an individual can apprehend stimuli of low intensity.

Sensory aphasia: see *aphasia.*

Sensory areas: regions of the cerebral cortex which are the final centres to which nerve impulses from the sense-organs are conveyed by afferent paths.

Sensory discrimination: ability to distinguish between stimuli differing qualitatively or quantitatively, and the degree in which such ability is present – the obverse of *difference threshold.*

Sensory organization: term employed by *Gestalt* psychologists for that organization which takes place in the sensory field, from the patterning of the stimuli, and the dynamic *self-distribution* of the field.

Sensory process: the process, or processes, as a whole, underlying sensation; the process, or processes, in the receptor.

Sensory reaction (sometimes called 'sensorial'): a type of response in a reaction time experiment in which the subject's attention is directed towards the stimulus, rather than the response; contrasted with *muscular* or *motor reaction.*

Sensual: usually employed with reference to excessive appetite for, and indulgence in, sense pleasures, particularly those of food and drink and sex. Must be distinguished from *sensuous.*

Sensuous: usually employed with reference to the special emphasizing of the sense aspect of experience; also used of tendency in some individuals to have affective or emotional experience from the sense aspect.

Sensum: sense datum; sometimes unnecessarily assumed as an intermediary between sense impression and percept.

Sentience: the capacity, or property, of receiving stimuli; the primitive (hypothetical) limit of consciousness.

Sentiendum: any quality of a perceptible object, considered, from the abstract point of view, solely as to its being capable of being sensed.

Sentiment: an emotional *disposition* (q.v.), centring round the idea of an object; not an experience, but part of an individual's make-up; sometimes expressed schematically, but not accurately, as *idea* + *affect*; older meaning, a complex and somewhat feeble emotion, still surviving in the expression *aesthetic sentiment.*

Sentimentality: trait, or characteristic, of an individual, whose actions are largely ruled by his *sentiments;* over-indulgence in the softer emotions, associated with the love sentiment.

Septum: a dividing partition.

Septum lucidum: the double-walled partition separating the anterior ends of the two lateral *ventricles* in the brain.

Sequela: a morbid condition, resulting from and following on an illness.

Sequence: a series of events, following on one another in time, and suggesting (usually) some sort of causal dependence on one another.

Serial: belonging to a series.

Serial behaviour: an integrated sequence of acts, as in a skilled performance, or the sequence of responses in the running of a maze.

Series: a group of items, objects, etc. arranged in a definite order of succession; employed particularly of a group of stimuli arranged in a sequence, as in the *serial method* of procedure, rather than presented simultaneously; also of the arrangement of experimental data.

Sessile: term employed of organisms which are fixed in position, as having inadequate or no organs of locomotion.

Set: a temporary condition of an organism, facilitating a certain more or less specific type of activity or response, as in *mental set* or *neural set.*

Set-up: arrangement of apparatus for a definite experiment, or series of experiments.

Sex: a fundamental distinction, relating to reproduction, within a species, dividing it into two divisions, male and female, according as *sperm cells* or *ova* (egg cells) are produced. In psychoanalytic theory *sex* and *sexual* are widened so as to include phenomena which have no direct bearing on reproduction, on the assumption that the pleasure derived is of the same order, is in fact essentially the same, in the case particularly of the young child, as that associated with sex phenomena in the strict sense; if in such cases *sensuous* were substituted for *sexual,* many of their views would be more readily accepted.

Sex character: any of the anatomical, physiological, or psychological characteristics, differentiating the sexes; classified into *primary,* those directly related to the reproductive functions, and *secondary,* those which play no direct role in reproduction.

Sex differences: used in mental assessment of any statistically significant differences in general mental activity, or in performance, between the two sexes.

Sex feeling: a general term covering feelings and emotions experienced by members of one sex towards the other sex, which are attributable to the difference of sex.

Sex (Sexual) sensations: a special group of organic sensations from stimulation of receptor organs in the *erogenous zones* (q.v.).

Sexual infantilism: retardation in development of sexual characters, primary or secondary, although age of puberty has been reached; psychoanalytically, an arrest of sexual development at one of the *pregenital* stages, or *regression* to one of the earlier stages.

Sexual instinct: employed in a wide sense, in psychoanalytic theory, to cover all the impulses included under *sexual,* as opposed to *ego instinct*; alternative term, *psycho-sexual instinct.*

Sexual latency: term applied, in psychoanalytical theory, to the period from the fifth or sixth year of childhood to puberty, on the assumption that this period between infantile and normal adult sexuality is a period during which the sex development apparently shows a pause, as far as overt signs are concerned.

Sexual reproduction: reproduction of new organisms by the union of male and female sex cells.

Sexual selection: selection for mating, by individuals of one sex, of certain individuals of the opposite sex, because of certain characters which in consequence tend to become predominant in the population, functioning therefore as a factor determining the direction of evolution.

Sexual trauma: emotional shock of a sexual origin and character, experienced in early childhood, and in early psychoanalytic theory regarded as a determing cause in the later development of *hysteria,* a view now generally abandoned.

Sexuality: usually employed with reference to the mental aspect of the totality of primary and secondary sex characters; sometimes used in a semi-pathological sense of over-development of sexual impulses.

Shade: employed in a technical sense, of colours darker than medium grey; the mixture with black, and thus with loss of saturation, of any colour.

Sham feeding: feeding animals with a gastric fistula, so that the food does not enter the stomach, in order to study the gustatory, apart from the gastric, effects of food.

Shaman: primitive dealer in magic and the supernatural; medicine man.

Shame: a complex emotional state, involving negative self-feeling or a disagreeable feeling of inferiority or defect, but, according to *McDougall's* views, incapable of being experienced until a *self-sentiment* has been developed.

Shamming: counterfeiting a certain activity, attitude, or condition, in the case of human beings or animals, in order to attain some objective, e.g. escape from an enemy.

Sharp: term employed of several types of sense experience, as of an intense and narrowly localized *pain,* a pointed contact, an intense acid taste; in music, a note slightly (or a semi-tone) higher than a given or standard note.

Shell-shock: name formerly given, but now discontinued, to temporary or prolonged nervous disorders, manifesting a variety of symptoms, developed through experience of war conditions in the field, and of a functional character.

Shock: sudden depression of the nervous system, or nervous exhaustion produced by violent emotion, accident, surgical operation, etc.

Short-circuit appeal: term used in connection with salesmanship, so far as the salesman's objective and its attainment depend upon *suggestion,* or the direct evoking of some instinctive impulse.

Short-circuiting: term applied figuratively to the cutting out of movements and actions, involving the facilitation and simplification of a process taking place in the acquiring of a piece of skill.

Shut-in personality: individual characterized by extreme *introversion;* an individual showing a tendency towards *schizophrenia.*

Shyness: discomfort in presence of other people, arising from intense self-consciousness; in *McDougall's* view, due to the simultaneous evoking of *positive* and *negative self-feeling.*

Sib: primarily applied to blood relationship: kinship; one of two or more members of the same family (*sibling*).

Side-window experiment: an experimental demonstration of binocular contrast, in which the subject stands in front of a window, with profile parallel to the window, so that one eye is illumined, and the other in the shadow of the nose; under these circumstances a sheet of white paper will be seen, when brought near the face, in two shades with the two eyes, the picture for the shaded eye being the brighter, and also yellowish in colour.

Sigh: a deep, prolonged, and audible inspiration, followed by a brief expiration; excellently shown in a *pneumograph* record.

Sigma: the Greek letter σ, employed (1) as the symbol for one thousandth of a second, and (2) as a contraction for *standard deviation.*

Sigma score: an individual's score, in terms of *sigma,* i.e. his deviation from the mean divided by sigma, with the sign plus or minus, according as it is above or below the mean.

Sigmagram: a graph showing distribution of scores in terms of sigma.

Signal experiment: a type of *learning* experiment, carried out either with human subjects, or with animals, where the subject requires to learn to make a specific response among a number of possible responses, to a specific stimulus or signal.

Significance: a type of meaning, where a present stimulus or situation has a meaning acquired through past experience.

Similarity: correspondence in some respect, or identity with regard to salient features, between one object and another, or others.

Similarity Law: formerly assigned as one of the *primary laws of Association* (q.v.), but now discarded by many psychologists in favour of the law of *organization* or of *thought relations.*

Simple eye: an eye with a single focussing arrangement, or optical system, as contrasted with a *compound eye* (q.v.).

Simplex inheritance: inheritance of a character through one parent only.

Simplicity canon: see *economy principle.*

Simulation: feigning, on the part of an animal or human being.

Simultaneous contrast: see *contrast.*

Sin: contravention of moral law, so far as that is regarded as divine law, or the law of a deity.

Single stimuli method: any experimental method where the subject is asked to report on each stimulus by itself, only one stimulus being given at a time.

Singularism: a philosophical theory, to the effect that the universe is explicable on the basis of a single principle, as contrasted with *dualism* or *pluralism.*

Sinistrad writing: writing from right to left, as in mirror writing or Arabic script.

Sinistrality: preference for the left hand in motor activity, or for the left one of some other double organ of the body, with respect to use (e.g. eye or foot).

Sinus: a hollow or cavity.

Siren: an arrangement for producing sounds by perforated discs, rotating in a current of air or steam.

Sitophobia: marked fear or *phobia* for food.

Situation: the objective conditions, giving rise to a stimulus pattern, towards which the organism acts or reacts.

Size-weight illusion: a standard illusion of sense-perception, by which objects of a large size are perceived as lighter than smaller objects of the same weight, provided the subject is aware of the size difference, visually or by some other perceptual cue.

Skeletal: referring to the bony frame; used with reference to striped muscle.

Skewness: a statistical term for a *frequency distribution* which deviates from bilateral symmetry, or where the *mean* and *median* do not coincide, owing to bunching of cases at one end.

Skiascope: an instrument for determining the degree of ocular refraction. Cf. *retinoscope.*

Skill: ease, rapidity, and precision (usually) of muscular action.

Skin: the outer covering of the animal body, consisting of two main parts, the *epidermis* or *cutis* and the *derma* or *true skin.*

Skin eroticism: psychoanalytic term for (erotic) pleasure from the experience of scratching or rubbing.

Skioptic response: response to a primitive type of vision, where the organism is sensitive to light and shade, or shadow only.

Sleep: a physiological state, not clearly understood, of relative immobility, and failure of adequate conscious response to stimuli.

Sleep-walking: see *somnambulism.*

Slip comparison: in *paired comparison* experiments, the comparison of the second member of a pair, not with the first member of the pair, but with a member of the preceding pair.

Slip of the tongue: lapsus linguae; the introduction inadvertently of a wrong word or phrase, irrelevant to the rest of the sentence, or changing radically its meaning, contrary to the conscious intention of the speaker, but interpreted by psychoanalysts as the expression of a repressed wish.

Slow motion: in cinematography the projection of a film at a much slower rate than its original exposure (usually in the ratio of one to eight), thus permitting of the analysis of the movements.

Smell compensation: a doubtful observation of *Zwaardemaker,* that two smells can cancel one another; not confirmed by other observers.

Smile: an incipient laugh; the facial expression that of a laugh, but more subdued, and without the sounds of laughter.

Smoked drum: a cylinder, covered with glazed paper, on which a layer of soot is deposited by a smoky flame, employed as a recording surface in a *kymograph.*

Smooth(ed) curve: statistical term for a curve drawn so as to eliminate minor irregularities and fluctuations.

Smooth muscle: muscular tissue consisting of small spindle-shaped muscle cells, forming the walls of blood-vessels and internal organs of the body; involuntary muscle.

Smoothness: a complex of tactual and movement sensations, characterized by uniformity of impression; applied by transference to tastes and sounds.

Snellen Charts (Types): printed charts with rows of letters arranged in varying sizes of type, for testing *visual acuity*.

Snow-blindness: a temporary condition of impaired vision, characterized by bright reflected light, as from snow, and by a red tingeing of all objects.

Sociability: enjoyment of, and tendency to seek, the company of other people.

Social: used with reference to the relation of an individual to others of the same species; or to aggregates of individuals forming more or less organized groups; also of tendencies and impulses concerning others.

Social adaptation: the act of adapting oneself, and one's behaviour, to the conditions and requirements of the community in which one lives.

Social adjustment, maladjustment: condition of fitting into one's community, or social milieu, and satisfying its conditions and requirements, or failing to do so, and being out of harmony, and more or less at war, with one's social surroundings, with possibly somewhat serious individual repercussions.

Social attitudes: attitudes towards the community, and other members of the community.

Social behaviour: behaviour with reference to social requirements, i.e. towards the community, and other individuals in the community.

Social consciousness: awareness of one's relations to the social group or community, and to the other members of the social group or community.

Social control: the influences exerted by the community and various institutions, organizations, and agencies, such as the school, on the behaviour of the individuals in the community.

Social decrement (increment): the loss (or gain) in the average work done by a group working together, as compared with that done by the individual members of the group, when working alone.

Social distance: the difference between two social groups, in the degree of cultural development; or the degree of antipathy manifested by individuals belonging to the one group towards individuals belonging to the other.

Social dynamics: the branch of sociology which treats of the progressive changes in time of social culture and social institutions, and the psychological processes involved, from a dynamic point of view, while *social evolution* is the descriptive account of these changes.

Social elimination: the social steps taken – functioning as a type of selection – to destroy or remove from active social participation individuals who are inferior, or seriously maladjusted.

Social facilitation: the increase in the efficiency of responses as a result of the social stimuli from others engaged in the same operations.

Social factors and forces: any of the social influences acting upon the individual, and eliciting social responses, i.e. responses to social relationships.

Social group: a collection of individuals feeling and acting in some degree as a unit.

Social heritage: the knowledge, expedients, habits, institutions, etc., handed down from one generation to another.

Social instinct: see *gregarious impulses.*

Social intelligence: the type of intelligence involved in an individual's dealings with other people, and with social relationships; high social intelligence is almost synonymous with *tact.*

Social medicine: a new and rather indefinite term, covering the study of factors affecting the welfare or health of society, so far as these can be considered as coming under the head of preventive medicine in a wide sense.

Social psychology: the branch of psychology which studies the psychological conditions underlying the development of social groups, the mental life, so far as it manifests itself in their social organization, and their institutions and culture, and the development of the behaviour of the individual, in relation to his social environment, or generally all problems having both an individual and a social aspect.

Social science: a general term covering all the sciences dealing with human relations.

Social selection: selective influences of social groups so far as they favour individuals and individual types in the *struggle for existence.* Cf. *social elimination.*

Social self: the *self* in his relations with other selves, in respect of behaviour and of development.

Social situation: the social environment, so far as it presents to the individual, at any time, a pattern of stimuli calling for his reaction or response.

Social status: the position assigned to an individual in his social group, as determined by the attitude towards him of the other members of the social group.

Social suppression: action taken by society to eliminate the influences of an individual in the social group, by punishment or otherwise, including the death penalty.

Social theory: any systematic attempt to account for the organization of society.

Social transmission: see *social heritage.*

Social will: the decision on a line of action or policy to be pursued, formed by the accredited agencies of a social group, and assumed to represent the will of the individual members of the group – not a separate will from that of the individual members, or a majority of them.

Socialization: the process by which the individual is adapted to his social environment, and becomes a recognized, cooperating, and efficient member of it.

Society: a group of individuals of any species, living in a community, in mutual intercourse with one another, and cooperating in the various activities of the community; sometimes used in a general and abstract sense of the essential factors underlying and constituting social organization and community life.

Sociodrama: see *psychodrama.*

Sociogram: a graphical representation of interpersonal relations within a social group. See *sociometry.*

Sociology: the science which studies the development and principles of social organization, and generally group behaviour as distinct from the behaviour of individuals in the group.

Sociometry: a development in the social sciences, which is a school of thought rather than a distinct branch, stressing the study of the dynamic interrelationships of individuals within a social group, and employing to a large extent spatial or geographical analogies and methods of representation.

Socionomic forces: influences, such as physical conditions in the environment, which, while not themselves social forces, nevertheless modify the operation of social forces, in a social group or community.

Socionomics: the science which studies socionomic forces and conditions.

Socius: the social unit as such, or in the abstract.

Socratic method: a method of investigation and instruction, by means of question and answer; the method pursued by Socrates.

Sodomy: an unnatural method of sexual intercourse between males.

Softness: a complex of tactile and motor sensations; employed, by transference, of *auditory* stimuli of low intensity, and also occasionally of stimuli – or impressions – in other sense departments.

Solidity: the spatial characteristic of possessing three dimensions; tridimensionality.

Solipsism: an extreme philosophical view of the idealist type, which reduces itself to the restriction of the universe to the individual and his own experiences, as the only certainty.

Soma: a general term, inclusive of all the cells in the body, except the *germ cells;* hence *somaplasm,* the protoplasm of the body, with the exception of the germ cells.

Somaesthesia: indefinite sensory experience of one's own body, from stimuli affecting mainly touch and temperature receptors on the surface of the body, but not excluding internal stimuli.

Somatic: in general sense, belonging to the body of the body cells excluding the *germ cells;* more narrowly of the body cells excluding the internal organs.

Somatic disorders: disorders of the body, excluding, and contrasted with, nervous disorders.

Somatic hermaphroditism: anatomical union of male and female sex organs, in one individual.

Somatic postures: attitudes of the body.

Somatology: the branch of science dealing with the constitution and physiology of the body.

Somatotonia: one of the personality types arising as a result of the correlation of physical and temperamental characteristics, the physique showing predominant *mesomorphy* (q.v.) and the temperament energy, assertiveness, and athleticism.

Somatopsychosis: a type of mental disorder marked by some delusion regarding the constitution of the body, as that it is made of glass.

Sommer tridimensional analyzer: an apparatus for recording movements of the forearm and fingers, analyzed into their two horizontal and vertical components, by means of levers recording on a smoked drum.

Somnambulism: walking, and carrying out other complex activities while asleep; at one time applied also to certain hypnotic phenomena, or phases of hypnosis, under the name *artificial somnambulism.*

Somnolence: drowsiness.

Sonant: voiced (of sounds).

Sonometer: an apparatus, employed in sound investigation, consisting usually of stretched strings mounted over a *resonance box.*

Sophism: fallacious argument, usually so propounded as to conceal the fallacy.

Sophistry: use of ambiguous or fallacious arguments, with a suggestion of intent to mislead.

Soporific: agent or influence such as a drug, inducing sleep.

Sorrow: one of the two polarities of the emotional life, the other being its opposite, 'joy'; regarded by older writers not as a special emotion, but rather as a group of emotions experienced in situations involving frustration or loss. Cf. *weeping*.

Soul theory: theory which regards mental phenomena as manifestations of the activity of an immaterial substance, or entity, distinct from the body; a philosophical or religious view, outside the field of positive science. *Fechner* attributed souls to all objects, including the sun, moon, and stars.

Sound: a mode of sensory experience, dependent upon waves of alternate condensation and rarefaction of air, and on the possession of an ear or sound receptor; violent alternations of condensation and rarefaction of air – or sound waves – may be experienced by means of touch receptors.

Sound cage (sound perimeter): an arrangement for studying the localization of sounds; the name given from the earlier forms, which were like a cage of wire, within which the subject sat; in the modern forms a telephone receiver, on an arm moveable in any vertical plane, and attached to a pillar moveable in the horizontal plane, is used, the subject sitting in a chair at the centre of the sphere round the surface of which the movement takes place, so that a sound can be made in any position relative to the subject's ears, except directly beneath the body.

Sound hammer: an electrical make-apparatus, for use in a set-up to measure reaction time to auditory stimuli, consisting of a hammer-shaped head of a lever, which strikes on a metal block, at the same time closing the chronoscope circuit, the movement of the lever being controlled by a separate circuit.

Sound key: see *voice key*.

Sound pendulum: see *Wundt's sound pendulum*.

Sound perimetry: the mapping, by a *sound perimeter (cage)*, of the subject's auditory space.

Sound-proof room: a room so constructed as to be relatively or absolutely impervious to sounds from outside.

Sound wave: the periodic alternations of air density producing sound for the human or animal ear.

Sour: a quality of taste sensations; sometimes used also of the stimulus.

Space error: the type of *constant error*, in psychophysical experiment, arising from the presenting of two stimuli to the subject, for comparison, in different relative positions with respect to the subject.

Space orientation: awareness of one's position in space, and adjustment accordingly, both mental and physical.

Space perception: perception of spatial order and spatial relationships of bodies, i.e. of position, direction, distance, form, and magnitude.

Space relations: direction and distance from the observer and from one another of objects in space.

Spaced repetition: a method of experiment or procedure, followed in learning for memorizing, where the material is presented at regular intervals, with a period of rest after each presentation.

Span of apprehension: see *attention span*.

Spark chronoscope: a pendulum swinging along a scale, the time interval to be measured being marked by moving a contact at the zero of the scale, and dotting by a spark a strip of paper, parallel with the scale, at the end.

Spasm: a convulsive contraction of a muscle or group of muscles.

Spasmophemia: stuttering or *stammering,* strictly the former, if a distinction is drawn.

Spatial threshold: the smallest distance between two points on the skin, simultaneously stimulated, at which the points can be discriminated as two.

Spearman foot-rule: a formula for calculating correlation coefficients which represents a shortening of the *'ranks' formula,* also due to *Spearman;* the formula is $R = 1 - \dfrac{6\Sigma(g)}{N^2 - 1}$ where g is the gain in rank in the second of the two series of marks (where there is a gain), N the number of cases, and R the coefficient.

Special ability tests: tests for the measurement of ability in special directions, or of a restricted group of abilities; rather loosely used for special *aptitude tests.*

Special senses: the four senses – sight, hearing, taste, and smell – with touch usually added, and sometimes temperature.

Specific ability: an ability specific to some particular test, which does not affect other types of test; the *s* of *Spearman's two-factor theory.*

Specific energy of nerves: the theory that each sensory nerve gives only one type of sensory effect and one quality of sensation, however it is stimulated.

Specificity: the characteristic of a quality, or process, that it is manifested only in one relatively specific set of circumstances.

Specious present: see *present.*

Spectral (chroma) scale: a scale of spectral colours in equal units of *just noticeable differences* in colour, differences of *brightness* (brilliance) being eliminated, from one end of the spectrum to the other (about 130 in all).

Spectral line: see *Fraunhofer's lines.*

Spectrocolorimeter: an instrument by means of which colours may be measured in numerical terms; a sample to be measured is matched with a mixture of spectral light, of known wave-lengths, and a standard white, the colour being specified in terms of the wave-lengths and the amount of white added.

Spectrometer: an instrument for the accurate measurement of the wave-lengths of spectral colours.

Spectrophotometer: a combination of *spectrometer* and *photometer.*

Spectroscope: an instrument for giving a spectrum, usually by a prism.

Spectrum: the band of colours, from a wave-length 400mμ to about 760mμ, obtained by dispersing white light by means of a *prism, diffraction grating,* etc. The range of audible tones, from a frequency of 16 c.p.s. to one of about 24,000 c.p.s., is sometimes spoken of as the *acoustic spectrum.*

Speech key: see *voice key.*

Speed: rate of movement or action in terms of time; the reciprocal of the time taken to perform an act, or move.

Speedometer: see *tachometer.*

Speeding-up: a term employed in industrial psychology for the employment of incentives and pressure in order to increase output, or diminish costs, or both.

Spell: a form of words employed to produce magical influence or results. Also employed in industry for a period of active work.

Sperm: the seminal fluid containing male germ cells, or *spermatozoa.*

Spherical aberration: failure of the rays of light from a given point to be refracted by a lens, so as to be focused at the same point, owing to the different refractions at the inner and outer zones of the lens. Cf. *chromatic aberration.*

Sphincter: a ring-shaped muscle, the contraction of which closes an opening.

Sphygmograph: an instrument for giving a graphic record of the pulse.

Sphygmomanometer: an arrangement employed to measure the blood pressure in the arterial system, by measuring (by means of a *manometer*) the amount of pressure that must be applied to an artery before the pulse ceases to be observable.

Spicy: a quality of smell sensations in *Henning's* classification of odours, e.g the smell of nutmeg.

Spinal animal: an animal in which the entire portion of the nervous system above the spinal cord has been put out of action.

Spinal cord: the mass of nervous matter, consisting of nerve fibres and cell bodies, with connective tissue, situated within the spinal canal.

Spinal ganglia: the groups of cell bodies of sensory *neurons*, forming swellings on the posterior nerve roots of the spinal nerves.

Spinal nerve: any one of the thirty-one pairs of nerves issuing from the cord below the *medulla.*

Spinal reflex: a reflex of which the whole nervous path is below the *medulla.*

Spindle: a type of *receptor,* so-called because of its shape, found in the *striated* or *skeletal* muscles and the tendons of the body.

Spirit photography: the production of photographs of persons, in which appear additional shadowy figures, assumed to be photographs of spirits.

Spiritism: belief in the reality of communication, by various methods, with disembodied spirits; popularly called *spiritualism.*

Spiritualism: a philosophical doctrine that the ultimate reality of the universe is of the nature of soul or spirit; popularly a semi-religious cult, adhering to a belief in communication with the spirits of the dead.

Spirometer: an instrument for measuring the air-capacity of the lungs.

Spite: strong prejudice against a person, which tends to manifest itself in minor injuries and annoyances.

Split-off consciousness: a rather loose expression, employed by *James* and others, to designate more or less organized groups of experiences, *dissociated* from the normal consciousness, and functioning sometimes as subordinate phases in the phenomena of *multiple personality* (q.v.).

Spontaneous: initiated without external stimulation.

Sport: an organism differing markedly from the type of its species.

Spot-pattern test: a type of test, in which the task is to reproduce, after a momentary exposure, a pattern formed by dots.

Spurious correlation: a correlation between two series of measurements which is partly due to factors other than those being investigated.

Spurt: an increase in the intensity of effort, or in the result due to it, occurring irregularly, and particularly in a period of continuous activity or work.

Squint: see *strabismus.*

Staircase illusion: a visual illusion of reversible or ambiguous perspective, in which a set of steps can be seen as from above or from below, and the two views keep alternating.

Staircase phenomenon: a phenomenon of muscular action, in which a muscle, subjected to a series of single, equal induction shocks, shows a rising series of contractions, up to a maximum.

Stakhanov movement: an industrial movement appearing in Russia about 1935, and characterized by the development of competition between individuals within a group, and between groups, all with a view to, and motived by, the furtherance of the purposes of the communistic state.

Stammering: strictly a series of irregular hesitations and repetitions in speech; now generally used in English as synonymous with *stuttering* (q.v.).

Standard: a model for reproduction; a base of measurement; unit of measurement.

Standard deviation: the square root of the mean of the squares of individual *deviations* from the mean, in a series; generally denoted by σ or S.D.

Standard error of estimate: the *standard deviation* of the differences between a series of estimates and the true value.

Standard score: see *sigma score.*

Standard stimulus: in a psychophysical experiment, involving comparison, that value of the stimulus with which the other values are compared; the stimulus chosen as the basis of comparison.

Standardized tests: tests which have been carefully selected, with reference to their objective, and the group for which they are intended, tried out, and arranged appropriately on the basis of the try-out, for which the method of administration has been exactly and unambiguously detailed, and careful instructions given with respect to the method of scoring, for which *norms* of performance have been made available, and of which the *consistency* and *validity* have been determined, and are known to be high.

Stanford achievement tests: a series of tests of educational level, in the basic school subjects, prepared by *Kelley, Ruch,* and *Terman*; in two sets, Primary and Advanced.

Stanford-Binet scale: known also as *Stanford Revision;* a revision of the *Binet Scale,* worked out by *Terman* and his co-workers, covering a wider range of *mental age* than the original scale, and with a constant number of tests (six) in each year group. Cf. *Terman-Merrill Tests*.

Stapes: the stirrup; one of the auditory *ossicles*, resting against the membrane of the *fenestra ovalis* or oval window.

Startle reflex: reflex, observed in the new-born child, and elicited, according to the results of investigation, with very young children, by loud sounds, withdrawal of support, pain, or experience of choking.

Static reflex: a postural reflex, or orientation to gravity, inclusive of the maintenance of pose (stance reflex) and the *righting reflex*.

Static sense: the sense upon which maintaining equilibrium depends, with its receptors in the inner ear. See *semi-circular canals*.

Statistical errors: inaccuracies that occur in actual measurement, in *sampling*, in treatment of data, and in calculation.

Statistics: the branch of mathematics which evaluates numerical data.

Statocyst: a receptor organ, which apparently represents the earliest appearance of an organ for the *static sense*, it consists of a sac, filled with fluid, lined with cilia or hairs, and containing small solid particles or *statoliths* (apparently analogous to the corresponding *membranous sac* in the inner ear of the higher vertebrates).

Stato-kinetic reflexes: postural responses during movement, maintaining the equilibrium of the body against gravity, speed of movement, etc.

Statoliths: small solid bodies in the *statocyst* (q v).

Statue of Condillac: Condillac's illustration of a statue, employed to show how the various aspects of the mental life may develop out of sensation; the statue was supposed at first to be endowed only with the sense of smell, and then the other senses were added; the illustration of a statue was not original to *Condillac*, and was also employed by other *sensationalists* (q.v.).

Steadiness tester: an apparatus employed to test and measure motor control, consisting of a metal plate, in which there is a graduated series of holes, into which the subject successively inserts and holds a metal stylus, without touching the sides; contact with these closes an electric circuit and rings a bell, or otherwise registers the contact, the timing of the subject's movements being controlled by a metronome.

Stentor: a trumpet-shaped protozoon, which lives as a free swimming, or alternatively as an attached or sessile, organism.

Stereo- (Gr.): prefix meaning usually 'solid'.

Stereognosis: perception of the solidity or tridimensionality of an external object.

Stereogram: a pair (usually) of pictures, which when viewed binocularly by means of a *stereoscope,* give a single impression of a picture showing relief, or distance, or tridimensionality.

Stereoscope: an instrument for combining two flat pictures by means of prisms or mirrors, when these are presented one to the right eye and the other to the left, so as to give the impression of solidity or tridimensionality.

Stereoscopic motion picture: a motion picture taken with two cameras or two lenses arranged so as to give a *stereogram,* employed in *motion study.*

Stereoscopic vision: binocular visual perception of depth or distance.

Stereotropism (-taxis): orienting response to contact with solid objects, frequently showing itself as a tendency to crawl into corners or holes.

Stereotypy: a pathological symptom of mental or nervous disorder, showing itself in continuous repetition of seemingly senseless words and syllables, or of certain postures and actions.

Sterilization: making an organism, male or female, incapable of reproduction.

Stern variator: a bottle-shaped brass vessel, with a movable bottom, giving a fairly pure tone when a current of air is directed across its mouth; variations of pitch are produced by sliding up the bottom, and are continuous throughout an octave; a scale is attached on which frequency can be read off.

Sthenic: employed to characterize feelings which are marked by excitement or increased nervous energy.

Stigma (pl. *stigmata*)*:* a distinguishing mark; any marked peculiarity of the body, especially those regarded as indicative of degeneracy; in plural, employed of marks resembling the scars on the hands and feet of Christ, alleged or recorded to have been shown on the bodies of saints and mystics; similar phenomena have been recorded in all ages up to the present day.

Stilling tests: a series of colour-blindness tests, in the form of plates or charts, with numbers printed on a background of confusion colours, so as to be easily read by those possessed of normal colour vision, but with difficulty, or not at all, by the colour-defective.

Stimulus: any energy change which excites a receptor; employed loosely of any object or event which has such an effect; if a stimulus is the normal stimulus for a receptor it is described as *adequate*; if it is not, and yet effective, it is described as *inadequate*.

Stimulus error: a type of error, occurring in psychological experiment involving introspection, in which the subject gives an account of the nature of the stimulus, in place of describing the experience.

Stimulus-response view: the view that psychological phenomena can be adequately and completely described in terms of stimulus and response.

Strabismometer: instrument for measuring the amount of deviation of the eyes in *strabismus*.

Strabismus: squint; the failure of one of the eyes to take up its proper position relative to the other in binocular *fixation*.

Stratton's experiment: a classical experiment, performed by *G. E. Stratton*, on the coordination of vision and tactual-motor experience; he wore a set of lenses over the eyes, which turned the visual field through an angle of 180 degrees, in order to study the development of the new coordination between tactual-motor space and this reversed visual field.

Stream of consciousness: phrase employed by *James* to describe figuratively an individual's conscious experience, with reference particularly to its continuity and its movement or flow.

Strength-duration curve: term sometimes employed in connection with the psychology of work of a graph showing the progressive decrease in amount of muscular work done over a long period, up to the point of extreme exhaustion.

Strephosymbolia: the perceiving of objects reversed as in mirror images.

Striate body: see *corpus striatum*.

String galvanometer: a type of *galvanometer* (q.v.), the essential part of which is a thin metallic thread in the field of a powerful electromagnet.

Striped muscle: sometimes *striate* muscle; term applied to a group of muscles, for the most part attached to the bony framework of the body; so-called because of its appearance; voluntary muscle.

Strobophotograph: apparatus for the photographic recording of sound waves, essentially of the nature of the *tonoscope*.

Stroboscope: a device for producing an *illusion* of movement, as in the cinematograph, by the exposure of a sequence of visual stimuli, separated from one another by brief intervals, such as are produced by A.C. light; though now more or less an interesting toy, it possesses certain useful features, and may be employed, for example, to measure speed of rotation, or as in the *tonoscope*.

Stroboscopic disc: a disc on which rows of radial lines are drawn, the rows being concentric, and the number of lines and spaces between varying from the outer row to the centre of the disc; when illuminated with A.C. light of 50 or 60 cycles, and attached to a rotation apparatus, such as a colour mixer, the disc, after calibration, can be employed to measure the rate of rotation, which is given by the row of lines, which appear stationary; a useful device for determining *critical rate of flicker extinction.*

Structural psychology: a point of view in psychology, or type of systematic psychology, which concentrates attention on the arrangement and composition of mental states and processes; *existential psychology.*

Structure: the composition, arrangement of component parts, and organization of a complex whole; employed by *Gestalt* psychologists of the organized wholes, forming units of experience, with reference to the positional and functional interdependence of their parts; may also be used of the mind or personality as a whole.

Structure-function: a property or activity belonging to, or dependent on, the influence or action of a whole as such, and not on the action of any of the parts in the whole.

Struggle for existence: somewhat picturesque phrase, employed by *Darwin,* to describe the conditions under which the *survival of the fittest,* i.e. the process of *natural selection,* will go on; where an individual has to compete with other individuals, or a species with other species, in an environment in which the conditions are such as to necessitate competition for nutriment, shelter, etc., those individuals and species best adapted to such conditions will tend to survive and reproduce their kind.

Stupor: a relatively unconscious and non-responsive state.

Stuttering: a disorder of speech, characterized by clonic and tonic contractions of the muscle systems involved in speech; usually employed, alternatively with *stammering,* to include both blocking, and convulsive repetition of speech sounds; a psychological, not physical, disorder.

Style of life: pattern of life; phrase employed by *Adler* and his school for an individual's method or technique, adopted in early childhood, and modifying his later course of life, for dealing with his feelings of inferiority, and achieving superiority.

SU: employed as abbreviation for *sensation unit.*

Subconscious: term employed, mainly by the French school of psychopathology, for processes of the same order as conscious processes, but occurring outside the personal awareness of the individual; often employed loosely, as equivalent of *unconscious*.

Subcutaneous sensibility: sensitivity to pressure stimuli, residing in the deeper layers of the skin, and the underlying tissues, as well as in the joints.

Subdural: underneath the outer covering (*dura mater*) of the central nervous system.

Subhuman: applied generally to animals and animal phenomena; behaviour below the human level.

Subject: the experiencing individual or *self*; the human being, or animal, upon whom an experiment is being performed.

Subjective: pertaining to, or arising from, the individual himself.

Subjective accent or rhythm: rhythm imposed by the individual on a succession of unaccented impressions.

Subjective sensations: sensations which are due to phenomena in the sense organ itself; sensations arising from stimuli within the organism.

Subjective psychology: sometimes applied to a psychology resting mainly or wholly on introspective data.

Sublimation: term, originally employed by psychoanalysts, of an unconscious process by which a sexual impulse, or its energy, is deflected, so as to express itself in some non-sexual, and socially acceptable, activity; often used loosely of any substitution of what appears to be a higher satisfaction for a lower.

Subliminal: below the *threshold* of perception; employed either of stimuli, or of stimulus differences; also employed of the acquisition of a habit, where the learning itself is not conscious.

Sublingual: below the tongue.

Submental: referring to the region below the chin.

Submission: the act of yielding to others; a type of behaviour on the part of an individual manifesting a tendency to submit to the dominance of others. Cf. *ascendance*.

Subnormal: below normal; frequently used of intelligence which is markedly below average.

Subservience: willingness, or tendency, to adapt one's behaviour to the interests, or the will of others.

Substantive states: term employed by *James* for what he called 'resting-places of thought', i.e. the definite objects, items, or data, thought of, as contrasted with the *transition states*, indicated in language by relational words, such as prepositions, conjunctions, and the like.

Substitute: term sometimes employed of a stimulus, or response, as an alternative to *conditioned* (q.v.).

Substitution test: a test – and also a method of experiment, in studying learning – where one type of symbol is continuously substituted for another type, for example numbers for letters, according to a prearranged system.

Subtraction method: a method of treating the results of *compound reaction experiments,* by subtracting from the time recorded the time given in simple *reaction experiments,* and taking the result as a measurement of the time taken for the additional process or processes.

Subtractive principle: the principle that apparent colour of objects, pigments, etc. is the complementary of the colour or colours absorbed, i.e. that the colour absorbed is the apparent colour subtracted from white light; applied in various ways to the colour obtained by mixing pigments, the colour obtained by transmitting white light through coloured screens superimposed, etc.

Successful: employed, in a semi-technical sense, of a response or act which leads directly to the goal, or is a definite step towards it.

Sucking: a reflex response, elicited in the newly-born child by the nipple between the lips.

Suckling: the whole series of responses involved in the infant's feeding.

Sudomotor nerves: the nerves controlling the secretion of sweat.

Sudoriferous glands: the glands which secrete sweat.

Sudorific: referring to, or causing, the secretion of sweat.

Suggestibility: readiness to accept *suggestion,* as a temporary or permanent characteristic of the individual, i.e. whether due to the temporary condition (hypnotized, drugged, etc.), or as a congenital characteristic.

Suggestion: a mental process which results in the uncritical acceptance, and realization, in act or belief, of ideas arising in the mind, as the effect of the words, attitudes, or acts of another person, or other persons, or, under certain conditions, dependent on processes in the individual's own mind – see *heterosuggestion* and *autosuggestion.*

Sui generis (Lat.): unique in its own class.

Sulcus: fissure.

Summation: term employed in two distinct technical senses, of the result produced by the adding of one stimulus or process to another: (1) in the one case, of the increased effect produced by two stimuli in immediate succession in eliciting a response, when neither separately would be of sufficient intensity to elicit one, as in muscle contraction, or in sensory excitation; (2) of an additional tone, produced when two tones of different frequencies are sounded together, the frequency of which is the sum of the two frequencies.

Super-ego: term employed by psychoanalysts to designate a structure in the *unconscious* built up by early experiences, on the basis mainly of the child's relations to his parents, and functioning as a kind of *conscience,* criticizing the thoughts and acts of the *ego,* causing feelings of *guilt* and *anxiety,* when the *ego* gratifies or tends to gratify primitive impulses.

Superior adult: an individual having an intelligence level equivalent to a mental age over 16; there has been considerable controversy regarding the level of the average adult, as expressed in *mental age;* expressed in I.Q., the level of the superior adult might be taken as from about 120 upwards, with general agreement.

Superior adult tests: tests devised specially for the testing of superior adults; usually *group tests,* but in the *Stanford revision,* six individual tests are given at the top of the scale for superior adult level, and in the *Terman-Merrill* tests, three grades of tests, for three grades of superior adult, are given, up to a mental age of over 22.

Superior child: a child with a high *intelligence quotient;* sometimes grades of superiority are assigned as 'superior', 'very superior' and 'near genius', but the limits tend to be rather arbitrary.

Superior intelligence: the degree of intelligence possessed by the upper 25 per cent of the population.

Superiority feeling: exaggerated self-valuation; not infrequently appears as a reaction or defence against an *inferiority feeling* or *complex.*

Superman: a hypothetical being, possessed of physical, mental, and moral characteristics beyond the limitations of the ordinary human being.

Supernatural: beyond, or outside, the bounds of natural law; not explicable by the known laws of nature.

Supernormal: above average, or normal, in respect of intellectual or other ability; sometimes employed in a sense approaching that of *supernatural,* but usually without the implication of inconsistency with natural law.

Superstition: a belief or system of beliefs, based on imaginary connections between events, and incapable of being justified on rational grounds; a reserved area of belief in influences, agencies, and forces whose existence is uncritically accepted; in the individual the tendency to accept such beliefs, and act upon them.

Supination: a rotary movement of the hand or forearm, bringing the palmar surface of the hand upwards.

Supposal: a mental attitude, allied to belief, but differing in that the individual is aware that his adoption of a certain view or theory is arbitrary and provisional.

Suppression: the process of dismissing from consciousness unpleasant memories, thoughts, or desires; distinguished from *repression,* as understood by the psychoanalysts, by the fact that it is conscious and voluntary; *Rivers* interchanges the meanings of the two words, so that Freudian *repression* becomes for him *suppression,* while *repression* is employed in the above sense of *suppression.*

Supraliminal: above the *threshold.*

Supraliminal differences method: see *mean gradations.*

Suprarenal: employed as alternative to *adrenal,* for the bodies situated over the kidneys.

Surdimutism: see *deaf-mute.*

Surface colour: the colour appearing as occupying the surface of an object; *body colour* as contrasted with *film colour.*

Surplus energy theory: a theory, proposed by the poet *Schiller* and supported by *Spencer,* which explains *play* activities as due to surplus energy, particularly as the expression of surplus energy in the young and growing organism.

Surprise: an emotional attitude or response of a more or less transient character. Cf. *startle.*

Surreptitious: the concealed introduction of unwarranted items among the data from which inferences are drawn.

Surrogate: term employed by psychoanalysts to designate a person or object introduced, as in a dream, as a substitute for a person or object whose identity is thus being concealed.

Sursumvergence: deviation of one eye upwards, with respect to the other, in fixation; measurement of the power of the eye so to deviate.

Survey tests: tests employed to give the degree and range of intelligence, or educational level, in a large group or whole population.

Survival of the fittest: a phrase employed to describe the result of the *struggle for existence,* in evolutionary theory; *natural selection.*

Survival value: the degree in which a characteristic or variation favours an organism with respect to *natural selection.*

Suspense: the temporary holding up of response, because of a conflict of motives, or the lack of sufficient data for coming to a decision.

Suture of nerve: artificial joining of the cut ends of a nerve trunk, in order that the portion attached to the cell body may grow out along the course of the nerve, while the other portion degenerates.

Swindle's ghost: a prolonged *positive after-sensation.* Cf. *Bidwell's ghost.*

Syllabism: the analysis of word-sounds into syllables, and the representation of these by syllabic characters – a *syllabary* – in place of an *alphabet,* as in the case of Japanese.

Syllable-span test: the employment of syllables, in place of digits, for the determination of the *memory span.*

Sylvian fissure: a deep fissure in the cerebral cortex, on the outer surface of each hemisphere, marking the division between the temporal and parietal lobes; frequently *fissure of Sylvius.*

Sym-, Syn-, Sys-: Gr. prefix equivalent to Lat. *con-,* meaning 'with' or 'together'.

Symbiosis: term employed of the social relationship between two organisms of different species, which live together, and contribute to each other's support.

Symbol: an object or activity representing, and standing as a substitute for, something else; in psychoanalytical theory, a representation by something not directly connected with it, of unconscious, usually repressed sexual, material.

Symbol-digit test: see *substitution test.*

Symbolism: systematic employment of symbols; in special sense, in psychoanalytical theory, of the employment of symbols to represent repressed material, so that the real meaning may not be recognized by the normal consciousness, in other words, may evade the *censorship,* as in *dreams.*

Symbolization: the process of employing symbols in dreams, myths, and the like; characteristically present also in neurotic symptoms.

Symmetry: term employed in *aesthetics* for the arrangement of parts in an artistic whole, so as to produce the effect of balance.

Sympathetic ganglion: one of the groups of cell bodies in the *ganglionic chain* of the sympathetic division of the *autonomic nervous system.*

Sympathetic nervous system: that part of the *autonomic nervous system* which consists of the *ganglionic chain,* lying outside and parallel to the spinal cord, with its nerves.

Sympathy: the tendency to experience the feelings and emotions expressed or manifested by those around one; contagion of feelings called by *McDougall primitive passive sympathy,* to distinguish it from *active sympathy,* which he regarded as the tendency to seek actively the sharing by others of one's own feelings and emotions.

Symptom: any deviation from normal functioning of an organ, or in behaviour, indicative of an underlying condition of physical or mental disorder or disturbance.

Synaethesia: phenomena in which sensations in one sense department carry with them, as it were, sensory impressions belonging to another sense department, as in *coloured hearing.*

Synapse: the region where the processes of two *neurons* come into close contiguity, and the nervous impulse passes from the one to the other; the fibres of the two are intermeshed, but, according to the general view, there is no direct continuity.

Syncope: swoon, or faint, owing to temporary cerebral anaemia.

Syncretism: term applied to a type of thinking, found particularly in young children, where accidental association takes the place of logical or causal connection.

Syndactylism: the condition of having two or more fingers or toes joined together.

Syndrome: a complex going together of the various symptoms of a disease; a symptom-complex.

Synergic: acting together of processes or influences.

Synonym-antonym test: a test where words are presented in pairs, and the subject has to indicate whether they mean the same or opposite.

Syntonic: a type of *personality,* emotionally responsive to the environment; chiming in with.

Systematic error: a type of error due to the method of collecting or treating data; often indicative of a *bias.*

Systematized delusions: delusions related to one another, in a single system or circle of thought.

Systematic sense: a general name covering the visceral or organic group of sensations.

T

T-scale: a scale used in interpreting test scores, with a range from 0 to 100 in percentiles, or from -5σ to $+ 5\sigma$, with a unit of measurement of $.1\sigma$, for unselected 12-year old children, with a mean score of 50 on the scale; scores so obtained are called T-scores.

T-type: tetanic type; a type of individual whose *eidetic imagery* is non-plastic and obsessive.

Tabes dorsalis: locomotor ataxy; a disease of the posterior columns of the spinal cord, with loss of muscular sensations, and consequent failure of coordination of movements, as far as the muscles in nervous connection with the affected segments of the cord are concerned.

Table turning: see *autoscope.*

Taboo (Tabu): used as noun, or adjective, or verb: general sense, negative precepts or prohibition, in connection with objects, dress, persons, words, acts, etc.; primarily the association is with the magical, or the sacred, and therefore dangerous, and by extension the unclean; psychoanalysts tend to use the term of prohibitions from without, imposed on the realization of powerful desires of a sexual nature.

Tabula rasa: a blank tablet; employed to describe the initial condition of the mind, before it is written upon by experience; a characteristic view in the early days of *empirical psychology,* in the 17th and 18th centuries.

Tachistoscope: an apparatus for the visual presentation of perceptual material for an extremely short time, so as to afford a single glance; various forms are used, the simplest depending on a falling screen or shutter, with an aperture which momentarily discloses the material being presented.

Tachometer: an instrument or device, of various types, for measuring velocity, linear or angular.

Tachycardia: excessively rapid heart-beat or pulse.

Tachyphemia: sometimes *tachylogia;* extreme rapidity of speech (usually morbid).

Tacit: of something assumed, agreed, or admitted, without being explicitly stated.

Tact: social intelligence; ability to understand and adjust oneself to the feelings and opinions of other people – in origin, largely dependent on emotional sensitivity.

Tactile: tactual.

Tactile circle: term employed of an area of the cutaneous surface, within which two points of simultaneous pressure are sensed as a single point.

Tactual: involving, or referring to, the sense of touch; used of sensations, stimuli, and type of imagery.

Talbot-plateau law: the principle that the same effect is produced on the retina by a given quantity of light, whether that falls on the retina as a steady light, or a periodically intermittent light, whatever the period, after *flicker* has been extinguished; usually illustrated by the *Talbot-plateau disc,* which is a white disc with concentric bands, each band showing black and white alternately, but with the same quantity of black and white, divided differently in each band, $1/1$, $2/2$, $4/4$, $8/8$, etc., this when rotated, so as to extinguish flicker, showing a uniform grey.

Talent: natural aptitude in some special direction.

Talisman: an object believed to possess magical protective power in favour of the individual possessing it or carrying it.

Tambour: a shallow, (usually) metal vessel, one side of which is closed by a thin rubber membrane, employed in obtaining graphic records of various processes, either as a specially adapted receiving tambour, or, with a light lever resting on it, as a recording tambour.

Tantrum: a violent display of bad temper, usually displayed by children as a means of obtaining or avoiding something.

Tanyphonia: abnormally thin voice.

Taphophobia: morbid dread of being buried alive.

Tapping board: a device for giving the *tapping test* of the motor capacity involved in speed of voluntary movement, consisting of a metal plate fastened on a board, which is connected up to an electromagnetic arrangement for counting or recording rate of tapping upon it with a metal-pointed stylo; in place of the ordinary board, a series of veeder counters may be mounted on a wooden base for direct reading.

Tarchanoff phenomenon: see *psycho-galvanic response.*

Tartini's tone: the *difference tone,* obtained with the major seventh, between the first overtone of the tonic, and the leading note.

Taste bud: a structure, containing the receptor cells for taste, in the *fungiform, circumvallate,* and *foliate papillae* of the tongue.

Taste tetrahedron: a schematic representation, by *Henning,* of the four fundamental tastes – sweet, bitter, salt, and acid – and their relations, by placing them at the four angles of a tetrahedron.

Tau effect: an illusion, affecting the perception of spatial intervals, due to the influence of temporal factors.

Taxis: an orienting response of organisms to physical forces, having direction; usually included under *tropism* (q.v.).

Taylorism: see *scientific management.*

Teasing: a form of social behaviour, playful or aggressive, in which one individual appears to try to annoy, by relatively slight annoyances, another.

Technopsychology: see *psychotechnology.*

Tectorial membrane: a membrane free at the one edge, lying over the *organ of Corti,* in the *cochlea;* assumed by some supporters of the *sound-picture theory* to be the locus of these, rather than the *basilar membrane.*

Tele-: Gr. prefix with the meaning 'end', 'purpose' or 'distant'.

Telegnosis: knowledge of distant events, alleged to be obtained by means other than reason.

Telegony: the influence of an earlier impregnation of a female, on offspring later obtained by another male.

Telekinesis: term employed in *psychical research* for movement of objects in the presence of a medium, apparently without contact, as a result of occult forces.

Telencephalon: the cerebral hemispheres, as the latest in development, of the parts of the central nervous system.

Teleceptor: see *distance receptor.*

Teleology: a doctrine emphasizing the character of vital, including mental, phenomena, as directed towards and determined by an end, goal, or purpose.

Teleostereoscope: an instrument which causes objects to be seen in exaggerated relief, and nearer than they actually are, the effects usually being produced by means of a series of mirrors, which cause an apparent increase in the distance between the eyes.

Telepathy: alleged communication, by other than known physical means, of thoughts, experiences, feelings, etc., from one mind to another at a distance.

Telephone theory: a theory of hearing, to the effect that the ear acts merely as a telephone receiver, the analysis taking place in the cortical centres.

Teleplasm: hypothetical substances emanating from the body of a medium, and taking ultimately the form of a person.

Telergy: the supposed or alleged direct action of the mind of one person on the mind of another.

Telesis: the attainment of an end, or the realization of a purpose.

Tel(a)esthesia: sensibility for events at a distance; in adjectival form – *tel(a)esthetic* – used of the taste or food sense of aquatic animals.

Teletactor: an instrument for transmitting sound waves produced

289

by speech to the skin of the deaf, in order to instruct the deaf in speech, the understanding of speech, and the appreciation of music.

Telic: intentional; on purpose.

Telic relationships: relationships involved in patterns of behaviour from a purposive point of view on the part of individuals. Gr. TEΛOΣ 'end' or 'goal'. The term '*tele*' is also employed for units of feeling, with similar relevance.

Telodendron: the end-brush of fibrils, at the distal end of the *axon* (usually) of a *neuron*.

Temper: the degree of strength of individual instinctive impulses, particularly the aggressive; employed also as synonymous with *temperament;* the units in the individual emotional systems of which *temperament* is a combination.

Temperament: (1) general nature of an individual, especially on the *orectic* (q.v.) side, generally used rather loosely in this sense; in the Ancient World four temperaments, attributed to the predominance of one or other of the *humours* of the body, were recognized – sanguine, melancholic, choleric, and phlegmatic – and there is still a tendency to emphasize physical, constitutional conditions and processes as determinants of temperament.

Temperament: (2) in music, a system of tuning keyed instruments so as to maintain constancy of relation between tones and semitones, thus facilitating change of key while maintaining the particular scale or mode, major or minor. See *scale.*

Temperature sensations (senses): a general term inclusive of sensations (and senses) of cold, heat, coolness, and warmth.

Temperature spot: employed inclusively of *cold spots* and *heat spots.*

Temporal: referring to (1) time; (2) location at the temples, or sides of the brow; (3) to a lobe of the cerebrum; (4) to a bone of the skull.

Temporal lobe: the lobe in each cerebral hemisphere, lying below the *fissure of Sylvius,* and more or less under the temporal bone.

Temporal maze: a maze in which the subject must pass through the same passages more than once, so that a temporal in place of a spatial sequence is learned.

Temporal sign: a characteristic of a memory by means of which it is located in time.

Tendency: a definite direction of progression of movement, or of thought, towards a goal or end; trend, either native (instinctive) or acquired.

Tendon: an inelastic cord of a fibrous connective tissue by means of which a muscle is attached to a bone.

Tendon sensation: a sensation depending on receptors situated within the tendon.

Tense: employed with reference to an attitude, or a situation, which is characterized by strain.

Tension: a feeling of strain; a general sense of disturbance of equilibrium, and of readiness to alter behaviour to meet some almost threatening factor in the situation.

Tension Law: a principle, formulated by *Delbœuf,* to the effect that change in the stimuli to which an organism is accommodated produces a *tension* in the organism, which constitutes the excitation of which a sensation is the mental accompaniment between certain limits of tension and sensation, beyond which limits the experience becomes some kind of distress.

Tension-relaxation: one of the dimensions of *Wundt's tridimensional theory* of feeling.

Teratology: the branch of biology dealing with malformations of the structure of organisms; the scientific investigation of monsters.

Terman-Merrill Tests: the latest scales of individual tests developed from the *Binet;* characterized by extensions of the *Stanford revision* at both ends, and by the provision of two alternative scales, practically equivalent to one another.

Terman Group Test of Mental Ability: a battery of verbal tests – ten in all – devised for the testing of children at the secondary school level, i.e. from 12 to 18.

Terminal organ: the special organ, in which sensory and motor nerves terminate, i.e. the *receptor* and *effector* organs respectively.

Terminal sensitivity: the highest intensity of sensation, in any sense department, which an organism is capable of experiencing.

Terror: extreme degree of fear.

Test: a standardized type of examination, given to a group or individuals; it may be qualitative or quantitative, i.e. determine presence or absence of a particular capacity, knowledge, or skill, or determine the degree in which such is present; in the latter case, the degree may be determined by the relative position of an individual in the group or the whole population, or by assigning a definite numerical value in terms of some selected unit; applied particularly in the qualitative sense to colour vision, in the quantitative to mental capacity, mechanical aptitude, educational level, sensory acuity, etc.

Test age: the rating in terms of *age, mental* or *educational*, based on the test score or level.

Test chart: a chart or card containing rows, graded as to size of the letters, characters, or pictures displayed, for testing visual acuity.

Test scaling: the grading by trial of the material selected for the formation of a test, with the determination of norms, usually in terms of score.

Test score: the value of the performance in a test, expressed usually in numerical terms.

Testimony: personal evidence in support of a statement of fact; by extension other forms of evidence; studied experimentally by *Stern's Aufgabe experiment* (q.v.) or variants.

Testis: a *gonad* producing male sex-cells.

Tetanus: continued tonic contraction of a muscle; produced experimentally by rapid succession of nerve impulses electrically excited.

Tetrachromatism: theory of four primary colours; colour vision marked by the ability to distinguish *Hering's* four primaries.

Tetrad equation: (more accurately 'tetrad difference') the equation taken by *Spearman,* as the criterion of hierarchical arrangement of *correlation coefficients,* and of the validity of the *two-factor theory;* the criterion is satisfied if, in a correlation table, two correlation coefficients in one column, r_1 and r_2 are taken, and in the same rows in another column r_1^1 and r_2^1, when these are cross multiplied the difference between the two products should not be significantly different from zero, i.e. $r_1 \times r_2^1 - r_2 \times r_1^1 = 0$.

Thalamus (optic thalamus): a mass of grey matter at the base of the cerebrum, containing important terminal and high level centres, both sensory and motor.

Thanatomania: homicidal or suicidal mania.

Thanatophobia: morbid fear of death.

Thaumatrope: stroboscope.

Theory of knowledge: epistemology.

Therapeutics: the branch of medicine concerned with the treatment with a view to cure or alleviation of disorders; the term *therapy* is also employed with a similar meaning, though emphasizing the practical measures employed, rather than the scientific basis. Cf. *psychotherapy.*

Therblig: a name given by the *Gilbreths* to any identifiable part in a series of movements, or actions, of a worker in his work, with a view to systematic *motion study*; the name is formed by the partial reversal of the letters in 'Gilbreth'.

Therm(o)-: Gr. word used as prefix with the meaning 'heat'.

Thermalgesia: state of an organism when a warm stimulus produces a pain sensation. Not to be confused with *thermalgia*.

Thermalgia: sensation of burning pain.

Thermanaesthesia: insensibility to temperature stimuli; the opposite of *thermaesthesia*, which is such sensibility.

Thermohyperaesthesia: excessive sensitivity to temperature stimuli.

Therm(o)aesthesiometer: an apparatus by means of which continuous cold or warm stimuli, at controlled temperatures, can be supplied, for punctate stimulation of the skin.

Thermoreceptor: sense organ responding to temperature stimulation.

Thermotropism (-taxis): orienting response to external thermal stimu-lation.

Thigmaesthesia: touch.

Thigmotropism (-taxis): orienting response to external contact.

Thinking: any course or train of ideas; in the narrower and stricter sense, a course of ideas initiated by a problem.

Third dimension: generally used of depth or distance.

Thought: see *thinking*.

Thought reading: see *mind reading*.

Thought transference: see *telepathy*.

Three-component theory: any theory of *colour vision* to the effect that it can be explained by three ultimate colour processes; represented, for example, by the *Young-Helmholtz theory*.

Threshold: or *limen:* that value on the stimulus scale of intensity, magni-tude, or, in the case of tone sensations, pitch, which just gives rise to sensation, or that difference between two stimuli, in intensity, mag-nitude, or pitch, which just enables them to be discriminated (RL or DL), i.e. *stimulus limen* or *difference limen*; by extension, applied also to bodily movement, as in rotation, the *threshold* being the *just appreciable rate*, or acceleration, positive or negative.

Thymus: a ductless gland, near the base of the neck, of unknown *endocrine* function; in man, atrophies after early childhood.

Thyroid: an *endocrine* gland in the neck, on either side of the *larynx* and upper *trachea;* the secretion maintains *basal metabolism* in the body; de-fect or enlargement has important effects, mental as well as physical.

Thyroid cartilage: Adam's apple; the large cartilage forming the front part of the *larynx*.

Tic: spasmodic or sudden twitch, generally of one of the face or head muscles, as a rule originating in some psychoneurotic disturbance.

Tickling: a sensory experience due to a complex of moving contact and pressure sensations, especially in certain regions of the body, with marked feeling tone, and usually with convulsive laughter and escape efforts.

Tilting Board: an apparatus for stimulation of the *static sense,* which consists essentially of a flat board, on which the subject lies, moving freely about a horizontal axis.

Timbre: clang tint; a qualitative aspect of a complex sound, or clang, or musical note from an instrument, or the human voice, dependent on the number and relative intensity of the *harmonics* or partials present in the complex, and affording the means by which we can distinguish the notes of one instrument from those of another, or one human voice from another.

Time: a fundamental directional aspect of experience, based on direct experience of the *protensity* (duration) of sensation, and on experience of change from one sensory event, idea, or train of thought to another, and distinguishing in experience beginning, middle, and end, as well as past, present, and future.

Time error: a type of *constant error* in psychophysical experiment dependent on order of succession of stimuli, where they are not presented simultaneously; according to convention time error is reckoned as positive when it has the effect of making the first of two stimuli greater or more favoured, negative when it has a similar effect on the second, the stimuli being objectively equal, or equally indifferent.

Time-limit method: a method of testing, as contrasted with the *work-limit method,* where a time-limit is fixed for the completion of a test, or series of tests, such that no one, or only a very limited number, of the testees can complete it.

Time sense: a somewhat loose term denoting our direct experience of the lapse of time, based, however, on the very definite impression we have of a time interval within the *sensory* or *specious present.*

Time-sense apparatus: an apparatus devised for the study of the accuracy of one's estimation of time intervals of short duration, and for the study of rhythm; the best known apparatus of this kind is the *Leipzig time wheel,* which consists esssentially of a metal arm moving at a regular speed round a circle graduated in degrees in which contacts can be placed.

Timidity: an individual characteristic of marked liability to experience fear in situations in which the average person experiences no such emotion.

Tingling: a sensory experience characterized mainly by rapidly inter-mittent tactual sensations.

Tinnitus: experience of ringing or buzzing in the ear in the absence of external stimulation.

Tint: variations of a hue in *brightness* (brilliance), towards white, with diminished saturation.

Tonal: referring, or related, to musical tones; having the character of tone.

Tonal bell: a bell-shaped wire model representing schematically the tonal series with its characteristics and inter-relationships.

Tonal gap: a region in the continuum of sensations of tone, where, for an individual, there is marked reduction of sensitivity.

Tonal Island: an island of hearing; the region of the tonal continuum between two *tone gaps.*

Tonal standard: a tone of definitely fixed and known pitch; an in-strument giving such a tone.

Tonality: usually equivalent to *octave quality,* it being a characteristic of the tonal scale for each tone, as it were, to repeat itself at octave intervals; sometimes employed of the characteristic of all tones as such, or even of all sounds.

Tone: the auditory sensation aroused by periodic sound waves; the interval between two successive notes in a musical *scale,* or one sixth of an octave. A *pure tone* is a note constituted by waves of one wave-length only, i.e. where *overtones* or *harmonics* are entirely absent, as opposed to a compound tone or *clang,* which can be analysed into components of different wave-lengths.

Tone deafness: poor ability, or inability, to discriminate differences of pitch; lack of a musical ear.

Tone variator: see *Stern variator.*

Tonic: the keynote of any scale; used also of a chord which has this note as its basis.

Tonic immobility: state of total stillness, characteristically set up in certain species of animals and organisms, in certain situations, or as a result of certain stimuli.

Tonmesser (Ger.) tonometer (q.v.).

Tonograph: a form of *sphygmograph,* for measuring radial pulse and blood pressure.

Tonometer: an instrument for producing notes of known frequency.

Tonoscope: an instrument for the visual analysis of complex sounds by applying the principle of the *stroboscope.*

Tonus: state of postural muscle contraction, or initiation of contraction, permanently present in living muscle while the nervous connections are intact; *plastic tonus* is a tonic condition of such a kind that the muscles remain contracted in the position in which they are placed by a manipulator.

Topographic: a term employed by psychoanalysts, following *Freud,* with reference to the localization of mental processes in the mental apparatus; *mental topography* means for them a localization scheme of the mind, employed for purposes of description and interpretation, in which they divide the mental apparatus into the *ego,* the *super-ego,* and the *id.*

Topology: the general mathematical science of non-metric spatial relationships, as of part to whole, or the being inside or outside one another of regions.

Topological psychology: the application to psychology of the notions and laws of topology, the whole being based on the conception of a psychological life space, and the interpretation of psychological phenomena on a regional basis in this life space. Cf. *sociometry.*

Toric lens: a type of spectacle lens with a concave surface towards the eye, so as to provide a wider field of vision, and with the front face ground into the form of a 'torus', that is, having two different curvatures, at right angles to one another, this latter characteristic distinguishing a toric lens from a *meniscus.*

Torpor: temporary unresponsiveness to normally intense stimuli.

Total colour blindness: achromatopsia or *achromatism.*

Totem: among primitive peoples, animal, plant, or other object held in veneration by a particular community, tribe, sex, or other group, as in a peculiar way symbolic of the group, and as its protector, treated in various ways in accordance with custom and tradition, and central in various semi-religious conventions and laws.

Totemism: the system of law and custom centring round the totem as a social and religious institution.

Touch: in wide sense, inclusive of sense experience both of *contact* and of *pressure*; in narrow sense, confined to the former.

Touch spot: a point on the skin specially sensitive to light pressure, as by a stiff hair, e.g. points directly over hair roots.

Toxic: poisonous; related to poisons.

Toxic psychoses: mental disorders due to the action of *toxins.*

Toxins: poisonous albuminous substances, produced by the action of bacteria, and exciting the production of *antitoxins.*

Toxophobia: morbid dread or phobia of being poisoned.

Tr: sometimes employed as a contraction for *terminal stimulus*, or upper *absolute threshold*.

Trace: term employed of the altered physiological condition, in the nervous system, resulting from any experience, and the physical basis of memory and learning, but of which the precise nature is unknown. Cf. *engram*.

Trachea: the windpipe.

Trachoma: a contagious disease of the *conjunctiva* of the eyelids, which may affect the eyeball itself, and cause blindness.

Trachyphonia: roughness or hoarseness of the voice.

Tract: term employed of a group or bundle of nerve fibres in the nervous system, with common origin and termination, but, possibly, mixed functions.

Traction sensation: sensation aroused by pulling out the skin.

Trade test: a test of proficiency in a skilled occupation, in the form of a series of tasks involving the performance of definite pieces of work in that occupation, and/or technical information with regard to the occupation.

Tradition: body of law, custom, story, and myth, transmitted or handed down orally from one generation to another.

Training: systematic action, designed to establish habits, abilities, and skills; sometimes used widely, of the education of the young generally; employed in special sense by psychoanalysts, of the preliminary analysis, before the therapeutic analysis begins.

Train of thought: sequence of associated ideas or images; in experiment equivalent to *continuous free association*.

Trait: an individual characteristic in thought, feeling, or act, inherited or acquired.

Trance: condition of *dissociation*, characterized by lack of voluntary movement, and frequently by *automatisms* in act and thought; illustrated by hypnotic and mediumistic conditions.

Transfer of training: the improvement of one mental or motor function, by the systematic training of another allied function; a highly controversial field, in which much experimental research has been carried out. Cf. *cross education* and *formal discipline*.

Transference: term employed by psychoanalysts of the development of an emotional attitude, positive or negative, love or hate, towards the analyst on the part of the patient or subject; also used generally, of the passing of an affective attitude or colouring from one object or person to another object or person connected by association in the experience of an individual person or animal.

Transformism (or *transformation theory*): a biological theory that in course of time one species may become changed into a radically different species.

Transmission: the passing on, by inheritance, of characteristics from one generation to another; or the passing on, from one generation to another, of customs, traditions, knowledge, and the like.

Transparent plane colour: mode of appearance of a colour in clear glass, through which objects are seen beyond.

Transverse: in general sense, lying across; employed of transverse vibrations in wave motion, when the movement of the particles in the wave are perpendicular to the movement of the wave; a line or axis perpendicular to the principle or longitudinal axis, as in the case of a limb.

Transvestism (*transvestitism*): the propensity or tendency to dress in the clothes of the other sex.

Traube-Hering waves: periodic changes in the pulse curve, indicative of pressure changes, alleged to be the basis of *fluctuations of attention,* and other psychological phenomena.

Trauma: any injury, wound, or shock, most frequently physical or structural, but also mental, in the form of an emotional shock, producing a disturbance, more or less enduring, of mental functions.

Traumatic neurosis: a *psychoneurosis,* precipitated by an emotional shock, as in *hysteria* or some *phobias.*

Trembling: slight or moderate involuntary and phasic contraction of groups of muscles.

Tremolo: periodic moderately rapid changes in the loudness, or pitch, or both, of a musical note produced by a musical instrument, or the human voice. Cf. *vibrato.*

Tremor: a continuous, rapid, muscular quivering or agitation, limited in its range, of limbs or body, associated with various relatively normal physical and mental conditions, such as fatigue or emotion, or with pathological conditions, usually of lesions in the *cerebellum* or *basal ganglia.*

Trend: line of direction of a series of events or types; inclination or tendency towards a specific kind of behaviour.

Trepan: see *trephine.*

Trephine: a special surgical instrument, hollow and conical or cylindrical in shape, for removing a part of the skull in a brain operation; as a verb, to operate with a *trephine.*

Triad: in music, a chord of three tones.

Trial and error: a type of *learning*, most characteristically shown in animal learning, and marked by the successive trial of various responses to a situation, ostensibly at random, until one is successful, and attains the goal; in repeated trials this successful movement comes earlier and earlier, until ultimately it is given as soon as the situation presents itself; it is doubtful whether entirely random response, and pure trial and error learning occur on the scale that some psychologists have asserted.

Tribe: a social group, based initially and primarily on kinship, speaking a common language, having common territory and name, with common social usages, religious beliefs, but generally lacking in any high degree of social organization or culture. The so-called *tribal self* is best regarded as the consciousness, in the individual, of himself as a member of the tribe, or of his membership of the tribe, rather than the psychical factors involved in the organization of the group considered figuratively as a *personality* or *self*.

Trichromatic theory: the theory basing colour phenomena on three *primary colours;* mainly a physicist's theory.

Trichromatism: normal colour vision; given that name on the basis of a *trichromatic theory*.

Tridimensional theory of feeling: Wundt's theory, that there are three dimensions in which feelings may vary, namely between pleasantness and unpleasantness, excitement and quiescence, and tension and relaxation.

Trireceptor theory: a theory of *colour vision,* corresponding, on the physiological side, to the *trichromatic theory*.

Tritanopia: partial colour-blindness, affecting the blues and yellows; blue or violet blindness; extremely rare as a congenital condition, but occurring fairly frequently as an acquired condition.

Tritone: a musical interval of three tones, or approximately half an octave.

Tromophonia: a tremulous voice.

Tropism: an orienting (and movement) response to physical and chemical agencies in cells, organs, and organisms, explicable (*Loeb*) in purely physicochemical terms; may be either positive or negative, with reference to the determining agency's direction, and may result, in the case of organisms, in actual movement, or in the assumption of a definite axial position.

Tropostereoscope: an apparatus devised to determine and demonstrate the influence of double images in the perception of depth.

True-false test: a mental test, usually intended to test the subject's range of information, where the subject is faced with a series of statements to be checked as true or false, and frequently scored by subtracting the number of those wrongly from the number of those rightly checked, to eliminate chance or random checking.

True score: the measurement which would be obtained by taking the average of an indefinitely large number of measurements of an individual on similar tests, under similar conditions, which is practically impossible, but can be approximated statistically.

Truism: a proposition the truth of which is so obvious as not to require statement or evidence in support.

TU (transmission unit): a logarithmic unit of sound intensity; two such units are in common use, the *decibel* (q.v.) and the *neper* (q.v.).

Tune: a rhythmical succession of musical sounds, forming a melody.

Tuning: a term employed in connection with cutaneous sensibility, for the maximum sensory intensity that can be evoked in each warm, cold, or touch spot, which cannot be increased by increase of stimulus intensity.

Tuning Fork: a two-pronged, tempered, metal instrument, adjusted to give sound waves of constant frequency, employed to give *standard pitch;* by means of riders, forks may be made variable, and employed to measure *thresholds; giant tuning forks* are made to determine the lower absolute threshold.

Turnover of Labour: the ratio of the number of changes to the number of full-year workers in a factory or business; the ratio of the number of new hands taken on in a definite period to the average number on the pay-roll.

Twilight sleep: a state of semi-consciousness induced by certain drugs.

Twilight states: conditions in hysterical patients, in which they are, in phantasy, detached from the normal environment, and have elaborate daydreams of a somewhat remarkable character.

Twin: a member of a pair of offspring produced at one birth; the pair may be *fraternal (dizygotic) twins,* of the same or different sexes, and usually not more alike than any two children of the same family, or *identical (monozygotic) twins,* of the same sex, and exceedingly alike in all characteristics.

Twitch: a sudden local convulsive movement.

Two-aspect theory: see *double aspect theory.*

Two-factor theory: Spearman's theory of intelligence, to the effect that all modes of cognitive activity, or types of mental performance, have in common one fundamental factor (g), while, apart from any group factors, they also depend upon a specific factor (s), not present in any of the others.

Two-point discrimination: see *spatial threshold* or *aesthesiometric index.*

Tympanic membrane: the drum of the ear, closing at its inner end the external auditory meatus. Often called *tympanum*, which is strictly the chamber behind.

Type: a class of individuals, having a characteristic or a pattern of characteristics in common, such as direction of interest, kind of imagery preferred, temperament, etc., on the mental side, or body build, on the physical.

U

Ultra-violet: beyond the violet; radiations of shorter wave-length than the violet end of the spectrum – shorter than 390mμ and not visible directly to the human eye, though possibly visible to some organisms.

Unanschaulich (Ger.): abstract; not perceptual, or imaginal.

Unconditioned reflex: innate or original reflex; a reflex elicited by its normal, or natural stimulus.

Unconscious: not having the characteristic of consciousness; with the definite article, 'the *unconscious*' is best understood as the aggregate of the dynamic elements constituting the *personality*, of some of which the individual may be aware as part of his make-up, of others entirely unaware, but all structural, rather than process; on process side, the inner mental dynamic, involving processes which are of a different order from conscious processes, and as such are incapable of becoming conscious processes, though influencing, and modifying these in all sorts of ways, and, to avoid confusion, better spoken of as *endopsychic* processes; often wrongly applied to processes of the same order as conscious processes but outside the field of personal awareness, which are more appropriately termed *subconscious* or *extraconscious.*

Understanding: apprehension of the meaning of phenomena, words, or statements; often employed loosely and indefinitely, as some sort of agency; general term, covering functions which involve apprehension of meaning.

Undoing mechanism: term employed by psychoanalysts for a ceremonial characteristic of the *compulsion neuroses,* by which a second
action is intended to rub out, as it were, a previous action, so that
it is as if the latter had never happened.

Unequivocal: having only one possible meaning.

Uniaural: employing, or with reference to, only one ear.

Unicellular organism: an organism consisting of only one cell; the
protozoa in the animal world.

Uniformity of nature: a principle or law applied to natural phenomena,
to the effect that with the same antecedents exactly the same consequences follow.

Unilateral: referring to, or involving, only one side of the body.

Unimodal: characterizing a *frequency curve,* or *distribution,* having only
one maximum frequency (or one high point).

Unipolar: having only one pole; employed of the cell body of a *neuron*
with only one process leaving it.

Unique: employed of the only example, or member, of a class.

Unison: term applied to a simultaneous sounding of notes of the
same pitch.

Unitary type: the type of individual whose *after-images, memory images,*
and *eidetic images* are closely similar in type.

Unit character: a character which is transmitted as a whole, or as a
unit, when inherited, and concerning which certain theoretical
conclusions regarding inheritance are drawn, which are still
matter of controversy.

Universal complex: a complex based upon emotional experience arising
in connection with a fundamental instinct, as against one based
upon incidental experiences.

Universe of discourse: the general field under consideration; the field
to which the topic being discussed belongs.

Univocal: see *unequivocal,* having only one meaning.

Unknowable: that which is essentially, or as such, beyond the capacity
of the human being or the human mind to know.

Unmusical: in a general sense, not musical; most frequently used of
individuals of poor musical capacity, and particularly of those
whose *pitch discrimination* is poor; not having a good musical ear.

Unpleasantness: a quality of *hedonic* experience.

Unreality feeling: the feeling, usually pathological, that an experience,
including the experience of oneself, lacks objectivity or reality.

Unreasoning: term employed of behaviour which is not influenced by,
or does not involve, reasoning; impulsive or automatic behaviour;

to be distinguished from *unreasonable,* which is employed of demands or claims for which there is no justification, or of the individual who makes them.

Unsociable: tending to avoidance of company of other people; must be distinguished from *unsocial,* which has the meaning, applied to an individual or an act, of not being in touch, or in keeping, with the social milieu, or social usage.

Unsocialized: lacking in social training, social feeling, or social habits.

Unspaced repetition: a type of procedure, in learning, where one repetition follows another without interval, pause, or rest, until the learning is complete; the most uneconomical type of learning.

Unthinkable: implying, of a proposition or generalization, that it essentially involves such inconsistency or self-contradiction that it is incapable of being either affirmed or denied.

Uraniscolalia: speech impeded by a cleft palate.

Uranism: homosexuality, involving also aversion towards the opposite sex.

Urban's Tables: a set of tables for facilitating the calculating of results in psychophysical experiments, employing *Urban's* modification of the *constant method,* or *method of right and wrong cases.*

Urethral erotism: term employed by psychoanalysts for sexual feelings in connection with the urethral region.

Urge: drive from within, or strong tendency towards the performing of some act.

Urning: a male who feels like a woman towards other males.

Urogenital: referring or belonging to the urinary and genital regions.

Use inheritance: the Lamarckian theory of the inheritance of acquired characteristics in so far as it emphasizes the transmission of characters brought about by use or disuse.

Use Law: see law of *exercise.*

Useful or *Serviceable duration:* that period from the beginning of the passage of an electric current, which produces a response of nerve or muscle, further duration having no additional effect (*Lapicque*).

Uterine life: period of life of a mammal in the *uterus* before birth.

Uterus: the organ in mammals in which the *embryo* develops.

Utilitarianism: the ethical, social, and economic theory which takes practical usefulness as the criterion of value; in the moral field, the view of the 'good' as 'the greatest happiness of the greatest number'.

Utility: usefulness of a character, function, act, etc., from a biological point of view, i.e. with reference to the preservation of the individual life, or the continuance of the species.

Utricle: a sac-like expansion, at the base of the *semi-circular canals,* in the vestibule of the inner ear.

Uvea: the *iris, ciliary body,* and *choroid* of the eye, considered as a unit.

Uvula: the appendage, hanging from the soft palate, at the back of the mouth cavity.

V

Vaginismus: spasm of contraction of the sphincter muscle of the vagina, usually *psychogenic,* and preventive of conception.

Valence: a term used generally by Gestalt psychologists for the attracting or repelling influence of objects or activities; and specially of the *colour* or *brightness* (brilliance) of a visual stimulus, in the sense of the capacity to evoke *colour* or *brightness* (brilliance) sensations.

Valences: the attracting and repelling aspects of the various regions of the *life space* (q.v.) in a *vector psychology* (q.v.) which represents the second part of a *topological psychology* (q.v.).

Validity: in a general sense, of an argument or theory, with the meaning that it holds true; in a special sense, in statistics, of the extent to which a test measures what it is intended or purports to measure, which is determined by the correlation between its results, and some other criterion of what it was devised to measure; e.g. the validity of an *aptitude test* would be determined by correlation with subsequent performance.

Value: quantitative measure in terms of some standard or unit.

Vanity: excessive, and usually misguided, self-satisfaction.

Variable error: a type of error incident to psychological or psychophysical experiment, due to a factor or factors varying in the course of the experiment, e.g. practice, fatigue, accommodation, etc.

Variability: term applied, in a general biological and psychological sense, to phenomena subject to change, continuous or discontinuous; in statistics, the amount of dispersion of the values in a frequency distribution, as measured by *standard deviation, mean variation, interquartile range,* etc.

Variance: term employed in statistics for the square of the *standard deviation,* or the mean of the squares of the individual deviations from the mean.

Variation: in biological sense, change in an organism or species due either to environmental conditions, or to heredity, or to mutation; in a statistical sense equivalent to deviation from the mean of a series.

Variational psychology: differential psychology (q.v.).

Varied response: a characteristic of animal behaviour, in efforts to attain a goal against obstacles, or in *trial and error learning*.

Variety: a subdivision of a species, in biological classification.

Vascular sensation: a sensory complex, attending abrupt changes in cutaneous circulation, and circulation changes in the underlying tissues, as, for example, in blushing.

Vasomotor centres: centres, in *medulla*, etc., which formerly were supposed to control muscle *tonus* in the blood vessels.

Vector: in physics and mathematics, a directed magnitude, or a magnitude having direction, e.g. a velocity.

Vector psychology: the part of topological or geometrical psychology which supplements the purely topological consideration by the dynamics of the situations, i.e. the play of the various tensions and forces within the life space.

Vegetative: term applied to functions concerned in growth and nutrition.

Velleity: a low degree of desire, or an incomplete or feeble *volition*.

Venereal: term applied to a group of diseases which are transmitted by sexual intercourse.

Vengeance: an act or series of acts directed by the intention to inflict injury on another, because of some injury inflicted by that other on oneself or one's friends.

Ventricle: one of the cavities within the heart, or the brain; in the human brain there are four ventricles filled with cerebro-spinal fluid.

Ventriloquism: a kind of speech without movement of the lips, so that the source of sound is wrongly located, and a suggestion may be conveyed, giving the illusion that it comes from other persons, or animals, or inanimate objects.

Verbal: characterized by being expressed in words, either orally or graphically.

Verbalism: thinking based on verbal associations, rather than real meaning connections; uncritical acceptance of verbal definitions, as if they were real explanations.

Verbiage: abundant, and even excessive, flow of words; overloading of sentences with unnecessary words, repetitions, and circumlocutions.

Verbigeration: repetition of words and sentences, without reference to their meaning.

Vergence: a word employed by ophthalmologists, as a general term covering movements in convergence, divergence, and sursumvergence of the eyes, particularly so far as they may be forced by prisms in front of the eyes.

Veridical: term employed particularly of dreams, which seem to correspond to events occurring at the time or later; of prophetic dreams or visions.

Verification: the search for, or the obtaining of, evidence, confirming the truth of a theory or hypothesis.

Vermis: the middle part of the cerebellum, between the hemispheres.

Vernier: an additional scale, moving on a larger scale, and so divided as to give fractions of the divisions of the latter.

Vertebrates: a division of the animal kingdom, comprising all animals having a segmented bony spinal column.

Vertical axis: the middle line of the body from head to feet.

Vertigo: the sensation of giddiness or dizziness, due normally to overstimulation of the receptors of the *static sense* in the *semi-circular canals.*

Vestibule: the part of the bony labyrinth of the inner ear, between the *cochlea* and the *semi-circular canals,* containing the *utricle* and the *saccule;* the term *vestibular system* is used of the whole neural mechanism involved in receiving the sensory data from the *static sense,* and providing for the making of the necessary responses for the adjustment of the equilibrium of the organism with reference to gravity, or other forces affecting it.

Vestige, Vestigial structure: the remains of a primitive structure in the body, now without function, but functioning in an earlier stage of evolution, of a particular organism (in the case of the human being, in prehuman ancestors), or at an earlier stage in its life-history.

Viable: capable of living, particularly of an organism in the earlier stages of its development.

Vibration: a periodic to-and-fro movement of a body or particle; a *double vibration* (v.d.) is a complete vibration to the starting-point; a *single vibration* (v.s.) half a complete vibration.

Vibration sensation: a sensory experience resulting from contact with a vibrating body.

Vierordt's Law: the principle that the *two-point threshold* on the skin varies inversely with the distance from the body axis, or with the degree of movement the part is capable of, e.g. in the case of the arm, the *threshold* diminishes from the shoulders to the finger-tips.

Vincent Learning Curve: a curve based on units representing a definite fraction of the time or the number of repetitions required to reach mastery of a problem; in this way one can make the curves of different individuals comparable, since the same units are represented in all.

Violet blindness: see *tritanopia*.

Viraginity: a type of homosexuality in a woman, involving not only the sexual feelings, but also the mental characteristics, which are those of a normal man.

Virtual image: an image that appears to be located at a point which no rays of light actually traverse, formed by a mirror or a lens.

Virulent: in general sense, possessing poisonous qualities; transferred, figuratively, to feelings or utterances; one of *Zwaardemaker's* classes of smell qualities, illustrated by the smell of morphine.

Visceral sense: see *organic sense*.

Viscerotonia: one of the personality types arising in the correlation of physique and temperament, marked on the physical side by *endomorphy* (q.v.), and on the temperamental by love of good living, delight in company, love of comfort, etc.

Visibility coefficient: the degree of visibility of different single wavelengths of light, or of a mixture of wave-lengths, relative to a standard, which is taken as the spectral energy, at maximum visibility, of light of a wave-length of $554\mu\mu$.

Visibility curve: a curve, showing the variation of *brightness* (brilliance) with wave-length, i.e. the plotting of the *visibility coefficients*, for different wave-lengths in the spectrum, the standard curve being that for the *photopic eye*, with normal vision.

Visile (Visual) type: an individual whose imagery is predominantly visual.

Vision: the sense of which the receptors are the *rods and cones* in the retina of the eye, and the adequate stimulus light waves of wavelengths between approximately $400\mu\mu$ and $760\mu\mu$ for the normal human eye. *Foveal vision* is vision due to stimulation of the *fovea centralis*, as contrasted with *marginal* or *peripheral* vision, where the stimulation is of the regions towards the margin or periphery of the retina.

Vision theory: a theory that attempts to give a systematic account of the phenomena involved in vision, and particularly of the phenomena of *colour vision*, of *dark adaptation*, and of the respective functioning of the *rods and the cones*.

Visual acuity: the degree of discrimination, as of separation of points or of apprehension of form, of which the eye is capable; usually determined practically by such tests as *Snellen's charts*, the visual acuity varying inversely as the size of the letters read at a given distance.

Visual angle: the angle subtended at the eye by any visual object, upon which the magnitude of the retinal image depends.

Visual axis: a straight line passing through the fovea, the nodal points of the eye, and the point of fixation.

Visual field: the total aggregate of the stimuli acting on the eye at any given moment, considered as projected upon a sphere whose centre is the eye; the experience of this field in its spatial aspect is known as the *subjective visual field*.

Visual Line: see *visual axis*.

Visual purple: a photochemical substance, found in the *rods* of the retina, which is rapidly bleached on exposure to light, and is believed to be the basis of *twilight vision* (q.v.); *rhodopsin*.

Visual span: the tridimensional world, as perceived by the eyes.

Visual yellow: a substance sometimes found in the retina, after the bleaching of the *visual purple*.

Visualization: the experiencing of visual imagery.

Vitalism: a philosophical and biological theory, characterized by the assumption of a non-material agency underlying vital phenomena.

Vitascope: stroboscope (q.v.).

Vitreous humour: the transparent, jelly-like substance filling the eye-ball between the retina and the lens.

Vividness: the liveliness of an impression or experience.

Vocabulary test: a type of mental test which aims at the determination of an individual's store of understood words; usually given by presenting the subject with a standard list of words, which he is required to define, or indicate which of a number of words given is nearest in meaning; in a more extensive investigation of his vocabulary the subject may be asked to check, in a hundred words, those of which he knows the meaning, and a correction applied by asking him to define or use the last ten of those he has marked.

Vocal cords: bands or ligaments in the *larynx*, by the vibration of which voice is produced.

Vocal register: the tonal range, or the pitch compass of the voice.

Vocal tone recorder: any apparatus devised to record the pitch of a note sung.

Vocality: vowel-character or attribute of a sound.

Vocational aptitude test: a type of test designed to determine an individual's natural suitability for a particular occupation.

Vocational guidance: see *guidance*.

Vocational selection: methods of selecting, by means of tests, etc., the most suitable individuals among those applying for employment in particular occupations; choosing individuals for occupations, as contrasted with choosing occupations for individuals, which is *vocational guidance*.

Voice: sounds produced by the vocal organs, particularly the *larynx*.

Voice-key: a reaction key operated by the voice, i.e. by the spoken sound. Cf. *lip-key*.

Volar: situated on the palm of the hand.

Volition: the conscious adoption by the individual of a line of action; self-conscious activity towards a determined end, manifested primarily in decision and intention; idea of an accepted end, with conscious activity towards it.

Volley theory of nerve action: a neurological hypothesis of nerve action, to explain both intensity and quality, particularly with respect to auditory sensations, on the basis of the results of investigation of action currents in sensory nerves.

Volume: tridimensional magnitude; psychologically of importance in respect of the volume attribute of sounds, regarded as a spatial datum.

Voluntary activity: activity accompanied by the idea of an end, and the desire to attain it; on the behaviour side marked by a longer *latent time* than reflex activity.

Volvex: an organism living in colonies; of biological and psychological importance, as forming a link between *protozoa* and *metazoa*.

von Frey's Aesthesiometer: see *hair aesthesiometer*.

von Kries theory: see *duplicity theory*.

Voodooism: a system of belief in magic and sorcery among natives of West Africa and Negroes in America.

Vorstellung (Ger.): The process by which an object is presented in perception or ideation, inclusive, therefore, of both *presentation* and *ideal representation*.

Vowel: a vocal sound, characterized by periodicity and complexity, and forming an element in speech.

Voyeur: an individual who obtains sexual gratification from seeing or watching sexual stimuli, objects, or acts.

W

w factor (will factor): a *group factor* (q.v.) in intelligent activity along certain lines.

Wakanda: the Sioux term for an impersonal, all-pervading, mysterious, supreme power in the universe; corresponding in many respects to *manitou* (q.v.), and in some respects to *mana* (q.v.).

Wake: a ceremonial remaining awake, during the normal time for sleep.

Wallerian degeneration: the fatty degeneration of the process of a neuron cut off from the cell body, which results in a condition that takes on certain stains, so that its course can be traced in a series of microscope sections; one of the important methods by which connections can be mapped out in the central nervous system.

Wanderlust (Ger.): impulse or tendency to leave home, or to move frequently from place to place; manifested in some children and adults.

Warmth: a quality of sensation, the stimulus for which is contact with an object at a higher temperature than the part stimulated, but below the level of heat.

Warm spot: a small area on the cutaneous surface, peculiarly sensitive to punctate stimulation, by objects above body temperature.

Warming-up: a characteristic process, occurring at the beginning of a continuous activity, or a series of experiments, extending over a period during which the subject's responses become progressively more efficient and constant.

Waterfall illusion: an illusion, appearing characteristically as an *after-sensation* of movement, when, after looking for some time at a waterfall, the eyes are turned on the surrounding country; the conditions may be imitated in a laboratory set-up, so as to produce the illusion.

Wave: a periodic to-and-fro movement of particles, transmitted to neighbouring particles, so that the whole movement advances continuously.

Wave-length: the distance between one crest and the next crest, or between two successive similar phases.

Weaning: employed figuratively, in psychoanalytic and general psychological literature, of the breaking up of a *fixation* or *transference* situation; used particularly of the breaking away from parent domination in the case of the adolescent.

Weber's Law: the formulation by Weber of the relation between stimulus differences and the perception of differences; the law formulated by Weber in these terms: 'in observando discrimine rerum inter se comparatarum, non differentiam rerum, sed rationem differentiae ad magnitudinem rerum inter se comparatarum, percipimus', i.e. in observing the difference between two magnitudes, what we perceive is the ratio of the difference to the magnitudes compared.

Wedensky effect: an inhibition effect, obtained with a nerve-muscle preparation, for which a critical point can be determined in the rate of the twitches with which a muscle responds to a rapid series of stimulations. Beyond this rate of stimulation the muscle responds with a single twitch, followed by complete relaxation.

Weighting: assigning definite proportional values to results in a series of experiments or tests, determined according to the significance of each, assumed or found, with reference to other data bearing on the object of the experiment or tests; any score or results, after being so treated, will be called a *weighted score.*

Weismannism: the theory of evolution, which asserts the continuity of the germ plasm, and, on that basis, denies the possibility of the inheritance of *acquired characteristics.*

Welfare work: supervision of the health, recreation, training, etc., of the employees in a factory or business undertaking.

Wernicke area: the area in the first and second convolutions of the temporal lobe of the left hemisphere (in right-handed persons), identified by Wernicke as the cerebral centre for the hearing and understanding of spoken language.

Wheatstone bridge: an arrangement for the determination of electrical resistance by means of a circuit, divided into two parallel arms, in one of which are two constant and known resistances, in the other a variable resistance and that to be determined. A galvanometer is placed across the two parallel arms from a point between the two constant resistances to a point between the variable and the unknown resistance. If the variable resistance is adjusted so that no deflection is shown on the galvanometer, the unknown resistance is given by its ratio to the variable resistance being the same as the ratio between the two constant resistances; if the latter are equal the unknown resistance is that shown on the variable resistance.

White matter: the parts of the central nervous system consisting mainly of *medullated nerve fibres* which give the characteristic white appearance.

Whole and part learning: general term inclusive of the two types of method employed in learning for memorizing – dealing with the whole material, by repeating over and over until learned, or breaking it up into sections, learning each separately, before taking them together.

Wiggly block: a rectangular wooden block divided by wavy-lined cuts into nine parts, employed in the study of *trial and error learning,* the subject being given the parts to put together to reconstruct the block, and the time being recorded.

Will: used generally, of the impulse to act in all its phases or stages of development, or more specially, of *volition* alone; when used with a capital letter, usually refers to the *personality* in action; hardly to be regarded as a specifically psychological term.

Will-temperament tests and *profile:* a series of tests, devised by *June Downey,* to reveal qualitative *temperamental* or *personality differences,* the result being represented in graphical form as a *profile.*

Window: term employed of two openings in the wall of the bony labyrinth in the inner ear – the *fenestra ovalis* and the *fenestra rotunda,* or the oval window and the round window.

Wish: in usual sense, ideal representation of a desired object or situation, accompanied by a felt impulse towards its realization; used by *Freud* and his followers, in a wider sense, of any specific impulse, trend, or motive force, regarded in and for itself, or in its own right.

Wish fulfilment: the realization of the aim of a Freudian *wish* or impulse, whether that is an acknowledged wish or impulse or not, and whether its realization is desired by the conscious personality or not.

Wishful thinking: acceptance of the thought that conditions are as an individual would wish them to be, and rejection of the thought that they are otherwise; the 'will to believe' Cf. *phantasy.*

Wit: an unexpected and ingenious turn of thought, or connection in thought, causing surprise and laughter; *Freud* distinguishes two kinds – harmless and aggressive, the latter being of the nature of attack directed against another.

Witchcraft: a form of magical power, usually of the 'black' type, attributed to certain persons, as the alleged reward of selling their souls to the devil.

Witness: an observer of a fact or event; one who gives testimony regarding a fact or event.

Wonder: an emotion excited by strange, novel, or impressive objects or occurrences.

Word: a sign, expressive, as the unit of language on the structural side, of some object, idea, or relation – its meaning; not the functional unit of language, which is a sentence or statement.

Word blindness: alexia (q.v.).

Word-building test: a form of mental test which consists in the forming of words from disconnected letters; the anagram is one type.

Word deafness: inability to understand spoken words, usually because of cerebral lesion; sensory *aphasia* (q.v.).

Word-reaction time: the interval between a stimulus and the verbal response, recorded by *voice-key.*

Word-span test: a test of the same type, and for the same purpose as the *digit-span test* (q.v.).

Work: serious activity with reference to a real world and real values, as contrasted with *play* activity.

Work curve: a graphical record of the mental or muscular performances of an individual, in successive uniform periods of time, extending over a considerable period.

Work-limit method: a test method, where every subject must cover the same material or ground, the time taken constituting part of the basis of measurement.

Worry: an emotionally coloured attitude of an unpleasant tone, akin to anxiety, and involving in part baffled mental activity.

Worship: practices representing an individual's attitude, and relations, to his deity.

Worth: subjective appreciation of the *value* of something.

Writer's cramp: a functional spasm affecting writing, usually involving intense contractions of the muscles employed.

Writing accent: characteristics of an individual's writing, especially natural characteristics, analogous to accent in speech.

Writing tremor: shaky movements in writing, arising from a variety of causes, such as senility, intoxication, writer's cramp, disorders of central nervous system, etc.

Wundt's fall (gravity) phonometer: an apparatus for determining *thresholds* of sound intensity, consisting essentially of ivory balls dropped from different heights by an electromagnetic release mechanism.

Wundt illusion: one of the geometrical optical illusions; an illusion of direction, where two objectively parallel lines are made to appear curved, by being crossed by lines radiating from two points at either side.

Wundt sound pendulum: an apparatus devised by Wundt, for determining *difference thresholds* for sound, consisting essentially of two wooden balls falling from either side on a wooden pillar through different angles, the angles being indicated in degrees on a semi-circular scale.

Wundt's principles of emotional expression: a reformulation of *Darwin's* principles, as (1) direct innervation, (2) analogous sensations, (3) relation of movements to images.

Würzburg School: the school directed by *Külpe* at Würzburg, studying experimentally the thought processes, imageless thought, and volition.

X

X-O tests: a series of three (or four) tests, devised by *Pressey,* for the investigation of emotional attitudes in children and adults, in which the subject is required to cross out certain words, and, going over the tests again, circle one word in each line.

Xanthic: yellowish.

Xanthogenic radiation: light stimuli giving rise to the sensation yellow.

Xanthopsia: condition in which all objects appear yellow, as, for example, jaundice, or under the influence of *santonin.*

Xenoglossia: term applied in *psychical research* to the reading, writing, speaking, and understanding, by a subject, of a real language, which he had never learned.

Xenophobia: morbid fear of strangers.

Y

Yellow: a visual sensation, psychologically fundamental, evoked by wave-lengths round $575.5\mu\mu$ or neon yellow.

Yellow spot: macula lutea (q.v.).

Yellow-sighted: heightened sensitivity for yellow, due to yellow pigmentation, after-effect of blue stimulation, or *xanthopsia* (q.v.).

Yerkes-Bridges Point Scale: a *point scale* of twenty tests, mainly selected from the *Binet tests*.

Yoga: a Hindu system of philosophy, and practice of asceticism, ending in a trance, interpreted as union with God.

Young-Helmholtz theory: a three-colour theory of *colour vision,* based on the assumption of three colour mechanisms in the retina – nerve fibres or photochemical substances – responding maximally to red, green, and blue or violet respectively.

Youth: the period of *adolescence,* especially later adolescence.

Z

Zee Chart: a time chart giving three curves: (1) showing amounts (data of various kinds) per unit of time, (2) a cumulative curve, based at each point on (1), and (3) a curve showing total amount for previous periods of the same extent.

Zeising's principle: see *golden section.*

Zeno's Arrow: an argument to show the impossibility of motion; 'the flying arrow rests'; depending on the assumption of discrete units of time and space; due to the Greek philosopher Zeno.

Zielvorstellung (Ger.): idea of end or purpose.

Zoetrope: stroboscope (q.v.).

Zones of Colour: bands in the visual field – or *retinal zones* – differing with respect to the colours seen; for normal vision a marginal zone where no colours are seen, an intermediate zone where only blues and yellows are seen, and a central zone with full colour vision.

Zooid: a member of a colonial aggregate of connected organisms.

Zoophilism (*-phily*): an excessive love of animals.

Zoopsia: hallucinations of vision taking the form of animals.

Zygomatic area: the upper part of the cheek in the vicinity of the cheek bone.

Zygote: a cell formed by the union of two *gametes* (q.v.).

MEANING AND PURPOSE
Kenneth Walker

A211

An analysis of the main scientific theories of the last hundred years and their impact upon religious thought and belief.

MAN THE UNKNOWN
Alexis Carrel

A181

A synthesis of what the various sciences have discovered about the nature of man, including a vigorous advocacy of the natural laws man must follow to be redeemed from the degeneracy of industrial civilization.

THINKING TO SOME PURPOSE
L. Susan Stebbing

A44

A plea for and a help towards clear and logical thought. The author advocates a strong resistance to rumour, slip-shod thinking and the slovenly misuse of language.

THE PERSONALITY OF MAN
G. N. M. Tyrrell

A165

An explanation of the present position of psychical research and a summary of the results it has so far gained.

NEW FRONTIERS OF THE MIND
J. B. Rhine

A206

A scientist's report on telepathy and psychic powers and phenomena, the main subject being the tests of psychical ability begun in America at Duke University in 1930.

NEW BIOLOGY

Edited by M. L. Johnson and Michael Abercrombie

NO. 7

NO. 8

NO. 9

NO. 10

One shilling and sixpence each

SCIENCE NEWS

Outstanding articles from recent issues include:

NO. 17

NO. 18

NO. 19

NO. 20

One shilling and sixpence each

THE PHYSIOLOGY OF SEX
Kenneth Walker

A 71

A straightforward statement of the facts of sex and its problems in the life of the individual and the community.

HUMAN PHYSIOLOGY
Kenneth Walker

A 102

A simple explanation of how the body works, not only in disease, but when functioning normally and healthily.

MAN, MICROBE AND MALADY
John Drew

A 73

An account of the various kinds of bacteria known to produce human disease, describing the conditions in which they live and explaining how they can be fought and repelled. This is a revised and enlarged edition.

ANIMALS WITHOUT BACKBONES
Ralph Buchsbaum

In two volumes – A 187 and A 188

The story of the amoebas, sponges, worms of all kinds, insects, and the other invertebrates which make up 95 per cent of the animal kingdom. Each volume has sixty-four pages of illustrations.

THE SCIENCE OF SEEING
I. Mann and Antoinette Pirie

A 157

A book about eyes of every kind -- those of insects, fish, birds, mammals and particularly human beings: describing how they are constructed and in what way they function.